CONFRONT AND CONCEAL

CONFRONT AND CONCEAL

OBAMA'S SECRET WARS AND SURPRISING USE OF AMERICAN POWER

DAVID E. SANGER

CROWN PUBLISHERS

NEW YORK

Cataloging-in-Publication Data is on file with the Library of Congress.

ISBN 978-0-307-71802-0
eISBN 978-0-307-71804-4

Printed in the United States of America

Book design: Nancy Field and Lauren Dong
Maps: Mapping Specialists, Ltd.
Jacket design: Christopher Brand
Jacket photography: Getty Images

10 9 8 7 6 5 4 3 2 1

First Edition

For Sherill

CONTENTS

Part IV
ARAB SPRING: THE REVOLTS, AND THE RISE
OF THE BROTHERHOOD

Part V
CHINA AND NORTH KOREA: THE REBALANCING

EPILOGUE

Prologue

THE WORM WAS LOOSE.

That was the mystifying, disturbing news rippling through Fort Meade, the headquarters of the National Security Agency, and across the Potomac at the CIA. Now, on a midsummer day in 2010, Leon Panetta, the CIA director, and two men responsible for overseeing the most sophisticated, complex cyberattack the United States had ever launched against an adversary descended the steps into the White House Situation Room to tell President Obama and his national security team that something had gone badly awry. America's most closely guarded covert operation targeting Iran's nuclear program—known to a small circle of officials by its code name, "Olympic Games"—was in jeopardy because of a careless error. Suddenly the malicious software Americans and Israelis spent years perfecting was being replicated across the Internet, and hackers had given it an ominous-sounding name: "Stuxnet." The men knew they would face blistering questions in the Situation Room: Obama and his team would demand to know whether the mistake was fatal to their carefully designed plan to undermine Iran's ability to produce nuclear fuel. The "worm" in question was a cyber worm, the product of years of cooperation between a small team of computer warriors at Fort Meade and their counterparts, half a world away, inside a military intelligence agency that Israel barely acknowledges exists.

For three years, Olympic Games had unfolded almost flawlessly. The Americans spent months devising the worm to strike directly at the tall, silvery centrifuges the Iranians were using to enrich uranium. To assess its powers, the Pentagon and intelligence agencies had quietly built a replica of Iran's Natanz enrichment plant behind the high walls of the Energy Department's national laboratories. There they tested the worm, at one point taking the rubble of a destroyed centrifuge and dumping it on the conference table in the Situation Room for Obama's predecessor, George W. Bush. It was then that the Israelis and the Americans went to work, inserting the worm using a special technique that leaped the giant electronic moat the Iranians had built around their system to protect it from outside invaders. Versions of the worm were deployed through the end of the Bush presidency, and days before the handover, the forty-third president of the United States invited the forty-fourth to the White House for a one-on-one talk, in which Bush urged Obama to preserve two classified programs, the cyberattacks on Iran and the drone program in Pakistan. The Iranians, Obama was told, were still clueless about why their centrifuges were blowing up. Obama took Bush's advice.

For a new president with little patience for technological detail, Obama was deeply engaged in planning America's covert attacks on Iran. After each major use of the new cyberweapon, Obama would meet in the Situation Room to assess the damage—and the delay to Iran's program—with the men overseeing Olympic Games. Often, they would bring with them "the horse blanket"—a giant, foldout schematic diagram of Iran's nuclear production facilities. Those meetings often ended with the president's authorization to proceed with the next step—sometimes a strike riskier and bolder than what had been attempted previously. Perhaps not since Lyndon Johnson had sat in the same room, more than four decades before, picking bombing targets in North Vietnam, had a president of the United States been so intimately involved in the step-by-step escalation of an attack on a foreign nation's infrastructure.

"From his first days in office, he was deep into every step in slowing the Iranian program—the diplomacy, the sanctions, every major decision," one of the president's senior aides said to me early in 2012. "And it's safe to say that whatever other activity might have been under way was no exception to that rule."

He was also acutely aware that with every attack he was pushing the United States into new territory. Only a few months into office, Obama was employing a remarkable offensive weapon whose future no one entirely grasped. At the same time it was Obama, more than any president before him, who was raising alarms about the need to harden America's own infrastructure against hackers, other states, or even terrorists who were contemplating cyberweapons that could turn out the lights in New York and Los Angeles, crash the stock market, interfere with navigational satellites, or bring down the air traffic control system. The Chinese worked harder at cyber than anyone.

"We discussed the irony, more than once," one of his aides confided in early 2012. Yet Obama believed that when it came to stopping Iran, the United States had no other choice. If Olympic Games failed, there would be no time and space for sanctions and diplomacy to work. The Israelis might well turn to a more primitive means of taking out Iran's facilities—an old-fashioned airstrike—and plunge the region into a war that the United States could not simply watch from the sidelines. Olympic Games was a new president's best shot at avoiding a new war, just as he was trying to end two others.

But the luck surrounding the covert plan could not hold out. Something was going to go wrong eventually, and when it did, it was a pretty spectacular screw-up. That day, it fell to Panetta; his deputy, Michael Morell; and Gen. James "Hoss" Cartwright to bring this news to the president and figure out what to do next.

The cyberwarriors had been swinging for the fences, they explained. They had devised a new version of the worm to destroy a particularly hard-to-target group of just under one thousand centrifuges at Natanz, and had inserted the worm remotely. Then, something had gone wildly wrong: An Iranian scientist had plugged his laptop into the computer controllers and the worm had hopped aboard. When he later connected the same laptop to the Internet, the worm broke free and began replicating itself, a step its designers never anticipated.

"We think there was a modification done by the Israelis," Obama was told during the briefing, according to one person who was present, "and we don't know if we were part of that activity."

Now the worm was acting like a zoo animal that had discovered his caretaker had left the cage door ajar. Suddenly it was everywhere, digitally replicating at blazing speed, showing up on millions of computers in Iran, Indonesia, and India. So far, Obama was told, nothing had been traced back to the United States or Israel. The first account of the worm's spread, written by a diligent computer-security blogger, reported that "a sophisticated new strain of malicious software that piggybacks on USB storage devices" was showing up around the globe. Within a day, Microsoft announced it was fixing a flaw in its Windows operating system that allowed the software to burrow into its architecture.[1] But it was only a matter of time, Obama was told, before the code would be pulled apart and features of it used in other cyberweapons, including those aimed back at the United States.

Sitting along the back row, Benjamin J. Rhodes could see what was coming next. Then thirty-two years old, an aspiring fiction writer who had set aside his ambition of following in Hemingway's footsteps to become Obama's national security speechwriter and later a deputy national security adviser, he injected a warning. It wouldn't take long, he told the group, before it became clear that the malicious code was aimed at Iran.

"This is going to show up in the *New York Times*," he told the group. (He was right, but it took a while.)

In the background, everyone could hear someone sucking air through his teeth. It was Joe Biden, the vice president, whose occasional outbursts were often a tension-relieving contrast with Obama's typically impassive reaction to bad news.

"Oh, goddamn," he said, according to the account of one participant. "Sonofabitch. It's got to be the Israelis. They went too far." (Another participant in the discussion room said that while Biden was "maybe a bit more demonstrative than the president was, that's not unusual.")

Obama asked the question that Panetta, Morell, and Cartwright dreaded: "Should we shut this down?" How much would the Iranians be able to tell from reading the now-leaked code? And what kind of damage could this software do outside of Natanz?

Panetta, Morell, and Cartwright said they thought the program should keep going—it was unclear how much the Iranians understood about the code, or how it worked. There was time to come up with new fixes, new approaches. But the answers Obama heard also contained a lot of "ifs" and "it depends."

"I don't think we have enough information," Obama concluded. He wanted real answers, and soon. But in the meantime, he said, don't stop the cyberattacks. It would take a while for the Iranians to sort it all out. Until sanctions began to bite harder—which meant, everyone in the room knew, until they began constricting Iran's oil revenue—the cyber worm was the best hope of buying some time, of slowing down Iranian progress.

That turned out to be a good call. Within weeks, the United States and Israel inserted another version of the amped-up worm into Natanz, and then a third. And suddenly, the giant electronic ears at the NSA picked up conversations suggesting that just shy of a thousand centrifuges had come crashing to a halt inside the underground cavern at Natanz.

Sooner or later, the Iranians would figure it out. But for now, the Olympic Games were still on.*

---

* See chapter 8 for a fuller discussion of the Olympic Games program.

◆

BARACK OBAMA CAME to office after a decade in which threats to the United States had dominated Washington's view of the world. Strategies for combating those threats had, in fact, *become* the dominant theme of American foreign policy, distorting the country's grander goals, preoccupying its leaders, and blinding it to greater opportunities. Obama vowed to get the country out of its defensive crouch. He promised to restore traditional American "engagement" by talking and listening to America's most troubling adversaries and reluctant partners. His supporters saw a welcome turn away from the "with us or against us" black-and-whites of the Bush years. His critics saw naïveté and softness. Both have been surprised.

This is a book about those surprises.

Obama entered the White House with higher expectations than any president in a generation, as the country looked to him to engage the world, and the world looked for him to repair damaged relationships and end an era of American arrogance. But it quickly became evident that engagement is just a tactic, not a real strategy. So perhaps the most striking feature of three and a half enormously consequential years in the redirection of American power has been the slow emergence of an Obama Doctrine, a redefinition of the circumstances under which the United States will use diplomacy, coercion, and force to shape the world around it.

Fortunately, Obama's strategy does not fit easily on a bumper sticker. But watching him in action for the past three and a half years, seeing how he has changed and adapted, the essence seems clear. When confronted with a direct threat to American security, Obama has shown he is willing to act unilaterally—in a targeted, get-in-and-get-out fashion, that avoids, at all costs, the kind of messy ground wars and lengthy occupations that have drained America's treasury and spirit for the past decades. The examples are clear: the bin Laden raid, the escalating drone strikes that have brought al-

Qaeda to the brink of strategic defeat, and—perhaps most important as a symbol of Obama's approach—Olympic Games.

Taken together, they are the expression of a strategy of confrontation and concealment, a precise, directed economy of force. It is also a strategy that quickly runs into limitations.

But there is another side to the Obama Doctrine. If a threat does not go to the heart of America's own security—if it is a threat to the global order but not to the country—Obama has been far more hesitant. He has declined to act unless partners with far greater interests at stake take the greatest risks, and contribute the greatest resources. For example, his approach to Libya—contributing American power for a short period of time, and insisting that other NATO nations and the Arab League be at the forefront of the fight—sent a message. So did the decision to extract the United States rapidly from Iraq—where American interests were few—and slowly from Afghanistan, where American interests are rapidly diminishing. In an age of reckonings, when so many bills have come due, Obama has made the case for an America that can no longer do it all. It must pick its fights.

Obama's willingness to use force frequently outrages those who think American arrogance and unilateralism still lives on—ask the Pakistanis, still fuming about the invasions of their sovereignty in the three-and-a-half-hour operation to kill the world's number-one terrorist as he operated in their midst, and demanding an end to the drone strikes that have become the new expression of the remote-control reach of American power. His insistence that others take the lead in using military force shakes allies who have relied on the United States to be their ultimate protector and who wonder whether America is no longer interested in playing the role of the "indispensable nation," the world's keeper of the peace.

But perhaps the biggest surprise of this presidency has been what we've learned about the instincts of the president himself. There was nothing in Obama's personal history and little in his campaign rhetoric that prepared his supporters or his allies for his embrace of hard, covert power, nothing that suggested he would dramatically escalate America's drone wars, or secretly launch the country into a new era of cyber combat. "He comes at issues completely differently than Bush did," said a senior official who dealt with them both for many years. "Obama worries far more about collateral damage, about the precedent the United States sets when it acts. But when it's decision time about whether to order a strike, or use a certain kind of weapon, he often comes out pretty close to where Bush did."

These are topics Obama almost never talks about in public. When he does, it is usually a series of allusions to the need for America to rely on a "light footprint" that enables it to fight its wars stealthily, execute its operations with the speed of the bin Laden raid, and then avoid lengthy entanglements. Those who have worked with him most closely say they are taken aback by something else.

"The surprise is his aggressiveness," one of the country's most experienced career diplomats told me during my travels for this book, after dealing with Obama on issues that ran from counter-terrorism to the cold, hard calculus of when to abandon longtime allies whose abuses invited the Arab uprisings.

It is an assessment that is echoed by both Obama's admirers and his detractors—from the Central Party School outside Beijing to the mosques in Tehran. The Chinese look past Obama's constant assurances that he welcomes their rise—a long-overdue statement by the United States, but also a highly calculated one—and wonder whether his idea of "engagement" is to enmesh China into one international institution after another until its freedom of action is constricted. To many Chinese, Obama's decision to establish a Marine base in Australia and deploy a new generation of ships in the Pacific amounts to a stealth containment strategy—and they are not entirely wrong.

Ayatollah Ali Khamenei, Iran's supreme leader, is similarly suspicious. Just months after Obama declared in his inaugural address that he was willing to "extend a hand if you are willing to unclench your fist," Khamenei declared that he "will not be fooled by the superficial conciliatory tone of the United States." And that was *before* his centrifuges began exploding in large numbers.[2]

The tension between these two facets of Obama's approach to the world—his embrace of working in coalitions to support shared goals, and his willingness to strike unilaterally, and often in secret—shone through when the president, somewhat to his embarrassment, was awarded the Nobel Peace Prize nine months into office. The Nobel committee was clearly hoping that his acceptance speech would point to a radically new direction for America—one that veered sharply away from the use of force. They were enthralled by Obama's embrace—as a long-term goal—of a movement to eliminate nuclear weapons around the world. They applauded when he described an America that had returned to a Wilsonian vision: "Agreements among nations. Strong institutions. Support for human rights. Investment in development."

But then, to their obvious discomfort, the newly minted peace laureate used the speech to justify why American presidents seem to reach so often for the force of arms. And he reminded them that he had no choice but to reach for hard power. "I face the world as it is, and cannot stand idle in the face of threats to the American people," he said.

ON MANY OF the hardest issues, Obama's idealism about what he could accomplish has run headlong into the more craven instincts of electoral politics—and oftentimes the craven instincts have won out. His promise to shutter the detention facility at Guantánamo Bay—repeated in his Nobel acceptance speech—collapsed entirely. One of his departed top aides said Obama's first-week-in-the-White-House declaration that he would close the facility within a year was a case of "the political imperative getting far ahead of any analysis of what it would take to get it done." It did real damage: Ask students on the streets of Cairo what stands out about Obama's policies, and they will complain about what they saw as lukewarm support for the Arab Spring and then ask why Gitmo is still open. Many add another failure, asking how a president who spoke so movingly about the plight of Palestinians during his first trip to the Middle East in 2009, and who said he could imagine Palestinian statehood by 2011, seemed to abandon that cause in the face of overwhelming opposition.

Ask Pakistanis about the signature achievements of the Obama presidency, and they will launch into the subject of civilian casualties from drone strikes. Ask the Syrian opposition, and they will describe an America of double standards that enters wars when they are relatively easy, as in Libya, but ignores carnage when the solutions could put American lives at risk. Even the Europeans, who were so eager to see George Bush return to Texas, and who massed at the Brandenburg Gate to hear candidate Obama in 2008, now grumble that there was more hope than change.

But they can no longer complain about 140,000 American troops in Iraq, or credibly charge that the United States was staying there to seize the country's oil. If there is a worry about Obama's instincts in South Asia, it is that the pendulum has swung too far away from the military interventions of the past decade. Many in the region fear that America will leave Afghanistan prematurely—and let the Taliban control large swaths of the country. From Thailand to Indonesia to Australia, leaders ask whether, despite Obama's talk about "rebalancing," America has the will or the resources to act as a counterweight to China.

Three and a half years into a presidency is far too early to come to lasting judgments about Obama's effort to refocus, and redirect, American power. At the equivalent point in the Bush presidency, Iraq and Afghanistan did not yet look like debacles. At the same point in the Nixon presidency, the president had not yet gone to China. In the Truman presidency, the concept of containment—what became the central strategy of the Cold War—was still an experiment.

And so is the Obama approach to the world. The bin Laden raid was his best-known gamble, winning him accolades for boldness and risk-taking. But as the account of his presidency that follows suggests, it was likely not the biggest, or even the most important, bet of his presidency.

Olympic Games is still being played; if Iran eventually gets the bomb, or if the president's vow to do whatever it takes to prevent that outcome leads to armed conflict, those events will define Obama's time. The president's mixed performance in the Arab Spring—successfully shoving out Mubarak and embracing change, but then committing precious little money or resources to the remaking of those societies—will be judged by whether dictators are replaced with liberal democracies or just another round of strongmen. (Iraq after the American pullout is not a reassuring example.) Obama's gamble that a rising generation of Chinese leaders does not want to go head-to-head with the United States, and can be lured into rule-based institutions rather than using their enormous stockpile of cash and military power to intimidate their neighbors, may represent his biggest roll of the dice.

"If we get China wrong," one of his most senior diplomats said to me, "in thirty years that's the only thing anyone will remember."

Getting it right begins at home. Obama's efforts in his first three years to marshal the country to face Chinese competition the way Eisenhower and Kennedy marshaled it to deal with the Soviet Union have hardly caught on. (The president's one effort to invoke the spirit of America's response to Sputnik, the Soviet satellite that took America by surprise, in his 2011 State of the Union address, prompted little action, and he has rarely repeated it.) In the aftermath of Iraq and Afghanistan, Obama finds himself fighting an undercurrent of isolationism—starting in his own party—that has driven America, once again, to look away from a number of the global challenges it faces.

The pages that follow are an effort to tell the story of the education of a president, who came to office with an enormous burden of old business to clean up, and who has only begun to cut a new trail. It is a story of rude discoveries, unfinished agendas, troublesome allies, and new adversaries. It is, in short, the story of a presidency in midstream.

PART I
AFGHANISTAN AND PAKISTAN

THE CURSE OF UNFINISHED BUSINESS

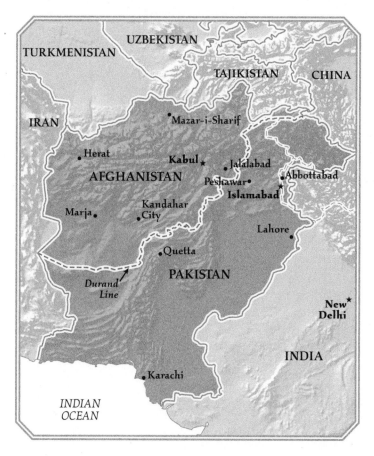

Chapter 1

Blowing Smoke

SECRET ISLAMABAD 002295

Money alone will not solve the problem of al-Qaeda or the Taliban operating in Pakistan. A grand bargain that promises development or military assistance in exchange for severing ties will be insufficient to wean Pakistan from policies that reflect accurately its most deep-seated fears. The Pakistani establishment, as we saw in 1998 with the nuclear test, does not view assistance—even sizable assistance to their own entities—as a trade-off for national security.

> —Anne Patterson, then US ambassador to Pakistan,
> in a secret cable to the National Security Council,
> September 23, 2009, disclosed by WikiLeaks

ON A SUNDAY MORNING IN EARLY OCTOBER 2011, PRESIDENT Obama's national security adviser, Tom Donilon, was driven through a wealthy suburb of Abu Dhabi. It was the kind of backdoor, no-photos diplomatic mission he enjoyed most: the quiet delivery of an urgent message directly from the president of the United States. A decade after 9/11, Donilon was overseeing the Obama administration's effort to end what he called the messiest "unfinished business" of the Bush years: Iraq and Afghanistan. Iraq was in its final chapter: in just a few months, the last American troops would drive out of the country on the same road they had driven in on, eight years before. Extracting Washington from Afghanistan—the "war of necessity" as Obama used to put it, before he reconsidered the phrase—was far more difficult. A promising-sounding game plan, to train the Afghan troops to defend their own country, was sputtering along. But precious few of the gains American troops had fought for seemed permanent. Obama's aides feared that the American withdrawal could lead to economic crisis and a Taliban resurgence.

Meanwhile, the relationship with the truly vital player in the region, Pakistan, had entered into such a death spiral there was a real possibility that American troops would be sent into the territory of an ostensible ally to hunt down insurgents targeting Americans.

At fifty-six, his hair thinning a bit, Donilon looked like a slightly disheveled version of the consummate Washington lawyer that he was. He had risen through the ranks of the Democratic Party as a superb political operator. In his early twenties, he managed the convention floor for Jimmy Carter; later he gained a reputation for getting presidential candidates through their debates.

Most of Washington knew Donilon as a canny political strategist, and political combat certainly made him tick. But the political world and the foreign-policy world in Washington often operate in different orbits, and what many missed about Donilon was his determination to live in both simultaneously. He dates that decision to one day when he was in his third year of law school and had lunch with Warren Christopher, the deputy secretary of state, whom he had gotten to know in the Carter administration.

"He came to lunch with this book, and he pushed it across the table to me," Donilon recalled. "He said, 'Politics is the easiest and most lucrative path for you. But you might consider another path.'" The book was an old copy of *Present at the Creation,* an account of the remaking of American national security after World War II, by Harry Truman's secretary of state, Dean Acheson. Donilon took it home and read it several times. (That copy is still on his bookshelf.)

He was hooked. For years, he could be seen carrying a battered L.L.Bean tote bag home, overflowing with ponderous articles on foreign policy and national security. When Christopher became Bill Clinton's first secretary of state, he installed Donilon down the hall as his chief of staff. And while Donilon returned to politics and law practice during the Bush years, he was clearly itching to get back into the game, constantly peppering old State Department colleagues, journalists, and academics with questions about how America's actions were perceived around the world.

Now he was present at a different creation—the effort to sustain and extend American power in a world of many more diverse threats, and new competitors, than Acheson ever could have imagined. As national security adviser, Donilon was the first person to brief the president of the United States on national security challenges every morning—he kept a precise count of how many such briefings he had done, a habit endlessly parodied by his staff—and relished special missions to deal with the hardest cases. This was one of them.

IN ABU DHABI, Donilon was accompanied by two of the most central players in the effort to find an exit from Afghanistan. One was the special assistant to the president for Afghanistan and Pakistan, Douglas Lute, the wry retired general who had served in the last two years of the Bush White House and stayed on, quickly becoming Donilon's guide to the wily ways of Afghan presidents, Pakistani generals, and the Pentagon bureaucracy. (Apart from Bob Gates, the secretary of defense, Lute was the only source of institutional memory in the White House for what had been tried, and what had failed, during the Bush years.) The other man in the car was Marc Grossman, Obama's recently appointed special envoy to Afghanistan and Pakistan. A soft-spoken career diplomat, he agreed, after the death of Richard Holbrooke, to take on one of the hardest jobs in Washington: finding out whether there was a way to reach a political accommodation with Mullah Mohammed Omar's Taliban, after ten years of war.

For a delegation of presidential envoys, it was a pretty unassuming motorcade: a couple of unmarked vans, rumbling past homes that looked like they belonged in Laguna Beach, one of the men later said. They were headed to a town house that belonged to a local intelligence agency friendly to the Pakistani government. It was the perfect place for a discreet meeting with the embattled, oftentimes embittered, commander of the Pakistani military forces: Gen. Ashraf Kayani.

Kayani is the most powerful man in Pakistan. When formal meetings with the Pakistanis were held for the cameras, Americans would sit down with the Pakistani president or prime minister and laud the arrival of a democratically elected civilian government. That was almost entirely for show. When they wanted to get something done, they ignored the civilians and called Kayani, who had risen through the ranks to become chief of the country's elite spy service, the ISI, or Inter-Services Intelligence, before becoming the head of the military. Kayani had clearly picked this venue so photographers and reporters would not know that he had slipped into town—Abu Dhabi, a favorite place for Pakistanis and Saudis making licit and illicit deals.

The meeting was Donilon's idea. After a year of crises—a trigger-happy CIA agent gone wild, the bin Laden raid, and a virulent rise of anti-Americanism—Donilon feared more trouble brewing. Just weeks before, a car-bomb attack on an American base in Wardak Province in Afghanistan had left seventy-seven Americans injured.[1] A few days later, an all-day attack on the American embassy in downtown Kabul, with rocket-propelled grenades, forced Ambassador Ryan Crocker to seek refuge in a basement safe room. Both attacks were quickly traced to the Haqqani network, a group that existed in the netherworld between an insurgent group and a criminal cartel, and lived unmolested in Pakistani territory.[2]

After the attack, the outgoing chairman of the Joint Chiefs of Staff, Adm. Mike Mullen, stood in front of the US Senate and delivered remarks that would have likely gotten him fired if he were not already halfway out the door. Mullen had been Obama's main interlocutor with the Pakistani military, but now, frustrated that more than twenty visits to the country had brought little change, he called the Haqqani network a "veritable arm" of the ISI.[3]

When Obama heard that his top military officer had made that charge in public, he was outraged—Mullen, he thought, was trying to save his reputation, to go out of office in a blaze of anger at the Pakistani military officers he had negotiated with for years. Obama didn't contend that Mullen was wrong, although the evidence that the ISI was directly involved in the attacks on Americans was circumstantial at best. But he knew that the accusation, in such a public setting, would trigger another round of recriminations with the country that had become the ally from hell.

When Donilon's team arrived, Kayani was already in the house, chain-smoking his Dunhill cigarettes. The out-of-the-way secrecy was pure Kayani, and the fact that Obama decided to send a high-ranking delegation to see him, not Pakistan's elected leadership, stroked his ego by reaffirming his primacy. Only a few short months before, Kayani had refused to deal seriously with the ambassadors and envoys from Washington—including Grossman—making clear he thought he deserved someone of higher rank. That would be Donilon, who played the role of secret interlocutor for Obama with the leadership of China and Saudi Arabia. (In fact, he had just come from a lengthy meeting in Riyadh with the Saudi king, trying to tamp down Saudi outrage at the American stance during the protests that ousted President Hosni Mubarak of Egypt.) But Pakistan was his toughest account.

Kayani was nothing if not unpredictable. To him, managing Americans meant following through with just enough promises to keep the brittle US-Pakistani alliance from fracturing. Polite and careful most of the time, he knew how to charm by offering up memories from his years in officer training in the United States. At other times, he was angry and bitter, lecturing the Americans about how often they had promised the world to Pakistan and promptly abandoned the country out of pique, anger, or a short attention span.

Though the Americans could have settled into a comfortable living room, Kayani insisted they sit more formally at a table. The general was clearly not in the mood for casual chitchat.

Donilon opened the meeting where Mullen had left off. "The ultimate responsibility of the president of the United States is to protect Americans," Donilon said in his clipped Rhode Island accent, reiterating something Obama had said to Kayani one day in the Roosevelt Room of the White House. Either Pakistan was going to deal with the Haqqani network or the Americans would. The message just sat there for a moment. Donilon went on. Why, he asked, would a man like Kayani, who grew up in the disciplined world of the Pakistani military, let a group of thugs hijack Pakistan's national security policy by waging war on America from inside its borders?

Then came the bottom line: "I know you want a guarantee from us that we won't undertake unilateral operations in your country again," a reference to the bin Laden raid. "I can't give you that." If seventy Americans had died in the bomb attack in Wardak the previous month, rather than just suffered injuries, "we wouldn't be having this conversation," Donilon said. It was a not-so-veiled threat that Obama would have been forced to send Special Operations Forces into Pakistan to attack the Haqqani network—national pride and sovereignty be damned.

"We're at a crossroads," Donilon concluded. "If this continues, you've really turned your fate over" to the Haqqani network.

When Donilon was finished, Kayani laid out his demands—and the chasm between them was obvious. The United States, he said, could never, ever again violate Pakistani sovereignty with an attack like the one they launched on Osama bin Laden's compound. That attack, he said, had been a personal humiliation. The Americans responded with silence.

"That was the tensest moment," one of the participants in the meeting noted, because it was an issue on which the two countries were never going to agree. Kayani moved on to his other concerns. The Americans were spending billions—approximately $12 billion in 2011—training the Afghan military and police.[4]

Should Afghanistan collapse someday in the near future—not an unlikely scenario—it would leave an armed, angry force just across the Pakistani border, Kayani said, many of them enemies of Pashtuns. And that would be a recipe for disaster. The Pashtuns are Sunnis, and they are also Afghanistan's largest ethnic group, about 40 percent of the population. But they live on both sides of the porous border between Afghanistan and Pakistan, a line of demarcation named after Henry Mortimer Durand, the British foreign secretary in the 1890s. The Durand line is a completely arbitrary boundary, an artifact of the British colonial era, that cuts straight through Pashtun tribal areas. The world may see the Durand line as a border between two nations, but the Pashtuns sure don't—particularly the Taliban. Today their leadership is living on the Pakistani side. But Kayani recalled that in the '90s, when they ruled Afghanistan, the Taliban systematically massacred non-Pashtun ethnic groups—specifically the Hazara, a Shi'a minority that has close ties with Iran.

If things fell apart, Kayani insisted, the Pashtuns in both Afghanistan and Pakistan could find themselves pitted against a force armed and trained by the United States. Had the Americans thought about that? Or the possibility that as the US forces pull out of Afghanistan, India—which had already invested billions in the Afghan government—would continue to extend its prowess in an effort to encircle Pakistan?

Having laid their cards on the table, the group of men went on to talk about their visions for Afghanistan's future and their troubled effort to negotiate with the Taliban. Donilon had sent ahead a document laying out the long-term American strategy, including a plan to keep somewhere between 10,000 and 15,000 American counterterrorism troops in Afghanistan, mostly at Bagram Airfield, a large base just outside Kabul, "to protect the interests of the US in the region." His meaning was clear: the United States would remain, and its troops would be ready to go over the Pakistani border if they needed to.

It was a conversation tinged with wariness on all sides, reflecting the distrust that permeated a relationship fractured by decades of betrayals. To Kayani, the three men in front of him represented a United States that had abandoned Pakistan before—during its wars with India, after the Soviets left Afghanistan, after Pakistan's nuclear tests. And to the Americans, the fact that Kayani spent five and a half hours blowing the refined smoke of his Dunhills into their faces said it all. The smoke cloud lingered, enveloping the men in a fog.

◆

If Kayani wielded secondhand smoke as a negotiating tool, it was one of the less lethal weapons at his disposal in his treacherous climb to power. From 2004 to 2007, when he ran the ISI, he excelled at managing what two successive American presidents came to deride as Pakistan's "double game." The phrase referred to Islamabad's habit of preserving its options by fighting on both sides of the Afghan War. But the phrase was misleading. It understated the complexity of Pakistan's position. Kayani's task was to maintain

Pakistan's tenuous, yet crucial, influence in Afghanistan and convince his own people (and fellow generals) that he was not letting the far more powerful India encircle Pakistan by expanding its presence in Afghanistan unchallenged.

"Kayani initially impressed me," Mullen told me, referring to his first meetings with the Pakistani general, "as someone who knew the totality of his country in a way that I don't know mine. He knew about its economics, he knew about its finances, he knew about its industries, he knew its people." And while Kayani did not have direct control over Pakistan's nuclear arsenal—roughly one hundred weapons and growing—the ISI played a critical role in keeping it safe.

Of course, "safe" meant very different things to the men in that room. To the Americans, it meant preventing terrorists from getting ahold of nuclear weapons or material from the world's most vulnerable arsenal. To Kayani, it meant, first and foremost, protecting that arsenal from the Americans, and making sure that, unlike that night in Abbottabad when they snuck in to kill Osama bin Laden, no SEAL team could seize or disable Pakistan's weapons. It was hardly paranoia. The Americans had an elaborate, well-rehearsed plan to do exactly that, which had been ramped up and revised when Obama came into office. At the same time, Obama stopped talking publicly about Pakistan's nuclear stockpile, knowing that even benign mentions fueled the ISI's paranoia. But all the quiet diplomacy, and offers of additional American help, heightened Pakistan's suspicions. And the more the Obama team examined the long-term threat of an expanding Pakistani arsenal—something Donilon had ordered up extensive studies about—the more the White House came to realize that the future of Pakistan was a far greater strategic threat to the United States than the future of Afghanistan. It was not an accident that by the end of Obama's first year, the goals in Afghanistan and Pakistan had been reduced to merely three. While the first key objective was to keep Kabul from falling back into the hands of the Taliban, the other two had little to do with Afghanistan: (1) disrupt, dismantle, and defeat al-Qaeda, and (2) prevent terrorists from working their way inside Pakistan's nuclear program. Neither of those problems was on the Afghan side of the border.

Kayani understood the American paranoia about a Pakistani meltdown, and he took advantage of it—which is one of the reasons he was the shrewdest survivor in the brutal Pakistani power game. As commander of the Pakistani military, he excelled at entertaining a parade of American visitors—senators, ambassadors, special envoys— who would arrive to lecture him about what Washington would no longer tolerate. Kayani would listen, take another drag on his cigarette, and try to get them to imagine how vulnerable both countries would be to terror groups if Washington ever made good on its threats to cut off Pakistan from the flow of money and arms the United States had been providing to fight terrorists. As he often told his own staff, the Americans talked a tougher game than they walked. Scratch beneath America's veneer of threats to cut off billions in aid or escalate strikes inside Pakistan's borders, and you would find a superpower that simply could not afford to risk breaking off relations. Not while Pakistan controlled the supply routes into Afghanistan, which—when tensions escalated—it shut off to remind Washington that its troops wouldn't last long without food and bullets. Not while Pakistan was a brew of 180 million people—nine times the population of Afghanistan—and home to several brutal insurgencies and the fastest-growing nuclear arsenal on earth.

As Lute often reminded his colleagues, "At the end of the day, breaking off relations with Pakistan or containing it might feel satisfying, but the next day you have to wake up and deal with them."

The three Americans told Kayani they had incriminating evidence about the latest two bold attacks against Americans in Afghanistan. Donilon had already spent hours poring through the intelligence, pressing the CIA and the National Security Agency— which routinely taps the ISI's cell phones—for every scrap that would tie members of Pakistan's elite spy service to the insurgents who had detonated car bombs and laid siege to the embassy. The case was circumstantial, as always. There was ample evidence that the ISI and others in the Pakistani military supplied the Haqqanis and gave them a free pass to cross the Pakistan-Afghanistan border along its most remote, dangerous stretches. But there was no smoking gun that the ISI had actually ordered the attack.

Always the lawyer, Donilon began making his case. He had a habit of starting each new argument with the phrase "Here's the deal," and then hitting three or four points. This time, Donilon listed the specific intelligence the United States had gathered. He described the Haqqani houses, places where the United States believed the attacks were plotted. He pointed to the madrassa in Miranshah—a religious school where extremist ideology was taught—that fed the Haqqanis with fresh recruits. The school, the United States had often reminded Kayani, is just a few kilometers from a Pakistani military outpost. Lute had often joked that if the Pakistani troops ever ventured out of their base for physical training, they could jog to the madrassa, touch its walls, and jog back.

Kayani took in the evidence silently, without pushing back. Well, Donilon thought, at least we're not bullshitting each other. He knows we have the goods—he knows that I'm as informed an intelligence official as there is in the world.

"We will undertake whatever steps we need to protect our forces," Donilon said. "We would prefer to act jointly. But if you refuse"—he could have said, if you agree and do nothing—"we will come in and do what we have to do." He did not need to add that the American model of success in this regard was Abbottabad, where seventy commandos infiltrated Pakistani airspace, landed forty miles from the Pakistani capital, killed bin Laden and his few protectors, and swept up his computers—all without setting off Pakistan's defenses. The unspoken message was, "We can do it again."

Kayani took another drag on the cigarette and blew a little

more smoke. Donilon, Lute, and Grossman knew what that meant. The Pakistanis had no intention of turning over or taking on the Haqqani network; it was their insurance policy for the moment when the Americans would inevitably leave.

And when Donilon, Lute, and Grossman got home—a seventeen-hour flight aboard a military jet—they knew their first stop: the dry cleaners. Getting the fumes out of their suits would be easy enough. Detoxifying the American relationship with Pakistan would be much more difficult.

Chapter 2
"Afghan Good Enough"

In a cramped office in downtown Washington where Barack Obama's skeleton "transition" staff was waiting to take over the powers of government, Doug Lute arrived one day with a set of PowerPoint slides to explain what was going wrong in Afghanistan.

No one knew the symptoms better than Lute, then still a three-star general. He spent the last two years of the Bush administration trying to manage the many tradeoffs as the Iraq War consumed the nation's military forces, its intelligence assets, even its newly deployed drones. When Lute heard his colleagues in the Bush White House deny that Afghanistan had been starved of resources in order to feed the Iraq beast, he rolled his eyes.

But it was the first slide that Lute threw onto the screen that day in the grimy office space near the Verizon Center, the sports arena midway between the Capitol and the White House, that caught the eye of Tom Donilon, who was preparing to become the president's first deputy national security adviser. "It said we do not have a strategy in Afghanistan that you can articulate or achieve," Donilon recalled three years later. "We had been at war for eight years, and no one could explain the strategy."

All new presidents like to exaggerate what a mess they were left with—Bush did it regularly in the first year after he took over from Bill Clinton—but in this case, there was little doubt. The financial crisis that broke in 2008 was the most immediate challenge, of course, but Afghanistan was the slow-burning disaster that Obama feared could, over time, consume his presidency, as Vietnam consumed Lyndon Johnson's and Iraq consumed George W. Bush's. It was bad enough that the Taliban were taking over large swaths of the country. But the real problem was that no one could identify exactly what the United States was trying to achieve. A full-blown democracy with the rule of law and respect for human rights? A divided country in which every warlord runs his own piece of turf? A state-in-name-only that survived on revenue from opium, minerals, and foreign aid? Something else?

"As Doug explained it," Donilon said, "no one could answer that."

SO IN THE first days of his presidency, Obama commissioned Bruce Riedel, a counterterrorism expert, to chair an interagency review of US policy in Afghanistan and Pakistan. Tall, bald, and heavy-set, Riedel seemed like just what an administration of rookies needed: an experienced insider, with years as an analyst at the CIA, who felt in his bones the convoluted tribal politics and deep sense of vulnerability that drove events in both Afghanistan and Pakistan. Over three decades, Riedel had been around for every cycle in which the United States had promised aid to the Afghans, abandoned the region, and threatened Pakistan as it raced for the bomb.

Riedel knew it would take the new president a year or so to get a feel for the strange rhythms of dealing with Pakistan's paranoia and Afghan president Hamid Karzai's volatility. He also knew Obama did not have the luxury of time to begin making decisions.

Obama's first hard call was waiting on his desk when he took office on January 20, 2009. Gen. David McKiernan—the four-star general who served as the top commander of US and NATO forces in Afghanistan, and whom Obama would soon jettison—had requested tens of thousands of additional troops to stem the Taliban tide. "It was kind of an urgent, five-alarm fire request," Ben Rhodes, one of Obama's young, inner circle of foreign-policy aides, told me. A presidential election was looming in Afghanistan, which, if it came off peacefully and cleanly, could serve as a turning point in the war. The extra troops, McKiernan said, would provide much-needed security. During the transition, the Bush team offered to approve the request and take the heat for sending more troops— Bush's approval rating already hovered in the low twenties, the lowest for an outgoing president in recorded history.[1] But Obama told them to hold off. The new president had campaigned on winning in Afghanistan—a "war of necessity," he argued then, to contrast it with the "war of choice" in Iraq. If there were going to be any major shifts in war strategy, he wanted to initiate them.

But it wasn't as easy as coming up with a new way forward for the beleaguered country. After more than seven years of war, Obama's Afghanistan was laden with serial instability, largely triggered by the Bush administration's distractions in Iraq. The Taliban did not waste that opportunity and had slipped back into the country while more than 100,000 American troops were fighting to retain influence in a new Iraq. When Bush talked about Afghanistan during the second half of his presidency, it was mostly as a poster child for what he called the "Freedom Agenda." He celebrated when Afghans first went to the polls to vote in 2004. He told audiences that girls were now going to school in Afghanistan, a line that always brought applause. But starting in 2006, Bush's own staff was warning him that he was failing to send in the troops and resources needed to keep Afghanistan from spinning out of control. Many in the Pentagon complained that the forces available were insufficient and that Bush had never fully grappled with America's strategic goals in the region. They could not say so in public, of course.

Eventually, Bush painted himself into a corner. With more than 150,000 troops in Iraq and a surge under way, he had no latitude to send more soldiers, or even Predator drones, to Afghanistan. And without the troops, his vow of building the country into a modern, democratic state, made in 2002 when he invoked the memory of the Marshall Plan, was empty.[2] Partly because of Afghan corruption and incompetence, partly because tribal leaders did not agree to central rule from Kabul, and partly because Bush had never sufficiently focused on Afghanistan, there was little progress to show despite seven years of war.

Obama entered office declaring that a new president, with a new vision, could break the cycle of American neglect, Pakistani duplicity, and Afghan dysfunction. He laid down an early marker of his own: having campaigned on fixing the war in Afghanistan, he would not make the mistake of employing the "light-footprint" strategy that Donald Rumsfeld, Bush's first defense secretary, had used in the first five years of the Afghan War. That strategy, one of employing minimal troops, had failed to stop the Taliban from gradually returning from their sanctuaries in Pakistan. "Obama set the parameters," Riedel recalled later. "He wanted an anti-Rumsfeld strategy. He wanted counterinsurgency."

So even before Riedel had time to complete his first, quick "strategic review," Obama decided to deploy 17,000 additional troops to Afghanistan, championing what he called "a new way forward."[3] But the "way forward" wasn't actually new; it was old-fashioned "counterinsurgency"—the slow, patient process of winning hearts and minds by building a government, promoting economic growth, developing the rule of law, and employing a host of other programs tantamount to nation building.

The deity of counterinsurgency, dubbed COIN by the military, was Gen. David Petraeus. A West Point student of history as well as of command (who also had a PhD in international relations from Princeton's Woodrow Wilson School of Public and International Affairs), he knew the enormous costs in lives and resources of a failed COIN campaign, having studied the effects of the United States' clumsy effort to employ counterinsurgency in Vietnam. For decades thereafter, there was strong opposition to counterinsurgency. George W. Bush derided "nation building" during the 2000 campaign. (Bush adamantly opposed using the military for "walking children to kindergarten," as he put it when I interviewed him at his ranch ten days before he took office.) But as Iraq spun out of control, and the conventional war strategy of simply killing insurgents failed, Bush discovered how little the American presence had kept a lid on Iraq's slow but steady descent. Eventually, Petraeus won Bush over. He laid out the case that the only alternative to counter-insurgency was an endless war, in which Sunni insurgents in Iraq would keep coming back, looking for vulnerabilities and waiting for the Americans to leave. Petraeus's theory gained traction in Iraq, especially when bolstered by the surge in troops. Whether that formula could translate to the very different territory of Afghanistan, though, was another question.

TWO MONTHS AFTER his inauguration, flanked by his national security team and top advisers for Afghanistan, Obama made his first big foreign-policy pronouncement: "I want the American people to understand that we have a clear and focused goal: to disrupt, dismantle, and defeat al-Qaeda in Pakistan and Afghanistan, and to prevent their return to either country in the future."

"Disrupt, dismantle, and defeat al-Qaeda" quickly became the new adage of the "war against al-Qaeda and its affiliates" (which was the line Obama used to replace Bush's vague, scattershot "global war on terror"). But this seemingly well-defined and limited goal had far-reaching implications. And in the half-hour speech that followed, Obama sounded an awful lot like a nation builder. "To advance security, opportunity, and justice—not just in Kabul, but from the bottom up in the provinces," Obama said, "we need agricultural specialists and educators, engineers and lawyers. That's how we can help the Afghan government serve its people and develop an economy that isn't dominated by illicit drugs. And that's why I'm ordering a substantial increase in our civilians on the ground.

"At a time of economic crisis, it's tempting to believe that we can shortchange this civilian effort. But make no mistake: our efforts will fail in Afghanistan and Pakistan if we don't invest in their future."

To drive home his point, Obama talked about a "civilian surge." "And that's why my budget includes indispensable investments in our State Department and foreign assistance programs. . . . Because it's far cheaper to train a policeman to secure his or her own village or to help a farmer seed a crop than it is to send our troops to fight tour after tour of duty with no transition to Afghan responsibility."[4]

After the speech was over, Riedel insisted the problem was more about Pakistan than Afghanistan. "If we were honest with ourselves, we would call this problem 'Pak/Af,' not 'Af/Pak,'" he told me. Almost all of Obama's top advisers later conceded that Pakistan was the far more potent threat. But the White House would not dare admit that publicly—even a rhetorical change would send the Pakistanis further into orbit. Instead, Obama called on Congress to end the years of on-again, off-again aid to Pakistan that only sowed more anger and suspicion toward the United States. Congress later responded by passing the Kerry-Lugar-Berman Bill—a bill that promised Pakistan a steady, predictable $1.5 billion per year in development assistance.[5] It was an effort to avoid the trap that Richard Holbrooke described to me just before he died in 2010: "The biggest problem we face is that the Pakistanis know that sooner or later, we're leaving. Because that's what we do. And that drives everything."

◈

OBAMA'S SPEECH WAS refreshing, but it was still littered with the easy phrases of the campaign trail. It described new initiatives and new organizations and suggested an end to the days when the United States changed its goals and its strategy every year. The new president described a strategy of huge investment in Afghanistan. Two years later—with a stagnant economy at home—it was a concept that would simply disappear from his speeches.

At defense secretary Bob Gates's suggestion, Obama also fired the US general overseeing the war, Gen. David McKiernan, in favor of a little-known general who could reimagine the mission of American and NATO forces in the country: Gen. Stanley McChrystal.

McChrystal—tall, gaunt, with leathered skin—lived an ascetic lifestyle, usually limiting himself to one meal a day, four hours of sleep a night, and a daily eight-mile run. He was a soldier's soldier. But McChrystal didn't possess Washington savvy. Unlike Petraeus, he did not spend weeks briefing committee chairmen on Capitol Hill or the White House's national security staff over lunches and dinners. Instead, he ran the most secretive branch of the military, the Joint Special Operations Command, or JSOC, home of the Navy SEAL teams and the Green Berets, among others. JSOC had become Bush's favorite branch of the military (as it would become Obama's) for the night raids it ran to find, capture, or kill high-value al-Qaeda and Taliban insurgents. The raids began as sporadic operations under Bush, but as Obama took over, the pace accelerated to ten to fifteen a night. They were highly effective in keeping insurgents on the run and making it far harder for them to train or plan.

But McChrystal was also an enthusiast of Petraeus's vision of counterinsurgency. The two men had forged a tight friendship over the years, and Petraeus described McChrystal as a "kindred spirit."[6] So, despite his past job commanding secret teams of "snake-eaters," as some Special Operations Forces called themselves, McChrystal strongly argued that the only way to bring the Afghan War to a satisfying end was through a comprehensive counterinsurgency campaign. The problem, he knew, was that counterinsurgency took a long time—most likely a decade in Afghanistan—and the American public, and the new president, might not have the stomach for that.

Obama made two other significant appointments for his Afghanistan team. Retired lieutenant general Karl Eikenberry, one of the first military commanders in Afghanistan to warn that Bush was ignoring the Taliban's resurgence, returned as a civilian to serve as the US ambassador. And the bullish diplomatic superstar who forged the Dayton Peace Accords—Richard Holbrooke—was appointed to be the State Department's special representative for Afghanistan and Pakistan. As the special representative, Holbrooke would try against all hope to replicate in Afghanistan his success in ending a war in the Balkans.

Obama exuded supreme confidence that this group, smarter and more focused about core American goals, could accomplish what Bush did not. What he could not anticipate was that his own team would be so divided on the right course to take, and his ostensible allies so recalcitrant.

As the number of troops in Afghanistan rose—Obama nearly doubled down in his first few months as president, raising the number of American forces in the country to 68,000 from 38,000—his team already showed signs of fracturing. Every one of them—Vice President Joe Biden, Secretary of Defense Robert Gates, Secretary of State Hillary Clinton, Special Representative Holbrooke, and Ambassador Eikenberry, to name just the most visible—was deeply experienced. But they were like an all-star team coming together for the first time, without the benefit of a few practices. The president had doubled the troop numbers before his team had hashed out what kind of future Afghan state was possible.[7] Obama soon worried that he had approved new forces before he had resolved the many contradictions that had long dogged policy in the region.

"The president approved [the troops]," an adviser told me one afternoon in the White House. "Then, the Riedel process happened, and I don't think the president was satisfied with that product. I think that he felt that the fundamental questions about what we're trying to achieve in Afghanistan, and how things were in Afghanistan, had yet to be answered."

A State Department cable dated April of 2009 that appeared on WikiLeaks demonstrated that Biden was particularly skeptical from the start that the United States could build a legitimate Afghan government. After meeting with Gordon Brown, Britain's prime minister at the time, an American diplomat who was taking notes summarized Biden's private view. "Currently there is little capacity for the Afghan government to execute many of the functions of government," the cable reported Biden saying. "In many areas of the country, local officials have close to no knowledge of how to govern or even basic knowledge of payroll or budget. . . . The idea of a strong rule of law under a centralized Karzai government was not realistic."[8]

But before the administration could tackle those problems, it faced an immediate challenge: a forthcoming presidential election in Afghanistan that many feared would not end well. There were roughly 38,000 American troops in Afghanistan when Obama took office; he deployed another 21,000, including 4,000 "training and advisory" troops, based on Riedel's recommendations, hoping their presence would help assure a credible election that would give the Afghan government the legitimacy it so sorely lacked.[9] But as Eikenberry warned in a cable back to the State Department in July 2009, a fair election that returned the mercurial Karzai to power could create far larger problems. Eikenberry was characteristically blunt as he described Karzai's paranoia and ineptitude: "Karzai remains deeply suspicious of US intentions and actions regarding key opposition candidates. . . . Karzai clearly expected (or hoped) to receive the same US support for his candidacy that he received in the 2004 election, and interprets our neutral stance in this election as evidence that the US is 'against' him."[10]

Even though administration officials were desperate to get rid of Karzai, attempts to nurture a serious opposition candidate failed. Dr. Ashraf Ghani, a technocrat and former executive at the World Bank, championed good governance, transparent institutions, and rule of law. He was coauthor of a book appropriately entitled *Fixing Failed States*. But Afghans viewed Ghani as more American than Afghan, and it was clear he would never get the votes needed to win. Dr. Abdullah Abdullah, previously Karzai's foreign minister, had fought with the Northern Alliance's top leader—Ahmad Shah Massoud—against the Soviet Union in the '80s and the Taliban in the '90s. But Abdullah was a Tajik in a country dominated by Pashtuns, and he lacked the family dynasty, tribal networks, and clan ties essential to winning the presidency.

Unsurprisingly, when the polls opened in August 2009, the Taliban unleashed a series of suicide bombings and rocket attacks across the country, and threatened to cut off the ink-stained fingers of anyone who voted. Turnout was low. Web videos showed election officials flipping through hundreds of ballots premarked for Karzai. The rampant fraud led Afghanistan's Independent Election Commission to disqualify 23 percent of the votes, putting Karzai below the threshold he needed to maintain his power.[11] Under the Afghan constitution, this mandated a runoff.

The Obama team froze. They had invested heavily in a fair election, and now had presided over a corrupt one. Karzai, characteristically, refused to participate in a runoff election, declaring himself the legitimate winner. And inside the White House, many feared that Obama would emerge looking like a rank amateur, endorsing a Karzai victory because the prospect of a power vacuum or a fractured alliance seemed much worse. They turned to the chairman of the Senate Foreign Relations Committee, John Kerry (who had hoped to be secretary of state), to fly to Afghanistan and shuttle between Karzai and Abdullah Abdullah, the runner-up, to broker an agreement for a second round of voting. (It was the first of many such missions to both Afghanistan and Pakistan for Kerry, and he reveled in the role of Obama's direct messenger.) Kerry and European allies stroked and cajoled Karzai to capitulate. Eventually, he was dragged into agreeing to a second round.[12] But as soon as he did, Abdullah Abdullah dropped out of the race, declaring that it would be neither free nor fair.

With its first foray into the democratic experiment in Afghanistan crumbling, the Obama administration simply embraced Karzai's incumbency. "Our sense was that after the election we'd know whether Afghanistan was taking a turn for the better or whether it was going in a downward trajectory," Rhodes said later. "And the elections obviously don't go particularly well." But as another one of Obama's aides told me at the time, "It's hard to say that we are sending your children off to fight and die for a guy who steals elections."

Despite his veteran national security team, it was clear that Obama was making rookie mistakes. The rushed review process for Afghanistan and Pakistan, the botched Afghan elections, and the fractures within his team raised red flags. So Obama declared that the time had come for a deep rethinking of Afghanistan and Pakistan policy that would, Rhodes said, "turn over every stone and question every assumption the United States has about Afghanistan and Pakistan, to agree on a set of objectives, and to agree on the resources that would flow from the strategies and objectives."

It sounded straightforward—the kind of hardheaded, start-from-the-facts analysis that would appeal to Obama's demand for depth and pragmatism. Obama told his staff he needed something he never got out of Riedel's review earlier in the year: a series of objectives in Afghanistan and Pakistan, and metrics to measure how well the United States was meeting them. But nothing in war or Washington is quite that easy.

The job was given to Doug Lute, who developed classified and unclassified measurements of progress, to be provided to Congress every few months. (The classified list added metrics for the security of Pakistan's nuclear arsenal.) The White House invited a few reporters over to the West Wing to explain how one measures progress in a war where the side that controls a town by day may not by night.

"We appreciate," Lute began, "that where we want to go with Afghanistan depends on having legitimate Afghan power." Given that the administration had just endorsed Karzai's victory, despite a highly dubious election process, Lute acknowledged that this would be a tough sell. But the new president was quickly realizing that the vision of building a modern, democratic state was beyond anything Americans could realistically accomplish. So how much would be good enough?

FOR OBAMA, THERE was a bigger question lurking beneath Lute's metrics: Was he slowly slipping into another Vietnam? It was a question that Donilon and Rahm Emanuel, Obama's first chief of staff, had debated endlessly: One weekend evening, after a family dinner at Donilon's house, Emanuel had seen a copy of Gordon M. Goldstein's *Lessons in Disaster* on the table in Donilon's library. A short book, it was a study of how a series of small bad decisions in Washington had slipped into a huge one called Vietnam. Emanuel had feared that Obama could be headed down the same path that LBJ took, in which a war abroad undercut his efforts to remake the country at home. The book soon became a must-read in the West Wing. What jumped out from the volume, Donilon told visitors, was that Kennedy and Johnson never tested the question of whether Communism was as monolithic as it was portrayed in America at that time. It was time to rethink similarly fundamental questions about al-Qaeda and the Taliban. Soon, several presidential historians received an invitation for a private dinner at the

White House. As they waited in a reception room for the president to arrive, they realized that almost everyone on the short invitation list had written about Johnson and his struggle to understand what he was getting into in Vietnam.

"The analogy of Lyndon Johnson suggests itself very profoundly," Stanford University historian David M. Kennedy told my colleague Peter Baker. "He needs to worry about the outcome of that intervention and policy and how it could spill over into everything else he wants to accomplish." Robert Caro, who is still writing the definitive multivolume biography of Johnson, knew that Johnson had debated Vietnam in the same room. "You had such an awareness of how things can go wrong," he said.[13]

The president listened, silently. "It was very typical of Obama," said a historian who was present at several such sessions. "You knew he was listening, but he held his counsel and mostly asked questions. You never knew quite what he was thinking." Obama understood that no analogy was a perfect fit; as Ernest May, the late Harvard historian, often warned, "History does not repeat itself, but it rhymes." The attraction of straight-line analogies had frequently led presidents astray. America went into Vietnam to stop the spread of Communism; it went into Afghanistan because its territory had been used to plot and launch a direct attack on the United States. The Vietcong had no reach overseas, Obama knew; al-Qaeda does, and elements of other insurgent groups would soon prove they did too. But al-Qaeda was not in Afghanistan anymore; it was in Pakistan.

One lesson of Vietnam did stick out that evening: quagmires often emerge not from a single, big miscalculation but from a series of smaller decisions, often when war goals are fuzzy. Obama knew that to fulfill his campaign promise to focus on the Afghan War, he had little choice but to accede to the Pentagon's longstanding requests for more troops. But despite his campaign pledges, he was growing skeptical about what could be accomplished by doubling the size of the force. "I think he hated the idea from the beginning," one of his closest advisers told me early in 2012. "He understood why we needed to try, to knock back the Taliban. But the military was 'all in,' as they say. And Obama wasn't.'"

OBAMA'S THREE-MONTH-LONG REVIEW of what it would take to reverse the momentum in Afghanistan and then get out—a strategy called "escalate and exit" inside the White House—would define his relationship with the military for the remainder of his presidency.

Over eight years and two wars, the Pentagon had gotten accustomed to working for a president who declared, publicly and repeatedly, that he would "listen to [his] generals" and "give them what they need." For Bush it was a great sound bite, and a way to cast opponents of the war in Iraq as unwilling to support the troops. It was also an abdication of civilian control. Over time Bush's statement of faith in the quality of the military's advice overwhelmed any fundamental reassessment of American objectives or interests. They were clear in the days immediately after 9/11: find the perpetrators of the crime. Three thousand days of mission creep followed. First came Bush's "Marshall Plan" phase: America was going to build a democracy in Afghanistan. Along with permanently eradicating safe havens for terrorists, it would educate girls, halt the drug trade, and curtail corruption. There was little effort to prioritize those goals, or even ask the question of whether they could be accomplished.

Obama's own team was deeply divided on how to define success. Biden, Donilon, Lute, and many of Obama's political advisers were ambivalent about what had become known as the "good war," despite Obama's call for something approaching nation building during the 2008 campaign. "This is a prescription for endless conflict," Donilon said to me one afternoon in the summer of 2009, after he had settled into the narrow, paper-stacked office he then occupied as deputy national security adviser. And while Obama was still publicly calling this a "war of necessity," Donilon was beginning to have his doubts.

After Obama appointed McCrystal, Obama gave him sixty days to assess the situation he found and report back to the White House, the first step in a top-to-bottom review of the strategy. Of course, even before that review began, a debate had broken out in Washington about how many troops would be needed to prevent calamity—thirty thousand? Forty thousand? Eighty thousand?

But while the Pentagon was thinking about how big to go in, Obama was already mulling over deadlines, time limits, and withdrawal schedules. Returning to the White House one day after visiting wounded soldiers at Washington's army hospital, he told his aides, "I don't want to be going to Walter Reed for another eight years."

Yet to get out, Obama had to redefine and drastically narrow American objectives. Implicit in his characterization of the conflict as a "war of necessity" was a commitment to fight until all of America's goals had been achieved. What played out over the next few months, though, was a new president's reassessment of whether the war was as necessary as he first believed.

"It was clear to McChrystal, Petraeus, and all the other commanders that soon Afghanistan would be the only war in town," one senior White House official told me several years later. "And so it was the last testing ground for counterinsurgency, and the last place where they could prove that this is the only strategy that would work."[14]

After spending his first months in office dealing with a raging global economic crisis, Obama was in a very different place from where he began on the issue of Afghanistan. The American people would soon lose patience with the soaring costs of the war, he thought. The fact that al-Qaeda was in Pakistan—not Afghanistan—was driven home every week by Biden, who was arguing for a bare-bones counterterrorism operation (which many administration officials deemed illogical and dangerous). Gen. James Jones, then still the national security adviser, had a pretty succinct summary of the situation at a dinner in the summer of 2009. "We've got maybe a year, eighteen months to turn this around. And then it's time for Plan B."

Obama's uncertainty about the mission was evident in the questions he posed in the first meeting with the National Security Council on September 13, 2009: Does America need to defeat the Taliban to defeat al-Qaeda? Can a counterinsurgency strategy work in Afghanistan given the problems with its government? If the Taliban regained control of Afghanistan, would a nuclear-armed Pakistan be next? It was only then that some in the military began to discover this was not a review meant to bless the current strategy; it was a review meant to find a way to the exit.

The jamming of the president began right away. Just after the first meeting to review the strategy, General McChrystal's secret report recommending a multiyear counterinsurgency campaign was leaked to Bob Woodward of the *Washington Post*. Obama and his White House aides fumed; if Obama chose another path, his opponents were now armed with the evidence that a young president, in his first major military decision, had overruled a commander who had warned of "mission failure" if he didn't get a large infusion of new troops. (The fact that Bush had left requests for more troops in Afghanistan unfulfilled was, by then, already long-lost history.)

Moreover, McChrystal's grim assessment of how effectively the Taliban were seeping back into Afghan society, while hardly unexpected, added urgency to the question of what it would take to avoid defeat. It was echoed in the Situation Room debate. Obama's two new envoys—Special Representative Holbrooke and Ambassador Eikenberry—warned of growing trouble, including the possibility of angry Afghans marching on the American embassy or outright civil war.

"There are ten ways this can turn out," Holbrooke told me during the Situation Room arguments, "and nine of them are messy."

McChrystal's leaked report contained no troop numbers. He handed his troop requests—in hard copy, no electronic versions—a few weeks later to Adm. Mike Mullen, the chairman of the Joint Chiefs, and Gen. David Petraeus, the regional commander—during a secret meeting in Germany. Soon, those numbers leaked too. With 80,000 troops, McChrystal calculated, he could run a robust counterinsurgency campaign throughout the country. With 40,000 he could take on the Taliban in their strongholds. With 10,000 to 15,000 he could train Afghan troops and pray they learned something. "This was classic Washington," one of Obama's national security aides told me. "An outrageous, unaffordable top number. A useless bottom number. And it was intended to force us to the middle option."

With some sarcasm, Secretary Clinton later described the military's presentation as "the Goldilocks option." But for weeks she and Secretary Gates engaged in bureaucratic warfare with Biden and the White House staff. The dispute was portrayed at the time as a stark choice between a "counterinsurgency" campaign that would secure the populations, Iraq-style, and a far more limited "counterterrorism" operation that used drone strikes and Special Operations Forces to kill or capture al-Qaeda and Taliban leaders. In reality, all the choices blended the two. And a little more than two years later, even the most passionate participants in that argument admit that it was both less stark and less important than it seemed at the time.

"That was such a foolish, unproductive argument, to be honest," Clinton told me one day in her office in January 2012. The focus, she said, should have been how to "fight, talk, build"—in other words, pound on the Taliban until they are marginalized or come to the negotiating table—all while rebuilding the country. Clinton's diagnosis of what was going wrong in the war was simple: "We were not fighting enough" to be able to force the Taliban to make a political settlement and forge real progress toward ending the war.

The friction between administration officials intensified on October 1, when General McChrystal was asked after a speech in London whether a narrower mission, like the one Biden proposed, would succeed. "The short answer is no," he said, drawing a sharp, personal rebuke from Obama for the public airing of the arguments.[15]

In truth, McChrystal wasn't the only one speaking out of turn; in the surge debate, White House discipline broke down, and after each meeting participants in the arguments were pressing their case to reporters, at least until Obama erupted with an anger few of his aides had seen before. "What I'm not going to tolerate is you talking to the press outside of this room," he snapped. "It's a disservice to the process, to the country, and to the men and women of the military." He made an impression: the leaking stopped for several hours.

By late October 2009, a consensus on the broad strategy had been reached. Gates put it succinctly: "We don't need to defeat the Taliban," he told me one evening during a dinner he held at Lincoln's summer cottage for a visiting top official of China's military commission. "We only need to degrade them. They need to be weak enough that the Afghan forces can deal with them alone." That soon became the mantra.

But right before the new strategy was announced, another critical leak emerged: Ambassador Eikenberry had sent a cable from Kabul complaining about President Karzai, repeating a warning that he had already expressed verbally during a secure video conference with the White House. Eikenberry's assessment was blistering, essentially saying that any American president who put the success of his strategy in Karzai's hands ought to have his head examined. Karzai, he wrote, "is not an adequate strategic partner," and "continues to shun responsibility for any sovereign burden."

"Sending additional forces will delay the day when Afghans will take over," Eikenberry continued, "and make it difficult, if not impossible, to bring our people home on a reasonable timetable."

The surge of forces would only "increase Afghan dependence" on the United States. Karzai's insular crowd of confidants, he wrote, "assume we covet their territory for a never-ending 'war on terror' and for military bases to use against surrounding powers." And he ended with a parting shot that he knew no one in Washington was truly prepared to confront: "Pakistan will remain the single greatest source of Afghan instability so long as the border sanctuaries remain. Until this sanctuary problem is fully addressed, the gains from sending additional forces may be fleeting."[16]

When the cable was published in the *New York Times*, Eikenberry feared his relationship with Karzai was over. He was right. But his characterization of Karzai appears as accurate today as the day he wrote it.

White House officials were stunned by the leak, and to this day Secretary Clinton still wonders aloud how the United States managed to send so many messages that undercut the Afghan president— even while she admits that dealing with him could be maddening. But by the time Eikenberry's cable arrived, Obama had already made up his mind. The only tenable solution, he believed, was a surge of American troops into the country. But he was already thinking about short deadlines: frustrated by the Pentagon's leisurely plans, he held up a chart in one session showing how forces would flow into Afghanistan over a year and a half, then stay for years to come. It looked like a long, flat bell curve. "I want this pushed to the left," he told a crowded Situation Room full of advisers, pointing to the bell curve. In other words, the troops should deploy sooner, and begin returning eighteen months later—just around the time the Pentagon plan had them arriving in full strength.

"What I'm looking for is a surge," Obama said. He turned to Petraeus, asking how long it had taken to get surge troops into Iraq three years before. (The answer was six months.) "This has to be a surge," Obama concluded. The Pentagon relented.

The biggest fight within the administration, though, came over

Obama's decision to set a deadline to start pulling the surge troops back out by the summer of 2011—whether they were successful or not. The divisions over that decision burn to this day. Generals fume that it undercut the effort. Gates opposed it. Clinton thought it was a mistake and still does; an internal deadline would have been fine, she believed, but a public one simply telegraphed to the Taliban and the Pakistanis when the United States would be leaving. The Taliban read the newspapers too, she pointed out.

In the end her concern—also voiced by Gates—seems prescient. The effort to explore the possibility of "reconciliation" talks with the Taliban sputtered along in low gear for years. It is impossible to know for certain how the pullout plan affected the Taliban's calculations, but interviews with Taliban taken prisoner by NATO suggested that the insurgents knew time was on their side, and they were simply waiting for the Americans to begin a significant withdrawal.

Donilon remains adamant that the president had no other choice but to set a deadline and stick to it. "We needed to do it, because it was the only way to retain discipline over the process, to make sure that we could accomplish our narrow goals and wind down the commitment in an orderly way, and make it clear to the Afghans that they had to be prepared to take the responsibility for security themselves," Donilon told me shortly after Obama made the decision. (In 2012, the White House was still holding regular meetings with the military to make sure they were on track for a full withdrawal of the surge forces later in the year, for fear that without constant supervision the Pentagon would drag out the process.)

AT WEST POINT in December of 2009, Obama publicly announced the surge. The recently deployed surge troops faced their first big test in Helmand Province, the hub of Afghanistan's drug trade, in a small town of 80,000 called Marja.[17]

To one senior American commander this battle was the "first salvo" in a new era of the Afghan War.[18] "It wasn't like we were fighting in Afghanistan for eight years, even though we were," Doug Lute told me one evening. "It was more like we were fighting a yearlong war, eight times in a row."

Marja was a "proof of concept" operation, a critical transition from the Bush era of "clear, hold, build" to Obama's version: "clear hold, build, and *transfer*." The addition was critical: Obama, as Donilon told me at the time, "doesn't want us taking territory that we can't hand over to the Afghans and that they can't hold on to." Otherwise the war would be an endless cycle of ground gained and ground lost.

Marja's beleaguered residents had grown tired of the Taliban, who had controlled the area with brute force for years.[19] But they were also wary of the men with guns that chased the Taliban off. They worried that any successes would be fleeting—and that it would only be a matter of time before the Taliban resurged, taking vengeance on anyone who had sided with the foreigners. In early 2010, no one was more attuned to the frustrations that Marja represented than Ambassador Eikenberry. "These people hate the Taliban, many of them, but they mistrust us," he said.

Over time the battle for Marja took on an aura beyond its relatively modest importance. The White House knew it could not afford a failure, and so Marja quickly became the largest military operation since the beginning of the Afghan War in 2001. But it also became a minefield of inflated expectations. Just as the operation was about to commence, General McChrystal boasted to reporters that as soon as the town was taken, there was a "government in a box, ready to roll in."[20] What he meant was that Marja would follow the classic counterinsurgency strategy—it would be infused with civil servants, judges, police, schoolteachers, and building projects—in an effort to win over the hearts and minds of the local population and provide an immediate, and viable, alternative to the Taliban.[21] Once the concept was proven, it could be replicated throughout the country. This was how the Taliban's momentum would be broken—one population center at a time.

Just before the offensive began, Obama's national security adviser, General Jones, traveled to Afghanistan and Pakistan to assess the situation on the ground. Jones barely knew Obama when the new president was elected; he was brought into the administration because he looked like what Obama needed—a hardened veteran who made traditionalists comfortable in an administration that had campaigned as Washington outsiders promising change. A retired four-star Marine general with an imposing six-foot-four physique, Jones was Central Casting's ideal of what a national security adviser should look like. A gracious demeanor matched his heavily lined face and untamed eyebrows.

For all his old-school qualifications—or perhaps because of them—Jones had a rough start in the Obama White House. He was an outsider in a West Wing filled with insiders. The true power flowed through those who had forged tight relationships in the closed world of the presidential campaign; Jones never saw the inside of the campaign bus. And after years in the military, Jones never seemed comfortable running the civilian decision-making system.

Instead, he left the meetings process to his deputy, Donilon, whom he clearly resented and regarded as a political infighter, not a strategist. That rankled Donilon, but he fought back by mastering the system. He managed the agenda for every Situation Room debate. He quickly became the most well-briefed, well-read official on any and every subject—how to undermine Iran, manage the exit from Iraq, plan drone strikes in Pakistan. More and more, Obama turned to Donilon for briefings, whereas Jones seemed happiest traveling around the world, as he'd done when he was NATO commander, meeting with presidents, prime ministers, and foreign ministers. "There was one moment," a member of Donilon's staff recalled, "when we were all headed into the Situation Room to handle some crisis du jour and there was Jim, in his bicycle suit, headed out the West Wing door."

As a result, the White House rarely let Jones talk to reporters. But one day, as the battle for Marja raged, Obama's aides agreed to let me and one of our White House correspondents, Helene Cooper, sit down with Jones to hear his assessment of the experiment in Marja, and its applicability to the rest of Afghanistan.

He painted a highly optimistic, some might even say fanciful, picture. But when I asked Jones about bringing this "government in a box" into Marja, ready to roll, he deftly avoided the question, describing instead the NATO mission he used to visit monthly. "As I left NATO, I did a study—and I said we're losing. We're not winning; we're losing. So to come a little bit full circle, the reason I'm encouraged is because all of the things I identified a few years ago have been incorporated into our new strategy and I see visible evidence of the fact that it's actually happening on the field."

But the reports from the field were contrasting pretty starkly with Jones's narrative. We pressed him more, citing examples of significant troubles—including President Karzai's latest bizarre threat, "If I come under foreign pressure, I might join the Taliban."[22]

In response, Jones stood up and uncorked a bottle of Chilean wine, a souvenir from his recent trip to the swearing-in of the Chilean president. It seemed like a deflection. The Marja operation, he predicted, would be a success and pave the way for "the year of Kandahar." By that, he meant a cleaning up of one of Afghanistan's largest and most dangerous provinces.

As it turned out, that prediction was optimistic. In the initial months after the Marines deployed to Marja, success was halting at best—and a symbol of how everything would take longer, and prove harder, than the White House imagined. Within a few weeks, the American presence had forced most of the Taliban to stay out of town. But "holding" was a lot easier than "transferring." As one of Jones's colleagues said a few weeks after the interview, "So we got there, and opened the 'government in a box,' and found that one guy walked out. And he didn't know how to govern." General McChrystal himself deemed Marja a "bleeding ulcer" three months after the operation.

As time wore on, the town finally began to stabilize. A year after the operation, local men were signing up to join the security forces, an act of bravery because it made them subject to assassination if the Taliban came back. Some local forms of government began to take root, and turnout for local elections was high. Marja proved that progress in Afghanistan was possible. It also proved that Afghanistan could not change the timeline Obama's team initially envisioned.

The slow pace didn't stop General Petraeus from asserting that, as Marja went, so would Afghanistan. But inside the White House the administration remained dubious. "There are tactical cases which seem promising as discrete bits of evidence," a senior administration official noted. "What's not clear is whether those cases can be put together to create a strategic trend. Marja looks a lot better than two years ago. But how many Marjas do we need to do, and over what time frame?"[23]

THE WARLORD AHMED Wali Karzai, half-brother of the president and the unchallenged font of power in Kandahar Province, embodied the paradoxes of the American experiment in the country—and was what ultimately led Obama to conclude that the effort to totally rewire Afghanistan was folly.

One of the most powerful men in Afghanistan, Ahmed Wali Karzai was the power broker who, from the time his brother was installed as the country's leader by the Bush administration, ran the most restrictive and strategically vital province in the country: Kandahar. While Hamid Karzai handled the Americans with his silken English and Afghan robes, Ahmed Wali Karzai handled the tribes, patching together alliances, enforcing deals, and cutting off enemies. Ahmed Rashid, a renowned Pakistani journalist, always regarded Ahmed Wali Karzai as "the practical operator while Hamid was the ethereal dreamer."[24]

This division of labor continued for nearly a decade. Hamid would fly to Washington, or join a meeting via a secure video teleconference with the president. Ahmed Wali would sit in his "poppy palace," cutting deals. If a tribal leader failed to support the Karzai government in Kabul, Ahmed Wali found a way to make sure that the American aid—which poured into the south after the surge in late 2009—was cut off.

"He didn't have to say a word about how that happened," one senior American official told me in the summer of 2011, with some admiration. "Everyone knew."

Despite being considered the king of Afghanistan's opium fields, Ahmed Wali quickly figured out that the kind of money generated by the poppy trade, while considerable, paled in comparison to the money the Americans and their NATO allies were willing to spend supplying the troops. He readily skimmed millions of dollars off those contracts.

For all these reasons, Ahmed Wali's relationship with the Americans was, as one would expect, volatile and complex. He worked for NATO and the CIA, for whom he ran a clandestine Afghan Special Operations team, and was simultaneously cutting deals with parts of the Taliban. Intelligence agents were drawn to him because he understood how power flowed and could get things done. After all, who else could the CIA turn to if it wanted to build a covert special-ops team that looked Afghan? "He was the ultimate 'asset,' for many years," one former top intelligence official who dealt with him told me.

The military had a more nuanced, less positive view. Yes, Ahmed Wali said he was willing to initiate peace talks with the Taliban, even if those talks went nowhere. Ahmed Wali, noted Lt. Gen. David W. Barno, who commanded American troops in Afghanistan early in the war, "had the family ties, the tribal connections, and the political and security muscle to get things done in and around Kandahar—and the coalition took full advantage of that power."[25] But the military also knew they were dealing with dynamite. Delegation after delegation to Kabul asked President Karzai to bring his brother under control—or get him out of the way. They were rebuffed, politely. "It was the one subject President Karzai would never discuss," one senior Bush administration official told me after Bush had left office. "He would smile but make it clear the subject was off limits."

Ultimately, the Americans both used and complained about Ahmed Wali Karzai because they believed they could not live without him, and yet they knew their long-term strategy for stabilizing Afghanistan could not survive while he was around. In many ways, Ahmed Wali exemplified the disconnect between the CIA and the military in Afghanistan. The CIA wanted to run a counterterrorism campaign; the military had orders to do counterinsurgency. And counterinsurgency was predicated on the emergence of an Afghan government that the people could trust. As one senior military official said to my friend and former colleague Dexter Filkins, "The only way to clean up Chicago is to get rid of Capone."[26]

Like Al Capone, Ahmed Wali made more than a few enemies. Indeed, the remarkable thing about Ahmed Wali Karzai was not that he figured out so many ways to profit from the war while playing all sides; the amazing thing is that he remained alive for more than nine years after the American invasion.

But Ahmed Wali's luck ran out on a Tuesday morning in July 2011, inside his poppy palace. Holding court, as usual, for a parade of officials and petitioners, he greeted Sardar Mohammad, a faithful associate who was so trusted he would often carry Ahmed Wali's young son into the family house. Mohammad was carrying a file, Haji Sayed Jan, a deputy of Ahmed Wali Karzai's, later recalled, and asked to see him alone. They walked into another room. Then

Mohammad took out a gun and, at point-blank range, shot Ahmed Wali Karzai twice in the head. Security guards rushed in and killed Mohammad even as he was squeezing off a third shot. As soon as Ahmed Wali Karzai was pronounced dead, his bodyguards took the assassin's corpse and strung it up in the middle of a busy central bazaar in Kandahar. That act proved that despite the billions NATO poured into the development of a basic justice system, Kandahar was still ruled by brute mafioso force.

In the end, President Karzai—erratic, emotional, and playing to his Pashtun constituency—gave Obama a way to extract himself from Afghanistan.

It was July 2010, when the temperature in Kabul regularly surpassed 100 degrees and the air was saturated with dust and debris. For the first time since the fall of the Taliban, the Afghan government was hosting an international conference in Kabul to map the nation's future.

There was reason for optimism. Nearly a decade after the Taliban's ouster, Kabul was once again a real city, a chaotic fusion of the modern and the medieval. By that summer, the city was a bustling, overcrowded jumble of marketplaces, businesses, restaurants, taxi drivers blasting hip-hop music, and billboards showing Bollywood stars promoting the latest cell phones. You could mistake some corners of the city for Bangkok circa 1980, or Beijing circa 1990. The building boom was almost entirely dependent on foreign money, much of it American.

Yet, Kabul's streets are still lined with donkey carts, open sewers, and herds of goats running alongside heavy traffic. The air smells of diesel fuel, making it difficult to take a deep breath outdoors. And the religious divide is evident as soon as you wander from the prosperous center of the city to the poorer outlying areas. On Kabul's university campuses and in businesses, supermarkets, and offices, most women wear headscarves and long tunics; a brave few venture out in fitted jeans, their faces fully made up and their headscarves pulled back defiantly, revealing swaths of hair. In the outdoor marketplaces, where anything from raw meat carcasses to electronic radios is sold, long-bearded men in turbans and kurta pajamas work alongside clean-shaven men with gelled hair and tight T-shirts. It's not unusual to see schoolchildren in blue-and-white uniforms and bright-blue UNICEF backpacks taunting one another on their way home from school. These are the images of Afghanistan that we rarely see.

In the poorer parts of the city, though, nearly all of the women walk around like pale blue ghosts with white netting over their eyes, and dry hands caked in mud. There, as in many of the rural Pashtun parts of the country, the burkas are the hallmarks of the Afghani practice of orthodox Islam.

Even in Kabul, the war is never far away. The capital is littered with sandbags, guns, barbed wire, and men in camouflage. Anybody affiliated with the UN, the US government, a foreign government, or any organization of clout is trucked around in caravans of armored vehicles, with the symbol of their organization clearly (and foolishly) marked on their car doors. The Afghan National Security Forces are scattered at checkpoints every few blocks, and guards search cars for bombs before letting expats back into their guesthouses. A tank graveyard, with the rusted remains from the failed Soviet occupation three decades ago, rests just outside of the city.

While bombings are not an everyday occurrence, the Haqqani network and other insurgents are out to prove Kabul is not safe. So almost every building is fenced in heavy steel, and getting into a café or restaurant is no easy task. First, you knock on the door of an unmarked building. Then a guard slides open a tiny window to check out how suspicious you appear. Then come several more doors, a reminder of how precarious the city's new freedoms feel.

For foreigners based in Kabul, the city is no place to go roaming alone. There's a roster of roughly six restaurants in the city that are formally approved by government and UN agencies—these are the places where expats are allowed to hang out and drink on the sly, and Afghans are explicitly prohibited from entering. The result, though, is social bifurcation: most foreigners, because of either cultural norms or legal requirements, rarely interact with Afghans outside of work.

That divide between Afghans and foreigners was never more apparent than during the "Kabul Conference" held in the summer of 2010. The idea of the conference, in the bureaucratese of the United Nations, was to settle on an "Afghan-led plan for improving development, governance, and security."[27] For the world leaders who flew into the capital city, the key part of that phrase was "Afghan-led."

The Taliban were there to greet them. Two days before the conference started, a suicide bomber on a bicycle detonated himself in the middle of a busy street, killing three people. Insurgents fired rockets at Kabul Airport as Ban Ki-moon, the UN secretary general, was landing for the conference, forcing his plane to divert to Bagram Airfield, where the United States kept its high-value detainees and its Predator drones. By the time the rest of the leaders arrived, the city was locked down, all shops were closed, and no one—expats, Afghans, or otherwise—was allowed to move. The Afghan National Security Forces in worn olive-green uniforms and caps were the only ones on the sealed-off streets, perching rifles behind sandbags and eyeing the few passersby.

But President Karzai ignored both the threats and the heat: he arrived in a white turtleneck, blue polyester coat, green robe, and sheep's-wool hat. It was remarkable he didn't pass out. Seated at the center of a table of world leaders, he read his statement in slow, stilted tones.

"I am committed to having the ability, by 2014, to reach the level of strength and ability and capacity in our own forces to provide for our own security." If the enormity of what it would take to fulfill that goal was affecting Karzai, he didn't show it. He never lifted his eyes from the sheet of paper in front of him. He adjusted his wire-rimmed glasses and continued: "We hope that the international community will help Afghanistan reach that objective. This is a national objective we have to fulfill—and we must."[28]

Secretary Clinton was one of several leaders sitting in silence during the proclamation. She clasped her hands, furrowed her brow, and planted her gaze firmly on her desk. Ban Ki-moon, the Korean-born secretary general of the UN, was expressionless, showing neither surprise nor mystification about how Karzai would get from point A to point B. Diplomats from seventy different countries surrounded the panel and listened closely with blank faces—some in pressed black suits with neckties, some with long white beards and turbans, some balancing bulky headphones on their ears. No one, it seemed, knew exactly what to make of Karzai's words.

The conference's final communiqué contained the words Obama's team would soon leap on to overrule American military leaders who wanted more time on the ground: "The international community expressed its support for the president of Afghanistan's objective that the Afghan National Security Forces should lead and conduct military operations in all provinces by the end of 2014."[29]

✦

BACK IN WASHINGTON it was obvious that Karzai's declaration was, as usual, more a hope than a plan. Karzai's periodic declarations that Afghan forces would soon control the country by themselves, or that all private security firms must leave Afghanistan, could easily be followed up by his periodic threats to join his "brothers" in the Taliban. Just months before, Eikenberry reported in a cable back to Washington that the two men, in their weekly meeting, had clashed about Karzai's "regular claim to senior US visitors that the United States has 'failed in Afghanistan'" and his regular condemnation of American-caused civilian casualties, while "failing to take any responsibility for Afghanistan's problems." In Eikenberry's view, Karzai's rants left visitors to "easily conclude that the US has accomplished little or nothing here and question why we continue to devote American lives and resources to the effort."[30] In another cable, Eikenberry warned of Karzai's fundamental incompetence, citing his "inability to grasp the most rudimentary principles of state-building."[31]

The numbers and reports from the field echoed Eikenberry's assessment that Karzai was out of touch with reality. Doug Lute kept a running list of heavily contested regions where the Afghan National Security Forces were prepared to take the lead in battling the Taliban, without significant assistance from international forces. "Outside of Kabul," he told his bosses, "there are only one or two areas where they can hold their own." (There were many others in uncontested areas where Afghan forces were taking the leading role.)

Just like the Bush administration, the Obama team put the best face on grim numbers. They reported to Congress that the number of trained troops and Afghan police was hitting, and exceeding, the targets—even in Afghanistan's volatile south. That was the good news. The bad news was that the Afghan forces suffered from such high rates of illiteracy, corruption, and drug addiction that maintaining a cohesive force was a huge challenge. The Americans would build checkpoints; the Afghan troops would man them sporadically. About 14 percent walked away from their posts every year.[32] To many American troops, progress seemed fleeting. To the American people, the war had become old news.

To Obama, the war increasingly looked like old business. Karzai's 2014 deadline, one of his advisers told me, "was our ticket out." General Jones, as he was being pushed out the West Wing door, told

Obama that the 2014 deadline set by Karzai was "a deal you should take." And so when the next summit came, in Lisbon in November 2010, all talk of "conditions-based" withdrawal ended. There were no longer conditions, just a withdrawal.

"My goal," Obama announced at a news conference, "is to make sure that by 2014 we have transitioned, Afghans are in the lead, and it is a goal to make sure we are not still engaged in combat operations of the sort we are involved in now."[33] What would happen if they were not ready for the task? The subject was not discussed in public.

Inside the Obama White House, however, it was talked about each day. John Brennan, the tough former CIA operative who was emerging as the most powerful single voice in the battle against al-Qaeda, argued for keeping just enough of an "enduring presence" in Afghanistan to assure that the "counterterrorism architecture" remained in place. The public line was that this would keep counterterrorism "capabilities, technology, sources, and partnerships to endure over the next many or several years."[34] What that meant, in real terms, was that any troops that remained in Afghanistan after 2014 would conduct only basic training, mentoring, and kill-or-capture operations. They would not be there to win hearts and minds. They would not be there to build schools or roads or clinics. Development would be left to the development professionals; the military would focus on what it did best.

There was another reason to establish an "enduring presence" in Afghanistan after 2014—a reason the White House did not want to discuss. It was Pakistan. The United States could live with an Afghanistan that was messy, even with some parts of the country under de facto Taliban control once the international forces pulled back. But stability in Pakistan—and the security of the Pakistani nuclear arsenal—was another story. The American forces in Afghanistan had a role as a "break the glass" emergency force if Pakistan, and its arsenal, appeared to be coming apart at the seams.

And by the time that Americans transferred combat operations to the Afghan forces, many of its partners would already be gone. While NATO's energetic secretary general, Anders Fogh Rasmussen, told the audience at Lisbon that "one thing must be very clear—NATO is in it for the long term," the calendar told a different story.[35] Many countries were already planning troop withdrawals that would precede 2014, and some had already begun. The Dutch had already quit Afghanistan by the time the Lisbon conference happened. Canada would be gone by the summer of 2011—a loss of about 3,000 troops. Later the French, after four of its troops were killed by a serviceman in the Afghan National Army, also announced they were leaving early. In combat terms, those numbers didn't mean much; they were a small fraction of the American presence. And since each NATO country determined its own rules of engagement, including whether it would conduct combat operations, many allied troops did not fight the insurgency. (Behind closed doors, the US military often joked that ISAF, the acronym for NATO's international security force, actually stood for "I Saw Americans Fight.") But the departures underscored the international fatigue with the war in Afghanistan. Countries that had once joined the effort to show their unity with the United States now believed the costs of solidarity far outweighed the benefits.

The message from the Lisbon conference was, in fact, very clear—but it was the exact opposite of what Rasmussen and Obama were attempting to convey: regardless of whether the Afghans were ready by 2014, NATO would no longer be around to build their country.

IN THE TWO years after Obama declared his "new way forward" in Afghanistan and Pakistan, he could certainly boast that the United States and its allies had some successes to put up on the scoreboard. The "benchmarks" that the data-driven Obama team assembled told part of the story. Some 85 percent of the population now had access to health care, a huge increase from the 9 percent that could find such care in 2002, just after the Taliban were driven out.[36] Access to education soared. Roughly 6.2 million children were now in school. Best of all, 40 percent of them were girls, who had been banned from education under Taliban rule.[37] A program to support local governance and development, called the National Solidarity Program, enabled Afghans to elect local representatives to guide community development and was championing widespread successes throughout the country. Millions of refugees who had fled during Taliban or Soviet rule were returning to rebuild their lives.

But benchmarks told only part of the story. Despite NATO's efforts, corruption and an absent Afghan government remained the norm. Karzai was not becoming more credible or legitimate in the eyes of his people. The opium trade continued to boom, lining the pockets of warlords and government officials alike. While the surge succeeded at "reversing the momentum" of the Taliban in the south, where American and NATO troops were present in the largest numbers, attacks by the Haqqani network were on the rise in the east, where troops were scarce. Lt. Gen. David Rodriguez, the day-to-day commander in Afghanistan, told me in the summer of 2010 that "our biggest challenge is durability."[38] The Taliban might retreat, but only temporarily. Assuring lasting change would require time and patience, two qualities that have never been American strengths when it comes to interventions overseas.

And the central problem that Obama had vowed to fix—making sure that neither the Taliban nor criminal gangs like the Haqqani network had a safe haven in the tribal areas of Pakistan—wasn't getting any better. When the surge forces were at their height in 2011, cross-border attacks in Afghanistan's eastern provinces by the Haqqani network, by NATO's count, increased fivefold over the previous year.[39] That was hardly the kind of statistic Obama could tout before Congress.

When Doug Lute conducted briefings with members of Congress or reporters in spring 2011, he sometimes gave voice to his inner pessimism. His first concern was an economic one: there was no way to replace the economic hole that the United States would leave in Afghanistan when it began to send its troops home. In the 2012 fiscal year, the Defense Department had asked for $12.8 billion to train, arm, and support the Afghan army and police—a figure that amounted to almost half of Afghanistan's GDP.[40] As Obama pointed out in a meeting where he stared at that number in wonderment, that was the biggest single item in the Pentagon's budget. It was bigger, for example, than spending on the Joint Strike Fighter, the next-generation aircraft to protect the United States.

The long-term projections, Lute told his White House colleagues, were not much better. It costs roughly $6 billion per year to sustain the 365,000 members of the Afghan National Security Forces.[41] Put another way, funding the army and police forces costs more than six times the country's entire budget of approximately $1 billion.[42]

"When you ask people what makes this a sustainable plan," Lute said one day, referring to the question of who would pay that kind of money after the eventual American and NATO withdrawal, "they just look at you. Because there's nothing to say. It's just not a credible model."

So while Obama may have inherited the Afghan problem, after he decided to triple-down at the end of 2009, he owned it. The question was how he could extract himself.

AT THE END of 2010, the White House organized a committee to narrow the goals even more—and find the president a path to the exits.

The group called itself "Afghan Good Enough." The committee's name was indisputably offensive; had its existence been known beyond the White House, it likely would have outraged many who served, and who feared that a "good-enough" mentality would abandon their hard-won gains.

The group was convened each week by Denis McDonough, the lean, insightful, sometimes sarcastic deputy national security adviser who had risen from the post of Obama's Senate aide to a member of the White House's true inner circle and was a first-class political operative. McDonough's main mission was to protect his boss, a skill he honed on Capitol Hill. After more than a year handling the public communications portfolio at the White House—a job he clearly did not enjoy—he went back to his traditional role as the man who solved problems and enforced control in the fractious administration. "Denis loves secrecy," one of his colleagues said. "He knows how to cut your nuts off if he thinks you are talking to too many outsiders. So 'Afghan Good Enough' was the perfect kind of mission for him."

The kind of conversations that took place within that group represented a realpolitik that no one ever admits to on Sunday-morning talk shows. "We spent the time asking questions like, How much corruption can we live with?" one participant told me later. "Is there another way—a way the Pentagon might not be telling us about—to speed the withdrawal? What's the least we can spend on training Afghan troops and still get a credible result?"

While the group was still meeting, a tragedy interceded—one that pushed the administration to downsize even faster. Richard Holbrooke, the diplomatic force of nature, collapsed one Friday morning in December 2010 while in Secretary Clinton's office. He was rushed down her private elevator and into a car to George Washington Hospital, just a few blocks from the State Department. During a series of emergency procedures, a procession of administration officials, from his loyalists to those driven to distraction by Holbrooke's constant calls and expansions of the boundaries of his authority, jammed into the hospital waiting room with Holbrooke's wife, Kati Marton. Obama called her repeatedly, leaving her to note archly, after Holbrooke passed away, that the president had placed more calls to her at the end than to Holbrooke during the previous two years.

Holbrooke's death accelerated the movement to Afghan Good Enough.

"Just think how big a reversal of approach this was in just two years," said one official who had worked closely with Holbrooke. "We started with what everyone thought was a pragmatic vision but, at its core, was a plan for changing the way Afghanistan is wired. We ended up thinking about how to do as little wiring as possible."

And within a year, Afghan Good Enough would have a strategic cousin: Pakistan Good Enough.

EVEN BY THE spring of 2011, Obama's commanders still did not fully believe that Obama intended to pull all of the 30,000-plus surge forces out of Afghanistan quickly, whether "conditions on the ground" were improving or not. While Biden, Donilon, Lute, and their allies had lost the initial battle in late 2009 to minimize America's "footprint" in Afghanistan, they won the long war. Petraeus either missed the turn in Obama's thinking or ignored it.

Obama had begun to make his point to the military a year earlier, in the summer of 2010, after Gen. Stanley McChrystal made the inexplicable decision to participate in a *Rolling Stone* profile on how he was conducting the war. In an article entitled "The Runaway General," Michael Hastings reported a series of profanity-laced conversations in which McChrystal and his staff were portrayed as openly disparaging of Obama, Vice President Biden, and other senior civilian officials. Before the article went to print, Press Secretary Robert Gibbs handed Obama a copy. Thirty-six hours later, McChrystal was out and Petraeus was in.

After McChrystal was fired, Petraeus was moved from CENT-COM commander (that is, Central Command, responsible for military forces in the Middle East, the Persian Gulf, and parts of Asia) to the head of NATO and US Forces in Afghanistan. As he took over, he made clear that he did not intend to administer a "graceful exit" out of Afghanistan. "For the first time," Petraeus said, "we will have what we have been working to put in place for the last year and a half."[43] He was there to win—whatever winning meant. Petraeus's assumption—which reflected the military's assumption—was that, as in Iraq, the surge would yield some significant benefits . . . significant enough that the president would not want to tinker with success.

But Afghanistan wasn't Iraq, and change wasn't coming as quickly as the deadlines Washington had set to satisfy the electorate. Counterinsurgency was working, more or less, in the key Taliban strongholds of Kandahar and Helmand, where the bulk of the surge troops were fighting. But these gains were fragile and would be lost if troops were withdrawn too quickly. Petraeus wanted as much time as possible to build the Afghan forces, consolidate the gains made in Afghanistan's south and southwest, and redistribute resources to secure Afghanistan's eastern border with Pakistan—where the Haqqani network was growing.

The military assumed the run-up to the decision about how fast to reduce the forces would look a lot like 2009: proposals from the commanders on the ground, lengthy interagency debates, lots of meetings in the Situation Room. They were wrong on all counts.

"My view of it is that the eighteen- to twenty-four-month agreement [for the length of the surge] was the Pentagon saying they could do it, in order to get the troops," one of Obama's most senior advisers told me one evening in the late spring of 2011 as Obama was pressing his aides for a sped-up withdrawal. "And Obama wanted it in writing. There is a seven-page memo that records all of this. They all signed up to it. And it was pretty plain: don't clear an area you can't transition in eighteen to twenty-four months."

"But the military never rallied behind that," he went on. "They thought that if we can establish this is working, we would not end up withdrawing. The way you do counterinsurgency is to do as much as it takes, for as long as it takes."

Soon after the 2009 surge was set, the official recalled, "I told the president that I thought the Pentagon signed on to the surge deadlines because they thought that if they needed more time later, there will be more time."

Obama responded, he recalled, by saying, "Well, I'm not going to give them more time."

WHEN IT CAME time to decide how fast to pull the surge troops out of Afghanistan, Obama had learned some bitter lessons. "The president expressly did not want to have a repeat of what took place last time. He talked to his national security advisers and made it very clear that we were going to do this low-key, and quietly," Ben Rhodes, by then Obama's deputy national security adviser for strategic communications, told me in the summer of 2011, a few weeks after Obama had publicly announced the timelines for withdrawal.

In essence, Obama decided that any outcome of the exit-strategy review process was going to be White House–driven. The State Department and Department of Defense would inevitably call for more time and more resources to fulfill their objectives. Strategic gains would invariably need to be consolidated; the opaque negotiations process with the Taliban would need more time to work. But in this review, Obama had a very distinct idea of where he was headed.

"The president said, 'I want to send a very clear signal about what we mean by transition. And you can't have a transition if you don't take any troops out during 2012, and you can't have a transition if you just say all of the things you're going to do for the Afghans,'" Rhodes said. "He said he wanted to be very clear about the fact that he was decreasing our resources. That set the tone for the review and made clear which direction he was going in."

In fact, the National Security Council principals (Gates; Clinton; the director of national intelligence, James Clapper; and the director of the CIA, Leon Panetta) were not allowed into the review process until just a few weeks before Obama officially announced his drawdown targets and timeline. Back in Kabul, before the meeting of the NSC principals, Petraeus's staff officers crafted options that would keep any withdrawals of US troops to a minimum. "Our hope is that we'll be able to get away with no combat troops getting pulled out this summer. But we recognize that may not be possible," an officer said.[44]

When Petraeus arrived in Washington in June and briefed his options to the president, he recommended limiting troop withdrawals to 2,500 to 5,000 by the end of 2011. The full surge, he insisted, shouldn't be recovered until the end of 2012—at the earliest. Petraeus wanted as many troops as possible in Afghanistan through the next fighting season, with a steep drop to follow once the fighting season was over.

"The president was pushing him," one of Obama's senior advisers told me, "asking, 'Why do you need two full fighting seasons before you begin your drawdown?' The president thought that the campaign plan was more ambitious than it needed to be, because it involved essentially doing what we were doing in the south, in the east."

The adviser continued: "And I think, from a purely military perspective, that you're led to a more maximalist objective of wanting to eradicate the enemy. And the president said that the goal of the Afghan campaign was not to defeat the Taliban militarily, or the Haqqani network militarily. He believed that we had a more limited set of objectives that could be accomplished by bringing the military out at a faster clip."

Privately, Clinton, Gates, and Biden voiced their concerns about the scale and pace of the proposed troop reductions. Clinton, like Petraeus, wanted to keep the surge troops around for as long as possible, but for different reasons. Clinton now had two main objectives for Afghanistan: to maintain all of the development progress forged over the past ten years and to achieve a credible, negotiated settlement with the Taliban. The latter objective would be much harder to achieve with fewer troops on the ground. To bring the Taliban to the negotiating table, or so the conventional wisdom went, they would need to feel like they were losing out on the field.

Biden, in keeping with his earlier positions on Afghanistan, wanted the surge troops out as quickly as possible—pushing for the full recovery of the surge by the beginning of 2012. But neither extreme seemed palatable to Obama.

After a short internal debate, Gates and Clinton came up with a different option: recover the surge by September 2012—as the summer fighting season wore down, but before the November 2012 presidential elections. Obama concurred. Ten thousand troops would return at the end of 2011, and the full surge of 33,000 troops would be recovered by September of the following year.

"The ultimate [drawdown] decision was a more aggressive formulation, if you will, in terms of the timeline than what we had recommended," Petraeus later testified before a Senate committee. "The fact is, there has never been a military commander in history who has all the forces they would like to have, for all the time, with all the money, all the authorities, and nowadays all the bandwidth as well."[45]

OBAMA WALKED UP to a wooden podium marked with a presidential seal couched between two American flags. The impeccable white halls, crystal chandelier, and red carpeting of the White House formed his backdrop.

This was no grand affair or cause for celebration. When Obama first announced his "new way forward" in Afghanistan and Pakistan in March 2009, all of his National Security Council principals and top commanders stood behind him. His speech announcing the surge in December 2009 was made before a large audience of West Point cadets, decked out in their gray uniforms. Now with two and a half years of his presidency completed, he stood alone, and his message was simple: American troops were being withdrawn from Afghanistan.

"When I announced this surge at West Point," he began, "we set clear objectives: to refocus on al-Qaeda, reverse the Taliban's momentum, and train the Afghan security forces to defend their own country. And I also made it clear that our commitment would not be open-ended, and that we would begin to draw down our forces this July. Tonight, I can tell you that we are fulfilling that commitment."

Obama stared directly into the camera and continued. "We will not try to make Afghanistan a perfect place. We will not police its streets or patrol its mountains indefinitely. . . . What we can do, and will do, is build a partnership with the Afghan people that endures. . . .

"Over the last decade," he concluded, "we have spent a trillion dollars on war, at a time of rising debt and hard economic times. Now we must invest in America's greatest resource—our people. . . . America, it is time to focus on nation building here at home."[46]

With that pronouncement, Obama shifted America's priorities—and his own—to a far greater degree than the White House was willing to admit. The conflict he came into office describing as a "war of necessity" had morphed into a "war of choice"—one that he decided to exit even if the job was far from complete, even if there was no assurance that gains made in the past decade could last. For the first time since 9/11, domestic needs—jobs, infrastructure, and debt reduction—trumped occupying and reinventing the land where the September 11 plot was created.

It was a pragmatic, cold calculus: Obama had learned, in the course of two years, that he could not remake Afghanistan. He had learned that he could not win hearts and minds with vast sums of military and civilian aid. He had learned that to preserve American interests in Afghanistan and Pakistan, he would have to use power in a manner more limited, more aggressive, and often more callous. He had come full circle in his ambitions for the country where empires and armies have met ugly stalemates.

He turned away from his podium and walked back through the low-lit marble halls of the White House—alone.

Chapter 3

The Bomb Scare

From the first days of the Obama administration, there was no question about what the ultimate nightmare in South Asia would look like: a missing nuclear weapon in Pakistan. But it was always something of a theoretical threat, the stuff of crisis scenarios played out at the National War College. That changed early in the first summer of Obama's presidency, when his intelligence briefers arrived in the Oval Office with the kind of fragmentary, maddeningly ambiguous evidence that gave a new president a taste of the panic and confusion that would surround hunting down a loose nuke in the world's most dangerous nation.

There was an "emerging intelligence picture," Obama was told, that a particularly virulent strain of the Pakistani Taliban may actually have gotten its hands on the ultimate terror weapon. But no one knew for sure exactly what the Taliban had—if anything.

The source of the scare was intercepted conversations from the TTP—the Tehrik-i-Taliban Pakistan—an umbrella group of insurgents formed in 2007 with the avowed goal of breaking the Pakistani state and restoring sharia law. As a result, it is the only Taliban group that the Pakistani military and intelligence services truly regard as a threat. So does the CIA, which was concerned about chatter within the group about targeting American cities, chiefly in retaliation for the drone strikes that were homing in on the group's leaders.

In the early summer of 2009, there was no doubt who the Predator drones buzzing overhead were gunning for: Baitullah Mehsud, the bearded, thirtysomething tribal leader whose control over South Waziristan would have won the envy of a Chicago mob boss. He had taken control of the area at a young age and used it as a base to run operations into Afghanistan. If the Americans could be exhausted there, he believed, Pakistan could be the next to fall. He was also a wily negotiator. In February 2005, he struck what President Pervez Musharraf, then the leader of Pakistan, called a "cease-fire" deal in which Pakistan pulled its troops out of Mehsud's area in return for a halt on attacks. In Washington the deal was regarded as a farce (not least because the Pentagon continued to "reimburse" Pakistan for military operations in the area that, by Musharraf's own account, had ended). The cease-fire lasted four months. Then Mehsud kicked into high gear. He was behind the plot that killed Benazir Bhutto, the former prime minister who had returned to Pakistan in late 2007 to challenge Musharraf for the presidency. It was assumed that her widower, the largely ineffectual current president Asif Ali Zardari, was high on Mehsud's hit list.

But no one thought Mehsud possessed the competence to handle a nuclear weapon, or the supply network to obtain one. Which is why the National Security Agency's experts were surprised to hear conversations among Mehsud's associates that, as one official characterized them to me, "strongly suggested they may have obtained nuclear materials, or a nuclear device."

The briefers who presented the evidence to the president emphasized their doubts. It could be a fully assembled bomb, the president was told, but that would have required a huge breach of the Pakistani arsenal. More likely, it was the makings of a "dirty bomb"—radioactive material that can be wrapped around some conventional explosives and used to pollute several blocks of a city, but doesn't cause a nuclear explosion. While the casualties would be low, the psychological effect from a dirty bomb would be enormous, particularly because in the public's mind, the difference between a radiological device and a real nuclear weapon is fuzzy at best.

A beat or two of silence hung over the room. As Obama knew well, this was a scenario that the United States had war-gamed time and again. The simulations rarely end well; for all the Pakistani paranoia, there is no good plan for sweeping up Pakistan's nuclear weapons, largely because on any given day it is not entirely clear where they all are. But in this case there was no obvious evidence of a breach of any Pakistani facility. Nor was there mention in the intercepts about where the weapon or material might have come from.

In the intercepts, Obama was told, several Taliban commanders talked about their acquisition in cautious, vaguely coded language. Over the course of many calls, they kept returning to the same subject.[1]

"It came up again and again," said one official who had read some of the intercepts. But exactly *what* they were talking about was elusive. Mehsud and his associates spoke in an odd dialect. And if the Pakistani government had picked up the same chatter, they had not shared it. This added to the complications. How do you find a bomb that may or may not exist without landing a nuclear search team that the Pakistanis, in their paranoia, will be certain was really sent to immobilize their own nuclear arsenal? And how do you get the cooperation of a country that has already declared, "Our security systems are foolproof"? Moreover, how do you count the nuclear assets of a country that is also trying to hide from Washington the tremendous pace at which it is upgrading and expanding its nuclear arsenal?[2]

No one was sure, of course, that the materials Mehsud's aides were talking about came from Pakistan's supply. But everyone knew that would be the first suspicion. "They are well on their way to becoming the world's fourth largest nuclear power," one senior American official said to me, reconstructing the harrowing few days that followed. "They're moving more nuclear material around the

roads and creating weapons in which we figured they could no longer separate the nuclear cores and the triggers," which is how the
larger nuclear weapons are stored, making an entire weapon difficult to steal. "So it's natural that's the first place we look."

Obama dispatched several of his senior officials, amid great secrecy, to approach the Pakistanis with the conversations they had
overheard. The initial response was unimpressive. "This turned out
to be an important shakedown cruise," said one participant in those
panicked few days as officials tried to cut through the fog of ambiguous evidence. "We discovered we had American officials who didn't
know the difference between a nuclear bomb and a dirty bomb. And
we had Pakistanis who just dismissed the report, and didn't seem
particularly interested in finding answers." To anyone who had reviewed the classified simulations Washington had run of a nuclear
crisis in Pakistan, this scenario was familiar: reluctant Pakistani officials, reams of unanswered questions, and missed signals.

DURING THE TALIBAN bomb scare, you could divide Obama's aides
into two camps. There were a few—at the CIA, at the Pentagon, and
in Obama's newly formed team—who had been through these fire
drills before. "You never want to get complacent, of course," one of
them told me later, "but you know that everyone's first reaction is
to think about the worst-case scenario, and then over time, as first
reports get questioned, the threat often dissipates."

Then there were the newcomers, who stayed calm mostly because the old-timers weren't running around with their hair on fire.
Still, as one senior military official reported, "For four or five days,
we were pretty focused on what it would mean" for one of the Taliban's most ruthless leaders to have his hands on anything nuclear.

The first and most important question was whether anything was missing from Pakistan's own facilities. On this, the
Americans had something of a window: soon after 9/11, the Bush

administration had begun a secret program to help Pakistan protect its nuclear facilities. When it started, the program represented quite a turnabout, since Washington had spent years imposing economic sanctions to prevent Pakistan from getting the bomb in the first place. But Bush, and Obama after him, had quickly concluded that it was a little late to be lecturing Pakistan about the virtues of atomic abstinence. Instead, it was worth investing in protection.

By the time Obama came to office, Bush had spent more than $100 million teaching the Pakistanis how to build fences around nuclear facilities, how to install electronic padlocks, how to track loose materials, and other techniques for keeping arsenals safe. According to both American and Pakistani sources, Obama doubled down on that program.[3]

But Pakistan was not exactly making it easy. It refused any technology or site visits that it believed would help Americans identify the location of Pakistan's weapons. And in February 2009, just weeks after Obama's inauguration, Anne Patterson, the American ambassador to Pakistan, had warned the new administration that diverting some highly enriched uranium or weapons-grade plutonium from Pakistan's stockpiles might not be as difficult as the Pakistanis insisted.

"Our major concern is not having an Islamic militant steal an entire weapon," she wrote in a classified cable that was part of the collection that WikiLeaks obtained and the *Times* and other newspapers ultimately published, "but rather the chance someone working in GOP [government of Pakistan] facilities could gradually smuggle enough material out to eventually make a weapon."[4] In other words, by shipping out a few grams of nuclear material at a time, insurgents could outwit a security system looking for major thefts. The Pakistanis, of course, dismissed such fears as ridiculous. When I went to visit Khalid Kidwai, the former general who runs Pakistan's Special Plans Division, which is responsible for the security of Pakistan's arsenal, a year before Patterson wrote that cable, his last words to me on the subject of the security of Pakistani nuclear weapons were pretty succinct: "It's perfect."

At least in public, Obama went out of his way during those first months to sound reassuring about the safety of the Pakistani arsenal—even if his answers caused anyone familiar with the details to cringe. In late April, three months after taking office but before the report about the TTP intercepts circulated, Obama was asked by NBC's White House correspondent, Chuck Todd, "Can you reassure the American people that, if necessary, America could secure Pakistan's nuclear arsenal and keep it from getting into the Taliban's hands, or worst-case scenario, even al-Qaeda's hands?"

The president stumbled at first with his answer, saying, "The Pakistani Army, I think, recognizes the hazards of those weapons falling into the wrong hands." When Todd pressed, Obama cut him off, snapping, "I'm not going to engage in hypotheticals of that sort. I feel confident that that nuclear arsenal will remain out of militant hands. OK?"[5]

Less than a month after President Obama's testy exchange, Anne Patterson sent another cable, classified "Secret," that drew a pretty stark picture of how deeply Washington and Islamabad differed on how to deal with the threat to the arsenal.[6] The ambassador's concern focused on a stockpile of highly enriched uranium—the kind used for bomb fuel—that had been sitting for years near an aging research reactor in Pakistan. In one of those great ironies of history, the fuel had come from the United States, decades before, under the 1960s' "Atoms for Peace" program. It was supposed to fuel a small research reactor. In those days, little thought was given to proliferation risks, and Pakistan seemed too poor and backward to join the nuclear race. The amount of fuel was not huge, Patterson reported: There was enough to build several "dirty bombs." In skilled hands, there might be enough fuel for an actual nuclear bomb.

But by May 2009, the American efforts to get the fuel back—it was no longer being used—had run into one blockade after another. Patterson's terse cable to the State and Defense Departments, among others, made it clear that the American effort to get the fuel out of Pakistan touched every nerve in the fraught relationship: mutual mistrust, broken promises, and a pervasive fear that any public talk about Pakistan's vulnerability would end whatever cooperation existed.

On May 27, 2009, Patterson reported that the Pakistani government was yet again dragging its feet on a year-old agreement to have the United States remove the material. Every time articles appeared in the American media about the safety of Pakistan's arsenal, she wrote, Pakistani officials would tell her, "The 'sensational' international and local media coverage of Pakistan's nuclear weapons made it impossible to proceed at this time." A senior Pakistani official, she said, warned that if word leaked out that Americans were helping remove the fuel, the local press would certainly "portray it as the United States taking Pakistan's nuclear weapons."[7]

So the fuel stayed where it was, waiting for something bad to happen.

FOR SEVERAL DAYS after the president's briefing about the Pakistani Taliban, officials scrambled to answer the most basic question: Was this real, or a hoax? "Mostly we had a lot of boasts and celebratory chats," among Taliban leaders exulting about their acquisition, one senior American intelligence official said. Yet there were reasons for skepticism. The Taliban seemed much less sophisticated than al-Qaeda, which had tried, and failed, to obtain nuclear materials and expertise from two senior Pakistani nuclear experts just before 9/11. "There were some in the intelligence community who just didn't believe this story," one senior official who had served in

Pakistan during the scare told me later as I tried to reconstruct an incident that remains, to this day, highly classified.

Obama decided he could not take the chance that the story was false: he ordered one of the US government's nuclear-detection-and-disablement teams to travel to the region in case it was needed for the search. But they dared not step into Pakistan itself, where the government would have a tough time explaining why there were foreigners with nuclear-detection equipment wandering around.

Obama's aides worried that if news of Washington's suspicions leaked, the Pakistanis would shut down altogether and the Indians—who had barely held back retaliating against Pakistan after a deadly attack in Mumbai the previous year—would mobilize and put their forces on high alert. That would inevitably trigger a Pakistani response, and the chance for miscalculations and deadly escalations would soar.

And there was always the risk that the TTP, realizing that the United States was on to the conversations, could issue a threat to make use of the weapon—even if none existed. If they included a threat to set it off in an American or Pakistani city, mass panic could follow. That could kill more people than a small explosion.

Several officials who were involved in the briefings told the president that, more than likely, the Taliban threat "focused on Pakistan itself." There had been a series of spectacular car-bomb and suicide attacks in Islamabad and the nearby garrison city of Rawalpindi, including one on the headquarters of the ISI.

Yet there was always the possibility, lurking in the back of Obama's mind, that the loose weapon—if there was one—could be headed for New York, Washington, or some other American city. It was a remote but reasonable concern. Though al-Qaeda was weakened, elements of the Pakistani insurgency were beginning to think about launching attacks of their own against the United States, as the administration was about to learn in the May 2010 attempted car bombing in Times Square, for which the TTP provided the training.

"It was a pretty tense series of conversations," one former senior intelligence official told me early in 2012. "We didn't know if the Pakistanis really knew what was going on. And if they did discover something was missing, how could we be certain they would level with us?" In the end, the Pakistanis responded: they surveyed their arsenal and reported back that nothing was missing.

Within days the crisis began to evaporate, though even today there are conflicting stories about why. One senior American official told me the Taliban had fallen for the oldest trick in the nuclear book: a scam, in which they paid dearly for some nuclear material that was completely useless in building a weapon. A senior military official had a different account: the mistake was the NSA's, which had trouble understanding the dialect in which Mehsud's associates spoke. "They were saying they had gotten something. But the word they used didn't necessarily mean it was nuclear."

But the effect on the administration was significant: The bomb scare underscored, more dramatically than anything else that first year, the fact that Pakistan could represent a far deeper strategic threat to the United States than Afghanistan ever will. Peering into the nuclear abyss so early in Obama's presidency, one official said, "created a lasting impression on all of us."

So now, every three months or so, the Americans try to meet the Pakistani nuclear establishment, as discreetly as possible. The United States is represented by Thomas D'Agostino, head of the National Nuclear Security Administration, and Robert Einhorn at the State Department; the Pakistanis are represented by General Kidwai and his staff. Because of the huge Pakistani sensitivities, the meetings are never announced, and to avoid discovery and the inevitable questions that would follow, they take place in cities where the participants can slip in and out unnoticed, from London to Abu Dhabi. One administration official said the process has impressed the White House with "how seriously the Pakistanis take nuclear security, perhaps more seriously than anyone else in the world." Nevertheless, US officials still fear things could rapidly spiral out of control if Pakistan ever imploded, an eventuality, he added, that "you can't handle with better training and equipment."

Chapter 4

Getting bin Laden, Losing Pakistan

Geronimo, EKIA.

> —*A transmission from the SEAL team in Abbottabad,*
> *Pakistan, the first confirmation transmitted to the White*
> *House that Osama bin Laden was, after a decade on the*
> *run, "Enemy Killed in Action"*

IN THE SPRING OF 2008, JUST AS BARACK OBAMA WAS OUTMANEU-vering Hillary Clinton for the Democratic nomination for president, two of America's top intelligence officials, Michael Leiter and Stephen Kappes, formed a special, highly classified cell inside America's spy community. They were determined to solve the most vexing intelligence failure of the decade: the Bush administration's inability to find Osama bin Laden and his deputy, Ayman al-Zawahiri.

"Our last decent sense of his whereabouts was Tora Bora, 2001," Leiter told me shortly after he had left as the chief of the National Counterterrorism Center, itself a creation of the intelligence failures of 9/11. He was referring to bin Laden's famous escape from the region, after a colossal misjudgment by the Bush administration gave Northern Alliance fighters, with the help of American Special Operations Forces, the primary responsibility for hunting him down in some of the world's most challenging terrain. Ever since, there had been rumors, promising leads, countless dead ends, millions of dollars spent, and nothing to show for it. By the end of his presidency, Bush rarely mentioned bin Laden's name in public, because it reminded the world that the president's "Wanted: Dead or Alive" advertisement had ended in a failed manhunt.

Together, Leiter and Kappes were the odd couple of the intelligence world. Leiter, who is fascinated by what makes terror networks click, still has the trim bearing of a Navy officer and is an urbane, intellectual Harvard Law School graduate and former Supreme Court clerk (for Justice Stephen Breyer). After his clerkship, Leiter served on the staff of the WMD Commission—the lesser-known cousin of the 9/11 Commission—which issued a searing report on how the United States blew the intelligence on Iraq, a conclusion that left many in the White House embittered and angry. (He once had to admit to Bush that he had never voted for him—a revelation that likely left the forty-third president, who relied on Leiter every day, a bit stunned.)

Kappes was a completely different animal—the ultimate intelligence operator. He had years of military service in common with Leiter; he was a former Marine. But the commonalities stopped there. Nearly a generation older, Kappes was the former CIA station chief in Moscow. He spoke Russian and was skilled in Persian, a rarity for the CIA. He had retired from the CIA once already, to go make some money, only to be dragged back when the agency was demoralized and under fire for everything from the nonexistent Iraqi weapons of mass destruction to the fierce argument over interrogation methods. Inside the Directorate of Operations, where he grew up, Kappes was a hero: he was the man who helped bring down A. Q. Khan, the Pakistani nuclear expert, in 2003—probably the best single operation the agency could boast of in a decade or more. And he worked with the British to pressure Muammar Qaddafi to give up his nuclear program, a move that seemed remarkable at the time, and looked brilliant years later, when Qaddafi could not wield a weapon to keep the West from helping topple his regime.

Both men were sufficiently obsessed with the failures surrounding the bin Laden hunt and knew that only new thinking—and new technology—would crack the case.

Soon they turned to the national laboratories, known for their work on nuclear weapons, for ideas about how to find a lone terrorist in Pakistan. The scientists had plenty of ideas—some good, some wacky. One stood out. Bin Laden loved nothing more than to make videos that kept his message alive, and someone had to be producing and distributing those videos. So the labs came up with the idea of flooding Pakistan with new digital cameras in hopes that bin Laden's videographers were eager for an upgrade. Each digital camera, the labs said, contained a unique signature with signals that are identifiable and, with luck, traceable.* Wouldn't it be the ultimate irony if bin Laden's next video threat to destroy the West became a beacon for a Predator drone strike? Within months, new cameras seeped into the distribution chain in Peshawar, where everyone in the tribal regions comes to shop. It was a pretty brilliant strategy.

Alas, it didn't work. It turned out that Osama bin Laden hadn't been in the rugged mountains of Pakistan for years. Instead, he was making his videos from a dank living room, barely a mile from where Pakistan's entire military leadership had been trained.

Leiter declines to talk about the cell that he and Kappes ran; the techniques they used, including the traceable digital cameras, are still relied on by the CIA and law enforcement officials, and remain highly classified.

But shortly after leaving government, Leiter said that the cell's efforts were something of a Hail Mary pass. "In the end," he said, "we knew the secret would be the couriers—you had to find the couriers."

He was right. The break came roughly a year later, in the sum-

---

* The program remains highly classified, because similar operations exploit the same technology. Some details have been omitted here at the request of government officials.

mer of 2010, when the National Security Agency captured a mobile-phone conversation between a longtime courier for al-Qaeda, Abu Ahmed al-Kuwaiti, and a friend he had been out of touch with for a long time.* To the untrained ear, it sounded like a typical catch-up conversation.

"Where have you been?" the friend asked. "We've missed you. What's going on in your life? And what are you doing now?"

"I'm back with the people I was with before," al-Kuwaiti replied.

His friend paused for a moment, and then replied, "May God be with you."[1]

To anyone who didn't know the pedigree of the participants, it wasn't much. But the conversation enabled the NSA to home in on al-Kuwaiti's whereabouts. Soon two Pakistani agents were able to pull up behind his white Suzuki, which had a distinctive rhino tire cover on its spare, in the bustling streets of Peshawar, the Pakistani city closest to the mountainous territory where bin Laden was believed to be hiding. Yet al-Kuwaiti did not head into the mountains that day. Instead, he headed east—across the Indus River—to Abbottabad. Northeast of Pakistan's capital, the small city is a wealthy, popular holiday destination for Pakistanis trying to escape the summer heat farther south. It is also the home of Pakistan's equivalent of West Point, which means that every military officer knows it well. The markets are jammed with current officers and retired generals, many of whom settled in the area.

As the courier approached the outskirts of Abbottabad, the CIA agents followed al-Kuwaiti to a whitewashed compound on a hilltop, just off Kakul Road in the middle-class neighborhood of Bilal Town—less than a mile from the entrance to the military academy.[2] To a Westerner, it hardly looked like a palace. "It is simply a concrete building with a wall sitting in the middle of a dusty cabbage

---

* The name is a pseudonym, not uncommon among al-Qaeda members.

field," my colleague Jill Abramson wrote after visiting there in the summer of 2011.[3] But it was a concrete building with an unusual history: nobody admitted to knowing who built it in 2005, and the records conveniently disappeared after the structure became infamous.* By some accounts, it was worth a million dollars, though that stretches the imagination. It was hardly unique, though; less than eighty yards away were some other large homes, including one owned by a serving major in the Pakistani military.

What made this building unusual were the twelve- to eighteen-foot-high concrete walls, topped with barbed wire and protected by two security fences. But even more unusual was the seven-foot "privacy" wall built around the third-floor balcony. Together with the opaque windows, there was no way anyone could see into the building or observe someone on the balcony. What or who was being hidden?

"It was clear this place housed someone big," said one senior official. "But that hardly meant it had to be OBL."

And it was also clear that in order to solve the mystery of who was inside, the United States was going to have to violate Pakistan's sovereignty in ways it had never before attempted, especially this close to Islamabad. "We didn't know who was there," the official told me later, "but we knew we were likely to kick up a shitstorm finding out."

When the agents who followed the courier's Suzuki communicated back about its destination, the compound became the subject of fascination—and utter mystery—inside the CIA. Yet it was impossible to keep 24/7 coverage, from satellites or drones, over the house. A couple of operatives set up a covert safe house from which

---

* The Pakistani government razed the building in February 2012, so that it would no longer be a tourist destination, or a symbol of national humiliation.

they could watch comings and goings from behind mirrored glass. They also used sensitive eavesdropping equipment to try to pick up voices from inside the house, and satellite radar to search for possible escape tunnels. But none of it yielded an answer about who was living upstairs.

Carefully, the agency began trying other techniques. Locals reported that people in "simple, plain clothes" started knocking on doors in the neighborhood, admiring the houses and asking for architectural plans because they wanted to "build something similar."[4] That was a risky ploy, but because so many military families come and go in the city, strangers were not unusual—and were rarely challenged. The CIA exploited that, using the transient nature of the place to its advantage. But every new surveillance strategy risked tipping off the occupants.

The mysteries grew. There were no phones or Internet at the compound; the occupants were either hermits or desperately afraid of being traced. Garbage was burned in the courtyard rather than collected on the street. And the couriers, it became clear, drove at least ninety minutes from the compound before they turned on their cells to make a call.[5]

In late summer 2010, just before Obama headed to Martha's Vineyard, his top intelligence advisers told him about the suspicious building, but couldn't confirm anything about its occupants. It was the first solid lead since the president had taken aside CIA director Leon Panetta in the spring of 2009 and told him, "We need to redouble our efforts in hunting bin Laden down. And I want us to start putting more resources, more focus, and more urgency into that mission."[6]

"I think that was a real wake-up call," Tom Donilon, who was part of the conversation, said to me later. "It sort of rocked the agency." That alone was surprising, since so many outside the CIA considered finding bin Laden to be job number one. For some, including a group of analysts who had focused on the couriers, it was. But there were so many other missions—in Iraq, in Afghanistan, in Yemen and Somalia—that the bin Laden effort had become a sideshow.

.After that conversation, Donilon drafted a memo from Obama to Panetta instructing him to create a "detailed operation plan" for finding bin Laden and to "ensure that we have expended every effort."[7] Now, a year later, Panetta's biggest worry was that once he told the president about the compound, the high-level attention would be overwhelming.

From that moment forward, there was a constant balancing act at work—everyone wanted to get in closer to the compound, but not so close that the occupants could be tipped off.

Then, the CIA rolled out the RQ-170 Sentinel, a sophisticated surveillance drone that had been outfitted with stealth technology. It could take high-altitude photographs and send real-time video while evading Pakistan's defensive radar. With its distinctive bat-wing shape, it was capable of flying high above the compound without detection by the Pakistani authorities.

Slowly, images of life inside the walls began to trickle in. A man—they called him "the pacer"—regularly exercised out in the courtyard, next to what the CIA called the "animal yard" (there were some animals kept there periodically). But despite the sophistication of the RQ-170 images, the CIA couldn't see his face or even estimate his height. At one point the White House asked the National Geospatial-Intelligence Agency, which provides and analyzes satellite imagery, to try to estimate whether "the pacer" was short or tall. It reported that the man's height was between five-foot-eight and six-foot-eight.[8] "Not the most helpful piece of intelligence," one official recalled later.

But the behavior around the compound seemed so bizarre that there was clearly something or someone in hiding. There were at least three families living inside, but only two moved in and out. Was it possible, after years of looking inside caves on the Afghanistan-Pakistan border, that bin Laden had become a recluse just thirty miles or so from Pakistan's capital? Could he, as Obama's counterterrorism coordinator, John Brennan, suggested at one talk, be "hiding in plain sight"?[9] Or was the idea that he was in a crowded city, where gossip flowed, just too far-fetched? "There were many reasons for skepticism," Leiter said later. And soon, he would be tasked to make the case that despite the obvious suspicions, there was an equally plausible case that Osama bin Laden was *not* Abbottabad's most famous, least-seen resident.

WHILE THE BIN Laden mystery simmered, Pakistan seemed on the edge of boiling over. Moderate politicians were suddenly under attack—and their assassins celebrated.

Salmaan Taseer was the secular, moderate governor of Punjab, known best, at least in recent years, for his campaign to rid Pakistan of its blasphemy laws, which mandate a death sentence for anyone convicted of insulting Islam. The laws were a leftover from Gen. Muhammad Zia-ul-Haq, who Islamized Pakistan in the 1980s, until he died in a mysterious plane crash. Of course, the standard for what constitutes an "insult" was entirely subjective. General Zia-ul-Haq had jailed Taseer, a quarter century ago, for Taseer's opposition to religious political parties in a supposedly secular Islamic state. Taseer argued incessantly for the laws to be repealed, and some of the new national leaders had backed his call—however timidly. To press his case, Taseer took up the cause of an illiterate Christian woman who had been sentenced to death for blasphemy, a case that seemed bizarre even by Pakistani standards.

Unsurprisingly, Taseer was the target of a continuous stream of death threats. Thousands of Pakistanis protested against him in the streets, burning his likeness in effigy. He sent out a Twitter message that described his plight: "I was under huge pressure sure 2 cow down b4 rightest pressure on blasphemy. Refused. Even if I'm the last man standing."[10] As Taseer's twenty-two-year-old journalist daughter,

Shehrbano Taseer, later said, "Times are such, if you believe something in Pakistan, you have to be willing to give up your life for it."[11]

Just a few days into 2011, Taseer was getting into his car at the Kohsar Market—a popular shopping and café spot for the city's elite in the country's capital. As he opened the door, one of his own bodyguards turned and pumped twenty-seven bullets into him. The assassin, Malik Mumtaz Qadri, who was twenty-six, made little attempt to escape. Instead he told a television crew that arrived at the scene shortly after the killing, "I am a slave of the Prophet, and the punishment for one who commits blasphemy is death."[12]

Taseer's assassination, though disturbing, wasn't what rattled the Obama administration most. It was that the bodyguard's fundamentalist tendencies were not detected before the murder.

It is unclear why Qadri, a member of the Elite Force of the Punjab police guard, was entrusted to protect anyone. In 2005, President Pervez Musharraf's new vetting system flagged Qadri because he was a follower of the religious party Dawat-e-Islami.[13] Investigators later found out Qadri had been detailed to Taseer seven to nine times and was also deployed to protect the prime minister and other leading ministers.[14] The fact that he got off twenty-seven shots—without being felled by one of his fellow bodyguards—raised the question of whether others were in on the plot.

Taseer's murder exposed the one question that kept administration officials working on Pakistan up at night: if Taseer's bodyguards weren't adequately vetted, how was anyone to rest assured that the thousands who protected the security of Pakistan's nuclear weapons were better screened? For years, Pakistani officials described a thorough vetting system to make sure that "fundos," as the Pakistanis call the fundamentalists, are not involved in protecting the country's nuclear assets.[15] A similar system, they said, was supposed to assure that armed bodyguards are loyal to the government, and to the officials they are supposed to protect.

Instead of punishment, Qadri received a hero's treatment. He was showered with cheers as he entered court for his trial. When Taseer was buried, Pakistan's president Asif Ali Zardari and other national leaders who had once supported his cause were suddenly too busy to attend his funeral. They withdrew their support for overturning the blasphemy laws, and let the fundamentalists and extremists win the day.

"What was once a problem confined to the borderlands is now an infection inside the entire body-politic of Pakistan," Bruce Riedel, who had conducted the first review of Afghanistan and Pakistan policy for President Obama, told me the week of the killing. Referring to General Zia, he added, "It is another reminder that Pakistan has had an Islamic jihadist dictator before, and he can be reincarnated."

Yet it would overstate the case to argue that the majority of the country was turning extremist. As Ahmed Rashid, an expert on the Taliban and radical Islamism, explained at the time, "We have a very, very severe polarization in the country. We have a small minority of extremists and small number of liberals speaking out, but the very large silent majority are people who are not extremist in any way but are not speaking out."[16]

BY THE SPRING of 2011, Obama's national security team was still divided on whether the intelligence on Abbottabad was good enough to warrant a strike. "We had a mysterious guy who liked to take walks in his compound, and was a recluse," said one participant. In the dry assessment that went to Obama, the most the analysts were willing to say was that "a key al-Qaeda facilitator appears to be harboring a high-value target."[17]

Obama understood their caution: after Iraq, going in and hitting the wrong house would be a disaster. Politically he would look like a mix of Jimmy Carter, who blew the Iran rescue mission, and George W. Bush, who dismissed intelligence that ran contrary to his gut. And the record in the region was not unblemished. In the last months of Bush's term, a Special Operations team made a rare foray into Pakistan, storming a compound in the tribal areas that it believed was the base of al-Qaeda militants. What was supposed to be a quick, in-and-out night raid turned into a full-scale firefight. Two dozen people were killed, including many civilians. The Pakistanis, angry about the incursion and under pressure because of the civilian deaths, issued dark warnings about what would happen if another such raid took place. It would become a familiar script once Obama took over.

Then, at the end of 2009, came the disaster at the CIA base in Khost. The CIA thought it finally had a lead on bin Laden's whereabouts through a Jordanian doctor who professed to be close to al-Qaeda's number two, the Egyptian-born Ayman al-Zawahiri. After months of nurturing, the doctor was invited to the not-so-secret Khost base to meet many of the top agency officials in the country. He was not searched at the gate, in an effort to treat him with respect and not alienate him. Once inside, he got out of his car and triggered a suicide vest that would have been easily noticeable on inspection, killing seven CIA employees. It was yet another massive deception in a frustrating search, and a bitter lesson of how even after eight years of war, the landscape remained murky.

Khost had been a tragedy and an embarrassment, so no one was going to rush into a raid on the Abbottabad compound. Obama told Panetta that he wanted to move "as soon as he concluded that the intelligence case was sufficient."[18] Panetta warned everyone that they still had a lot of work to do. Obama later said he took Panetta's point, but warned against the danger of overcaution. "The intel guys had been burned so many times, even before Iraq, there was worry they might freeze," one White House official told me later.

Later, Obama recalled, he instructed his intelligence team: "Even as you guys are building a stronger intelligence case, let's also start building an action plan to figure out if in fact we make a decision that this is him, or we've got a good chance that we've got him, how are we gonna deal with him? How can we get at that?"[19]

Such work had already begun months before. In February 2011, CIA director Leon Panetta invited Vice-Admiral William H. McRaven, commander of the Pentagon's Joint Special Operations Command, to come to the CIA's headquarters in Langley, Virginia. There they began to prepare for the option they suspected Obama would demand—inserting a strike force to either snatch bin Laden or put a bullet through him. McRaven's elite forces had already captured or killed many of America's most wanted, including Saddam Hussein. If there was a raid, Panetta told him, it would be run jointly with Special Operations and overseen by the CIA.

In the internecine world of American intelligence and the most secret branch of the military, Panetta's gesture was rife with symbolism. Tension between the agency and Special Operations was palpable around the world as their separate missions often collided. (The CIA can do its work under a "finding" from the president to conduct covert actions, including against friendly nations like Pakistan; the Special Operations Command adheres to the different legal strictures that guide the military.)

The very fact that the Langley meeting happened, many commented later, was a sign of how much had changed in the years since 9/11. The CIA's commando squads were increasingly indistinguishable from Special Operations Forces; as one intelligence official put it to me, "What we're doing now is more like the operations run by the OSS," the World War II–era Office of Strategic Services. Yet just a few years before, one insider said to me, "It was unimaginable this kind of session would be held, especially on CIA turf." To Panetta, it was clear from the start that McRaven, who had literally written the book on American Special Operations, would be central to any attack on the Abbottabad compound. That wasn't clear to many others in the CIA, who wanted to bag the biggest trophy in terrorism themselves.

Yet at the time, it was also not clear there would be a raid. Gates and Biden thought the best way to deal with the compound would be to obliterate it with a bomb. "That was a view they held to the very end," one senior administration official involved in the discussions told me. It was an option Obama never liked; he wanted irrefutable evidence that bin Laden had been eliminated. Even then, the same bloggers who never believed Obama was born in Hawaii might never believe bin Laden died in Abbottabad.

Downstairs from Panetta's suite, several CIA operatives were already working on new ideas to confirm bin Laden was inside the compound. What they really needed were DNA samples—if not from bin Laden himself then from some of his children there. So they concocted the ultimate ruse—a vaccination program.

No one has paid a steeper price for the effort to locate bin Laden than Shakil Afridi, a doctor who had aided the United States by seeking to collect DNA from the residents of the bin Laden compound.

Afridi was hired along with a team of nurses and other health workers to administer hepatitis B vaccinations throughout Abbottabad. The vaccinations were real. But the object of the operation was not what it seemed, something the doctor himself may have not known. And in the end, like the plan to flood Pakistan with digital video recorders, this was a brilliant idea that never worked. The doctor did get inside the compound briefly, but he never saw bin Laden or administered vaccinations to any of the family members.

He was picked up for "questioning" by the Pakistanis days after the raid, along with others suspected of cooperating with the Americans. Soon the questioning took an ugly turn, and a government commission urged he be tried for treason for helping a foreign power execute a secret operation that violated Pakistani sovereignty. It was the ultimate example of how far the so-called American–Pakistani alliance had plummeted. Rather than launch a serious investigation into how the world's most wanted terrorist could be living within an hour of Islamabad, under the noses of the military, the ISI focused instead on a doctor who was doing what the spy agency claimed it was doing: hunting al-Qaeda leadership.

A few weeks after Afridi's arrest, Mike Rogers, a bear of a man who is the chairman of the House Intelligence Committee, flew to Pakistan to urge the Pakistanis to release Afridi. The United States was willing to take him if his life would be endangered in Pakistan, he and other officials said.

But Gen. Ahmed Shuja Pasha, the head of the ISI at the time, brushed him off. He told Rogers that he was personally offended by the bin Laden raid; it hurt not only the country's national pride but his own. Pasha is far less refined than General Kayani, the military chief; he alternates between reasonableness and nationalistic bluster. And he had a list of demands, among them that the United States reveal all its intelligence operations inside Pakistan. Rogers told him, as others had, that it was something the United States simply could not do. The operations would be compromised as soon as the ISI knew of them.

And on Afridi, the news was even worse. American intelligence reports indicated he was being tortured. Not only would the Pakistanis not release him, some Americans were convinced they would kill him. "Here is a man who was trying to save his country from being overtaken by fundamentalists," one official told me later, with disgust in his voice. "And they thank him by hanging him by his thumbs." In the late winter of 2012, Hillary Clinton was still arguing for his release, complaining publicly that the Pakistanis had "no basis" to hold him. Pakistan ignored her.

ONE MORE COMPLICATION drove up—literally—on the streets of Lahore. His name was Raymond Davis.

Davis was a CIA security officer, a former Special Operations

soldier with, as one of his agency colleagues later put it, "more tes-
tosterone than judgment." He was being paid $200,000 a year by
the CIA, apparently through a shell company he set up several years
ago called Hyperion Protective Services. And he was the kind of
operative who drives the Pakistani government to distraction: the
CIA never told the government he was in the country, and never
discussed his mission, which included reconnaissance against Pakistani terror groups such as Lashkar-e-Taiba, which was behind the
famous Mumbai attack in 2008.

Davis's most marketable talent seemed to be his knowledge of
Pakistan's backstreets and dark corners. He was at home operating
in Islamabad and other Pakistani cities, even those where an American from Virginia stands out. His car, no surprise, was laden with
the accoutrements of spycraft: a semiautomatic 9mm Glock pistol,
seventy-five rounds of ammunition, an infrared flashlight, a long-
range walkie-talkie, two mobile phones, a digital camera, a survival
kit, and five ATM cards. (One can only conclude the CIA's accounting department hates those extra bank charges.) As investigators
later determined, Davis had been busy. His camera held photos of
Pakistani defense installations, which, to the CIA's embarrassment,
were ultimately broadcast on Pakistani national television.

Three weeks after Taseer's assassination, on January 27, 2011,
Davis was driving a rented white four-by-four through an industrial
area in the city of Lahore where few foreigners venture. A bulky Cau-
casian in his mid-thirties, he was pretty conspicuous, but he seemed
comfortable in the neighborhood. He stopped to get some cash
from an ATM and got back into his car. As he was driving, he spotted
two motorcyclists following him in traffic. His mind immediately
turned to the ISI, which, in a giant game of Spy-and-Counterspy,
would have had plenty of interest in following him and others from
the CIA station in Islamabad. Then Davis got stuck in traffic.

The two motorcyclists pulled ahead of him and spun around.
They dismounted and pointed guns right at him. Was it a robbery?

Or were ISI thugs trying to scare him out of Lahore or out of the country? Or was it a kidnapping attempt by the Taliban? Davis had neither the time nor the inclination to find out. He grabbed his Glock and shot through the windshield, hitting and killing both motorcyclists with five shots each.

Then he did something truly remarkable. Rather than hit the gas, he opened the driver's door, got out, let off a couple more rounds, and walked over to the two young men who were sprawled across the road.

Seemingly unfazed, Davis took out a cell phone and photographed the dead men. He could sort out later whether they were two unlucky thugs who had just chosen the wrong victim or whether they were ISI agents. The only thing that was evident to him before he got back into his car was that they were dead.

Davis put in a distress call to the US consulate in Lahore, and soon an unmarked Toyota Land Cruiser raced out of the building to find their man and bring him in before the Pakistanis got him. Instead, the second car made the incident far worse. As the Toyota careered the eight miles from the consulate to the shooting locale, its driver veered the wrong way down a one-way street. In seconds, he ran over a motorcyclist. By the time they got near the crime scene, Davis was already in custody.

Suddenly Davis was in a police interrogation room with officers yelling at him in a mixture of English, Urdu, and Punjabi. Davis's training kicked in: he managed to hold a camera between his feet so he could document the interrogation. He portrayed himself as a diplomat.

"I need to tell the embassy where I'm at," he told the police officers. They asked in Urdu for his name. "Raymond Davis." "From America?" they asked. "Yes," he said, though with no passport, he could not prove it.

"I just work as a consultant there," he insisted.[20]

There was no particular reason to believe his misleading answers.

Now, having killed two Pakistanis in broad daylight in one of the country's biggest cities, his fate would become the latest test of wills between the two countries.

THE NEXT DAY, Davis was escorted through a crowd of screaming protestors to a Punjabi court. Without a lawyer or translator, and over the protests of the State Department, he was charged with murder. Washington's first reaction was reflexive: no one would confirm that the American's name was Raymond Davis, or say what he did at the embassy.[21] Despite a flurry of phone calls from Panetta and Adm. Mike Mullen, the chairman of the Joint Chiefs of Staff, to their Pakistani counterparts, the government in Islamabad refused to release Davis. Pakistan's public opinion would not allow it.

While Mullen was making the case to Pakistan for Davis's release, he was astounded by Washington's farcical explanations of what Davis was doing there. The cover story could not pass the laugh test. The US government was asking the Pakistanis to believe he was just an unlucky diplomat who happened to be robbed, and fought back. Meanwhile, Pakistan's front pages were filled with accounts of Davis's expertise, his weapons cache, the number of shots he took, and his accuracy with his 9mm Glock.

Mullen's job was to ask General Kayani to get Davis released. He asked, but as Mullen commented to associates later, if the roles were reversed, no American prosecutor would have let him walk either.[22]

The issue became a cause célèbre in Pakistan. Local lawyers called for a trial, and the Lahore High Court blocked any attempts to hand over Davis to American authorities. President Zardari was forced to go on television and declare that Pakistan alone would decide Davis's fate.

"This was the problem from hell," one American official said months later, "because we knew that if we had to do a raid in Abbottabad [to kill bin Laden], we'd never get Davis out." A US congressional delegation that arrived in Islamabad soon thereafter made a plea for Davis's release and warned that the dispute could endanger US military aid. They were escorted back to the airport and arrived home empty-handed.

By early February, Davis was formally charged with murder. At the *Times,* we had confirmed that Davis worked for the CIA, but a senior official inside the Obama administration asked the paper to withhold that fact until he was out of the country. As Bill Keller, the *Times'* executive editor at the time, explained later, "He was asking us not to speculate, or to recycle charges in the Pakistani press. His concern was that the letters C-I-A in an article in the *New York Times,* even as speculation, would be taken as authoritative and would be a red flag in Pakistan."[23] Already American flags and effigies of Davis were being burned in the streets. The widow of one of the men who was killed committed suicide by drinking rat poison. Crowds chanted, "Blood for blood." It was the beginning of what one American diplomat later called "the year from hell" in Pakistan.

WHILE LEON PANETTA was trying everything to secure Davis's release—eventually traveling to Islamabad to negotiate a deal in which the United States would pay "blood money" to the victims in return for Davis—the case for moving in on the compound in Abbottabad was gaining speed. It was also gaining doubters.

On March 14, President Obama called his national security advisers to the White House to review the attack options for Abbottabad developed by McRaven, the CIA, and the Pentagon.[24] They ranged from the bluntest of instruments—an airstrike that would take out not only the compound but perhaps much of the neighborhood—to a risky insertion of commandos to find and kill bin Laden.

Both Defense Secretary Gates and Vice President Biden—the two veterans on the team who knew how much could go wrong— were already leaning toward bombing the site. "From the start, there was a lot of talk about Desert One," said Donilon, who was a just-out-of-college political aide in the Carter White House when that rescue mission in Iran went horribly wrong. Gates himself said he was conservative about these things: he had seen the high price of unanticipated consequences too many times in four years of missions in Iraq and Afghanistan.

But the pull to send in Special Operations was hard. Obama wanted to know for certain that they had killed bin Laden; if there was a crater at the site, the world would never know for sure. Moreover, Obama had grown comfortable with the Special Operations Forces in a way no one expected. Adm. Eric T. Olson, who had made his own wetsuit at age nine, headed the Special Operations Command and now was the longest serving Navy SEAL still on duty, known as the "Bullfrog." To Olson, a potential raid on the Abbottabad compound was hardly as risky as Desert One; as he and others knew, the force had been created to make sure such a disaster never happened again. In the decade since 9/11, the Special Operations Command had almost doubled to 58,000. And they were busy: with ten or fifteen raids a night, "this was becoming habit," Olson said shortly before retiring in the summer of 2011.

But as everyone in the room knew, even if the operation was straightforward—a big "if"—dealing with the Pakistanis would not be. Should they tell them about the compound? Should they offer to work with them, so that they could claim some credit? The idea was discussed very briefly, and then instantly discarded. There was story after story of the ISI warning potential targets of joint raids to get out of town. The NSA's computers were filled with intercepted conversations in which ISI officers played both sides of the war.

The reality was that not one person in President Obama's team wanted the Pakistanis to be in the loop. As one senior administration official told me, "No one was really saying let's notify the Pakistanis. I am not aware of anybody who took that position." Another senior adviser to Obama put it this way: "We believed that if there was any leak, it would have been picked up by al-Qaeda and Osama bin Laden would have been out of there." The ISI, the Americans believed, was incapable of keeping a secret; better to anger it, or even have a breach in the relationship, than lose the best shot in years.

Obama decided not to make a decision. He sent McRaven off to refine the plan for a raid; he wanted to see every detail. But meanwhile, the Pentagon was asked to come up with a more precise bombing plan, one that would wipe out the compound but not risk taking out the neighborhood. To the very last moment, Gates and Biden would argue that bombing would be the optimal way to go.

ON MARCH 16, the decision over whether to proceed with an attack became a little less complicated. After Lt. Gen. Ahmed Shuja Pasha, the head of the ISI, visited Washington, a quiet deal was struck. Raymond Davis was released. The "blood money" solution—reportedly $2.3 million—combined with the political pressure that Pakistani politicians put on their highly pliable courts, did the trick. Davis was rushed out of the country to Kabul and the United States, and, presumably, told to put away his Glock and never let his head pop up on the public radar again. (He failed at that—a few months later he was arrested in Colorado for allegedly assaulting someone he thought was taking his parking spot.)

In retrospect, the incident put a chill between the CIA and the ISI. "The question the Pakistanis asked was, How many other Raymond Davises are there driving around Pakistan that we don't know about?" one Obama administration official said to me. Suddenly the Pakistanis were insisting on renegotiating their fundamental understandings with Washington. From this point forward, they said, temporary American "diplomats" get a one-month visa. Then, they have to leave the country. That crippled a plan to essentially flood Pakistan with more CIA operatives. The ISI also demanded a list of every American intelligence official in the country and an end to the drone strikes. Yes, they said, back when Musharraf was running the country, Washington and Islamabad had a secret agreement to allow drone strikes. But that was before production was ramped up and the number of drones mushroomed, and with them the anger of the Pakistani populace. Now, from far, far away, a drone could be launched to strike Pakistan. The Americans pretended they never heard that last demand. To Obama, the drones were the only thing in Pakistan that was working.

WITH THE DAVIS issue over, more or less, the plan to take out the compound went into overdrive. On March 29, McRaven and Panetta brought a more detailed plan to the White House that called for flying two helicopters of Navy SEALs directly into the compound. But Obama's advisers remained divided. Gates reminded his colleagues that when Eagle Claw—the ill-fated 1980 Delta Force mission to rescue the Iranian hostages—was presented to the Carter White House, "they said that was a pretty good idea too."[25]

Gates and Gen. James Cartwright, the vice-chairman of the Joint Chiefs and one of Obama's favorite strategists, preferred the option of using B-2 bombers. "There was an argument that in some ways a bomb was less of an affront to Pakistani sovereignty than sending in a team," Donilon recalled later. But the initial plan— two-thousand-pound bombs—could take out a neighborhood filled with women and children. The Pakistani outrage would know no limits, especially if the supposition that bin Laden was in residence turned out to be wrong. "It would have created a giant crater," one senior intelligence official told my colleagues in the Washington bureau of the *Times,* "and it wouldn't have given us a body."[26]

Another option was armed, unmanned drones. But that would still destroy any chances of obtaining additional material from the compound, including evidence about how bin Laden communicated.

Panetta began giving voice to his private worries about what could go wrong. "What were they going to confront? What were they going to find? Would they be . . . could they be locked into that compound because of the Pakistanis suddenly attacking that compound and putting them in a very difficult position?"[27]

Nonetheless, a helicopter assault gradually emerged as the favored option. James Clapper, the taciturn director of national intelligence, kept repeating his mantra that while the raid was risky, it would make use of "skilled human beings making decisions, not dumb bombs." And so on April 10, McRaven's team selected twenty-four SEALs and told them to report to a densely forested area in North Carolina.[28] What they found was a crude replica of the Abbottabad compound, with walls and chain-link fencing marking the layout. For the next five days, the SEALs practiced entering and exiting the American-built model. Then they moved to a stretch of desert in Nevada, at roughly the same elevation as Abbottabad, and practiced roping in.

One evening they had visitors: Adm. Mike Mullen, along with Bullfrog Olson and McRaven. The questions began to fly. What if a mob surrounded the compound? Were the SEALs prepared to shoot Pakistani civilians? If a helicopter was shot down inside Pakistani territory, how would that be handled and explained? For Olson, this was no tabletop exercise: he'd received the Silver Star for valor during the disastrous 1993 "Black Hawk Down" episode in Mogadishu, Somalia, when an attempt to capture two senior aides to a notorious warlord went wrong. The images of the bodies of American soldiers being dragged through the streets became the icon of ill-thought-out American interventions. He remembered the outcome as well: the United States left, and Somalia became a breeding ground for pirates and al-Qaeda affiliates.

◈

TEN DAYS BEFORE the raid, Obama started to get nervous. The latest strategy presented to him called for sending only two helicopters to the compound; a "backup team" if anything went wrong—a crash, a firefight with Pakistani troops—would stay on the Afghan side of the border, more than an hour away. What happens if the Pakistani police or military arrived and tried to interfere? The Navy SEALs would just talk themselves out of the situation, McRaven said. That struck Obama as hopeful to the extreme. If the SEALs were captured, or even locked inside the compound, it would be the Davis standoff all over again. As a senior administration official later put it to me, "Some people may have assumed we could talk our way out of a jam, but given our difficult relationship with Pakistan right now, the president did not want to leave anything to chance. He wanted extra forces if they were necessary."[29]

Extra forces meant, of course, an even bigger violation of Pakistani sovereignty. That's what happened. Under a revised plan, the backup helicopters would also fly into Pakistani territory, and refuel at a remote Pakistani site. Of course, that created yet another place to be detected. The SEALs were to avoid any confrontation if at all possible. But if they had to fight their way out, they were authorized to open fire on America's putative allies. As one senior administration official described the preparations, "We were heavied-up."

Back in Washington, Donilon insisted that his team prepare several volumes of tabbed notebooks, with a script for every telephone call that would have to be made at specific times for every scenario. According to one senior administration official, they rehearsed the calls like they were preparing for a live TV program: "Zero hour, zero hour five, zero hour ten, Admiral Mullen calls Kayani, X calls Y. . . ." What if they didn't answer the phone?

"Well," another official said, "then we're screwed."

✦

AS WORD OF what was being planned gradually seeped beyond the small group in on the planning, Leiter began to worry about the quality of the evidence. From Iraq forward, he had seen what happens when wishing something to be true overcame hardheaded analysis. He went to John Brennan, the counterterrorism czar at the White House, and told him that there was no room for shortcuts: "Let's make sure we've learned lessons from previous tricky intelligence problems."[30] The evidence had to be "red-teamed"—examined by outsiders with nothing invested in the operation—so that every assumption could be tested.

They had already created a "red team," Brennan replied, which consisted of two national intelligence officers and two CIA officers. Leiter looked at the list and countered that none of them ever did counterterrorism. Well, Brennan responded, time is getting short.

Leiter went to Donilon. "I felt that it was important that we basically took people that had nothing to do with working up that case. They weren't tied to any operational outcome. They weren't tied to any organizations that were principally involved. But frankly, they knew a lot about terrorism." Donilon agreed, and so did Mike Morell, Stephen Kappes's replacement as the deputy director of the CIA, who had risen through the ranks of analysts, not operatives. They told Leiter to put together a team to "murder board" the evidence and come up with the best case for why bin Laden might *not* be in the compound. But he should hurry. He might only have days.

Leiter locked a team of his best in a room and gave them all the intelligence that was available to the people who had made the previous assessments.

The review didn't take long. "It turned out you could do it in days because there was not reams and reams of evidence," Leiter told me a few months later. It started with the couriers, who had deep links to senior members of the al-Qaeda leadership. There was the odd house in Abbottabad, with its high cement barriers. There was the mystery about the family living inside the compound. And there was "the pacer." That was all the evidence they had to work with.

On April 26, the Tuesday before the raid, Leiter descended into the Situation Room to give a sense of what he had found. Mike Morell was there, along with the top national security team. Earlier, Morell had summarized Leiter's job this way: make the best case you can that bin Laden is *not* there.

We're not done studying the evidence, Leiter told Obama. But there are three big possibilities, all of which need to be considered.

The first, he said, was that bin Laden had used the house in the past, or might just use it occasionally. After all, why would he want to sleep in one place night after night? He noted that the United States had aerial coverage of the house only a few hours each day. It was simply not possible to keep a constant eye on the house with satellites and drones—meaning they could easily miss bin Laden coming and going. "Everything points to this house being associated with bin Laden," he said, "but nothing says he is there every day." At the same time, there was no evidence he left often—or ever. (After the raid was over, the after-action reports concluded bin Laden had not emerged from the compound in six years.)

There was a second possibility: the house could be associated with another "HVT," or high-value target. It wasn't Zawahiri—there was good evidence, still deeply classified, that he was somewhere else. The house might have been a hiding place for a steady procession of "number threes"—who had a high attrition rate because they usually made the mistake of using cell phones, a beacon for Predator drones. Or al-Qaeda associates.

There was the third scenario, Leiter warned, and it was the ugliest. Obama had to be prepared for the possibility that the house had nothing to do with al-Qaeda. It could be just another drug lord. Or a rich Dubai prince hiding his money, his business, or his mistress.

Leiter came back two days later and presented his conclusions at the final National Security Council meeting before the raid. Obama was in the room to hear the results. "Mr. President, of this team of four analysts, the range of certainty that it's bin Laden ranges from forty percent to seventy percent." But Leiter added that he thought all the statistics were crap. Whatever the numbers were, "they are thirty-eight percent higher than what we've had for ten years." But in a play on how George Tenet, the CIA director during the Iraq invasion, once famously described the chances that Saddam Hussein possessed WMD, Leitner added, "This was not, pardon me, George, a slam-dunk."[31]

Privately, Leiter wondered why it had taken the intelligence agencies so many years to focus on Abbottabad. The city had been a home to the couriers from the days of Abu al-Libbi, the suspected mastermind of the 2006 plot to blow up ten transatlantic flights and the number three in al-Qaeda at the time. (It was that incident which led to the rule restricting the amount of liquid passengers can take onto commercial flights.) Pervez Musharraf, Pakistan's former president, had even written in his memoirs about the search for al-Libbi's couriers there.

The president listened to Leiter and then said, "We are looking at essentially four possibilities here: You go in and get him and it's pretty clean. You go in, he's not there but you get out clean and you probably just say 'nothing to see here.' You go in, he's there but it's really messy—a lot of people die, there's a firefight, maybe the ISI shows up, but it's successful in that you get him. And then the fourth option was just catastrophe and there are any number of things under that—US hostages taken, significant US casualties, helicopters down . . . the imagination can fill it in."

Obama thought trying to attribute percentages to these scenarios was "a bit weird." "At the end of the day," he told the room, "it's fifty-fifty." Not great odds. But it was "the best evidence we've had since Tora Bora."

Leiter's own view was that it was worth waiting for stronger confirmation of bin Laden's presence in Abbottabad. While Panetta had privately told Obama that it was impossible to collect better intelligence without risking exposure of what the United States suspected, Leiter believed others in the intelligence agencies who thought there was more that could be tried.[32]

As one senior administration official told me, "It was always a question of risk. Is it worth the risk? One of the arguments was that it's not worth the risk unless we have greater certainty that bin Laden was there. . . . So Leiter wanted to wait and do more collection. Biden was a little bit in that camp too."

Vice President Biden's own account confirms his qualms. In late January 2012, Biden recalled that Obama "went around the table with all the senior people, including the chiefs of staff, and he said, 'I have to make a decision. What is your opinion?'"

He started with Donilon, then Clinton, then other senior officials, including Panetta, who was closest to the details. "Every single person in that room hedged their bet except Leon Panetta," Biden later said. "Leon said go. Everyone else said, forty-nine, fifty-one." Obama ended the meeting, at seven p.m., saying that he would sleep on it.

"I'm not going to tell you what my decision is now—I'm going to go back and think about it some more. . . . But I'm going to make a decision soon."[33]

JUST SIXTEEN HOURS later, at 8:20 a.m. on a Friday morning, Obama met with Donilon and Denis McDonough, Donilon's chief deputy and Obama's longtime aide from the Senate, in the Diplomatic Room of the White House. Obama was in a windbreaker, headed to his helicopter.

"It's a go," Obama said. "We are going to do the insertion. Write the orders." For those who knew Obama best, it was a surprise. He was usually cautious to the extreme, especially when it came to inserting ground troops. He knew the evidence was still circumstantial. He also knew that he could be betting his presidency. If bin Laden wasn't in the compound, he would be Jimmy Carter without the peanut farm.

But it was a situation he had been thinking about for a long time. During the presidential campaign, a woman from Nashville had asked the young senator from Illinois in a debate with the Republican candidate John McCain if he was willing to pursue al-Qaeda leaders inside Pakistan, even if that meant violating the sovereignty of an ally. He replied, "If we have Osama bin Laden in our sights and the Pakistani government is unable, or unwilling, to take them out, then I think that we have to act and we will take them out. We will kill bin Laden. We will crush al-Qaeda. That has to be our biggest national security priority."

Now, confronted with the reality, everything looked far murkier than it was on the campaign trail. Obama knew that the only way to figure out whether bin Laden was "in our sights" was to send commandos in to look. When they gamed it out, though, the possible reactions in Pakistan were pretty grim. In the Situation Room, Donilon, Brennan, and Obama had discussed whether crowds in Islamabad might overrun the American embassy, or whether Pakistan might break diplomatic relations with the United States—and fully sign up with the Taliban. Now it was up to Donilon—the careful lawyer and perpetual worrier—to issue the orders with rules of engagement that Obama hoped would limit the risk of any of those outcomes. By late Friday morning, the SEAL team was ready to go.

But the weather had other ideas. Later that day, Donilon had to call the president and tell him that cloud cover would force a delay. And Obama could not exactly sit in the Situation Room and guide preparations: he was scheduled to speak that Saturday evening at the White House Correspondents' Association Dinner, a scripted annual event in the jammed ballroom of the Washington Hilton where reporters strain their necks to see what celebrities their competition brought to dinner. The president is supposed to laugh at his own foibles, pretend to enjoy himself, and score a few political points.

President Obama opened his speech with the words, "What a week." The audience broke into laughter, thinking he was talking about what was arguably the stupidest moment of the presidential campaign to date: Donald Trump's continued questioning about whether Obama was born in the United States. Obama had just produced his "long-form" birth certificate, but that kept the cable television channels distracted, full of drivel. Obama used the evening to skewer Trump for his buffoonery, which dominated the headlines as the SEAL teams were getting ready to go.

The president's national security team was nothing if not disciplined that night. At the *Vanity Fair* after-party at the grand French embassy, Donilon and other key players were out until midnight, mingling with reporters. When Donilon finally excused himself, he turned to a reporter who had known him for years and said he had to get some sleep. "I've got this thing tomorrow."

In retrospect, there were a few hints. The following day, May 1, all West Wing tours were canceled so that no one would ask why the vice president or secretary of state was wandering around on a Sunday afternoon. Rather than risk having a large staff of cooks around, a staffer was sent to Costco for pita wraps and potato chips, a menu that seemed more fitting for a baseball game than a targeted assassination. Obama went to play golf that morning at Andrews Air Force Base.

While he was still on the course, his advisers gathered in one of the large conference rooms in the Situation Room complex. The room was connected via video link to Panetta at CIA headquarters in Langley and McRaven in Afghanistan. Next door, in a much smaller room, Brig. Gen. Marshall Webb, an assistant commander on the Joint Chiefs of Staff, took a seat at the end of a long table and turned on his laptop. He was looking at the only video feed in the White House showing real-time footage of the target, which was being shot by an unarmed Stealth RQ-170 drone flying more than fifteen thousand feet above Abbottabad.[34] Obama entered the Situation Room just after two p.m. as Panetta was going over the operation one last time.

UNDER THE COVER of a moonless and cloudless evening, two MH-60 Black Hawk helicopters lifted off from Jalalabad Airfield in eastern Afghanistan. Aboard the aircraft were two pilots and a crewman from the 160th Special Operations Aviation Regiment known as the Night Stalkers, twenty-three Navy SEALs, a Pakistani-American translator, and a dog named Cairo, a Belgian Malinois. The SEALs aboard were in their thirties, seasoned veterans who were not likely to be trigger-happy. Cairo was there to check for explosives and booby traps and sniff out secret rooms like the ones Saddam Hussein kept in his compounds. For the translator, however, all of this was new—he had been pulled from a desk job before the mission and had learned from the SEALs how to descend a fast rope from the helicopter.

As the Black Hawks crossed the border into Pakistan, they were not picked up by Pakistan's radar system. "It was a little like us on Pearl Harbor Day—they had their radar off," one of Obama's aides told me later. "It was the first of several examples of incompetence that broke our way." Just in case, the helicopters had been modified to mask heat, noise, and movement; the Hawks' exteriors had sharp, flat angles and were covered with radar-dampening "skin."[35]

Forty-five minutes after the Black Hawks took off, four MH-47 Chinooks left from the same runway to provide the backup that Obama had insisted on. All headed toward Abbottabad, but two peeled off, staying on the Afghan side while the other two landed on a dry riverbed in a wide, unpopulated valley in northwest Pakistan—still unbeknownst to the Pakistanis. Once on the ground, they kept their engines going so they could provide additional support if the Pakistanis scrambled fighter jets.[36]

Around four p.m., Panetta signaled that the Black Hawks were approaching the compound. The plan was for the national security team to stay in the large conference room and receive updates—so that there was no perception that the White House was running the operation. But that lasted only until the president said, "I need to watch this," and walked across the hall to the smaller room, taking a seat on a collapsible chair next to Brigadier General Webb.[37] The rest of the group quickly followed him: Vice President Joseph Biden, Defense Secretary Gates, and Secretary of State Hillary Clinton. Then everyone else poured in—nobody wanted to be left behind. This standing-room-only crowd soon became the most famous image of the raid.

They sat in virtual silence—Obama in an open-neck shirt and jacket, leaning forward to catch every flicker of movement. But little could be seen, and the sound transmissions were a confusing babble. Panetta narrated: "They've taken off . . . they've crossed into Pakistani airspace . . . they're thirty minutes out . . . they're twenty minutes out." Obama later said that the forty minutes that followed were the longest of his life, except for when his infant daughter was ill with meningitis. On his right sat Biden, fingering his rosary. Crammed around the table were far less familiar faces—counterterrorism czar John Brennan; Denis McDonough, the deputy national security adviser; and one of the analysts who had been central to finding and following the courier's car.

MORE THAN SEVEN thousand miles away, the first Black Hawk was preparing to land in the courtyard of the compound in Abbottabad. Almost immediately, things began to go wrong. As the pilot descended, the downwash of his helicopter bounced off the compound's walls and shot back up, forcing the helicopter to lose its lift. McRaven said later they had planned for that possibility, but the result was that the commandos could not rappel to the roof of the main building from the chopper. "The pilot told us he struggled just to get over to the animal yard to land," said one official who later met the SEALs. He wedged his controls forward and told everyone to brace for a hard landing. But then he clipped the wall, leaving a broken rotor on one side and the main body of the chopper on the other. He bounced hard into the compound's animal pen.

The pilot of the second Black Hawk watched helplessly. He landed in a field just outside the compound. It was not exactly a textbook operation—the element of surprise was gone. In the Situation Room, visions of Desert One danced in the heads of many. Biden, remembering what Gates had said at one of the earlier meetings about Murphy's Law and helicopters—whatever can go wrong will—declared, "Murphy just showed up."

For the next couple of minutes, the president and his advisers sat in silence—waiting. If Obama saw the end of his presidency unfolding in the animal yard, he never let on. "It was silent, but people were making nervous eye contact," one participant said. "There wasn't a lot of talking as people were waiting to hear from these guys."

"The suspense was not visual; it was what McRaven was going to say," the official reported. "He would only speak in increments of minutes, so there were long stretches when you didn't really know what was going on."

After what seemed like a lifetime, McRaven's voice came across the speaker: "Everyone is accounted for." For the time being, the worst-case scenario had been averted. McRaven, one NSC official told me, was instantly "the coolest guy in the room."

The SEALs now had to blast their way out of the animal pen

and into the main section of the compound. Using C-4 explosives, they blew the door off the metal gate of the pen and a second locked gate. The team outside the courtyard was about to blow a hole in the wall as well when one of his fellow SEALs saw there was an easier way: he opened a door. They streamed into the courtyard facing the guesthouse, then split into two teams.*

What followed could hardly be called a firefight. Abu Ahmed al-Kuwaiti, dressed in a white *salwar kameez,* ran into the guesthouse and emerged with a gun. He was killed on the spot. The other team headed for the inner courtyard and the main house. Abu Ahmed's brother—a stocky, mustachioed man in a cream-colored *salwar kameez*—appeared with an AK-47 at the front door of the house with his unarmed wife, Bushra.[38] The SEALs shot both of them dead.

Then, the teams joined forces and they started to clear the floors of the main house. After checking the ground floor, they blasted their way through a gate on the stairs that blocked off the entrance to the second floor. At the top of the landing was Khalid, bin Laden's twenty-three-year-old son, firing an AK-47. He was quickly shot.

The lead SEAL heading up the stairs was stepping around Khalid's body when he spotted a man peering out from behind a bedroom door. He was tall, bearded, and wearing a tan *salwar kameez* and prayer cap. It certainly looked like "Crankshaft," the code name the JSOC had given Osama bin Laden.

◈

WHAT FOLLOWED NEXT will be a debate for the ages. When the team opened the bedroom door, bin Laden stood in the middle of the room, unarmed but shielded by two women. One was screaming in Arabic. Jay Carney, the White House spokesman, would later tell as-

---

* Note to reader: Some confusion still exists as to the exact details of the raid.

sembled press that she "rushed the US assaulter."[39] One SEAL shot her in the calf and then in a moment of selflessness, wrapped his huge arms around both of the women to shield the rest of the room in case anyone detonated suicide vests. Nothing happened—they were lucky. The team had caught the household by surprise—no suicide vests, no booby traps. It seemed that after six years of living inside the compound, bin Laden never expected the Americans to break down his door.

Within milliseconds, another shot was fired. A 5.56mm bullet hit bin Laden in the chest. In quick succession, a second shot hit his head above the left eye. As bin Laden collapsed onto the floor, the women screamed. The SEAL reported into his radio, "For God and country—Geronimo, Geronimo, Geronimo . . . Geronimo EKIA."[40]

McRaven relayed the message to the Situation Room. In approximately eighteen minutes, bin Laden had been found and killed. President Obama was self-contained to the extreme: "We got him," was all he said.[41]

The SEALs still had much to exploit, and not much time. The helicopters and firefight had woken the neighborhood, and the Americans feared it would not be long before the Pakistani forces figured out what was happening. Without realizing the significance of what was under way, a consultant who was taking a break in Abbottabad began tweeting the events live. "Helicopter hovering above Abbottabad at 1AM (is a rare event)," he wrote. Then, "A huge window shaking bang here in Abbottabad Cantt. I hope its not the start of something nasty :-S."[42] Neighbors approached the mysterious compound; the "translator" who had been posted outside in a *salwar kameez* and a flak jacket underneath pretended he was a plainclothes policeman. "Go back to your houses," he said in Pashto. "There is a security operation under way."[43]

The team had to move quickly. One group gathered the surviving women and fifteen children who were living in the compound. The SEALs bound their hands with flex cuffs and herded them to a safe place against the exterior wall facing the remaining Black Hawk. The translator questioned them but gained minimal new information.

Two other members of the team executed the much-rehearsed plan for bin Laden's body. A medic from the support Chinook that had been scrambled in after the crash of the Black Hawk took two bone-marrow samples, which were shipped out in separate helicopters so that if disaster struck, the administration could still prove they got bin Laden.

Meanwhile, a third group of commandos swept up a huge trove of the CDs, DVDs, flash drives, and hard drives pried from bin Laden's computers. These were the documents—equal to "a small college library," Donilon later said—that told the story of an ailing, isolated bin Laden who struggled to get his junior commanders to execute orders, fretted that his organization had a growing public-relations problem, and took solace watching videos of himself. They were immediately leaked by the Obama administration to portray bin Laden as a diminished, sad figure—the washed-up jihadi. As Leiter later said to me, "Bin Laden really wasn't the CEO of a multinational corporation. He was the slightly out-of-touch coordinator of a broad, dysfunctional family who were frankly operating more on their own agendas than his agenda."[44]

The immediate problem was to make sure that the stealth helicopter was not left in a condition where it could be useful to the Pakistanis—or, more to the point, their friends in Beijing. The pilot of the downed helicopter smashed up the instrument panel and radio with a hammer, and then, using explosives with extra C-4 charges, the team blew up the helicopter, much to the astonishment of the handcuffed women and children.*

---

* This effort appears to have failed. According to accounts later produced by intelligence agencies, Chinese agents were allowed access to the helicopter before it was shipped, in pieces, back to the United States from a Pakistani air base near Islamabad.

After thirty-eight minutes, with no American casualties and a dead Osama bin Laden, SEAL Team Six headed back toward Afghanistan, stopping briefly to refuel with the other Chinook before crossing the border. "We don't think the Paks saw us until we were over the border again," one American official told me later. The whole process—in and out of the country—had lasted about three and a half hours, and the Pakistanis had still not scrambled any forces.

McRaven and the CIA station chief met the team on the tarmac at the Jalalabad Airfield. Photos were taken of bin Laden. Because no one had a tape measure, a six-foot SEAL had to lie next to his body to assess his height. The absence of something quite that basic led Obama to give McRaven a plaque with a tape measure on it as thanks for the operation.[45]

Later the administration said it had been fully prepared to arrest bin Laden rather than kill him, had he not "resisted." And in fact, there were two specialist teams on standby on a naval ship— one to bury his body at sea, and one composed of lawyers, interrogators, and translators in case he was captured alive.[46] But that seemed more a cover story than reality. Enormous planning had gone into the burial at sea to make sure that there was no grave, like the one in Tikrit for Saddam Hussein, which has become a pilgrimage destination for admirers. And no one in the administration wanted to make bin Laden the most famous occupant of Gitmo and turn the question of when, and how, to put him on trial into a cable television soap opera.

But some formalities had to be observed. John Brennan, the former station chief in Riyadh, made a courtesy call to one of his friends in the House of Saud. Did the Saudi government have any interest in taking the body of the most infamous of the famed bin Laden family? Or should the United States proceed with its plan to give him a Muslim burial at sea? The question answered itself.

"Your plan sounds like a good one," the Saudi replied.[47]

By then bin Laden's body was already on a V-22 Osprey headed to the USS *Carl Vinson,* a thousand-foot-long nuclear-powered aircraft carrier sailing in the Arabian Sea, off the Pakistani coast.[48] Brennan would later say that after consulting with Islamic experts, "The disposal of—the burial of bin Laden's remains was done in strict conformance with Islamic precepts and practices."[49] Osama bin Laden's body was washed, wrapped in a white sheet, and placed in a weighted bag. The White House later described a ceremony lasting fifty minutes, in which a military officer read prepared religious remarks, translated into Arabic by a native speaker. Then, according to the official account, "the body was placed on [a] prepared flat board, tipped up, and the deceased body eased into the sea."[50]

The man who had terrorized America for a generation was gone. President Obama alone had made the risky decision to conduct the raid—imagine the reaction if the result was a dead Dubai prince. His decision and its result cemented his national security credentials. It also insulated him from the critique that he, and his party, is soft on terrorism; when one of the Republican presidential hopefuls charged him with a policy of appeasement, Obama shot back, "Ask Osama bin Laden and the twenty-two out of thirty top al-Qaeda leaders who've been taken off the field whether I engage in appeasement."

But the cost was high: the problems with Pakistan were just beginning.

In the endless debates inside the White House about how the Pakistanis would react to the bin Laden raid, the administration got just about every prediction wrong.

There was no attack on the American embassy in Islamabad. Some in the Situation Room guessed that the Pakistanis would sever diplomatic relations with the United States. That didn't happen either.

But perhaps the most important thing that the administration got wrong was the source of Pakistan's anger—and that would come to dominate the rest of Obama's dealings with the country. "We thought that Pakistan would be embarrassed because we discovered and killed bin Laden in a garrison town, the closest thing they have to West Point, and a short drive from the capital," one senior American official told me later. "We were half right: they were embarrassed, but it didn't have anything to do with bin Laden. It had to do with the fact that we were able to fly in and out, undetected, for a three-and-a-half-hour operation." And the ramifications of that ugly realization were just beginning.

AT FIRST, the shock in Pakistan was so great that it looked like Obama might get off easy. After hesitating a bit to work their way through their prepared script of calls—"Donilon was nervous," one participant recalled, "and wanted to go through what we were going to say one more time"—the outreach to the Pakistanis began.

"We could call this a joint operation," Admiral Mullen told his counterpart, General Kayani, in the first call. But Kayani demurred, offering a congratulations and urging Mullen to announce the news immediately so that the Pakistani government could begin managing the story at home. Kayani told Mullen, "You gotta get this out. The sun's going to come up here in a couple of hours, and I'm going to have a very hard time explaining this."

The sovereignty breach would be a huge issue, Kayani predicted, but if the word got out fast "it would be easier for us to explain it to our people if they know it's bin Laden." In other words, don't let the conspiracy theories set in; don't let them wonder why there are black helicopters in the night. When Obama called President Zardari, the Pakistani president was "effusive in his congratulations," one official told me, and began recalling the moment of terror when his wife, Benazir Bhutto, was assassinated. But as news of the raid filtered through the almost feudal Pakistani elite, attitudes changed. Never had the military, the strongest institution in the country, been so humiliated since it lost three wars to India. Many turned on Kayani, saying this is what he got for casting his lot with the Americans. "The officer corps was pissed," one of Obama's top aides said to me.

And they got even more pissed as the Americans, who had been so disciplined in the months leading up to the raid, made the situation worse with a series of triumphalist-sounding comments. There was a huge and understandable hunger among the media for a play-by-play of the hunt for, and demise of, the world's most wanted man. As day broke in a stunned Washington, John Brennan was rolled out in the White House press room to describe events that he only understood in fragmentary detail—much of it, as it turned out, suffered from the inevitable wild inaccuracy of first reports. And so a White House that had conducted the raid itself with enormous discipline began to offer contradictory, uncoordinated descriptions of how it went down.[51]

Brennan gave the impression that bin Laden was armed and died in a firefight; almost as soon as the seventy-nine SEALs involved were debriefed, the world learned that only Abu Ahmed al-Kuwaiti, the courier, got off a shot. Brennan said bin Laden used a woman as a human shield; it turned out she actually rushed the SEALs. Brennan described the al-Qaeda leader as living a luxurious lifestyle in his Abbottabad villa. While he lived better than many in Pakistan, the pictures of his apartment actually revealed something closer to squalor. At the Pentagon, top officers fumed at Brennan's blow-by-blow description of how the SEALs operated; they believed that the former CIA officer had given away operational secrets never shared outside the tribe. (In fact, it appears no real secrets were divulged.) No one was angrier than Mullen himself, who still fumed about that news conference nearly a year later.

The president's spokesman later blamed these mistakes on the "fog of war," as the White House responded in too much haste while "information came in piece by piece."[52] That was understandable, but the reaction in Pakistan grew uglier and uglier with every revelation of how long the operation had been planned and how the country's leadership was deliberately kept in the dark. The White House pushed back, arguing that the real violation of Pakistan's sovereignty was committed by bin Laden, who ran his terror syndicate from inside the country for nearly a decade. But it was to no avail. By Wednesday of that week, Gates went to see Donilon, offering up a barbed assessment of how the White House had handled the aftermath of the raid.

"I have a new strategic communications approach to recommend," Gates said in his trademark droll tones, according to an account later provided by his colleagues.

What was that, Donilon asked?

"Shut the fuck up," the defense secretary said.*

IT WAS GOOD advice, perhaps, but a bit late. With every new detail—how long the SEALs were inside Pakistan, how they refueled on Pakistani territory without being detected—the television commentators in Islamabad stoked the public anger. By the Friday after the raid, with emotions overflowing, the leaders of the two most powerful institutions in Pakistan—the military and the ISI—were called to their parliament for a humiliating dressing down by Pakistan's politicians, a rare event in a country where no civilian leader has ever ruled without being overthrown by the military.

For nearly eleven hours, Kayani and his successor at the head of the ISI, Lt. Gen. Ahmed Shuja Pasha, faced a barrage of questions from more than four hundred members of the parliament as to how the American forces had entered Pakistani territory undetected, operated unimpeded, and left unchallenged. Kayani and his generals were ready with a PowerPoint presentation that included

---

* Donilon reports no memory of that exchange.

photographs of the members of al-Qaeda captured by the ISI since 9/11, to make the point that Pakistan had been deeply involved in the fight against al-Qaeda. But that wasn't the issue—they were clueless about this operation.[53]

To spare Kayani the embarrassment, Pasha blamed an "intelligence failure" to detect the Americans. To any American who tuned in, it had the faint whiff of what American admirals said when they had to explain why the radar was off at Pearl Harbor, or what Bush administration officials told the 9/11 Commission about how America had been caught unawares that September morning.

Pasha said he had twice offered to resign, and twice been refused by Kayani. Then he gave the parliament what it hungered for: a rousing denunciation of the United States, which was met by thumps of approval from the legislators banging on their desks. He told them that the United States had let Pakistan down at every turn and now Obama had "conducted a sting operation on us" by not informing Pakistan of the raid in advance.[54]

Kayani sat in silence; when he couldn't bear it anymore, he left the chamber to smoke. But the session lasted so long that he ran out of cigarettes. It went on until two in the morning, ending with a resolution condemning the Abbottabad raid as a violation of sovereignty and a demand for a review of the partnership with the United States "with the view to ensuring Pakistan's national interests were fully respected."

What really had Kayani worried, though, was that the American raid exposed huge holes in the Pakistani defenses, rekindling the old paranoia. Within days of the raid, members of the Pakistani parliament insisted on an independent inquiry asking whether "the military could defend Pakistan's borders and its nuclear arsenal from being snatched or attacked by the United States or India."[55] (Kayani shared that concern, and issued orders to move elements of the arsenal around the country—an order the Americans immediately detected.)

When Sen. John Kerry, the chairman of the Senate Foreign Re-lations Committee, showed up in Islamabad less than two weeks after the bin Laden raid, Kayani was still seething. He used a private session with Kerry and Pakistan's president and prime minister to demand a written assurance that, under no circumstances—even chaos in Pakistan—would the United States enter the country to grab or secure the country's nuclear treasure. Kerry, thinking he was using a figure of speech, said he was prepared to "write in blood" that the United States has no intention to go after the arsenal.

"Immediately the Pakistanis tried to get us to write a statement using the term 'blood oath,' or something like it, that ruled out ac-tion against the arsenal under any circumstance," one participant in the trip told me. Kerry, of course, had no authority to issue such a statement. After much debate, the two sides settled for a declara-tion that the United States has no "designs" on Pakistan's weap-ons, which of course meant nothing. The Pakistanis immediately called in the press and read a statement declaring that Kerry "says he can write with his blood that the US has no interest in Pakistan's nuclear assets, though it is the United States' desire to see that they remain well protected and secure."[56] The reassurance was dutifully reported in Pakistan the next day.

TWENTY DAYS AFTER bin Laden was killed, a group of heavily armed insurgents stormed the Mehran naval air base, located just off of one of the main boulevards of Karachi, the most populous city in Pakistan. The attack lit up the night sky and set off a prolonged gun battle with Pakistani security forces.[57] As crowds gathered at the entrance gate to watch the fighting, flames and thick smoke could be seen billowing up from two P-3C Orion surveillance air-planes, surveillance crafts that the United States had sold to Paki-stan in 2010.

Just as in Abbottabad, the Pakistani forces were caught flat-footed. It took hours for them to mount a response. The staccato of gunfire punctuated the night before a massive explosion from one of the planes' fuel tanks rattled the city. It took sixteen long hours for Pakistani forces to retake control of the base, with many dead. One insurgent blew himself up; two managed to escape without a trace.[58]

It quickly became clear this was no random attack—this was an inside job. Pakistani officials had long advertised that the Mehran base was one of the country's most secure. Yet the attackers, carrying rocket-propelled grenades, penetrated its interior from three different directions. Clearly, they knew the base's layout, enabling them to bypass security posts and surveillance cameras.[59]

Nonetheless, Pakistan's military got lucky that night. The Mehran naval base is about fifteen miles away from an air force base where Pakistan is widely believed to keep a large depot of nuclear weapons. Had the attackers chosen to target the air force base instead, the Pakistani military might have woken up to a repeat of the earlier scare, this time with real weapons on the loose. In any event, the embarrasment over the attack left a journalist named Syed Saleem Shahzad dead in a culvert.

Shahzad knew how to push the ISI's buttons; he had written at length, sometimes with more accuracy than at others, about the ISI's connections to fundamentalist groups, or of missions gone awry. His fatal error after the raid on the base came when he posted a story describing vague evidence that al-Qaeda, not the Pakistani Taliban, was responsible for breaching the base and torching the planes. "Al-Qaeda carried out the brazen attack . . . after talks failed between the navy and al-Qaeda over the release of naval officials arrested on suspicion of al-Qaeda links," Shahzad wrote.[60] If true, then the insider threats that Washington so often warned about—and that Pakistan so often dismissed—were real.

Shortly after posting his story, Shahzad was on his way to another interview about the Mehran attack, but he never made it. His bruised and bloated body was later found washed up a few miles downstream from where his abandoned car, a white Toyota Corolla, was found. Still wearing a suit and tie, the body had become stuck in the grates as the water from a canal flowed into the top of a dam.[61] While the crime has never been solved, it bore all the hallmarks of Pakistan's intelligence agencies. The ISI denied any involvement.[62]

The combination of the Mehran attack and the cover-up that followed called into question whether the Pakistani military's assurances could be trusted. How hard would it have been to mount a similar attack across town, where the nuclear weapons were stored? "We don't think it would be that difficult," a retired Indian general who has spent much of his career studying the Pakistani nuclear program told me in Delhi at the end of 2011.

The fact of the matter is that insurgents in Pakistan don't need to steal a complete, working weapon to achieve their goals. Part of a weapon will do. Even without a nuclear core in hand, terrorists with a credible story about infiltrating the Pakistani nuclear storage areas could easily convince the world they have a crude nuclear capability.

Imagine, another Indian official told me, if Lashkar-e-Taiba, the terror group created by the ISI to fight a proxy war with India, had claimed to have a nuclear weapon when they laid siege to luxury hotels in Mumbai in 2008, killing scores of locals and hotel guests. "Quite simply," the official told me, "we would have had to think twice about the counterattack." Indian nuclear forces would have been put on alert. And soon there would be the threat of nuclear strike and counterstrike, a replay of the terrifying standoff nearly a decade ago.

"They don't have to be truly successful to become powerful," the Indian official said to me. "They just have to convince the world that the Pakistanis lost one of the crown jewels."

It was a telling comment. During the Cold War, America worried about super-empowered countries—China, the Soviet Union—that could decide to use their nuclear weapons against the United States or its allies. Pakistan is the reverse problem. Pakistan, as Obama told his staff late in 2011, could "disintegrate" and set off a scramble for its weapons. It was his biggest single national security concern, he told them—and the scenario he had the least power to prevent.

THE BIN LADEN raid will certainly go down in the history of counterterrorism as an extraordinarily bold presidentially ordered attack, with the president himself amending the tactical plan. In American military annals, it probably compares best with the ambush of Adm. Isoruku Yamamoto, the Harvard-educated commander who oversaw the attack on Pearl Harbor. Just as Yamamoto's death in 1943 sped Japan's defeat, bin Laden's killing accelerated al-Qaeda's decline, though as Obama later boasted, the terror group "was on its [knees] well before we took out bin Laden because of our activities and my direction."[63]

If the raid had gone wrong—and there were many moments where it could have—we would view Obama's presidency entirely differently. Luck helped, but in the end Obama's team applied a renewed rigor to the search, and discipline to the debate over how to proceed. The president overruled far more experienced foreign policy professionals, and got it right. And the success allowed him to close a chapter in American history. It ratified his decision to stop talking about a "war on terrorism" and talk instead about a war to dismantle al-Qaeda.

But in its aftermath, the administration has buried the question it aired briefly after the raid: How could the world's most wanted man live that close to the capital of a key American partner, outside the gates of its military academy, without a deep support structure? A review of the NSA's tapes of conversations among Pakistan's top officers—who are monitored frequently—found no evidence that Kayani or Pasha knew about bin Laden's whereabouts. "We just came up with nothing," said one official who had studied the intercepts. But the material found inside the compound shows that bin Laden was in contact with Mullah Omar, the leader of the Taliban, and with militant groups like Lashkar-e-Taiba that the Pakistanis listen in on every day. They also found evidence that bin Laden sought a way to kill Obama, but it was all talk, it appears, and no plan.

In the interest of restoring a semblance of peace with Pakistan, American officials stopped publicly asking hard questions about who inside the country knew of bin Laden's whereabouts or how some of his children could have been born in a public hospital in Pakistan long after the September 11 attacks. It was reminiscent of how the Bush administration stopped asking questions about how A. Q. Khan, operating from a base about forty miles from bin Laden's hideaway, could have sold off Pakistan's nuclear technology to the world's most desperate states. In both cases, the White House lived in the hope that by avoiding a rigorous inquiry that was bound to embarrass Pakistan, they would somehow win Pakistani cooperation in the future.

It proved a bad bet in the Khan case, and there is little evidence that, in the aftermath of the bin Laden case, it will turn out any better.

CHAPTER 5

THE LONG GAME:
GETTING OUT, WITHOUT REALLY LEAVING

In November of 2010, the month before he died, Richard Holbrooke put the final touches on a plan for negotiating an exit strategy for a war that had already cost nearly fifteen hundred American lives and nearly $400 billion, and that still had no end in sight.

The master diplomat's plan drew heavily from the crowning experience of his diplomatic career: ending the war in the Balkans in 1995, when he locked the presidents of Serbia, Bosnia, and Croatia into an air base in Dayton, Ohio, and emerged with a peace accord many thought was unachievable. Those negotiations only happened after the United States and NATO bombed the parties to the negotiating table, as Holbrooke would often remind people, applying the kind of intense military pressure that made a political solution between foes the best of several bad choices. It was a grueling, brutal process. But even as Holbrooke finished his outline for a combined military and political strategy for Afghanistan, he told me in our last conversation that he had his doubts that the Obama administration had the will or the persistence to create the conditions for a Dayton-style deal in Afghanistan—or that he could get the Americans, the Afghans, and the Taliban into one room.

"This will be far, far harder than the Balkans, and anyone who thinks it won't be isn't paying attention," Holbrooke told me about ten days before he died, when we ran into each other after breakfast at a hotel in Georgetown. He called for another cup of coffee and laid out a two-or-three-year vision for how he hoped to maneuver each of the parties to the negotiating table—stroking the egos of some, embarrassing others, cajoling and threatening more than a few. It was pure Holbrooke: one part hubris, one part raw determination, one part canny three-dimensional chess. But he acknowledged two big holes in the strategy.

"At least in the Balkans I knew which thugs to talk to," he said. In Afghanistan, the list of players was too long: "You need Karzai, and he's impossible; you need Mullah Omar," the Taliban leader, whom he considered more dangerous—and a more urgent target—than Osama bin Laden. "You need the Taliban, the Haqqanis, the Northern Alliance, and then you need the Pakistanis," who, he predicted, would try to blow up the talks. He knew the chances of getting past decades of hatreds and rivalries were vanishingly small.

The second big vulnerability in the strategy, he said, was Obama himself. He could not tell if the president really believed in a peace deal, or just wanted to get out of Afghanistan as quickly as he could. "I just don't know," he said before he took off, late to a meeting, and, as always, leaving more questions hanging in the air as he disappeared with his cell phone pressed to his ear.

More than a year after his death, the only certainty is that America will leave Afghanistan—save for a small force behind high walls—with al-Qaeda mostly crippled, but the grand experiment of remaking Afghanistan largely in tatters. The American conceit that Afghanistan would emerge a very different place—after a decade of occupation, a new constitution, a Western-trained military, and a reinvented economy—collapsed in the Obama years. "For the first two years" of the Obama administration, "we'd land in Afghanistan and talk about building a new Afghanistan," said one official who worked with Holbrooke until his death. "And in the last twelve months, we land there and someone says to us, 'The British tried and left, the Soviets tried and left, and now you've tried. You just haven't left.' " But the most difficult questions raised by Obama's circuitous route to an Afghan exit—the road from "war of necessity" to "Afghan Good Enough"—will not be answerable until after the vast majority of the American force departs.

After years of training and billions in investment, a significant portion of it wasted, will the Afghans prove they have the firepower and will to hold the most contested areas of the country? If a settlement with the Taliban, and other insurgents, is achieved—a big "if"—can the weak Hamid Karzai and his successor enforce the deal and strengthen the legitimacy of the government? And could Washington live with an Afghanistan in which some cities and provinces are effectively under Taliban control?

Ask those questions in Washington and you get something of a shrug, from Democrats and Republicans, diplomats and generals. It is a shrug that says we gave it more than ten years, and it's time to move on. It is a shrug that avoids the hardest question: Was this all worth it?

EVERY DAY DURING the two years he worked from his suite on the ground floor of the State Department, Richard Holbrooke fought one battle to bring a group of unsavory enemies to the negotiating table, and another to influence a strategy being run from the White House. From the first months of his tenure, it was clear his relationship with Obama was strained at best. He had backed Hillary Clinton for the Democratic nomination, whispering to journalists that Obama just didn't have the experience for the job. That got patched up, but Obama bristled at Holbrooke's lectures and thought he was mired in the glory of his past accomplishments and grandiose visions of his role in Obama's diplomatic universe. White House aides suspected he was a leaker, the highest sin in the Obama White House. When Gen. Stanley McChrystal was fired in the summer of 2010, there was a movement inside the administration to fire Holbrooke as well, and start totally anew.

But Hillary Clinton protected him, and she thought that without Holbrooke's drive, a diplomatic solution was impossible. So Holbrooke and his team would churn out position papers, one after another, describing pathways to the negotiations. "He did this pretty strategically," Vali Nasr, a former adviser to Holbrooke, told me. "What he had in mind was that you needed a truly regional solution—one that involved the Taliban and Afghanistan, but also Pakistan and India and Iran. And he knew he never had a mandate for that. So he would put together these fairly narrow solutions, trying to socialize the White House to the narrower idea of negotiations. And it was a struggle, because for two years the whole discussion at the White House was troop numbers and surges and the military approach to the war. Richard actually believed that the Taliban was willing to break with al-Qaeda, and there was a grand bargain to be had."[1]

And if there was a grand bargain, Holbrooke thought he was the man to broker it. Holbrooke subscribed to what Tom Donilon later called a "great-man theory" of how diplomacy gets done in the world—that passionate individuals matter in getting a deal done, often more than the details of the transaction. There is no doubt about what Holbrooke wanted: another Dayton accord, rife with diplomatic high drama, that might end with a deal that the Taliban, Karzai, and all the regional players could sign. Holbrooke's wife, Kati Marton, made that clear a few months after her husband's death. Soon after the bin Laden raid, Kati told my colleague Nick Kristof that in Holbrooke's mind, "The whole policy was off-kilter, way too militarized. Richard never thought that this war could be won on the battlefield. He was dreaming of a Dayton-like setting somewhere, isolated, no media, no Washington bureaucracy. He was a long way from that, but he was dreaming of that."[2]

What seemed like a dream to Holbrooke had the potential to be a nightmare for the White House. As they looked forward to Obama's reelection campaign, his advisers could easily imagine what Obama's opponent would try to do with the narrative of Obama publicly negotiating with the same enemy that had spilled American blood.* Even Obama's national security staff, many of whom had worked with Holbrooke for years, admired his successes but feared that, once let loose, he would become a renegade negotiating machine—and they worried he would not protect the president from the charge of striking a deal that appeared to give ground to the Taliban. Holbrooke had the political acumen not to press the point. As Nasr recalled, Holbrooke also "knew that if he suggested a Dayton accord, or anything that would look like the agreement in the Balkans, it would get shot down at the White House because it would look like he was putting himself at the center of it."[3]

But Holbrooke died before negotiations got off the ground. Even in his final hours, he bickered with his doctors, who were desperately attempting to calm him down. "You've got to relax, Richard," one of his doctors told him.

"I can't relax," he said, before the twenty-one-hour surgery that he would never wake up from. "I'm worried about Afghanistan and Pakistan."[4]

One of the many unknowns of the Obama presidency is whether the denouement of a decade-old war—an Afghanistan that is still broken and vulnerable to the return of the Taliban, and a Pakistan that is still paranoid, angry, and growing more nuclear than ever—would have come out differently if Holbrooke had lived long enough to implement his own plan. But the plan Obama's team is now attempting is, at its core, the one that Holbrooke outlined

---

* It turned out to be a legitimate fear: in the Republican debates, Mitt Romney, the former Massachusetts governor, denounced the idea of negotiating with the Taliban.

the month before his death. And in the opening days of 2012, after months of maneuvering, the Taliban had agreed to set up offices in the tiny, garishly wealthy Arab state of Qatar, a tiny sliver of absolute monarchy that had deftly avoided any hint of an uprising during the Arab Spring. But Karzai initially objected, fearing that the Americans would hijack the process, and threatened to set up his own talks in Saudi Arabia. Pakistan didn't like it either, realizing, as one senior American official put it to me, that Qatar was selected because "it's a place where the Pakistanis have very little influence," and thus limited ability to damage the process.

ONLY A FEW pictures of the one-eyed mullah Mohammed Omar are known to exist, but for a man few say they have seen, he has amassed and retained an astounding amount of power. Nearly eleven years after an American invasion cast him out of Afghanistan, Omar is in exile in Pakistan, where he runs the insurgency from afar. At the ·height of the Taliban's power, from 1994 until the 2001 invasion, Mullah Omar's rule was known for its exceptional ruthlessness, amputating thieves' hands and stoning adulterers. Public executions became sporting events, in front of crowds in Kabul's stadium.[5]

But Omar was the ultimate survivor. He'd lasted through decades of war and targeted attacks from his rivals. When the American invading force hunted for him, Omar moved his operations to Pakistan, and while his rough whereabouts were well known, the United States never seemed able to target him. The Pakistanis, still seeing the Taliban as their best proxy for ensuring influence in Afghanistan, would not touch him.

Holbrooke once told Steve Coll, perhaps the best chronicler of the insurgencies that have gripped the region, that "Mullah Omar is incredibly important" to any solution to the war.[6]

Over time, members of Obama's negotiating team came to agree: "Whoever you talk to—Pakistanis, Afghans, other people—it does all go back to Mullah Omar," one key American negotiator in Qatar told me early in 2012. So did leaders of the despised, but powerful, Haqqani network that launched brutal attacks against international forces on Afghanistan's eastern border with Pakistan, and the 2011 attack on the US embassy in Kabul. Siraj Haqqani, a son of the network's leader, told the BBC Pashto service, "Mullah Omar is our leader and we follow him. . . . You should not expect us to say anything other than what [Omar decides]."[7]

"He is the Ho Chi Minh of the war," Vali Nasr liked to say, referring to the North Vietnamese leader who sat under an open-air canopy in Hanoi with a single black telephone from which he commanded an insurgency that ran circles around a far larger American force.[8] In the end, Nixon was forced to deal with Ho to end the war. And Holbrooke, who as a young diplomat got his start in Vietnam, knew that sooner or later the Obama administration would find itself in the odd position of negotiating, at least indirectly, with a man who still has a $10 million bounty on his head.[9]

That job of negotiating with Omar, at least indirectly, fell to Marc Grossman, Holbrooke's successor. A serious, methodical diplomat, Grossman came to the process with plenty of determination but none of Holbrooke's diplomatic theatrics. He also has none of Holbrooke's frenetic air. Gone were the eighteen-hour days, the cell-phone calls from early morning to midnight, the mix of endless meetings and parties in the Hamptons. "It's like they put Valium in the coffee," said one of the staffers who stayed on. "You get your weekends back, but you wonder if he can drive people who hate each other back to the table."

Holbrooke rarely went a day without spinning reporters. When Grossman flew commercial to Qatar to meet with Mullah Omar's former executive assistant, Tayyab Agha, and a half-dozen other Taliban representatives, he held no press conferences and said virtually nothing about the meeting.

They spent much of the time talking about a prisoner

exchange—five Taliban members held at Guantánamo Bay who, over many congressional objections, would be swapped for a single American soldier who had wandered off his post and ended up a captive. It would be a while, if ever, before they got to the question of whether a political resolution was possible.

"I don't know whether these people are reconcilable or not," Grossman told Bill Keller and me in his State Department office before the talks began. "But the job we've been given is to find out."[10]

The secrecy surrounding the talks in Qatar reflected the huge risks, both political and strategic. The very prospect of a political settlement seemed ambitious at best. The United States had to facilitate a negotiation not just between the Afghan government and Karzai, but between the Afghan government and Afghanistan's two other major insurgencies: the Haqqani network and Hezb-e-Islami Gulbuddin. And negotiations between Afghan insurgents and the Afghan government could not occur in a vacuum. All of the major regional players—India, China, Iran, the Central Asian Republics, Turkey, and the Gulf states—had significant stakes in the outcome in Afghanistan, and would be needed to enforce a settlement. And the most essential regional player, Pakistan, also happened to be the most duplicitous.

In the months ahead of Grossman's trip, even Obama's own team was divided. After fighting for a decade, most of the American military leadership was adamantly against premature "reconciliation" with Afghan insurgents. While their talking points read that the only solution to the Afghan conflict was a political solution, their training taught them the enemy had to see inevitable defeat before a political settlement was possible. As the surge wound down, that turning point was nowhere in sight. "We fought the Pentagon every step of the way on this," one senior American diplomat told me.

But over time, Obama and Donilon grew impatient with the Pentagon argument, and allowed Clinton and Grossman more room to test the Taliban's intentions. The Taliban will never be knocked backward to the military's satisfaction, they argued. Clinton viewed the military's opposition as a "reflexive reaction against the idea that there could be any sustainable, workable peace with these guys—with the Taliban." The military, she said, believed that the Taliban "needed to be defeated first."

But Americans were clearly tired of a war that cost $119 billion in 2011, the high-water mark of Obama's surge.[11] And the strategic advantages of staying the course were becoming as opaque as an Afghan sandstorm. In the beginning of the Obama administration, Obama often said that a stable Afghanistan was necessary to defeat al-Qaeda and prevent its return there. But three years later, al-Qaeda was nearly dismantled, and the Taliban posed little threat beyond Afghanistan and Pakistan. What was to be gained by another five years of combat?

"We can hold the minimal objective of ensuring there's not a Taliban overthrow of the government," one of Obama's top aides told me in December 2011, while building an Afghan military capable of securing the country as Americans withdraw. "We need not overdefine our objective, and we need not do what we did in Kandahar—the very methodical COIN campaign. We don't need to take that all over the country. And that's the 'good enough' concept."

After Marc Grossman took over as Holbrooke's replacement, the first thing he told his staff to do was to get advice from people who had actually negotiated an end to war. In late April 2011, they had their chance: Henry Kissinger was back on the seventh floor of the State Department, reminiscing about diplomacy in a public forum with Hillary Clinton.[12]

When the public discussion was over, Kissinger went behind closed doors to talk to Clinton's staff, including many who were attempting exploratory talks with the Taliban.

At eighty-eight, Kissinger remains the wily dean of American diplomacy, and while he looks half-asleep at times, his chin sometimes resting on his chest, his insights have grown more acerbic with age. His retelling of history sometimes involves a bit of rewriting as well, as if he is adjusting the historical interpretation of his time in office while he still can. Yet the combination of his reputation and his analysis means he always attracts a large and respectful crowd—and he is too old to care whom his advice offends.

"You should never be negotiating a peace when the opposing force knows you are leaving," Kissinger said to Obama's senior negotiators that day in April. "Your leverage will wither away each day that the peace talks are dragged out." In public, a few months later he reiterated, "If you negotiate while your forces are withdrawing, you're not in a great negotiating position."[13]

Of course, by then Obama had already announced that the surge troops would begin withdrawing in the summer of 2011, and he was just weeks away from announcing that by September 2012, the surge would be over. He was already violating Kissinger's first warning. "We couldn't tell if he knew what the president had already said and was ignoring it, or if he was just giving us his best advice," said one of Clinton's top aides.

Kissinger had a second piece of advice: beware troop withdrawals. "He said they are like eating popcorn," another young staffer, a disciple of Holbrooke's, remembered later. "Once you start, you just can't stop. Particularly in an election year."

◆

"YOU KNOW IT'S a messy war when you can't recognize the enemy—even when he's sitting across the negotiating table from you," Robert Baer, a former CIA field officer, wrote at the end of 2010.[14] He turned out to be more correct than he could possibly know.

Previous efforts to negotiate with the Taliban had not gone exactly as planned. Early in 2010, while Holbrooke was still alive, senior officials working on Afghanistan thought they were on the verge of a major breakthrough. Mullah Akhtar Muhammad Mansour, known as the Taliban's "Commander of the Faithful" and one of the most senior commanders in Mullah Omar's inner circle, had agreed to start reconciliation talks.

Mansour was a mysterious figure. American military commanders, diplomats, and spies had never seen him; neither had most Afghan officials. But Mansour seemed like the real thing. The more he talked, the more NATO officials flew him around in official aircraft, even taking him to meet President Karzai in Kabul. Naturally, they gave him a big wad of cash to make sure he would stay involved in talks.[15]

The Obama administration was so certain of its negotiating partner that it asked the *New York Times* to omit his name from an article for fear his life would be jeopardized.

Mansour talked a great game: the Taliban were tired and wanted to see an end to fighting, he said, a line that played perfectly into the American narrative. Mullah Omar was ready to come to the table, he promised. Over three high-level meetings with US and NATO officials, his demands, relayed by surrogates, seemed surprisingly modest: The Taliban leadership had to be able to leave their hiding places in Pakistan and return to Afghanistan. Foot soldiers needed jobs. And prisoners held by Americans needed to be released. There was no demand that all foreigners must vacate the region, which is usually the Taliban's first agenda item.

But as officials later discovered, there was one central problem: Mullah Mansour wasn't actually Mullah Mansour. It wasn't until the third meeting that someone figured out there was something strange going on, when a former colleague of the real Mansour was seated at the table and looked quite confused. "He said he didn't recognize him," said another Afghan official. This Mansour—whoever he was—was never seen again. He took the money—$150,000 by some accounts—and ran, leaving the Americans to wonder whether they had been talking to a real Taliban agent who was testing the waters, a phony sent by Pakistan's ISI to determine America's real intentions, or just a very talented scam artist. I asked an administration official what the reaction had been after someone had to tell the president that the United States had been taken for a ride.

"The most common reaction you hear goes along these lines," one senior official told me a year after the incident. "We have the biggest CIA station on the planet in Afghanistan. And they can't tell us we're negotiating with the wrong fucking guy?"

It was an embarrassing incident, but mostly harmless. The next fraud ended in tragedy.

AT SEVENTY-ONE YEARS old, Burhanuddin Rabbani had seen Afghanistan at war for three decades. He had been a commander of the mujahideen for many years (some Americans had gotten to know him when he was an ally in the war against the Soviet Union). But as old age set in, he became widely respected by factions of the fragmented Afghan society and was a natural as the leader of Afghanistan's new High Peace Council, the body Karzai appointed to lead the peace negotiations on the Afghan government's behalf. The council reached out to insurgent commanders in Afghanistan and Pakistan, making the case for joining negotiations and supporting the government. Rabbani took it upon himself to travel throughout the country, setting up reconciliation councils in each province, and to persuade neighboring countries to engage in the peace negotiations.[16]

Just before leaving on a trip in September, Rabbani had been in talks with a man named Esmatullah, who also said he came from the Quetta Shura Taliban, Mullah Omar's headquarters. His taped messages, outlining a peace deal, had been sent to President Karzai, who talked about them with President Obama during a trip to Washington.

While Karzai was still in Washington, Rabbani was returning to his home in Kabul and learned that Esmatullah was waiting for him with "a very important and positive message from the Quetta Shura."[17] After five months of talks, he was a trusted figure; he was allowed to sit in Rabbani's home and wait for his return. When Rabbani got back, the reunion was short: Esmatullah was ushered into the room with Rabbani, and, as he greeted the elder statesman, he placed his turbaned head on Rabbani's chest. Then he triggered a bomb, which was hidden in his turban. Rabbani was killed instantly.

Again, it was impossible to verify exactly who Esmatullah represented. The Haqqani network? The Taliban? A splinter group? "This is a lesson for us all that we shouldn't fool ourselves that this group, who has carried out so many crimes against the people of Afghanistan, are willing to make peace," offered Dr. Abdullah Abdullah, a Tajik Northern Alliance leader and former presidential candidate. "We are up against people who don't believe in humanity. They assassinate people on the streets of Kabul, they assassinate those who are trying to achieve peace."[18]

Even the savvy, seen-it-all American ambassador, Ryan Crocker, issued a sobering statement after the Rabbani funeral, conceding that the attack "raises very serious questions as to whether the Taliban and those who support them have any real interest in reconciliation."[19]

BY EARLY 2012, twice burned, the White House was understandably nervous about trying again. This time the Taliban interlocutor was Tayyab Agha, Omar's former executive assistant, who arrived in

Qatar with some promising words: "The Taliban want peace like all of our Afghan brothers and sisters," he said. "We believe in Islam, and we believe that Afghanistan should be an Islamic state. But the Taliban do not think that they can bring a true Islamic state only by force. We can bring those changes in many ways—by negotiating, by speaking."[20]

But administration officials wisely kept expectations low. At the end of January, Marc Grossman repeatedly emphasized that the "Taliban have not explicitly said that they would participate in peace talks."[21]

In fact, "peace talks" were a long-term goal, not an immediate one. In Situation Room meetings about the talks, White House officials said they couldn't imagine a political settlement any sooner than 2014, when the NATO operation was supposed to end. More immediately, what Obama wanted was a credible enough cease-fire that would give the Afghan forces a bit more time and training.

Even today, it is questionable whether a political settlement with the enemy Americans spent a decade chasing is possible. At the beginning of 2012, one of Clinton's top aides said it was "fifty-fifty at best that the peace talks even get off the ground." Already Clinton herself had taken a step back from what were once the "preconditions" for the talks—that the Taliban lay down arms and renounce violence, break ties with al-Qaeda, and become part of the political process. Now, the renunciation of ties with "international terrorists"—code for separating from al-Qaeda—is the administration's only precondition. (American intelligence officials, tapping into the Taliban's internal debates, picked up indications in early 2012 that the Taliban's military and political wings were arguing with each other about whether the group's ties to a diminished al-Qaeda were worth the cost.) The rest of the administration's "preconditions" were demoted to desired "outcomes." Whether it was desperation to begin the process or recognition that under any withdrawal scenario the Taliban will be a powerful force, it was clear that the United States did not enter these conversations with the upper hand.

But the main advantage to the negotiations was the dissention and disruption it created within the Taliban's ranks. "The leadership of the Taliban's heads are spinning," one senior diplomat told me. "They don't quite know what Mullah Omar has authorized or not." As a result, the official added, "we have a long time before we get into a room with the Taliban and with the Afghans."

IF YOU HAD to pick a winner coming out of the decade-long experiment in Afghanistan and Pakistan, you would be hard pressed to find one. Obama scored one tremendous victory: his determination to narrow America's goals resulted in a far greater focus on decimating al-Qaeda. He accomplished that goal with a combination of precision drone strikes and a growing sophistication inside the Special Operations Command about how to fight an enemy few understood in the early years after 9/11.

While the Special Operations Forces' capabilities had been growing for a decade, there was little in Obama's personal history—and little in his presidential run—to suggest that he would be able to focus those resources in a way the Bush administration had not. Obama can go into the 2012 campaign making a legitimate argument that by reconceptualizing America's objectives and avoiding distractions, he was on the cusp of destroying al-Qaeda's old leadership. The enemy that seemed ten feet tall on September 12, 2001, was almost vanquished. "There are a lot of critiques of how we do business," Donilon said to me once early in 2012. "But no one can say we don't execute."

The narrowing of focus came at a cost, however: America backed away from many of the promises it made—many of them unwise or unachievable—to the Afghan people. The fact that Obama, in the fourth year of his presidency, is beginning to negotiate with the Taliban is recognition that there is no other way to prevent Afghanistan from falling back into a civil war. And it will mean making concessions to some of America's most hated adversaries. Under the best of circumstances, the Taliban and other insurgents may push for a revised constitution that allows them greater autonomy and governing power along the Afghanistan–Pakistan border. Under the worst circumstances, they may skip that step and simply take control of provinces by brute force and impose their radical ideology on the local population.

In 2002, in the days when American hubris was at its height, President Bush talked about radically changing Afghanistan's society and institutions, and building a modern state where none had ever existed. Obama came into office employing some of the same rhetoric, and poured billions of additional resources into Afghanistan. Unlike Bush, however, Obama quickly recognized his folly and kept walking that vision back until it became a vanishing part of the American effort. Obama's new plan—to keep a small force of perhaps 10,000 to 15,000 Special Operations Forces, engineers, drone operators, and others hunkered down in a few bases around the country as an "enduring presence"—marks a reversal of the American strategic calculus in the region. When the United States prepared to invade Afghanistan, it forced Pakistan to choose between allying with the Taliban and al-Qaeda or allying with Washington. With a gun to his head, Pakistan's military dictator Pervez Musharraf made the only choice he could, and his country became a platform to launch the invasion of Afghanistan.

In 2012, faced with a very different world, the United States is now turning that strategy on its head. The "enduring presence" in Afghanistan is intended as a platform to allow American Special Operations Forces and drones to go anywhere in the region:

to strike into Pakistan if al-Qaeda revives or a nuclear weapon gets loose; to move into Kabul if it looks as if the Afghan government is going to fall; to deal with Iran. That was the essence of Donilon's message to General Kayani during that smoke-infused meeting in Abu Dhabi. It is the right strategic concept—for the United States, at least.

But what about the Afghans? What will endure from America's effort to transform a country that prides itself in outlasting its invaders? With luck, most of the 2.4 million Afghan girls now going to school will still be able to do so after the United States leaves. But the country will be reeling from the loss of the American presence; the World Bank estimates that 97 percent of Afghanistan's $28 billion gross domestic product depends on development aid and in-country spending for foreign troops.[22] A senior State Department official said that it will cost roughly $4 billion per year in assistance just to maintain two-thirds of the Afghan security forces, which is many multiples of Afghanistan's federal budget. A diminishing portion of that will come from the American Congress; if Iraq is any guide, as soon as the troops leave, American interest will fade.

But the United States has a moral responsibility to the Afghan people, and Obama needs to talk about that honestly—to adjust expectations to reality. The withdrawal will mean lost jobs or diminished income for the millions of Afghans who came to depend on the revenue generated by feeding, transporting, and translating for foreign troops. After so many years of loose talk in Washington about Marshall Plans and aid packages, the president needs to negotiate an agreement with both parties in Congress about what America will provide to Afghanistan over the next five or ten years, and stick to it. And, most important, Obama needs a bipartisan, publicly declared strategy to fund the Afghan security forces after American troops withdraw—or risk repeating a grievous mistake of his predecessors, leaving behind hundreds of thousands of unemployed, armed, and angry young men.

In the early spring of 2012, no such strategy existed: Obama's aides said he did not want to spend more than $2 billion a year on the Afghan forces; the effort to get Europe and Asia to chip in at least as much was faltering. Suddenly everyone was discussing shrinking the size of the Afghán forces by at least 100,000.

And even if negotiations with the Taliban move ahead, it is very possible that a decade from now, visitors to Afghanistan will see few traces—apart from military hardware and bases—of the American experiment there. Tribal warlords, local strongmen, Pakistanis, Iranians, and Indians will all have greater influence. And it seems safe to assume that as Americans leave in large numbers, the war in Afghanistan will continue in some form. The NATO-backed Karzai government never managed to extend its writ far beyond Kabul's city limits, and isn't likely to once the Americans are gone.

This may be an outcome America can live with. The chances that Afghanistan will once again become a breeding ground for international terrorists who can attack the United States are now minimal; the United States has far greater surveillance capability, and many more tools to attack terrorist training centers, than it did before 9/11. Afghanistan is no longer the "war of necessity" it was several years ago, and a large military presence in Afghanistan is no longer strategically justifiable. Nor is it tenable. The Afghan reaction after word got out that some American troops mistakenly burned Korans at Bagram Airfield in February 2012 touched off days of rioting and the killing of several Americans, including two officers who worked inside Afghan ministries and were shot by an Afghan intelligence official. The level of mistrust ran so high that it was clear Americans would always be looking over their shoulders in Afghanistan, always worried about whether they could trust their own allies. The calculus in Washington was simple: the cost of the war was too high, the returns on any resulting peace, too low.

"A STABLE AFGHANISTAN is not essential," Holbrooke often said in the last year of his life. "A stable Pakistan is essential."[23] Of course, America had rarely known a stable Pakistan. But the awful year with Pakistan in 2011 had one benefit: it clarified, for any who were confused, that Holbrooke's argument was right. Afghanistan could fall to the Taliban, and it would be a black mark on American diplomacy and the military, just as the fall of Saigon in 1975 was for a previous generation. Strategically, though, it would mean little. But if Pakistan fell, the United States could not afford to be a spectator and simply pray that those nuclear weapons were safe.

It is no wonder that at the end of 2011, Obama admitted to aides that it was Pakistan that still worried him the most. The country had never gone through a truly peaceful transfer of power, until Musharraf's military dictatorship gave way to the weak civilian rule of President Zardari. Its elected government is toothless. "If there is one image of Zardari that will stick with me," said one retired official who dealt with him often, "it was the split screen of those awful floods hitting the poorest people in Pakistan" in the summer of 2010 "while Zardari is shown arriving at glorious weekend places in Britain and France."

Yet as America identifies all that is wrong with its ostensible ally—how it plays both sides of the war, how rampant the corruption is, or how scheming the military and intelligence services are—it is easy to forget that the United States has more than its share of responsibility for taking the relationship to new lows. "The concept at the beginning of 2011," a senior State Department official said to me, "was still to build a strategic relationship. But then, like clockwork, we triggered a crisis every two months."

After the Raymond Davis shootout in early 2011 came the bin Laden raid. Then US forces made a huge and deadly mistake in November on a remote mountaintop border post in Pakistan's Mohmand tribal region, which borders Afghanistan. Through a fatal mix of bad intelligence and poor communication, US troops confused Pakistani soldiers for insurgents who they believed were firing on them. They called in a helicopter gunship and killed twenty-four people in a prolonged series of strikes that were so withering, there was little left to the victims' bodies. (Not surprisingly, the Pentagon has suppressed its video of the incident.) Americans blamed Pakistanis for failing to notify them of the Pakistani border posts; Pakistanis declared the killings an "act of deliberate aggression."[24]

The American ambassador to Pakistan, Cameron Munter, advised Obama to apologize on behalf of the American people, but Obama's advisers demurred. At the time, an investigation into what went wrong had just been launched, and responsibility was unclear. When, later, the United States was found largely responsible, it seemed too late. The moment was lost, and the incident had entered Pakistani folklore.

But scratch deeper, and it's exactly the kind of tragedy that happens too often in a relationship fraught with mutual distrust and suspicion. Pakistan immediately closed all NATO supply routes to Afghanistan and called for a total reevaluation of the strategic partnership.

"The tragedy at Mohmand," Sherry Rehman, Pakistani ambassador to the United States, later said, "really served as an end-line trigger that called for a fundamental reset. It was indeed shocking for the Pakistani nation to see the flag-draped bodies of twenty-four soldiers martyred in the line of active duty on the international border with Afghanistan, at the hands of our allies."[25]

At the same moment the American debate on strategy for Pakistan veered between abandonment—Who would want to ally with a country that so regularly undercuts US interests?—and engagement. The truth is that while both approaches would feel temporarily satisfying, the feeling wouldn't last long.

Abandonment, or isolation, is not a policy; it is an act of desperation. It would mean that when a nuclear weapon goes loose, when al-Qaeda tries to revive itself in Karachi, when insurgents attack

Afghanistan from the border or head into India, the United States would have essentially no leverage with the Pakistani government. True, Washington often feels as if it has no leverage now. But real abandonment would mean Pakistan would have to look elsewhere for a superpower partner, and there is no question where it would turn: toward Beijing. The result would likely be a vast escalation of the confrontation between India and Pakistan—just at a moment when the two are talking to each other in civil tones—and an expansion of Chinese influence in South Asia. It is bad enough that the Chinese gave A. Q. Khan the designs for their early atomic bomb. If China became Pakistan's patron, the Pakistani military would be encouraged to overrule the civilian government at every turn. After all, the Chinese don't like dealing with messy democracies.

The alternative the Obama administration now discusses is periodic engagement—a transactional relationship that almost amounts to work-for-aid. In reality, it is a form of "Pakistan Good Enough." Rather than treat Pakistan as a "major non-NATO ally," the administration wants to reduce the rhetoric to fit reality, limiting cooperation to individual projects—enhancing trade relations within the region, for example—which can work if they are in the interest of the ISI and Pakistani military.

This approach—some call it "mitigation"—has three goals. The first is helping Pakistan keep its arsenal safe—while improving the American ability to find and immobilize the weapons if that effort fails. The second is to keep the Pakistani civilian government from being toppled, by the army or extremists, through various forms of assistance. And the third is to keep up the pressure on insurgents and al-Qaeda operatives, mostly with drone strikes.

But "mitigation" is all about self-defense. There isn't much in it for the Pakistanis. And it is easy to forget that for all its double-dealing with the Taliban and other insurgent groups, Pakistan has been a major loser in the region's wars. Since the US invasion of Afghanistan, 30,000 Pakistani soldiers and civilians have died—

what my colleague Bill Keller rightly calls a 9/11 of their own every year.[26] While drone strikes have been successful in knocking off some al-Qaeda and Taliban leadership in Pakistan, they have generated massive amounts of anti-US sentiment throughout the rest of the country because they are, justifiably, viewed as a violation of Pakistani sovereignty.

That is entirely understandable. If Canada or Mexico were running drones over US territory to wipe out suspected criminals or terrorists within our borders—declaring they were accomplishing what American forces could not or would not—it would be the source of round-the-clock outrage on cable television. Ambassador Rehman made the point after first arriving in Washington that the issue of raids inside Pakistan has become the hottest political issue in Pakistan because it is a symbol of "subversion" of the country and "is so repeatedly and unfortunately associated with the United States' growing footprint in Pakistan."

And when Pakistanis look at America, they also see something else: an ally in Washington that urgently makes non-negotiable demands on their country when Washington needs them, and then gradually loses interest. In 2008, early in his time as chairman of the Joint Chiefs of Staff, Adm. Mike Mullen sent off his staff to prepare a presentation from the Pakistani vantage point—he wanted to know how the United States' renewed attempt at engaging Pakistan would appear to the Pakistanis. Mullen's team briefed him as if he were General Kayani, and presented a report whose title said it all: "The Fourth Betrayal." It described the three times the United States had abandoned Pakistan over the past half century: when India invaded in 1965 and again in 1971, and when the United States abandoned the region following the Soviet pullout from Afghanistan in 1989. They anticipated that the withdrawal from Afghanistan would be yet another betrayal in a long history of disappointments.

The Americans, of course, have a similar list of betrayals:

Pakistan's secret pursuit of the bomb in the '80s; its protection of A. Q. Khan when he was providing nuclear technology to North Korea, Iran, and Libya; and perhaps, if they could ever prove it, its harboring of Osama bin Laden for so many years in Abbottabad. It has become commonplace in Washington to dismiss the Pakistanis as serial prevaricators who will only respond to threats. But that's an attitude; it's not a policy.

Obama's response has been to say very little about his vision of America's future with Pakistan, because honesty would be bound to enrage all sides. If he chastised Pakistan for adding to its nuclear arsenal in the most dangerous ways—with smaller, easier-to-hijack weapons—it would likely only encourage the Pakistanis to build more. If he talked about reviving the idea of a stable aid package to Pakistan, there would be an uproar in Congress that he is funding the country that made a nest for the world's number-one terrorist.

In April 2012, the Pakistanis confronted Obama with one of the greatest challenges to the Obama Doctrine yet. Up until that point, the United States had justified its more than 250 American drone strikes inside Pakistan's tribal areas by claiming the agreement of the Pakistani government to conduct the operations.[27] But the reality was that the approval—never officially made public—came from General Kayani and his military colleagues, not from the country's elected leadership. It was a tenuous approval at best. Then, when the Pakistani Parliament conducted a broad reassessment of its relationship with the United States, it voted overwhelmingly to bar all American drone strikes on Pakistani territory.

The demand posed a predictable challenge to Obama's insistence that he could secure American vital security interests with a lighter footprint, while respecting the sovereignty of a democratic nation. If he capitulated to the Pakistanis and ceased the drone strikes, it would lift the pressure on al-Qaeda, just as bin Laden's dispirited followers were on the verge of what the White House called "strategic defeat." If Obama continued the drone strikes, he would be undercutting the authority of the one nascent democratic institution in the country. Unilateral drone strikes conducted in defiance of the Pakistani government would be perceived, quite literally, as an act of war.

It was easy to see the seeds of the next crisis brewing. At a minimum it proved what the State Department called the Ruggiero Rule, named for Frank Ruggiero, a veteran diplomat who conducts many of the negotiations with the Taliban: if anything looks like it is going well with Pakistan, Ruggiero often told his staff, just wait forty-five minutes.

So three years into his presidency, the arguments over how to deal with the Pakistanis still rage. "On this issue, more than any other, you get such disparate accounts from different parts of our government," one senior State Department official conceded to me.

There is only one certainty in Pakistan's relationship with the United States: there will be more crises. One lesson of 2011 is that a "strategic partnership" is simply not possible in the coming years: it sets expectations that neither side is prepared to fulfill. But while every crisis will be accompanied by renewed calls from Congress to punish Pakistan by withholding aid, it makes sense for Obama to continue to press the case for some consistency, especially with civilian assistance. The Pakistani public may be deeply anti-American these days, but they are not responsible for the duplicitous actions of their intelligence services and military. Cuts to civilian assistance programs will simply reinforce the narrative of betrayal.

TEN YEARS LATER, we have learned some hard lessons. The United States had no choice but to invade Afghanistan in 2001, and Pakistan was given no choice but to follow the Americans' lead. But our inability to mold Afghanistan into a full-fledged democracy and Pakistan into a full-fledged ally should have been predictable, and serves as a cautionary tale about the very clear limits of American power in reshaping the world to our will. In the end, we fared better than the British and the Soviets in Afghanistan. But it is not clear that the surge Obama reluctantly approved in 2009 made enough of a lasting difference to justify the huge human and financial costs.

That is not an argument for getting out completely—for abandoning Afghanistan a second time and fulfilling the Pakistani narrative of the "Fourth Betrayal." The reality is that America will need a lasting presence in Afghanistan—both to keep it from falling apart and to keep a cork on a nuclear Pakistan—for years, maybe decades, to come. The force need not be large. But it has to be large enough to be credible, the strategy that worked in Europe for seven decades after the end of World War II and that has worked on the Korean peninsula since 1953. The president needs to explain the logic of keeping a force there—to the Afghans, to the Pakistanis, and, most important, to the Americans, whose instinct is to call for immediate withdrawal. To do otherwise would be to lose all leverage in the region, a mistake history suggests we cannot afford to make again.

PART II
IRAN

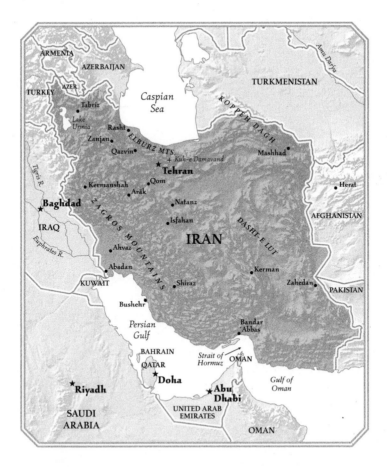

THE ZONE OF IMMUNITY

CHAPTER 6

THE SECRET WAR

COMMUTING TO WORK THROUGH THE CHAOTIC STREETS OF NORTH Tehran is never easy, but it is particularly nerve-racking these days for the accomplished scientists of Shahid Beheshti University.

For years, Shahid Beheshti has been one of several Iranian campuses that serve two purposes: one public, one hidden. For the bright students who flock to its urban campus for science and engineering, it is part of a national mission to restore the Persian people to their historic role as the Middle East's most influential power. To the West's intelligence agencies, the campus is an academic cover story. The handful of scientists who have been recruited as spies, or lured to the West as defectors, have described how Shahid Beheshti's best minds were funneled into working on the most challenging problem of all: designing nuclear triggers and small, efficient nuclear warheads that fit atop an Iranian missile. For years, the Mossad and the CIA have tracked the university's scientists as they travel throughout the West, searching for the technology and parts Iran needs to complete their nuclear ambitions. Thanks to a mix of incompetence, sabotage, and sanctions, that program has already taken a decade longer than it should have.

For several years the university has shown up, usually without explanation, on the West's list of targets for sanctions; the British once went so far as to list the university as a center for "scientific research on nuclear weapons."[1] The Iranians, not surprisingly, have contended that all those charges are deliberate falsehoods, part of an elaborate effort to stifle the reemergence of Iranian influence in the Middle East, and around the world. In fact, sanctions had only a modest effect on the work at Shahid Beheshti and universities like it; with remarkable dexterity, the organizations and laboratories working on the nuclear program shifted to different outlets or morphed into new organizations.

Starting in 2010, however, the scientists began to wonder if sanctions were the least of their problems. That was when Israel's Mossad painted a huge bull's-eye on the campus, turning its scientists into targets.

Majid Shahriari and his wife drove into the crossfire of that escalating confrontation one fall morning in Tehran in November 2010. They were on their way to the campus, accompanied, as usual, by a bodyguard. Iranian officials have never explained why the forty-year-old academic and father of two required twenty-four-hour protection. But Shahriari's publications offer an important clue: he was an expert on neutron transport—the physics at the heart of nuclear chain reations. It is a field critical to understanding the behavior of nuclear-reactor (and nuclear-weapon) cores. Senior Iranian officials would later reveal that Shahriari was involved in a "major project" with Iran's atomic energy agency, although they never explained what it entailed.[2]

Around 7:40 a.m. on a cold Monday morning, the couple was stuck in traffic, their car crawling through the wealthy neighborhood of Aghdasieh, near the palace where American-backed Shah Mohammad Reza Pahlavi spent his last ten years of rule before the revolution caught up with him. As Shahriari's car finally nudged forward, a motorcycle wound its way through the traffic and pulled up alongside it. Suddenly, a faint "click" of a magnet being attached to the driver's-side door could be heard. Then, the motorcyclist sped off.

The huge explosion came a few seconds later. Pictures of the wreckage, replayed over and over on state-run television that night, showed that the bomb's powerful blast focused almost entirely on the driver's seat of the couple's Peugeot, where Shahriari had been sitting. He died almost instantly. His wife, sitting beside him, survived, though today she bears a scar on one cheek and struggles to walk with a cane.[3]

On the other side of town, twenty minutes later, a nearly identical attack played out against Fereydoon Abbasi, Shahriari's close friend and another nuclear scientist at the university. A longtime member of the Islamic Revolutionary Guard Corps, the elite organization that oversees what investigators suspect is the military side of Iran's nuclear program, Abbasi was a bigger target. But he was a lot luckier that day. Perhaps because of his military training, he reacted instantly to the click of the magnetic bomb and pulled himself and his wife out of the car just before it was consumed in a fireball. He was hospitalized, but emerged relatively unscathed. Today, in the words of one foreign diplomat who has dealt with him, he is "an angry man, more determined than ever."

Abbasi is now the public face of Iran's atomic energy program, and he keeps a large picture of his friend Shahriari in his office. "He tells everyone that they were targeted by the Mossad," said the diplomat, who has visited him recently. "And he's probably right." Unimpeded by a UN travel ban, Abbasi uses his official passport to travel to conferences around the world, offering assurances that Iran's interest in nuclear technology is entirely peaceful. A year after surviving the attempt on his life, Abbasi led the charge that the International Atomic Energy Agency's accusation that Iran was experimenting with possible bomb technologies was simply "fabrication." The evidence the IAEA described—drawings of warheads, the calculations of efficient nuclear detonation heights, the work on nuclear triggers—were all, he insisted, part of an effort by Israel and the United States to justify in advance an attack on Iran's nuclear facilities and of plans to bring down the regime.

◆

BY THE FALL of 2011, nearly three years into Obama's presidency, it was clear that the secret confrontation with Iran was kicking into a new, far more intense phase—a "state of low-grade, daily conflict," in the words of one of Obama's top advisers. At the White House, the parade of strategy sessions on Iran was constant, though never publicly announced. Sometimes the sessions included Israeli officials, beamed in by secure video. "I don't think you've ever seen the intelligence and military coordination happen at a more intense level in any previous administration," Donilon told me, shortly after another delegation of visiting Israeli senior officials left his office. But there was a strange dance to the coordination. Because of a political ban on assassinations—which dates back to the CIA's scandals in the 1970s—the American officials were prohibited from aiding Israel in the targeting of scientists, or even from providing information about individuals who the US believes might then be targeted. So the sticky-bomb attacks in Tehran—the last of which Secretary of State Hillary Clinton publicly condemned—were off-limits. And the Americans were careful not to ask too many questions about the huge, unexplained explosions wreaking havoc in Iran with increasing frequency.

The most spectacular of those is still a bit of a mystery. In November 2011, thirty miles west of Tehran, a huge blast wiped out the leading missile-development site where Iran's newest long-range missile was being prepared for testing. In a flash, the entire base was destroyed, killing seventeen people, including a man almost no ordinary Iranians had ever heard of: Gen. Hassan Tehrani Moghaddam. For years, he had been the leading force behind Iran's most advanced missile efforts, and the one pressing for a weapon that could reach Western Europe and, eventually, the United States. He was among Iran's best-guarded officials. And, as an Israeli officer noted to me a month after the blast, "he just happened to be sitting in his office" when the base disintegrated around him.

Another Israeli plot—this one involving explosives planted by Iranian agents trained by the Mossad? Or, given the huge size of the explosion, a freak accident, similar to the kind that has struck some American rocket facilities over the decades?

At the White House, officials were quick to say that whatever happened, it was not the work of the United States. "We simply have drawn a line and don't do kinetic activity inside Iran," one official said, while expressing little doubt this particular explosion was the work of the Israelis. Across the Potomac, the intelligence agencies were more cautious. "I'd say 51/49 it was not an accident," one senior intelligence official told me a few months after the plant lit up the sky. "But it would have been very hard to pull off an explosion that big." It was in the category, the official said, of "things we don't ask about."

When Moghaddam's funeral was held a few days later, Iran's supreme leader, Ayatollah Ali Khamenei, showed up to pay his respects. The next day, the Iranian press hailed the missile expert and his colleagues as "martyrs," a term which, in context, could describe an unlucky victim of an accident as easily as an assassination target.

WHATEVER THE TRUTH about what happened at the missile base, there were two purposes behind the assassinations and explosions. One was obvious: to slow Iran's ability to develop and deliver a weapon by hitting its hardest-to-replace assets, and its brainpower. In that regard, it was quite similar to the effort the Office of Strategic Services (the predecessor to the CIA) launched during World War II, when it picked off scientists it feared were getting Nazi Germany closer to secrets of the Bomb.[4]

But the second purpose was almost entirely one of psychological warfare. The Israelis were determined to sow fear into Iran's most elite scientific circles. The allure of working in Iran's most secretive, best funded project must have been strong. Israel was trying to make the fear of a sticky bomb even stronger. It is impossible to know, from the outside, whether this strategy was working—or whether it simply was feeding Iran's sense of victimhood and doubling its determination. The Iranians had other worries, too. The International Atomic Energy Agency, the world's nuclear inspectors, had gained possession of drawings, internal e-mails, and scientific notes from the nuclear program that were slipped out by traitors. Stories swirled that some scientists had made it to the West and were being protected by the Americans, the Israelis, and the Europeans. For Iranians, said one American intelligence official, "the big question has to be, What else do our enemies know? The location of secret facilities? How to sabotage a new generation of equipment?"

As the pace of sabotage and "accidents" accelerated, the Iranians had a difficult choice to make. Declaring that some of these explosions, including the devastation at the missile base, were true accidents bore its own risk. It made the people running Iran's most prized national program look, in the words of one senior American official, "wildly incompetent." The alternative—denouncing the West for sabotage and spying—would acknowledge that the West was deep inside Iran's treasured nuclear program.

IT WASN'T JUST the Iranians who ran into technical troubles in the desert. So did the Americans.

In December 2011, the CIA "borrowed" a stealth, unarmed RQ-170 drone from the Pentagon's collection in Afghanistan for a secret mission over Iran.

No one has talked openly about the objective of the flight, but it was part of a three-year-long program to check out the hundreds—perhaps thousands—of tunnels that are laced throughout the country, some of which are believed to hold hidden elements of Iran's nuclear program. It is all part of a system the Iranians call "passive defense," dispersing and burying their most critical facilities, making them hard to bomb.

"They will be scattered in the mountains," one former chief of the Iranian Atomic Energy Organization boasted several years ago. "We will be using the passive defense so that we don't need to have active defense."[5]

The stealth drone is America's best means to get into those mountains and identify potential targets. "All standard planning steps," said one senior administration intelligence official.

But of course there was more to it than that. The RQ-170 was the drone that the Americans hovered over Abbottabad for weeks, undetected, recording patterns of life about Osama bin Laden's lair in Pakistan. When the existence of the stealth version of the plane was revealed in the aftermath of the bin Laden raid, officials like James Clapper, the director of National Intelligence, were outraged—partly because they knew it was only a matter of time before the Pakistanis and the Iranians figured out how else it was being used. That turned out to be the least of Clapper's RQ-170 problems.

As the borrowed drone sped over a remote corner of Iran, it developed a problem with its speed sensor, according to a senior intelligence official who was fully briefed on the incident. "It showed the plane going fifteen thousand miles an hour, or something like that," he said, exaggerating the true figure (which has never been revealed) to make a point. An automatic system kicked in, overriding the commands of the pilots running the drone by remote control, and landed the plane fairly gently in a sparsely populated area of Iranian grazing land.

The controllers looked at each other in horror. They had just watched helplessly as one of America's most top-secret planes, largely intact and coated with unique, cutting-edge materials that give it the ability to absorb radar signals and defy interception, settled in among the goats.

"This hadn't really happened before, at least in a place where we worried about losing the damn drone," one military official re-counted to me later. "You could almost hear people shouting, 'Oh, shit, now we've done it.'"

The question of what to do next went to the president. Do you send in a SEAL team to rescue it? "A few of us remembered back thirty-three years or so," one senior official said, recalling the fa-mous "Desert One" disaster when Jimmy Carter, also in an election year, tried a hostage rescue in Iran. "That wasn't going to happen."

There was talk of just dropping a bomb on the downed drone, but it turned out the special radar-absorbing material melts at an extraordinarily high temperature. The government's drone experts feared even the rubble would be useful to the Russians or the Chi-nese.

Obama decided that doing nothing was the safest course, and for a brief while some officials lived in the hope that none of the herders in the area would find the wreckage, or understand its im-port. That strategy failed in only a few days, and the stealth drone ended up on the streets of Tehran. It quickly became a televised propaganda symbol, demonstrating that Iran was under perpetual surveillance by an unmanned air force sent by the Great Satan.

As Obama headed into his reelection campaign, the White House insisted that no president had ever before inflicted this much pain on the Iranians, both fiscal and political. "The Iranians are more isolated than at any moment in their history since the 1979 revo-lution," Donilon insisted. That was probably true; sanctions had made it hard for Iranian ships to enter foreign ports, for Iranian airplanes to get refueled abroad, to obtain new investments to drill for oil, and even to conduct some routine banking transactions. Inflation was getting out of control and the Iranian currency was tanking. At the end of 2011, Congress—in one of the few issues that unified the perpetually divided Democrats and Republicans—voted unanimously to require Obama to cease engaging in any transactions with Iran's central bank, a step the president had resisted taking without proper escape hatches for key American allies, which are reducing their purchases from Tehran. But soon the European Union announced an embargo, and the Iranians, out of pique, announced they were cutting off shipments to Britain and France. Oil prices began to rise.[6]

But the Iranians had put some points on the board, too. In the three years since Obama came to office, Iran had manufactured enough fuel to make at least four weapons, though it would require additional enrichment before it was usable in a bomb. The Iranians had made enough progress in Obama's time in office that, as Harvard's Graham Allison put it, it was "as if the Iranians had moved the ball to the twenty-yard line."

So from Washington to the Middle East, the mystery came down to this: How long would it take the Iranians to turn that fuel into weapons? On that question the Americans and the Israelis had different clocks running—and, naturally, none of them were ticking at the same pace.

In the early spring of 2012, Obama's aides insisted they still had plenty of time. If the Iranians made a political decision to race for a bomb—what the nuclear gurus call "breakout"—they would have to throw out international inspectors, almost inviting the destruction of their facilities before they could manufacture their first bomb. If they attempted to deceive inspectors with hidden facilities—"sneakout"—then "we're pretty certain we would detect it," Gary Samore, President Obama's counterproliferation chief, told me. In the meantime, White House officials were preparing new sanctions and covert action to knock the timeline back even further.

But White House officials blanched a bit in December 2011 when Leon Panetta, who left his post at the CIA to become defense secretary, suggested that despite all the roadblocks Washington had thrown in the way, Iran could move to a weapon fairly quickly if it made a political decision to do so. "It would be sometime in around a year they would be able to do it," Panetta said. "Perhaps a little less. The one proviso is if they have a hidden facility somewhere in Iran," in which case a nuclear weapon may be within their reach sooner.

WHEN THE HISTORY of this era is written, Iran may be the most challenging test of the emerging tenet of the Obama Doctrine that asserts adversaries can be effectively confronted through indirect methods—without boots on the ground, without breaking the Treasury, without repeating the mistakes of mission creep. In Iran, Obama tried three approaches at once: engagement, sanctions, and covert action. Engagement failed—the Iranians were not interested, at least until a flurry of negotiations resumed in mid-April 2012. Sanctions have exacted a harsher and harsher price on the Iranian people but so far have not broken the will of the leadership to press ahead with their nuclear program. Covert action was more successful. Israeli assassinations and sabotage have not only made scientists wonder if every trip to work may be their last, they have made them fear that every new line of imported computer code could be the beginning of a new round of destruction.

Yet the mixed messages emanating from the White House belied the reality that nobody was entirely sure whether America was winning its covert war with Iran. "I don't know anyone around here who doesn't believe the Iranians are headed for a bomb," one of Obama's advisers said matter-of-factly, as talk of air attacks and war swirled around Washington early in 2012. The problem was that after billions spent slowing them down, it was still impossible to discern Iran's intentions. A working, deliverable nuclear weapon? Or just the option to build one? "It's still like you are climbing Everest in a fog," one of Obama's senior advisers said to me. "You've got no fucking idea who's going to make it to the top first."

The Israelis were equally in the dark, but more paranoid and driven by a clock that ticked faster and more loudly. Fearful that the cyber sabotage program may have run its course, they held a series of increasingly urgent meetings with their American allies throughout the winter and spring of 2012—to warn that they may need to bomb Iran's facilities during Obama's reelection campaign, an event many fear would plunge the United States back into a conflict in the Middle East.

"When Bibi says this is an existential threat," one senior Israeli intelligence official told me, referring to Prime Minister Benjamin Netanyahu, "he means this moment is reminiscent of 1939" and the rise of Nazi Germany. To the Americans, he said, "it is more like 1949," when the Soviets tested their first nuclear device. That brought many confrontations that veered toward catastrophe, most notably the Cuban Missile Crisis. But with skill, sabotage, and diplomacy, the Soviets were contained.

The Israelis' deepest fear was that Obama believed that ultimately Iran would succeed in its quest, and that America had a Plan B: Soviet-like containment. Inside the White House, the president was wrestling with exactly that question—whether what worked in the Cold War could work in the Middle East.

Chapter 7
"Cut Off the Head of the Snake"

THE SATELLITE PICTURES FROM JUST OUTSIDE THE HOLY CITY OF Qom appeared on the screen during one of President-elect Obama's first detailed briefings about the dimensions of the Iranian nuclear threat. The image was of a massive construction site, on a mountainside military base, surrounded by anti-aircraft guns. From the tunnel entrances, Obama was told, it was abundantly clear something very big was being dug deep into the mountainside. From the few human spies that had reported back, a picture was emerging of just what it was: a new facility to produce nuclear fuel, more than 150 feet under solid granite, deep enough to give the Iranians some confidence that Israel and the United States would not be able to reach it.

It might be vulnerable, Obama was told, but only if it was hit—probably several times—with a bunker-busting bomb so huge that the weapon was still under development for the American arsenal: the 30,000-pound Massive Ordnance Penetrator, called "the MOP" by the acronym-obsessed Air Force. It was created to burrow into the most hardened nuclear sites—North Korea was what the designers had in mind at first—but it wouldn't be available until well into Obama's first term.

Oh, and just one more thing, the briefers added. No one had ever tried anything quite like this. "There was always the possibility it might just bounce off the top, and we'd have to hope the concussion was big enough to stop work in the chamber below," one intelligence official said, recalling the discussions that took place in Obama's first days in office. "It might well work, but there are no guarantees."

When those first pictures of Qom appeared—long before the Iranians began to enrich uranium deep under that mountain—Obama could not have envisioned that this mysterious hole in the ground would become the focal point of a struggle between him and Israel's hard-line prime minister, Benjamin Netanyahu. And the battle over how to deal with it—whether to risk letting production ramp up there or to strike it before it became the invulnerable heart of the Iranian nuclear program—would rival the differences the two men had on how to handle the Israeli-Palestinian peace talks. It would become a struggle over if, and when, to go to war.

Exactly three years after seeing those first images, Obama would find himself engaged in a running argument with Netanyahu and his defense minister, Ehud Barak, over whether the Qom plant created a "zone of immunity" for Iran—a place where the Iranians could take their time building a bomb, finally freed of the fear that one night they would wake up to find their most precious nuclear sites had been turned into a smoking pile of rubble. That is what had happened to Saddam Hussein in Iraq in 1981 and Bashar Assad in Syria in 2007. Qom was ordered up by the Islamic Revolutionary Guard Corps to make sure the same fate did not befall Iran.

In retrospect, I had an early hint of the Qom discovery in the summer of 2008, before Obama's briefing, but at the time I did not know its name or its precise location, nor did I foresee the dimensions of the challenge it would present to the next president. Over lunch, a senior American intelligence official had strongly hinted to me that they believed they were on the trail of at least one, and perhaps several, secret nuclear sites. "I'm not saying we saw centrifuges spinning on the edge of the Caspian Sea," he said, just as Obama was preparing to accept the Democratic nomination for president. "But," he added cryptically, "there was a secret enrichment program too."*

A few weeks after his initial briefing, Obama got a "deeper dive" about Qom, according to one official involved. With guidance from the Israelis and Iranian scientists who had been recruited by Western spy agencies, the site had been found a few years earlier. At the CIA and the Pentagon, officials marveled at what a brilliant place it was to put the facility: Throughout the Islamic world, Qom has been known as the site of a famous shrine and the center of Shi'a scholarship. The supreme leader, Ayatollah Ali Khamenei, studied there, as did his predecessor. Grand Ayatollah Seyyid Ali al-Sistani of Iraq did as well. In other words, it could not be bombed without headlines racing around the world that the Americans and the Israelis were blowing up one of the holiest cities in Islam.

If finished, Obama was told, Qom would give the Iranians a better-protected version of its larger enrichment facility at Natanz. That facility had been exposed in 2003, and international inspectors now crawled all over it. For that reason, the United States and Israel had been hunting for a second Natanz for years. Or, as Gary Samore, Obama's most senior aide on counterproliferation, put it so succinctly in 2009, "If the Iranians are getting a bomb, it's not coming from Natanz—it has to be from someplace else."

The question of what to do about it had been considered so

---

* This quotation first appeared in *The Inheritance* (Crown, 2009), page 6, to alert readers that the United States suspected the existence of at least one hidden enrichment facility in Iran. Before publication of *The Inheritance*, I learned more details, but the Bush administration asked that some specifics about the discovery be withheld. I agreed to the request, as did editors of the *Times,* but we proceeded to publish a story describing how President Bush had denied Israel technology it requested that would have enabled it to conduct a broad bombing campaign against Iranian sites. The story noted that "several details of the covert effort have been omitted from this account, at the request of senior US intelligence and administration officials, to avoid harming continuing operations."

urgent in the last years of the Bush administration that President Bush had been presented with a highly risky, but very tempting, proposal to make sure the Qom plant never opened. As Bush's presidency entered its last year, satellite photographs showed that just outside a tunnel entrance, workers were stacking up the giant cement pads that would support the centrifuges. The pads were awaiting transport down into the huge facility.

But while they were still outside, the military had come up with an ingenious plan: insert Special Operations Forces into Iranian territory—a huge risk—with an engineering team to plant technology into the pads that could aid the United States later in destroying the centrifuges. "As a tactical matter, it would have been enormously tricky, but it was presented as perhaps our only shot," said one person familiar with the operation. Another called it "a suicide mission."

Bush balked. Even though he was the author of the "preemption doctrine," the idea of inserting forces inside Iran gave Bush's team heartburn. The firestorm that would erupt if any of those forces were taken hostage or killed on Iranian soil was too large to be worth the risk.

And so now Obama, in his first months as president, faced his first decision about what to do about Iran. He could expose it to the world and see if the stunned Iranians could come up with an explanation. But if he blew the whistle too early, he feared, the Iranians could claim that the construction site was intended for some benign purpose. Instead, Obama decided to pocket the discovery until he could use it to maximum negotiating advantage. Meanwhile, he would test the proposition that Iran's supreme leader could be persuaded, through direct engagement, to give up the country's pursuit of a bomb project.

ON MARCH 20, 2009, exactly two months after Barack Obama's inauguration, Iranians tuning into Voice of America on their illegal satellite television dishes saw something remarkable: an American president directly addressing them and their rulers. Beamed in to evade Iranian censors, Obama's message was a deliberately reassuring one. After three decades of unrelenting hostility between the two countries, a new president with a new approach to the world said he wanted to reset the relationship between Tehran and Washington. He assured the Iranians he was determined to engage them in direct unconditional dialogue.

In his four-minute message marking Nowrūz, the festive Iranian holiday that means "new day" in Persian, Obama made several allusions to starting the new year with a dialogue unlike any since the Iranian revolution. He deliberately avoided specifics, and never made direct mention of the country's ominous nuclear ambitions. Nor did he refer to Iran's government as "the regime," which was his predecessor's preferred term.

"The United States wants the Islamic Republic of Iran to take its rightful place in the community of nations," Obama said, a nod of respect to the country's deeply embedded national pride as Persian subtitles flashed in white on the bottom of the screen. "You have that right—but it comes with real responsibilities, and that place cannot be reached through terror or arms, but rather through peaceful actions that demonstrate the true greatness of the Iranian people and civilization."[1] To underscore the point, Obama closed with a quote from one of Iran's most beloved poets on the oneness of humanity and, in stilted Persian, wished the Iranians a happy new year.

The symbolism was groundbreaking. The results in the years that followed were not. With Iran, North Korea, and Cuba, promises of engagement mean little if the charm offensive's target is unwilling to engage back.

In fact, Obama had expected that his outreach would likely fail. He had to reach out, he thought, because the mullahs could well calculate that their own survival required an end to the escalating sanctions that had begun under the Bush administration. But even if they did not yield, as one of Obama's top advisers put it to me soon after moving into the West Wing, "we can't get the rest of the world to turn the screws unless they believe we made a serious, bona-fide offer for a diplomatic solution."

So even before the satellite broadcast was transmitted, Obama's diplomats and the Treasury Department were at work on a Plan B—more sanctions, and smarter ones—that would eventually chip away at Iran's oil revenues, the seemingly bottomless pit of dollars that kept the regime alive. And over at the CIA and in Israel, Plan C—covert action—was already well under way.

IRAN DOMINATED OBAMA'S first efforts to recalibrate American foreign policy, and its interests in the Middle East. "There were more meetings on Iran than there were on Iraq, Afghanistan, and China in year one," one of Obama's top aides told me in 2011. "It was the thing we spent the most time on and talked about the least in public."

Obama considered Iran one of Bush's biggest strategic blind spots: for the United States, Iran is far more strategically vital than Iraq. Yet Bush seemed paralyzed. Having wrongly accused one country of secretly building weapons, Bush could not sound the alarm about another. Hillary Clinton recalled at the end of 2011 that one of the first decisions was to cease "publicly disparaging" the Iranians—no more "axis of evil" proclamations. Instead, Obama, whose name literally translated into "He is with us" in Persian, would talk directly to the Iranian people. Washington would no longer regard sitting down to talk with an adversary as a sign of national weakness. "Not because we thought it would necessarily work," as Clinton later said, "but because we knew that without trying, we'd never get the allies to sign on to a much, much tougher approach." As Obama's most formidable opponent in the Democratic primary elections, Clinton had dismissed Obama's promise to engage with

Iran and other rogue nations within the first year of his presidency as "frankly naïve."[2] Now tasked with implementing Obama's strategy—and dealing with its consequences—her State Department went into overdrive. Clinton talked publicly about engaging the Iranians while she visited capitals around Europe to prepare for sanctions that would target the Revolutionary Guard and, ultimately, Iran's central bank, which handles oil transactions.

Whatever Obama's charms, the mullahs were unimpressed. The president's secret letters to Supreme Leader Khamenei were returned with diatribes about America's many offenses over the past three decades. "There was nothing suggesting interest in a real dialogue," one official told me as details of the letters leaked. Khamenei saw nothing new in this different-looking president and predicted that he would keep America's boot on Iran's throat. "Obama's is the hand of Satan in a new sleeve," asserted Hossein Shariatmadari, who had been handpicked by Khamenei to edit the hard-line conservative newspaper *Kayhan,* which became the leader's unofficial mouthpiece. "The Great Satan now has a black face," Shariatmadari told the *Telegraph* after Obama's inauguration.[3]

Khamenei himself took the hardest line, just a few days after Obama's New Year's message, ticking off a list of American crimes stretching back to the days of the Shah. "Now the new US administration is saying, 'Let's forget about the past. We want to conduct negotiations with Iran,'" Khamenei proclaimed in a speech interrupted—and complemented—by the ritual chants of "Death to America" from women in black chadors and men waving banners bearing the supreme leader's visage. "They are saying, 'We are extending our hand to Iran.' Well, what kind of hand are they extending? If they are extending an iron hand concealed in a velvet glove, then it has no positive meaning."[4]

OBAMA'S OTHER HOPE was to win over US allies in the region, who had said for years they wanted an end to Bush's "you're either with us or against us" approach. In fact, Obama's outreach to Iran had an unexpected effect on many allies, at least in the beginning: it completely unnerved them.

The most predictable reaction came from the Israelis, who were anxious from the start that Obama would be too soft on Iran. In the administration's first days, an Israeli delegation visited Dennis Ross, the longtime Middle East negotiator, at a barely furnished office he had set up in the State Department. This outreach program is fine, they told him with barely hidden disgust, but given the progress in Iran's nuclear program, Israel might have to take military action in a year, maybe a year and a half. "It was the same message, the same timeline they always give," Ross remembered later with a smile. "I felt like I had never left."

The WikiLeaks diplomatic cables revealed how apoplectic America's Arab allies were that the United States would be too soft in its approach to the Iranians. In the last days of the Bush administration, the king of Saudi Arabia, among others, began to despair that the US invasion of Iraq had taken America's eye off the bigger problem of Iran.

Sometimes the warnings were extremely stark. In April 2008, the Saudis had a tense meeting with American officials. They provided a dire warning that Iran had gone too far. Of course, it was a problem that Abdullah Al Saud, the Saudi king, wanted the United States to solve for him—without much Saudi help.

The WikiLeaks revelations exposed the degree to which the Saudi royal family had become fixated on Iran. In one crucial cable, Adel al-Jubeir, the Saudi ambassador to the United States, reminded an American diplomat in Riyadh about what the king had said to American leaders in private sessions.

In his cable back to the State Department, the diplomat explained that "Al-Jubeir recalled the king's frequent exhortations to the US to attack Iran and so put an end to its nuclear weapons program. He told [America] to cut off the head of the snake." And, the diplomat added, al-Jubeir insisted that working with the United States to roll back Iranian influence in Iraq is a strategic priority for the Saudi king and his government.[5]

It is not clear whether the publication of that cable, revealing the depth of the Saudi royal family's desire to destroy the Iranian regime, helped prompt a clumsy Iranian assassination plot on American soil in 2011. That fall, the Justice Department revealed what it described as an effort by Iran's Qods Force, one of the most elite units of the IRGC, to kill al-Jubeir by blowing up one of his favorite posh Georgetown restaurants while he was dining. The whole scheme seemed out of a very bad late-night movie: the Iranian agents tried to hire a member of a Mexican drug cartel who, as they later discovered, was on the payroll of the US Drug Enforcement Administration.

The Saudis have revealed little about their own investigations into the plot. One US official who reviewed the evidence remarked, "As you can imagine, it makes the Saudis think we are only a step or two away from war."

King Abdullah's hatred for the Iranians was hardly a secret, but the impulse to "cut off the head of the snake" was widely shared in Sunni nations. The king of Bahrain, a Sunni who feared Iran would try to spark an uprising among the Shi'a majority in his tiny country, chastised the Americans for not launching a military attack, though he, too, was not exactly racing to provide arms or personnel. In Jordan, officials had a favorite, if squishy, metaphor for Iran: "an octopus whose tentacles reach out insidiously to manipulate, foment, and undermine the best-laid plans of the West and regional moderates."[6]

Those "tentacles," the Jordanians contended in a meeting with Americans in April 2009, included Iran's support for Hamas and Hezbollah, as well as a sometimes-pliant Iraqi government. The Iranians, they warned the new administration, were unlikely to erase their memories of US engagement in Iran and acquiesce to a new phase in relations simply because the Americans wanted to talk. In one cable, the American ambassador to Jordan, R. Stephen Beecroft, warned the new administration in April 2009 that Jordan's leaders "are careful not to be seen as dictating toward the United States, but their comments betray a powerful undercurrent of doubt that the United States knows how to deal effectively with Iran."[7]

Nonetheless, Obama persevered with the outreach. In early May, just a month before a presidential election in Iran, he sent a private letter to Khamenei, through the Swiss embassy in Tehran, which represents American interests in the absence of direct diplomatic relations.[8] The letter contained all the predictable calls for cooperation and improved relations; in return Obama got what one aide described as "a diatribe about the United States, taken out of Friday prayers." And while the United States made no secret of its distaste for Iran's president, Mahmoud Ahmadinejad—whose annual trips to New York for the opening of the United Nations sessions created mirth, amazement, and gridlock—it carefully avoided taking sides when Ahmadinejad was up for reelection.

Obama reminded his aides that the CIA had meddled plenty in Iranian politics in the '50s through the '70s, and the lingering memories in Tehran were bitter. So the new American president—not yet burned by his dealings with Iran—sounded a lot like a football coach dutifully reminding players that it's not about whether you win or lose, but how you play the game.

"Whoever ends up winning the election in Iran, the fact that there's been a robust debate hopefully will help advance our ability to engage them in new ways," Obama told reporters the day of the Iranian election.[9]

THERE WAS IN fact a robust debate going on in Iran that gave Obama hope—false hope, it turned out—that the country was on the cusp of change. Mir-Hossein Mousavi, Iran's prime minister during the 1980s, had mounted a strong campaign with a moderate message, winning the support of former reformist president Mohammad Khatami and legions of young volunteers, particularly women. An architect and former journalist with a professorial air, Mousavi had emerged from twenty years of near-retirement in the hopes of cutting short Ahmadinejad's presidency. Like the Americans, he saw Ahmadinejad as a charlatan—something he was happy to tell Ahmadinejad to his face. In live, televised presidential debates hosted on state television—the first of their kind in the history of the Islamic Republic—Mousavi went on the offensive, saying Ahmadinejad's foreign policy was tinged with "adventurism, illusionism, exhibitionism, extremism, and superficiality."[10] The debate became personal, with Ahmadinejad accusing Mousavi's wife, the well-known professor and artist Zahra Rahnavard, of entering graduate school without taking the required entrance exam. Mousavi grew visibly angry toward the end of the debate and accused Ahmadinejad of leading Iran into a dictatorship.

Mousavi was no antiestablishment candidate. But on the street, Mousavi's campaign electrified Iran's youth. For weeks leading up to the election, Iranians flooded into the streets cheering and clad in green, the campaign's signature color, to register their support. At times, the mood in Iran's biggest cities resembled a street carnival, lines of cars filled with young people honking their horns late into the night. Mousavi supporters chanted English slogans set to Persian melodies, like *"Ahmadi Bye Bye, Ahmadi Bye Bye!"* while clapping in unison. Videos posted online showed men and women dancing openly in the streets, utterly forbidden behavior in the Islamic Republic. Young, photogenic, and fashionable Iranian women marched for their candidate in green headscarves, their manicured fingers signing a "V" for victory—a new, camera-friendly symbol of Iranian politics.

It ended badly. Far worse, in fact, than anyone in the White House had expected.

Just hours after the voting booths closed on June 12, 2009, the Interior Ministry declared Ahmadinejad the winner with 63 percent of the vote, and the same young people who had attended rallies in the weeks and days before the election now took to the streets shouting accusations of election fraud. Within days, the protestors, still in green, but now with their faces obscured with surgical masks and rags, began clashing in bloody street battles with government riot police bearing electric batons. The supreme leader, seeing the threat to his own rule playing out on the streets, abandoned his usual pretense of being above the political fray and declared that Ahmadinejad's landslide win was entirely legitimate. On June 15, hundreds of thousands—by some estimates, up to three million—poured into Iran's streets in by far the biggest protests since the 1979 revolution.

No one knew it at the time, of course, but in this non-Arab country, the protests became the first hint of the revolutionary fervor that would soon sweep the region. All the elements were there: protestors capturing images and sounds of chanting crowds and brutal police assaults on their mobile phones, then uploading them immediately on Twitter, YouTube, and Facebook, always several steps ahead of the Iranian authorities. "We just hope the people of the world hear our voice," said Bashu, a twenty-eight-year-old opposition supporter two days after the election, in an interview with a reporter. He opened his shirt to show long, red welts on his chest, marks left by the chains of a government militia member.[11]

In this first uprising of Obama's presidency, the rookie president initially reacted with a caution that many of his aides later regretted. The street uprisings were a window of opportunity to show American sympathy, if not outright support, for an organic movement for regime change in Iran. But fearful that the United States would be blamed by the Iranian leadership for trying to manipulate the election—as the CIA did there decades ago—Obama was unwilling to even suggest that the results were fraudulent. "My understanding is that the Iranian government says that they are going to look into irregularities that have taken place. We weren't on the ground, we did not have observers there, we did not have international observers on hand, so I can't say definitively one way or another what happened with respect to the election," he told reporters.[12] Repeatedly, Obama emphasized that he wanted to avoid being perceived as intervening in Iran's domestic politics. "Now, it's not productive, given the history of United States–Iranian relations, to be seen as meddling—the United States president meddling in Iranian elections," Obama said on June 16 in the Rose Garden.[13]

At that point, Obama was still hopeful that his engagement strategy could bring Iran's leaders to the negotiating table; harshly criticizing the regime may have put him in the Bush camp he had so eagerly tried to distance himself from. Three years later, aides regarded Obama's Iran missteps as a key moment in the education of a new president. "It turned out," one of Obama's senior national security aides said to me later, "that what we intended as caution, the Iranians saw as weakness."

THE REPRESSION ON the streets only got worse. On June 20, a twenty-six-year-old woman, Neda Agha-Soltan, a philosophy student and aspiring singer, was driving in Tehran with her music teacher. They stopped their stiflingly hot car on Kargar Street and stepped out for a breath of fresh air and to observe the unrest on the streets from a distance. Suddenly, a gunshot rang out and Neda, as the world soon called her, collapsed to the ground, shot in the chest—the music teacher later said he believed she was shot by a sniper perched on a rooftop across the street.[14] Amateur videos posted on YouTube showed her falling, surrounded by men attempting to staunch the bleeding from her chest. Neda's eyes roll to the side as ribbons of blood pour from her nose and mouth. A man next to her screams, "Neda, don't be afraid. Neda, don't be afraid. Neda, stay with me. Neda, stay with me!"

The videos capturing her death were watched more than a million times on YouTube. The brutality of her death, juxtaposed with pictures of the beautiful, smiling young woman in happier times, transformed Neda—whose name means "voice" in Persian—into a symbol for all those who were killed at the hands of the Iranian security forces.[15] After the Neda videos went viral, Obama finally spoke publicly about the uprising. He condemned "the threats, the beatings, and imprisonments of the last few days," while adding that "the United States respects the sovereignty of the Islamic Republic of Iran and is not interfering with Iran's affairs."[16] Inside the White House, however, a fierce debate broke out about how strongly Obama should side with the protestors—a prescient discussion that would deeply affect how Obama reacted to the Arab Spring eighteen months later. "The first instinct, of course, was to get entirely behind the people on the streets," one of Obama's top aides at the time told me after leaving the White House. "But then this sense of caution kicked in—maybe an overcaution."

Obama was clearly stung by the criticism that he was coddling the Iranian regime, and for the first time, the White House invited me in to talk with Obama's Iran team about its calculus. It was a revealing moment. Over the course of an hour, the people Obama listened to on a day-to-day basis floated in to make the president's case for going slowly. Dennis Ross, who by then had moved to the White House to bolster the effort on Iran; Tom Donilon, then still the deputy national security adviser; and Denis McDonough, a former Capitol Hill aide who was close to Obama from his days in the Senate, ushered me into a conference room adjacent to the Situation Room to argue that the best way for Obama to support the protestors would be to do so from the sidelines. The president did not want to give the IRGC and the dreaded "Basij"—plainclothes enforcers of the regime who would beat people in the crowds—the material they were looking for to charge that the CIA was behind the protests. "If the president came out and endorsed the protestors," one of them said, "we'd see people hung up as spies. It's that simple."

THERE WAS ANOTHER reason for the administration's reluctance to throw American support behind the opposition: basic distrust of the mullah's political opponents, including the opposition leader, Mousavi.

An artist and architect, with a trim white beard, Mousavi certainly galvanized the opposition. But he was a "reformer" only in comparison to the virulently anti-American clerics. As Vali Nasr, a scholar and adviser to the administration has pointed out, Mousavi—a creature of the Islamic Revolution before he split with its leadership—did not embrace the Green Movement's drive for truly fundamental change, evidenced in its later slogans and protests. Mousavi is a cousin of Khamenei's and publicly yearned for a return to the days of Ayatollah Khomeini—hardly a time when freedom of expression and civil rights had flourished in Iran. Most important, the Americans did not trust that Mousavi would turn back the clock on enriching uranium, the key to Iran's bomb program.

In fact, the nuclear problem got its start in Iran when Mousavi served as prime minister. "The difference between Ahmadinejad and Mousavi in terms of their actual policies may not be as great as has been advertised," Obama said in one interview. "Either way, we are going to be dealing with an Iranian regime that has historically been hostile to the United States."[17] In short, Mousavi, armed with nuclear weapons, might be as dangerous as Ahmadinejad. It could have been the case that Obama and his aides figured the adversary you know is better than the reformer you don't.

The WikiLeaks cables suggest the administration had yet another reason for distancing itself from the Green Movement: many doubted it was going to last long or bring about real change. A January 2010 assessment of the "Green Path Organization" from a diplomat at the State Department's Dubai listening post offered a nuanced take on the movement's strengths and weaknesses and the motivations of its diverse members. "Outside of the active GPO core group there is a larger, relatively passive group, whose support now mostly manifests itself in anonymous shouts of 'God is Great' from night-time North Tehran rooftops or who scrawl or stamp anti-regime slogans on ten thousand Toman currency notes." But they would only fight the regime, the cable concluded, if the prospect of victory "became more real to them than the prospects of blows from a Basiji baton."[18]

Indeed, the Basij did a ruthless job of stamping out the immediate post-election unrest. Firsthand accounts from Tehran in the two weeks after the protests began were filled with stories of Basijis beating protestors with batons, clubs, and electric prods, and in some cases shooting them dead. Their brutality stunned even a hardened Iranian citizenry. "Please go home," one regular security officer reportedly told protestors. "We are scared of the Basijis too."[19]

In fact, the rise of the Basij (which means "mobilization" in Persian) marked the big change that was occurring in Iran during Obama's first year: the military was essentially taking over Iran, in what Hillary Clinton would later compare to a silent coup.

The Basij had been launched in the first years of the Islamic Republic, as a quasi-militia that recruited from local mosques and middle and high schools. During the long and brutal war with Iraq in the '80s, it delivered young and old to the battlefields, and suffered thousands of casualties. Then, in the '90s, the Basij turned into a dependable tool of domestic repression when the newly minted supreme leader Khamenei and then-president Akbar Hashemi Rafsanjani attempted to shore up their own legitimacy by associating with the heroes of the war with Iraq.

Soon, like other units of the IRGC, the Basij was bought off.

Eventually, the IRGC and its units dominated construction, tele-communications, auto-making, energy, banking, and finance.[20] As the most popular branch of the IRGC, members of the Basij also got into the best universities and snagged government jobs. "There should be a difference between the people who have gone to the fronts and sacrificed their lives for the revolution, and others," the speaker of the parliament, Mehdi Karroubi, said in 1989 of the Basij. "In all sectors, priority should be given to the people who have gone voluntarily to the fronts."[21] Karroubi could not have imagined that twenty years later, as a reformist candidate for president, that same force would attack his car, beat his supporters, and trash his home with stones, bullets, and paint.

In the end, both the payoffs and the ideological training succeeded in keeping the mullahs in power: the Basij were loyal, effective, and brutal in suppressing the most significant unrest Iran had seen in thirty years. If dissent existed within the Iranian security forces—of the kind that later plagued Egypt and Libya—there was no sign of it in Tehran.[22] Just a week after the election, demonstrations were already smaller, and despite continuing clashes for the next six months, the protests' numbers never again matched the scale of those in the days just after the election.[23]

The Iranian resolve to maintain that brutality was only reinforced when the mullahs saw, eighteen months later, what happened to leaders in Tunisia and Egypt who, for all their authoritarian inclinations, did not have as disciplined and brutal a force at their disposal.

The Persian Summer may have been largely forgotten, but for Obama's education as a president, it was an important practice run for the Arab Spring revolutions that followed. It did not spark the Arab Spring: Tehran's youth had many different grievances from their counterparts in Tunisia, Egypt, Libya, and Syria. But many of the early elements of what became familiar later were there. A restive youth movement, despondent about its prospects for the future, chose Facebook and other social media as its weapon of choice and took to the streets to demand change. And on the other side of the world, Obama's initial hesitance to side with the protestors in Tehran contributed to the perception that he was inconsistent in his approach to Middle Eastern dictators.

Ordinary Iranians who had celebrated Obama's victory a few months before their own elections were puzzled. One confidential source who visited American diplomats on June 15 reported that Iranians were surprised by the "muted reaction thus far of the United States and EU governments."[24] On November 4, 2009, on the thirtieth anniversary of student activists seizing American hostages, Green protestors took to the streets of Iran, chanting a new, catchy Persian slogan. It wasn't what you might have expected: *"Obama, Obama, you're either with them, or you're with us."* [25]

GARY SAMORE'S OFFICIAL title at the National Security Council is President Obama's coordinator for arms control and nonproliferation. But by the middle of 2009, he came to realize that his job would be entirely different from what he would have imagined when he worked under Bill Clinton at the White House years before. "Ignore the title," he told me in 2010, as the daily reality moved in on him. "My job comes down to a single thing—to keep Iran from obtaining a nuclear weapon."

With his shock of unruly salt-and-pepper hair, White House aides joked, Samore looks a bit like a younger version of Dr. Emmett Brown (played by Christopher Lloyd), the scientist in *Back to the Future*. He knows his nukes, but he is able to mix a detailed discussion of centrifuge technology with a lengthy analysis of internal Iranian politics. Most important, he believed that if Iran manages to build a nuclear weapon, Obama's goal of moving toward the elimination of nuclear weapons would be set back by years, if not wiped out entirely. A domino effect would sweep across the region, Samore feared; sooner or later, Saudi Arabia and other Gulf states would be tempted to follow. It would be the ultimate irony, he knew, if the president who came to office talking about scaling back the nuclear weapons that dominated the last half century presided over an era in which they spread through the world's most volatile, terror-prone region.

Few people have ever come to the job more prepared: Samore had moved seamlessly between the open and classified worlds, teaching at Harvard, then moving out to the Lawrence Livermore National Laboratory in California, where he spent the mid-'80s in the famed "Z Division," the special projects area where America's nuclear-weapons designers worked. "It was pretty intense for a political science student to be alongside these guys," Samore later said. "It's a whole different world." Then he went to the State Department, and ultimately was assigned to negotiate with the North Koreans as they were speeding toward a bomb of their own. It was a searing experience: he witnessed up close the American declarations about stopping North Korea from getting a nuclear weapon, then the silence from Washington when it got one.

During the Bush administration, Samore was working for a leading think tank in London where he wrote some of the best analyses of Iran's nuclear program. Perhaps not understanding where he had been—or certainly where he was headed—the Iranians even allowed him into the country for a not-very-informative tour of their nuclear infrastructure. He also had a scary, firsthand view of terrorism in action: when Pakistani terrorists took over the grandest hotel in Mumbai in 2008, killing dozens and ultimately torching the place, Samore was upstairs in a guest room with his wife and young daughter. They were trapped for hours before escaping out a back stairway as the inferno spread.

I first met Samore three decades ago, in his days as a graduate student, when he taught a small group of college students in an undergraduate seminar. Samore is no nuclear alarmist. More prescient than those in power at the time, he had been highly skeptical that Saddam Hussein possessed nuclear weapons when those at the highest levels of Bush's administration were convinced. While outside of government, he was nevertheless aware of the 2007 National Intelligence Estimate that concluded Iran had worked intently to develop a bomb until late 2003, although it supposedly had since suspended its efforts. But he had not seen the intelligence gathered by European, Israeli, and American agents and the documents that had been slipped out of the country by dissident scientists. Once he did, he told me, he was convinced "they had a full-scale Manhattan Project running" through 2003, when it was suspended. As Samore acquainted himself with the classified assessments of Iran's progress during the eight years he had been out of government, he found himself somewhat stunned.

"You know, you come into something like this assuming there is a strong case that Iran's ambition is to build a bomb," he told me at the end of 2009. "But it's truly astounding when you see the details, the effort they have put into it."

Samore, of course, could not discuss those specifics, save for the ones the IAEA made public. But over time, many have leaked out, and a few have been published. There were the remarkable plans and videos, including some showing what it would take to detonate a weapon high above a city, replicating how Little Boy was triggered over Hiroshima. There were elaborate documents for the kind of experiments one would conduct only if trying to build nuclear triggers that would set off a precision detonation. And then there was the pattern of specialty steel and other material purchases that were needed for advanced centrifuges. Most worrying were the detailed descriptions of the work of the mysterious man at the center of Iran's efforts to build a weapon: Mohsen Fakhrizadeh.

It was Fakhrizadeh, ostensibly a professor, who oversaw the

efforts to build warheads and detonation systems and to solve the myriad problems in building small, powerful nuclear weapons. He kept renaming and reorganizing projects to stay one step ahead of the inspectors. He had never been interviewed by the IAEA. As one inspector said to me, "When we arrive, we always hear that he's out of town." While the CIA had followed Fakhrizadeh for years, his name has almost never been uttered in public by American officials outside of classified hearings.

To Obama's team, the fact that Fakhrizadeh was still in business—though not running as active a program—was evidence of how Bush ran out of gas on Iran. Several sets of escalating sanctions, banning scientists from travel (Fakhrizadeh and his lieutenants included) and punishing individual Iranian companies had failed to have much effect. Meanwhile, polls showed that Ahmadinejad was admired throughout the region—mostly for standing up to Washington during the Bush era when few dared to.

Samore concluded that the scales needed to be tipped in the other direction. "The Iranians calculated they have the upper hand," he told me later. "Our job was to shift that, to convince them there is no way out" of constant inspection, escalating sanctions, constant embarrassment—and unpredictable attacks on their nuclear infrastructure.

At the same time, Samore often said that he was surprised at the level of Iranian incompetence. The British, the Indians, the Pakistanis, the South Africans, and many others had mastered the art of enriching uranium in far less time, oftentimes in only three to five years. The Iranians, in contrast, had been at this project for decades, and screwed up many of the most basic steps. Part of the problem was that they had bought an outdated, poor design from Abdul Qadeer Khan, the rogue Pakistani metallurgist who built the biggest black-market operation in history for selling nuclear weapons technology.[26]

But their troubles were worsened by American, Israeli, and European sabotage that had undercut their efforts. Samore helped launch some of that work during the Clinton administration, when the covert action really began in earnest, slipping the Iranians bad designs and diverting parts they ordered so that flaws could be built in before they were shipped on to Tehran. And he knew more could be done.

JUST AS THE protestors were facing off against the Basij in the summer of 2009, a little-known Iranian researcher by the name of Shahram Amiri left his university post to go on what he said was a pilgrimage to Mecca—the duty of every good Muslim. He made it as far as the Saudi city of Medina. Then he disappeared.

After a few days, the Iranian government was claiming that the young researcher—who was thirty-two, with a wife and young son back in Tehran—must have been kidnapped. The Saudi authorities were asked to search for him, and when they got to his hotel room, his clothes and some shaving implements were still there. If he left, they reported, it was without luggage. It was probably around then that the Iranians realized they had a big problem: Amiri was likely in American hands. While he was not as senior as the top defense official and former IRGC general who defected in 2007, he had visited some of Iran's key facilities.[27]

The United States ignored the kidnapping charge in public— even after the Iranians complained to the secretary general of the United Nations—and dismissed it in private. As Secretary of State Hillary Clinton said much later, Amiri arrived in the country "of his own free will."[28]

In fact, he had arrived, but the story was not quite that simple. Within a year, the Amiri defection would turn into a spectacle and prompt a propaganda war, after the young scientist had second thoughts about leaving Iran. Today, some in the CIA still question whether he was a double agent; their counterparts in Iran probably wonder whether he was a triple agent. If nothing else, the whole episode illustrates how desperate the United States is to gain insights into the innermost operations of the Iranian nuclear program—the kind of secrets you can't learn from flying a stealth surveillance drone over the desert. Of course, they were trying that, too.

IF HOLLYWOOD WERE making a movie about the shadow wars between Iran and the United States, Shahram Amiri would never have been chosen by Central Casting for the role of Iranian spy. Clean-shaven, square-jawed, and baby-faced, Amiri often bumbled and possessed an air of nervousness—then again, he had much to be nervous about.

Exactly how much Amiri did know remains a bit of a mystery. As a "specialist in nuclear radiation measurements," which is what the Iranians later called him, he would be unlikely to have access to the most vital information. Regardless of what role he actually played, Amiri had seen a lot, traveling from one nuclear site to another. And one critical element of his biography remains beyond dispute: for years he worked at Malek-Ashtar University in Tehran, where Iranian officials insist he was an expert on radioactive isotopes used in medical reactors.[29]

Like Shahid Beheshti University across town, Malek-Ashtar is one of the academic centers that intelligence officials believe covers for nuclear-weapons research. Less well hidden than it should be, Malek-Ashtar sits in northeast Tehran, near an army garrison and a long-suspected nuclear development site, which was visited by inspectors a decade ago. There, the inspectors picked up traces of highly enriched uranium, which the Iranians never fully explained. The weapons area, called Lavizan-Shian, was razed by Iranian bulldozers in 2003 and 2004, raising concerns that the Iranians wanted to make sure that if the inspectors showed up, all they would find was fresh dirt.[30] In 2006, UN sanctions targeted one of the university's top officials, Lt. Gen. Mohammad Mehdi Nejad Nouri, for his alleged connections to Iran's nuclear program. So it was no surprise that the CIA was desperate for an insider at Malek-Ashtar. Young and impulsive, Amiri became that man. He was recruited, several intelligence officials later told me, two or three years before he disappeared in Saudi Arabia. And he was an important source—but not the only one—about Iran's decision to suspend its nuclear-weapons program in 2003, not long after the invasion of Iraq.

"He was the one who told us about the 2003 suspension," said one senior official. At the time the National Intelligence Estimate was published, the whole notion that the Iranians, for political reasons, had slowed the bomb program seemed mind-boggling. (Today, according to the IAEA, there is evidence the work has resumed, but not at the pace or with the organization that marked the earlier effort.)

Amiri was also a critical source for the CIA on the internal Iranian debate over whether the country really needed a nuclear weapon at all—or whether it could make do with a "threshold capability"—that is, the technology, fuel, and expertise it would need to assemble a bomb in a matter of weeks or months. There is much to be said for walking just up to the line: it allows Iran to stay within the confines of the Nuclear Nonproliferation Treaty—which, as the Iranians rightly point out, Israel never signed—and remain a non-nuclear-weapons state. Meanwhile, the whole world would know that status could change with a few turns of the screw. Samore once described this approach as "cheating within the treaty," the perfect phrase for a situation in which Iran could assert it was a non-nuclear-weapons state yet have all the influence that comes from being one.

Outsiders have debated for years whether Iran's only goal is to walk up to the threshold. But it was Amiri, in his debriefings, who explained the ongoing debate in Iran. As one official familiar with those debriefings later described it, "There is a major dispute under way in Iran right now, between those who want to build up to the

line—to be just a few months from a weapon—and those who simply want a civilian capability, which always preserves the possibility
of breakout" and a race for a bomb.

Mohsen Fakhrizadeh, the mysterious scientist running the
weapons side of the program, wants to move to a full weapon "as
soon as possible," the official said—no surprise, since he vigorously
opposed the 2003 decision to suspend weapons work. Others in the
IRGC, however, think that racing for a bomb is simply too risky.
If they are caught, they know, the Israeli bombers will be overhead
in a matter of days, perhaps with backup from the United States.
Pragmatic conservative Akbar Hashemi Rafsanjani, Iran's president
from 1989 to 1997, has also argued that "it is simply enough to
have a civilian capability."* But it is an argument that Rafsanjani
and others cannot utter in public; it would seem to acknowledge
weakness to the West. The ultimate finish line in this race, therefore, is always a bit ambiguous.

Amiri was clearly not in the inner circle. But he offered glimpses
into the debates. Mostly he measured radiation at different sites
and took on other scientific projects. But it was all enough for the
CIA to be certain they had to get Amiri out of Iran. The half-life of
any Iranian scientist who works secretly for the West is pretty short;
inside the CIA, there are still shudders about the fate of another
scientist who helped smuggle out a laptop that he had filled with
critical scientific data about the nuclear program that, to this day,
has given the best insights into Iran's progress. His family made it
out of the country with the information; he was not as lucky, and
has never been heard from since. It was a mistake no one wanted to
repeat with Shahram Amiri.

---

* This view was described in interviews with senior officials in 2010, after Amiri
had returned to Iran. Rafsanjani has been under increasing attack in Iran,
though more for what he has said about freedom of expression than about the
future of the nuclear program.

By early 2009, one official told me, "there was just too much leaking out" that might have pointed back to Amiri. But the young scientist was reluctant to leave Iran: his marriage was under severe strain, he had a young son, and he could not imagine living apart from him. The agency volunteered to whisk the whole family out of the country. Amiri said his wife would never agree to leave.

Eventually, Amiri decided to make the move—alone. It helped that the CIA promised him about $5 million and a new identity. All Amiri had to do was head for his pilgrimage to Mecca; arranging for "disappearances" on such trips is hardly a new scenario to American intelligence officials. By the time the Iranians woke up to what was happening, Amiri was already in the Washington area, being debriefed by officials who had been running his case for years but had never met him. When he was judged sufficiently drained of information, he was placed in the National Resettlement Program—a blandly worded title for the CIA's equivalent of the witness-protection program, for foreign spies who make it to US soil. Within months, Amiri was in Tucson, under somewhat dubious cover as a graduate student. Unfortunately, it was a cover that would not last.

WITH THE PROTESTS all but extinguished in Iran in the summer of 2009, Obama turned back to the question of how to pressure Iran to give up its nuclear program. Since engagement had been a failure, he stepped up his alternative approach: encirclement, on the way to military containment.

The first public hint of the change in approach came from Secretary Clinton, who suggested in July 2009 that the United States would consider extending a "defense umbrella" over the Middle East.[31] While it had long been assumed the United States would protect its closest allies in the region—not only nuclear-armed Israel but also Saudi Arabia, Kuwait, Bahrain, and others—her statement was an implicit acknowledgment that diplomatic engagement alone would not work; it had to be backed with a more ominous threat. But Clinton's wording also seemed to suggest that Obama was preparing for the day that Iran might get the bomb—and that the rest of the region might follow. That was the beginning of troubles with the Israelis, who suspected Obama was not willing to draw a line in the sand.

"I was not thrilled to hear the American statement yesterday that they will protect their allies with a nuclear umbrella," said Dan Meridor, the Israeli minister of intelligence and atomic energy. It is "as if they have already come to terms with a nuclear Iran. I think that's a mistake."[32]

Secretly, Obama was taking another step to contain the Iranians: he accelerated the deployment of a series of new missile defenses around the Gulf. Following a plan laid out by Gen. David Petraeus—who would soon be sent to Afghanistan, and then become director of the CIA—Obama authorized putting Aegis Cruisers on patrol in the Gulf at all times, equipped with advanced radar and antimissile systems designed to intercept medium-range missiles. It was something of a half measure because those systems could not defend against the Shahab-3, Iran's medium-range missile. Then again, American intelligence agencies believed it would be a few years before the Iranians figured out how to arm the Shahab-3 with a nuclear warhead, meaning the United States would have time to come up with something better.

Perhaps the most fascinating part of the plan, however, involved the placement of secret Patriot missile batteries up and down the Gulf. With prompting from Washington—which began in the Bush administration—at least four countries signed up to buy the missiles or to allow the American military to set up the antimissile batteries and man them around the clock. Naturally, few of the Arab states wanted to admit to cooperating with Washington on containing Tehran, for fear of angering the Iranians and their own Shi'a populations. But Qatar, the United Arab Emirates, Bahrain, and Kuwait all allowed them in. (Saudi Arabia and Israel already had similar equipment of their own.) "We didn't have a choice," one senior official of the UAE told me one day in Washington after we had published news of the installations in the *Times*. "We are highly vulnerable to the Iranians; they know it and we know it. But there was no reason to rub their faces in it."

But as one senior American official told my colleague Eric Schmitt and me, the goal of the missile batteries went beyond merely deterring Iran. A second goal, he said, "is to reassure the Arab states, so they don't feel they have to go nuclear themselves." And, he admitted, "there is certainly an element of calming the Israelis as well."[33]

Any reassurance to Arab states and Israel was about to get much more difficult, however, with the exposure of the secret site at Qom.

OBAMA'S EFFORTS TO build an international coalition to pressure Iran were making little headway; Secretary Clinton had called for "crippling sanctions," and the Chinese and Russians had yawned. The White House pressed the outgoing chief of the IAEA, Mohamed ElBaradei, to release, in public, evidence that Iran was working on a weapon. While some of that evidence had leaked out to the *Times* and elsewhere, ElBaradei feared that publication would make the agency appear biased toward the West. He resisted. "We had strong indications, but no solid case," he told me later. "We didn't want to give the Iranians an excuse to shut down" all cooperation.

But evidence of Qom was something Obama could release on his own. He had been holding back, yet as he arrived at a UN Security Council meeting in New York in late September 2009, Iran forced his hand.

World leaders had gathered at the UN to discuss closing the

loopholes in the Nuclear Nonproliferation Treaty that had enabled countries to turn peaceful nuclear programs into weapons projects. Iran was the most prominent example, in Obama's mind, of the treaty's weaknesses.

Obama took the unusual step of personally sitting as the chairman of the Security Council meeting—a first for a US president. Obama's presence there sent a clear message: with the Bush administration gone, the United States planned to reestablish the United Nation's authority—and in particular, the credibility of the tattered Security Council. He talked more like the law professor he once was than the president he had become. "This is not about singling out an individual nation," Obama said. "International law is not an empty promise, and treaties must be enforced."[34] His words marked an important departure from the impotent approach the UN had been pursuing. North Korea had been in violation of the Nuclear Nonproliferation Treaty since 1994 and had suffered no consequences. It was also a message that contained a twist of irony: Obama had been unable to convince the Senate to ratify the decade-old Comprehensive Nuclear-Test-Ban Treaty. Regardless, Obama determined he needed to take a stand.

In a private meeting with Hu Jintao, China's president, Obama described the intelligence about the Qom facility and warned that he would soon make it public. It was in China's interests, he said, to stop Iran's nuclear program early, before a confrontation developed. "We've been trying to convince him that if this gets out of control, China's own interests—especially in oil—will be hurt, so they better get involved," one of Obama's aides told me. It was hardly the first time the Chinese had heard that argument, but it was the first time they had seen the evidence of Iran's secret work. Hu, characteristically, was expressionless.

None of us traveling with Obama knew anything about this, of course; the press briefings were completely uninformative. But right around the time Obama was meeting with Hu, I received an unexpected call from a diplomat in Europe with some surprising news: the Iranians, he said, had gotten wind of the fact that the cover was about to be blown on a secret new facility they were building. In order to avoid the embarrassment of being caught, they had just rushed a letter to the IAEA describing, in the vaguest terms, the fact that they were building an underground enrichment site, and at some point they would open this future enrichment plant to inspection. Their letter had arrived just as ElBaradei was headed to New York. "We stuck it in his jacket pocket," my caller said, "and told him to read it on the plane."

The story was a big one—this was the first indication of those secret plants the intelligence officials had hinted at more than a year before. I started putting out calls, pressing sources for details. There were long silences at the end of the phone. The issue was too classified to discuss, I was told. Well, I said, it wouldn't be in a few hours, after we wrote a story describing the Iranian letter and the secret facility. It was one of those moments when, like during the WikiLeaks disclosures one year later, you could hear diplomatic and intelligence bureaucracies forced to change gears.

I flew to Pittsburgh that afternoon, Obama's next stop, for a G-20 economic summit meeting that most of the world's major leaders would be attending. As often happens when the president travels, there was a dinner organized with a number of other reporters and several of Obama's political aides, including David Axelrod and Rahm Emanuel. The talk was mostly politics and the economic downturn. But just as coffee was being served, a senior official in the National Security Council tapped me on the shoulder. After dinner, he said, I should take the elevator to the floor of the hotel where the president had his suite. "We'll talk about Iran," he whispered.

OBAMA WAS NOT back at the hotel when we gathered that evening outside his suite. But most of the rest of the national security staff was present and armed with the intelligence that had been collected over many years about Iran's secret site.

As they laid it out on a coffee table in the hotel suite, it was clear that this new site was relatively small: it had enough room, they estimated, for three thousand centrifuges. That is not enough to make fuel for a nuclear power reactor, but plenty, as Samore put it later, "for a bomb or two a year." The fact that it was built on a military base said everything you needed to know; it reopened the question of why the military was so involved in a program that the Iranian government has said is entirely civilian. In fact, the United States had watched the construction of the facility for several years, long before Obama came to office. Via satellite photos, the United States had mapped the construction of the building—useful if it ever had to hit it. Since then, "we've been building up the case," one official added. It was clear from the details that the United States had interviewed scientists who had been inside the underground facility; it was only later I learned that one of them was Amiri. The Israelis had played a crucial role in gathering the intelligence. The Russians—usually among Iran's biggest defenders—were totally in the dark.

Obama, I was told, had informed President Dmitry Medvedev just a few hours before. "The Russians were truly pissed," one official told me later. "They thought the Iranians had embarrassed them."

We spent an hour reviewing the evidence. I probed them to reveal how the facility was discovered and received evasive answers. (Later I was told it was discovered by the United States during the Bush administration, but confirming its purpose took years.) Then I went down to my hotel room and began writing the story, knowing it was too late to make the next morning's papers. Instead, we devoted the front of the *Times'* online edition to the revelation. When Obama appeared on a stage the next morning with the president of France, Nicolas Sarkozy, and the prime minister of Britain, Gordon Brown, the news of the revelation had already circled the globe.

"They are going to have to come clean and they will have to make a choice," Obama said. The alternative to giving up their program, he insisted, would be to "continue down a path that is going to lead to confrontation."[35]

It seemed, for a while, that Obama's new leverage might work. Within days the Iranians volunteered to tell the IAEA about "the location of the facility" and then added, cryptically, "and others." Inspectors, they said, would be let in. But the Iranians suspected that this revelation would blow over: other facilities had been exposed before, and ultimately went into operation.

◈

JUST DAYS LATER, the Iranians met the United States and its allies in Geneva, the first real, direct discussion of the nuclear standoff between the two countries since Obama became president. The direct engagement Obama had attempted at the beginning of his presidency was finally coming full circle, although it came, at this point, with less of an outstretched hand. The Iranians had been arguing for months that they could not stop producing uranium, as the UN demanded, because they needed it to keep a small research reactor running in Tehran that produced medical isotopes that were used to treat cancer patients. The argument didn't hold: Iran did not have the capability at that time to fabricate the fuel into a form that would work in the Tehran reactor. (It is one of the many ironies of the Iran standoff that the Tehran reactor was given to Iran by the United States in the Shah's day, another part of the "Atoms for Peace" program. It was an important lesson: the half-life of uranium 235 is a lot longer than the half-life of a corrupt regime, meaning the best-intentioned gift can come back to haunt you.)

Iran's explanation, though, gave Robert Einhorn, the longtime proliferation specialist now on Clinton's staff at the State Department, an interesting idea. Why not offer to "swap" much of Iran's enriched uranium for specialty fuel that could be used in the research reactor—and that would be very, very difficult to use in a bomb?

The offer, he knew, would put Iran in a tough spot. If Iran turned down the deal, it would essentially be admitting that its fuel was intended for a weapon. If it took the swap, it would have to give up the fuel it had spent years producing—fuel that could produce a single bomb. It would take Iran at least a year, maybe more, to make an equivalent amount, giving the United States some time to negotiate a solution. As Dennis Ross said to me, "We couldn't stop their clock, but we could reset it."

It almost worked. In a day of diplomatic drama in Geneva, the Iranian delegation agreed to the deal in principle and to opening up the newly revealed Qom site to international inspectors. A few weeks later, the talks moved on to Vienna to work out the details. After threats, walkouts, and a declaration by the Iranian negotiator that he had a headache and couldn't talk about the subject anymore, a final accord was struck. Iran would ship its fuel to Russia—a country friendly to Tehran—and would get back specialty fuel rods that could be used in a reactor but not a weapon.

But as the talks ended, the Iranian negotiators insisted that any final deal had to go back to Tehran for approval by Iran's clerics, a process they warned could take weeks. Within days, a heated debate broke out in Iran, pitting President Ahmadinejad against his political opponents and ultimately the supreme leader. Ahmadinejad argued that Iran should take the deal. Tired of being blamed for the poor performance of the economy, Ahmadinejad likely felt the deal may have been the breakthrough opportunity to bolster his power. But his political opponents denounced him for falling for an American trap. What if Iran allowed its precious fuel to be shipped out of the country, the opponents warned, and then got cheated by the duplicitous Western powers?

Conspiracy theories abounded. Hard-line politicians dug in. Alaeddin Boroujerdi, the head of the Iranian parliament's national security committee, told a state news agency, "This option of giving our enriched uranium gradually or in one go is over now."[36] Ahmad Khatami, the Tehran Friday prayer leader who called for punishing election protestors "without mercy," expressed doubts that Western powers would hold up their end of the deal in exchange for the uranium.[37]

While the debate dragged on in Tehran, American intelligence agencies were trying to intercept message traffic between Ayatollah Khamenei and other power centers inside the country. The officials would not reveal how they tracked his communications. "But in the end," one senior official who had reviewed the intelligence told me a few months later, "it became clear that it was the supreme leader himself who killed this whole thing."

It was a telling episode in both Tehran and Washington. The Iranians, caught up in their own domestic struggles and an almost reflexive distrust for the West, were clearly not interested in any negotiated solution that would enable them to keep reactors running, while foreclosing their easiest pathway to a bomb. "My personal opinion is that the Iranians have the intention of having nuclear weapons," Defense Secretary Bob Gates confessed. They may have not "made a formal decision" to manufacture weapons, he added, but clearly they wanted to keep their options open.

Obama had reached the end of the road for his engagement strategy. He kept repeating that his offer was still open, but the momentum in the administration had shifted to sanctions and covert action in an effort to avoid an open war now that direct engagement had failed.

Over at the Pentagon, Gates thought the White House was living in a fantasy that its current strategy—engagement, sanctions, periodic covert activity—would amount to a real solution. For decades he had been a voice of warning about Washington's vulnerability to what he called "strategic surprise." Gates believed that the White House lacked a realistic, comprehensive strategy to stop Iran from assembling all the major parts it needs for a nuclear weapon—fuel, designs, a detonator. Once it had those in place, it could declare itself a virtual nuclear power, or conduct a nuclear test.

Gates knew the power of this critique. If it ever leaked, the Israelis would seize on it to declare that even Obama's own team believed he did not have a tough-minded strategy, and the president's political opponents would portray him as weak. So Gates made sure there were only a few copies of the memorandum he wrote to the White House in January 2010, making his case and proposing a new set of military initiatives to contain Iran's power should it get that close to a bomb. And in fact, when the details of the memorandum were described to my colleague Thom Shanker and me and published on page one of the *Times*, the White House issued a blitz of denials. Gates, the most savvy of Washington players, acknowledged that he had written the memo "to contribute to an orderly and timely decision-making process, not to criticize the White House."[38]

In what turned out to be his last months as national security adviser, Gen. James L. Jones told me that we were overinterpreting Gates's critique. "On Iran, we are doing what we said we were going to do," he declared the day after we published news of the memorandum. "The fact that we don't announce publicly our entire strategy for the world to see doesn't mean we don't have a strategy that anticipates the full range of contingencies—we do."

But the questions Gates was raising were profound, and they persisted long after he left Washington in 2011. If Iran decided to go to the threshold of assembling a nuclear weapon, how would we know they stopped short of assembly? And, he asked in the memorandum, how would we know if Iran gave the fuel, parts, or technology to a terror group like Hezbollah? From his years at the CIA, he knew that intelligence just wasn't that timely, and often not that precise.

But something else was going on, too. "Gates was always of the view that at the end of the day, if everything we tried to do to stop a weapon failed, we were not going to go to war to keep Iran from becoming a nuclear weapons state," one of his former colleagues, who sat in on the debates that the memo touched off, recalled to me early in 2012. On that point, Gates had history on his side: the United States considered, and rejected, taking military action to stop China from becoming a nuclear weapons state. It never seriously thought about it in the cases of India, Pakistan, and, astoundingly, North Korea.

Implicit in Gates's memo, then, was a question Obama debated in private in the Situation Room: Could America live with a "nuclear capable" Iran, one that could build a weapon quickly?

A FEW MONTHS after Gates sent in his memo—but before its existence became public—I asked Obama whether, in his mind, there was a difference between a nuclear-capable Iran that stood at the threshold of becoming a nuclear power and one that had a fully developed weapon.

He stopped for a moment, weighing the implication of his answer. Clearly, it was a problem he had spent a lot of time thinking about—but one he had never talked about in public.

"I'm not going to parse that right now," Obama simply said.

But over the next two years—as Iran added to its stockpile of fuel and conducted tests of the missiles it might one day want to arm with a warhead—the question kept coming back, again and again. With the democracy movement crushed, the nuclear program progressing, and the sanctions biting, but not hard enough, Obama knew he needed a game-changer. The hope was manifesting itself in the form of a computer worm that was, at least for a while, America's and Israel's most closely guarded classified program.

CHAPTER 8
OLYMPIC GAMES

WHEN THE CENTRIFUGES FIRST BEGAN CRASHING IN 2008 AT THE NA-tanz enrichment center, the crown jewel of the Iranian nuclear program, the engineers inside the plant had no clue they were under attack. That was exactly what the designers of the world's most sophisticated cyberweapon had planned.

The idea, hatched in Washington and Jerusalem, was to make the first breakdowns seem like random accidents and small ones at that. A few centrifuges—the tall, silvery machines that spin at the speed of sound to purify uranium—raced out of control, seemingly for no reason. With a little luck, they would blow apart, forcing the Iranians to shut down the whole plant and spend weeks figuring out what went wrong.

"The thinking was that the Iranians would blame bad parts, or bad engineering, or just incompetence," one of the architects of the earliest attacks told me later. A mechanical failure seemed entirely plausible. Iran purchased its centrifuge designs from A. Q. Khan, the rogue Pakistani who sold himself as the father of the Pakistani bomb, to speed their ability to make enriched uranium. In fact, the evidence suggests it set them back by years. The design he peddled, called the P-1 for Pakistan's first attempt at a centrifuge, was so deeply flawed that even the Pakistanis stopped using it years ago. The P-1s had developed a reputation over the years as the Ford

Pintos of the nuclear world, subject to periodic, random explosion. Bad ball bearings could cause a catastrophic failure. So could a tiny blip in the electrical system. But the Iranians were determined to keep them running until they could design and build a better one on their own.

A few weeks would go by and then there would be another breakdown—and then another. Each seemed to be caused by a different flaw. And that, too, could be easily explained: fearing inspectors and foreign plots, Iran's nuclear engineers had spread the work of assembling the machines to scores of small shops, where they could be easily hidden. Secrecy was vital; no one in Tehran wanted to repeat the embarrassment they suffered years ago, when IAEA inspectors found an entire assembly operation behind a false wall of a clock factory.

It was particularly difficult to manufacture the delicate rotors at the center of the machines. The rotors are the most vital single part: they spin at terrifying speeds, and each rotation of each centrifuge creates a slightly more purified version of Uranium-235. But they are very temperamental. Spin them up too quickly and they can blow apart. Put on the brakes too fast and they get unbalanced. When that happens, the rotors act like a metallic tornado, ripping apart anything in its way—including any human beings unlucky enough to be working in the enrichment center at the time.

This was exactly the vulnerability that nuclear experts and computer engineers inside the United States and Israeli governments decided to try to exploit in 2007 and 2008. What if they could somehow secretly take command of the specialized computer controllers that run the sprawling centrifuge plant at Natanz? What if they could implant some code that would lie dormant for weeks or months, waiting for a chance to wreak havoc? And what would happen if one day, when the Iranians thought everything was running smoothly, the code would kick in to order those centrifuges to speed up too quickly or slow down too fast, creating exactly the kind of instability that sometimes happens naturally? And how long would it take the Iranians to figure out that someone, somehow, had gotten inside their system?

Those questions ultimately led to the creation of one of the most secret, compartmentalized programs inside the US government. The details of "Olympic Games" were known only by an extremely tight group of top intelligence, military, and White House officials. The intent of the operation was twofold. The first was to cripple, at least for a while, Iran's nuclear progress. The second, equally vital, was to convince the Israelis that there was a smarter, more elegant way to deal with the Iranian nuclear problem than launching an airstrike that could quickly escalate into another Middle East war, one that would send oil prices soaring and could involve all the most volatile players in the region. "We told the Israelis that if you bomb Natanz, it will take the Iranians two years to replace it—but they will do so deep underground; you won't be able to get it the next time, and you'll make them want the bomb even more," one participant in the program told me. "But if you do it this way, they won't see it, and the longer we can go before you have to bomb it."

It was a brilliant theory. But no one knew whether it would work, or for how long. When President Bush held his one-on-one meeting with President-elect Obama days before the transfer of power in early 2009, he told him the program could mean the difference between peace and war with Iran. Obama, at first, may have had his doubts. But he did know that it would be the most dramatic field test in history of a new weapon in America's arsenal—a weapon that of course could, sooner rather than later, be turned back on the United States.

"THE MOST ELEGANT cyberattacks are a lot like the most elegant bank frauds," one of the early architects of Olympic Games told me in 2011, as I began to delve into the question of how Washington was making use of a new technology—offensive cyberweapons—which it spends billions of dollars on each year and steadfastly refuses to talk about.

"They work best when the victim doesn't even know he's been robbed."[1]

The origins of the cyberwar against Iran goes back to 2006, midway through George W. Bush's second term. Bush had often complained to his secretary of state, Condoleezza Rice, and his national security adviser, Stephen Hadley, that his options regarding Iran looked binary: let them get the bomb or go to war to stop it.

"I need a third option," Bush told them repeatedly.

When that option emerged, it came from inside the bowels of the US Strategic Command, which oversees the military's nuclear arsenal. Since its creation, the command has focused almost exclusively on how to improve and defend "the triad"—nuclear weapons based in silos in the United States, in bombers that carry the weapons, and aboard the "boomers" of America's submarine fleet. But it became increasingly evident to the general commanding those strategic forces, James Cartwright, that these weapons of the past were of little utility in the kinds of conflicts the United States found itself in today. That was equally evident to Mike McConnell, the last director of national intelligence under Bush. Cartwright set up a small cyber unit within his operation that later blossomed into the United States Cyber Command, which now is the centerpiece of the Defense Department's offensive cyber capability. McConnell, meanwhile, worked to build up the capacity of the National Security Agency, the huge intelligence agency that has a lock on much of the government's best offensive cyber talent.*

So both at the sprawling nuclear command base in Nebraska

---

* US Cyber Command is based at Fort Meade, Maryland, so that the Defense Department's operations are alongside those of the NSA. Gen. Keith B. Alexander, who is the director of the NSA, is also the commander of what the Pentagon calls USCYBERCOM.

and inside the NSA's headquarters at Fort Meade, Maryland, the United States began thinking in detail about how cyberweapons might be used against the infrastructure of another nation—grinding its machinery, its electric power systems, or its markets to a halt.

It was an entirely new territory for the Defense Department, which for the first time in decades was thinking about a weapons system it didn't know how to build. And while cyber issues are hardly new to the NSA, its mission was to collect intelligence, not fight wars or execute covert actions. Naturally, turf wars broke out at various agencies in Washington over who should be responsible for cyber offense and cyber defense—a battle that has never been fully resolved.

But the Iran problem would not wait. In 2006, Iran resumed the uranium enrichment at Natanz after negotiations with the Europeans and the United States floundered. President Mahmoud Ahmadinejad made no secret of the country's plans: he took Iranian reporters on a tour of Natanz and described grand ambitions to install upwards of fifty thousand centrifuges. For a country that had only one nuclear reactor—whose fuel came from Russia—it seemed hard to justify as a civilian energy project. For years to come, Iran would have no place to burn the reactor fuel it is spending billions to produce. But the fuel's other utility—if it was ever enriched to bomb grade—seemed obvious.

The solution that Cartwright and others presented to Bush, Hadley, and Rice was straightforward: buy some time to deal with the Iranian nuclear program by, in the words of one senior intelligence official, finding new ways "to throw a little sand in the gears." No one had high expectations. The United States had only attempted relatively minor cyberattacks before, for example on an al-Qaeda cell in Iraq—nothing very sophisticated. If this plan worked, they thought, perhaps it could slow the Iranian program by a year or so. Along the way, the United States would learn about this new form of weaponry. But Rice and Hadley, in particular, saw Olympic Games as the best bet to forestall an Israeli attack. They saw no other option: when they asked the CIA to bring them, one more time, the array of "kinetic options"—physical attacks on Iran's facilities from the air or the ground—none of them looked workable. "It was a very short conversation," one participant in the review said later.

Bush immediately seized on the cyber idea and issued the orders to allow it to go forward. "It took us about eight months [to put together the first plan]," one of the key players told me, much of it spent with lawyers trying to make sure that the code they were writing did not violate the laws of armed conflict. The cyberattack had to be as accurate as the best guided missile—it couldn't take out hospitals or schools; it had to be focused on Iran's centrifuge plants. It had to be stealthy, leaving no "fingerprints." And somehow, it had to get inside the heavily guarded Natanz facility.

Soon, an attack plan was developed that bore little resemblance to any that past generations of military planners had ever taken through the northwest gate of the White House. The first step was to develop a bit of computer code called a "beacon" that could be inserted into the computer systems at Natanz to map their operations and determine how they controlled the centrifuges. Eventually the beacon would have to "phone home"—literally send a message back to the NSA's headquarters that would describe the structure and daily rhythms of the enrichment plant. The most important task would be to understand how the centrifuges were connected to what are called "programmable logic controllers"—specialized computers that run the fast-spinning machines, guiding their speed and controlling every aspect of their operation. The good news for the American cyberwar strategists was that these controllers are virtually undefended; like the first personal computers, they were designed in an era when no one ever thought that they might come under attack. They carried no virus protection, not even something as simple as Norton 360. As the designers of the attack knew, if they could get inside the controllers, they would likely have free rein to take control of them.

But getting in, and getting out again, required thinking a bit like a bank thief casing a well-protected vault. While there were few electronic protections, there were plenty of physical protections around Natanz, and a lot of paranoid Iranian officials who knew that their centrifuges were the target of saboteurs from the West. They knew from bitter experience.

OVER THE YEARS the Iranians had been the subject of repeated sabotage—but almost all of it was conventional stuff, the kind of industrial trickery that the CIA had specialized in from the earliest days of the Cold War. Nearly a decade ago, the United States and others had tinkered with power supplies sent to Iran from Turkey; when the equipment was installed at Natanz, an unstable electrical wave surged through the delicate centrifuges and caused them to blow up. It didn't take the Iranians long to figure it out and find another supplier. Gholam Reza Aghazadeh, one of the more hapless previous chiefs of Iran's nuclear program, implored his workers, "Build these machines even if they explode ten times more."[2]

After the Iranians caught on to the power-supply trick, the United States turned to inserting small defects into Iran's supply of critical vacuum pumps. The pumps were secretly diverted to the Los Alamos National Laboratory in New Mexico—home of America's first secret nuclear program—for "improvement" before they were delivered to the Iranians. And the list went on.

It had already occurred to the Iranians that the computer systems running the centrifuges at Natanz were huge targets. But they solved that problem in the same naïve way that many American corporations, power stations, or even the US military once relied on in a more innocent age: they made sure to not connect them to the Internet. Instead, they were surrounded by what engineers call an "air gap," meaning that the only way to get at the computers was to get inside the plant and work on them directly.

So the first challenge was to leap the gap. And the second was to implant the beacon.

It quickly became evident to the Bush administration that if the mission was going to be successful, the Israelis had to be involved—both to leverage their technical expertise, which rivaled the NSA's, and to take advantage of their intelligence about operations at Natanz. The Israelis would also have to be convinced that the new line of attack was working—and that the threat of airstrikes could be put off. Soon the American and the Israeli intelligence partnership kicked into high gear. Olympic Games became part of the weekly conversation between security officials from the two countries, conducted over secure video lines and with visits to Washington and Jerusalem.

"This was really unusual, because you have two intelligence agencies that don't usually play well with others," said one former American intelligence official who had worked extensively on Iran. But current officials dispute that, saying that Iran has brought American and Israeli intelligence and defense officials closer together than at any time in their history. And while "the bug," as some of the Americans called it, was first designed by a small cell of cyberwarriors at the National Security Agency, soon there were improvements, and new versions, coming out of Israel's famed Unit 8200, the country's NSA equivalent.*

Where the Israelis could also contribute, in the eyes of the Americans, was in penetrating the Iranian scientific community. As the assassinations, defections, and a flow of documents had made evident, the Israelis had informants deep inside some of Iran's most critical nuclear and missile projects. That was essential because the only way the beacon, and ultimately the malicious software itself, would leap the air gap would be with the help of scientists, engineers, and others who had access to Natanz.

---

* In meetings between officials in Washington and Jerusalem, the unit handling the Israeli side of the attacks was just referred to as ISNU, for Israel Sigint National Unit.

"We had to find an unwitting person on the Iranian side of the house who could jump the gap," said one participant in the planning. Fortunately, he said, between Israeli and American intelligence agencies "we had a pretty good idea who was going in." Soon there was a list of targets, from the scientists who worked inside the program (some of whom were listed, in public, in the annexes to United Nations sanctions lists) to technicians from Siemens, the giant German electronics firm whose programmable logic controllers, conveniently, had been purchased by the Iranians, who wanted their centrifuges run by the best available technology.[3]

The trick was to get the beacon into those programmable logic controllers. The best way was on small thumb drives—which could be plugged directly into ports on the controllers—or on laptop computers. Frequently, the engineers at Natanz work on program updates on their laptops, and then connect them directly to the controllers. "That was our holy grail," one of the architects of the plan said. As it turned out, it didn't take long to jump the air gap. "It turns out there is always an idiot around who doesn't think much about the thumb drive in their hand," one of the architects of the plan later told me.

It took months for the beacons to do their work and report home—complete with maps of the electronic directories of the controllers, and what amounted to blueprints of how the centrifuges spinning in the basement in Natanz were connected to their electronic control systems. According to one person involved, it helped that Siemens was maintaining the system every few weeks, updating the software. "Siemens had no idea they were a carrier," one official told me. (American officials insist that the United States steered clear of the Siemens engineers, for fear of jeopardizing their relationship with Germany's intelligence service. But those diplomatic niceties apparently did not stop the Israelis.)

Soon it was not an issue: the Iranians, suspicious of the German engineers, banned them from access to Natanz, either directly or remotely.

With the data from the beacons in hand, the NSA and the Israelis set to work developing the bug itself, an enormously complex computer worm. It became a large operation, one that involved far more than just programmers well stocked with Diet Cokes. The bug had to be tested, and to test it they needed the P-1 centrifuges. Fortunately, the US government possessed a few—thanks to the "Mad Dog of the Middle East."

When Muammar Qaddafi gave up his nuclear weapons program in late 2003, he turned over everything A. Q. Khan had sold him—which investigators at the IAEA believe was similar to the package he had sold to the Iranians. (The Libyan treasure trove included a not-quite-complete Chinese bomb design that dated to the 1960s, and was clearly transferred to Pakistan years ago.) Since the IAEA didn't know where to store sensitive nuclear equipment, the centrifuges ended up at the heavily guarded Oak Ridge National Laboratory in Tennessee. They were still inside long, wooden boxes—some stamped KHAN RESEARCH LABORATORIES. Qaddafi's nuclear team had looked at the prototypes and the design plans that came with them and apparently given up. But Iranian engineers had been more diligent, and they set about building their own variant of the P-1.

Soon the military and intelligence officials overseeing Olympic Games managed to borrow a few centrifuges for what they delicately termed "destructive testing." Those first, small-scale tests were a success: only when Bush saw the remnants of a destroyed centrifuge was he convinced the program could work. Soon, from small factories around the country, the United States was secretly producing its own P-1s, perfect replicas of the centrifuges that the Iranians were using. The Siemens controllers were widely available on the open market; they are a common, fairly inexpensive piece of hardware used in an incredible variety of manufacturing plants; no one would raise an eyebrow when front companies were sent out to buy them.

But there was concern that any large-scale test to run and destroy these outdated centrifuges would give away the project, so the work was spread out over several of the Energy Department's national laboratories, from Oak Ridge to the Argonne National Laboratory in Chicago to the Idaho National Laboratory, where—in one of those wonderful ironies of history—the US government has set up a center to help American companies defend themselves against cyberattacks.

"We had banks of these [centrifuges] we were building," one participant told me. Soon began the "destructive testing," an effort to see if the bug could do what it was intended to do: transmit a command that would lead large numbers of centrifuges to run out of control and ultimately self-destruct.

The tests grew more sophisticated; the bug was tried against mockups of the next generation of centrifuges the Iranians were expected to deploy, called IR-2s, and successor models, including some the Iranians still are struggling to construct. It was ready to be tested in Iran—once again inserted by embedding it on laptops and thumb drives headed into Natanz.

Once there, the worm sat, waiting and watching. It recorded what the "normal operation" of the plant looked like. This was critical, because there was a feature of the worm that would be familiar to moviegoers who watched the comedic remake of the thriller *Ocean's Eleven*. In one of the most memorable—and hilarious—scenes in the movie, a team of extraordinarily talented thieves lay the groundwork for their heist by tapping into the circuitry of the security cameras that monitor activity inside the vault that is supposed to hold the winnings from three of Las Vegas's biggest casinos. Then, as part of an elaborate con, they broadcast previously recorded footage onto monitors in the casino control room. The casino's operators are deceived; meanwhile, the vault is cleaned out.

The worm did something very similar—and fooled the operators of Natanz just as George Clooney's character deceived a slimy casino operator. For weeks before the attack happened, the bug recorded the electronic signals indicating that the centrifuges were operating normally. Then it played those back just as the computer worm was taking control, spinning the centrifuges to enormous speeds, or slamming on their brakes. The plant operators were clueless. There were no warning lights, no alarm bells, no dials gyrating wildly. But anyone down in the plant would have felt, and heard, that the centrifuges were suddenly going haywire. First came a rumble, then an explosion.

"This may have been the most brilliant part of the code," one American official acknowledged. Later, word circulated through the IAEA that the Iranians had grown so distrustful of their own instruments that they assigned people to sit in the plant and radio back what they saw. "This really freaked them out," one official familiar with the operation of the plant old me.

For the longest time, the Iranians did not seem to understand that more than just bad luck, and bad parts, were causing the problem. "Even then, it took a while for them to figure out what exactly was happening." To keep them off balance, the participant said, "we kept changing the modalities of the attack," churning out new versions of the bug. The idea was not only to slow Iran's ability to produce enriched uranium; it was to mess with Iran's best scientific and military minds.

"The intent was that the failures should make them feel they were stupid, which is what happened," the participant in the attacks said. When a few centrifuges failed, the Iranians would close down whole "stands" that linked 164 machines, looking for possible sabotage in all of them. "They overreacted," one participant in the

American-Israeli attacks said. "And that delayed them even more." A few months later, Israeli and American officials began sharing reports of finger-pointing inside Iran's scientific infrastructure. "We soon discovered they fired people."

Later, imagery recovered by the nuclear inspectors from the monitoring cameras installed at Natanz—which is how the IAEA keeps track of what happens between visits—showed the results. There was some evidence of wreckage, but it was clear the Iranians had also carted away centrifuges that had previously appeared to be working well.

"Previous cyberattacks had effects limited to other computers," Michael D. Hayden, the former chief of the CIA, told me, declining to say what he knew about these attacks when he was in office. "This is the first attack of a major nature in which a cyberattack was used to effect physical destruction. And no matter what you think of the effects—and I think destroying a cascade of Iranian centrifuges is an unalloyed good—you can't help but describe it as an attack on critical infrastructure."

"Somebody has crossed the Rubicon," Hayden observed. "We've got a legion on the other side of the river now. I don't want to pretend it's the same effect, but in one sense at least, it's August 1945," the month that the world first saw capabilities of a new weapon, dropped over Hiroshima. That was a deliberate overstatement—this was a weapon of precise destruction, not mass destruction—but Hayden's point was an important one. In the hands of others, it could become a weapon of mass destruction.

BY THE TIME Barack Obama had settled into the presidency, Olympic Games was the best hope the United States and Israel had in slowing the Iranian nuclear program. Bush had launched a critical effort, Obama's team agreed. At the insistence of Defense Secretary Robert Gates, the program had been shifted over from military command to the intelligence community. That meant that President Obama had to review and renew a set of presidential findings that would allow the United States to attack the nuclear infrastructure of a country with which we were not at war.

It was Obama's introduction to the new world in which he would soon be immersed. In the days before his inauguration, he had already been through the usual briefings every new president gets—the lesson about how to use the nuclear codes, carried in a briefcase, "the football" that would be near him at all times. General Cartwright, who conducted that briefing, has often told the story of Obama's reaction: after Cartwright talked him through the nuts and bolts of how to order the launch of nuclear weapons, Obama said he wasn't sure he would remember it all. Would Cartwright be able to come back in a few days, after the inaugural hubbub died down? Of course, the general said. A few days into his presidency, Obama passed word on to Gates: "You know that guy who scared the shit out of me? Can I talk to him again?"

But within a few weeks, a second team arrived, and the education of the president about cyberweapons began. Large foldout maps of the Natanz plant were spread across the Situation Room, as a series of officials went through the details of where the United States could implant technology to get at the centrifuges. Various options were described—from interfering with the plant's electrical supply to attacking the controllers—along with assessments of the preliminary results of the bug's first attacks on Natanz. Soon those diagrams of the Iranian enrichment process were showing up every few weeks in the Situation Room, marked to indicate where there were vulnerabilities. "Iran has been one of the president's highest priorities, and it's fair to say there wasn't a major strategic or tactical decision made without him," one White House official told me. Obama had choices to make about when and how to launch the next attacks. He listened and asked a few questions, but he was not as interested in the technological details as Bush had been, his briefers sensed.

What animated the new president were questions about the implications of this new weapon. What kind of collateral damage might occur? If a cyberattack focused on compromising the power grid that supplied Natanz, as the Bush administration had contemplated, might it trigger some other, unanticipated harm to civilians? "We didn't want to be cutting off the electricity to hospitals," one participant in the discussions with Obama said. What were the chances the Iranians would figure out the source of the attacks, and how might they respond? Obama thought it highly unlikely the Iranians would be able to respond in kind—the country's cyber capabilities appeared less than impressive—but they could certainly pull off "asymmetric attacks" on American troops, on Israel, on Saudi oil facilities. How well had the United States and its allies hardened their bases and oil facilities in case they became the natural target?

Obama also insisted, early on, that the bug had to be "unattributable," meaning he wanted the program to remain totally covert, for as long as possible. "He recognized there was a risk of attribution," one official said. "That's always a risk. But it's worth taking because of the need to effect the program."

In fact, for months before Obama took office, the Iranians appeared to have their suspicions. The NSA was increasingly successful at tuning in to the exchanges between Iranian scientists, engineers, and their superiors. "They were having a hard time understanding which of their problems were of their own making and which were not," one official said. Moreover, accounts of President Bush's approval of new ways to undermine the Iranian program, including attacks on its computer systems, appeared just as the Bush administration was packing up in January 2009. And at both the Pentagon and inside the intelligence agencies, some of the creators of the bug believed that it might be even more valuable if the source of the attacks became known, because the Iranians would get the message that Washington could pierce its systems repeatedly.

"The thinking was that the longer it could stay unattributable, the better," a participant in the discussions with Obama told me. "But we had to be ready to work in an environment where the Iranians knew exactly who was doing this to them, to make the point that we could come back and do it again."

As they settled in, many in the National Security Council grew uncomfortable simply extending Bush's covert program without a full review of its implications. Tom Donilon ordered a detailed review of all of Bush's old findings on Iran and the authorizations for covert action, with an eye toward reviewing and rewriting them so that Obama didn't run into a problem with a program that was simply on autopilot. (Most presidential findings are reviewed annually anyway, but this was a far more thorough scrub.) But up on the executive floor of the CIA, and deep in the bowels of the National Security Agency, the architects of Olympic Games feared that if the old findings were withdrawn, the activity would have to stop while Obama's team rewrote the others. In the intelligence world, "people started to go nuts," one official involved said, "because we'd have to pull everybody out and we'd erase the knowledge we had gained."

Eventually that problem was solved, and the Bush findings were simply amended. But over the course of 2009, more and more people inside the Obama White House were being "read into" the cyber program, even those not directly involved. As the reports from the latest iteration of the bug arrived, meetings were held to assess what kind of damage had been done, and the room got more and more crowded. The good news was that with each hit, the Iranians were losing more centrifuges, or spending so much time avoiding new problems that they could not focus on expanding their program as fast as they had hoped.

Then, in the early summer of 2010, trouble hit. Big trouble.

Several weeks before public reports appeared about a mysterious new computer worm, carried on USB keys and exploiting a hole in the Windows operating system, the creators of the bug realized that random copies were floating around the globe. They were found disproportionately in Iran, Indonesia, and India. But how had it happened? Why was a computer worm that had been painstakingly designed to release itself only if detected by computer controllers connected to a specific array of centrifuges at Natanz suddenly zipping through the Internet like a newly released videogame?

The answer appeared to be one that Microsoft and every software manufacturer has discovered sooner or later: poorly tested new releases of software can generate all kinds of unanticipated results.

In this case, the problem lay in a torqued-up new version of the worm. In the spring of 2010, the White House, the NSA, and the Israelis had decided to swing for the fences. They had a specific, large array of centrifuges at Natanz in their sights—a critical array of nearly a thousand machines whose failure would be a huge setback for the Iranian project. A special variety of the worm was developed that would go into Natanz. The program was supposed to detect the presence of the centrifuge controllers and deploy itself. The Israelis had put the finishing touches on the ingenious program.

As American officials later reconstructed events, an Iranian scientist had plugged his laptop into the controllers at Natanz, and the worm hopped aboard. The bug had identified the network it was on—the centrifuge system—and began to do its work. But when the laptop was later unplugged from the secret network and reconnected to the Internet, the worm apparently did not recognize that its environment had changed. That's when things began to go haywire.

"The program began to think of the Internet as its little, private network," said one official who was briefed on what went wrong. It started propagating its code. Suddenly, the secret worm that the Americans and Israelis had invested millions of dollars and countless hours perfecting was showing up everywhere, where it could be picked apart.

"There is a lot of question about who was at fault," said one official. "But there is no question it was a fuck-up." The initial blame was put on the Israelis, who were the last ones to have their hands on that version of the code. But later analysis suggested that the Americans might have been equally at fault.

The release led to a series of panicked meetings. Was Olympic Games over? Or would the world be sufficiently confused about the origins of the worm that American deniability could be preserved?

Inside the Pentagon and the CIA, there were meetings about whether the United States would be accused of being among the first to use a cyberweapon against a sovereign state. Obama and Vice President Joe Biden called for briefings, and had to be persuaded that the virus would not hurt anything beyond its intended target. "The real damage was that we all had egg on our faces," said one official, "and now we were closer to the possibility that the Israelis would feel that this cyber experiment was over and they had to bomb."

Within weeks, as predicted, news stories started to appear, first in the technical press, then in mainstream newspapers. Soon, this worm had a name: "Stuxnet." (The name was an amalgam of some key words found in the software code, but they had no real meaning. The term "Stuxnet" had never been used by the United States or the Israelis.) Suddenly a worm no one had ever seen coming appeared on front pages around the world. Conspiracy theories abounded: It was the work of Russian criminals; of Chinese cyberspooks; of Israel, because of a number that seemed to refer to the date of the assassination of an Iranian-Jewish philanthropist who was killed in 1979. And of course, some thought it was so sophisticated it had to be the work of the United States.

Within days, the code was being picked apart by experts from Silicon Valley to Germany, where Ralph Langner, an independent computer security expert, began dissecting the bug with his staff and running it through the bank of Siemens computer controllers he kept in his chalet-style offices. "It's like a playbook," he told me when I went to visit him just after Christmas 2010 in Hamburg. He described a worm that had what he called a "dual warhead." While it was widely spread, it kicked into effect only if it found the specific controllers that were connected to a configuration that fit the array of centrifuges at Natanz. "The attackers took great care to make sure that only their targets were hit," he said. "It was a marksman's job."

The very fact that Langner had a copy of the bug indicated that the marksman had missed a shot. Deciding they had little to lose, the Americans and Israelis issued another version of the code, this one with the error fixed. Then another one. The third time was a charm. In Natanz, 984 centrifuges came to a screeching halt.

IT DID NOT take long for the IAEA inspectors, who were clueless about the origins of the attack, to discover that about a fifth of Natanz's operating centrifuges had been taken offline since Stuxnet hit. It took months to get them working again. In the meantime, the Iranian Atomic Energy Organization announced that its engineers were trying to protect their facilities from the worm, even while denying it had done much damage. "The effect and damage of this spy worm in government systems is not serious," declared Reza Taghipour, a top official of Iran's Ministry of Communications and Information Technology.[4]

In Washington, a new debate began. Had the creators of this cyberattack on Iran erred by focusing too intently on a narrow set of Iranian vulnerabilities—those spinning centrifuges—instead of other areas? What else could this cyberweapon hit? And in the end, what was accomplished?

◆

FOR ALL THE fears in the Situation Room that early summer day in 2010 when the president learned of the mistake that begot Stuxnet, there is no reason to believe America's cyber wars have ceased. Iran remains the number-one target. Some senior officials in the US government express dismay that we had not used this cyber capability, even in an earlier, primitive form, against North Korea's nuclear infrastructure once it began enriching uranium.

But the harder question to resolve is how successfully the bug prevented the Iranians from their goals. A senior American defense official estimated to me that it caused a year or two of delay, mostly because the Iranians shut down their facilities for fear that other attacks were on the way. Perhaps because the attack was the intelligence community's project, its estimate of success is more generous: its officials told the White House that Olympic Games delayed Iran's progress by two to three years. In fact, it's almost impossible to know the truth. But one fact is clear: Natanz was built to hold fifty thousand centrifuges. Today, after nearly a decade of continuous work, the Iranians have installed about a fifth of that number.

Still, a review of Iran's production records, released by the IAEA, suggests that by speeding up the centrifuges that were still working, Iran's output of enriched uranium did not decline. In short, Stuxnet was a setback, but not a crippling one.

Olympic Games put additional time on the clock, however. It gave Obama a chance to rally the allies to push for more effective sanctions, cut off oil revenues, and close down banking relationships. What it has not done, at least so far, is force the mullahs to give up their project. Olympic Games was not cost-free, however. The United States lost a bit of the moral high ground when it comes to warning the world of the dangers of cyberattacks. The next time the Chinese are confronted with evidence that they are launching cyberattacks against the US or its allies, Beijing is bound to offer up an easy one-liner: "So?

Explain how what we may be doing is different from what you did in Iran."

IN SEPTEMBER 2011, the Department of Homeland Security invited reporters for the first time to the cyber-emergency response center it built in Idaho Falls. Just on the edge of town, DHS installed a simulated chemical company and connected its equipment to computer controllers built by Honeywell, Siemens, and other major manufacturers. Then they set up a "red team"—a simulated competitor chemical company with the mock name of Barney Advanced Domestic Chemical, or BAD—to attack the system and try to bring it down.

It wasn't a fair fight, or a lengthy one. In cyberattacks, all the advantages lie with the attacker—the element of surprise, the ability to hit multiple weak spots at once, the mystery of where the attack is coming from. A team of "defenders" trying to protect the mock chemical company was quickly overwhelmed; when you walked downstairs, a small automated chemical factory appeared to be in chaos, with liquid spills occurring all the time, mixing machines shaking, black smoke pouring out for effect. The operators of the machinery were unable to shut any of it off, because the attackers had taken control of the electrical system too.

"We're connecting equipment that has never been connected before to this global network," Greg Schaffer, a DHS official, told us. "As we do, we have the potential for problems. That, indeed, is a space our adversaries are paying attention to. They are knocking on the doors of these systems. In some cases, there have been intrusions."

Of course, the Stuxnet virus was on the lips of each reporter, with everyone in Idaho Falls assuming that government officials knew more about it than they were saying. They probably didn't;

only later did I learn how closely held Olympic Games had been kept. But they knew enough to have the wisdom to declare their ignorance of Stuxnet's origins (and to demonstrate a remarkable lack of curiosity on the subject). It's not clear at all that they knew that a few miles away, behind high walls, the Idaho lab had been the place where the United States was testing out some of its P-1s in a classified effort to conduct exactly the kind of attack they had gathered us to warn against. The closest they would come to discussing Stuxnet was to comment on its importance as a wake-up call: it was a "game-changer," said Marty Edwards, who runs the control systems security program for DHS. Several years before, Edwards had invited Siemens to undergo a study of the vulnerability of its systems; a year later, those exact same vulnerabilities were exploited by the bug that the United States and Israel designed. Now, Edwards and others were fretting that elements of Stuxnet were being pulled apart by experts around the world, and that inevitably those elements would be used against the United States.

As Ralph Langner later said to me, "Now that Stuxnet's in the wild, you don't need to be a rocket scientist. You've got a blueprint of how to do it."

WHILE A SUCCESSION of computer worms were wreaking havoc in Natanz, Shahram Amiri, the Iranian scientist who had disappeared in Saudi Arabia, was settling into a new life in the southwest United States. He had taken on an entirely assumed identity—and he was miserable.

Even before Amiri defected through Saudi Arabia, the CIA had offered to attempt to bring his family with him, a senior intelligence officer told me. It was not possible; apparently Amiri's wife, from whom he was increasingly estranged, balked. So he had decided to come alone. At first, he was so busy being debriefed and discovering life in the United States that the pain of separation was eased. But eventually the debriefings wound down and doubts and fears set in.

Amiri missed his young son desperately and over time could not resist the temptation to call home. He quickly discovered that the Iranian intelligence agencies, now aware that he had defected, were putting his family under huge pressure. By some accounts, they seized the family's passports so they could not join him. On one of Amiri's calls, Iranian intelligence officials answered and threatened to hurt his seven-year-old son. His only option, the Iranians told him, was to make a videotape claiming he had been kidnapped.[5]

By early April 2010, the pressure was just too great. So Amiri sat down in front of a webcam and repeated the story the Iranians had been pushing: "I was kidnapped last year in the holy city of Medina on June 3, in a joint operation by the terror and abduction units of the American CIA and Saudi Arabia's Istikhbarat," Amiri said. He described being drugged and tortured. Finally, he asked for help.[6]

Curiously, Iranian state television did not broadcast the video for two months. In the interim, Amiri had apparently felt pangs of guilt about bending to the Iranian authorities. So he told his American handlers about the webcast. It was hardly the first time a defector had reconsidered: Washington was full of stories of spies who returned to the cold, including the case of a Soviet defector who met his handlers in Georgetown, then ran out of a restaurant only to end up back in Moscow a few days later, to the CIA's huge embarrassment.

Eager not to be blindsided by the Amiri video, the CIA decided to fight YouTube with YouTube. Just hours after the Iranian broadcast, a well-shaven Amiri showed up on the Web telling a very different story. Sitting down in front of professional cameras in a well-furnished, warmly lit library, Amiri now contradicted most of what he had said in the earlier webcast.

In Amiri's revised story, he had come to the United States voluntarily to pursue a higher degree. "I am free here and I assure everyone that I am safe," Amiri said. He never quite explained why his family remained at home, and watching the two videos back-to-back makes your head spin.

American officials later said the CIA had meant to get ahead of the Iranians and air their video first, but had screwed up the project.[7] As the propaganda war accelerated, Amiri's wife, Azar, told Iranian state television that the second video looked staged. "His deliberate method of speech showed that he was reading text; he wasn't speaking of himself, he was reading," she said. "How can a man with a child in the first grade . . . so easily say he is pursuing graduate study and will return when it is over?"[8]

Iranian state TV broadcast a third video three weeks later, with Amiri once again reverting to the story that he had been kidnapped. This time, he said, he had escaped from US custody and "could be rearrested at any time." He described his second video—the one in which he said he was pursuing his studies—as "a complete fabrication." Later, a senior American intelligence official told me that Amiri had spent weeks telling his handlers he had made a huge mistake defecting to the United States and just wanted to go home and be with his son. The Americans told him the stories of what had happened to Soviet defectors who returned home in the Cold War—only to be tortured or imprisoned. They explained what they thought happened to other Iranian scientists who had been detained on suspicion of revealing nuclear secrets. None of it registered. "He was just very emotional," the official said. "He kept saying, if I can only see my son's face for five minutes, I don't care if everything else you have warned me about comes true."

The rules of the resettlement program are clear: if a defector wants to return home, the United States has no legal basis to hold him. By July, Amiri had made his way back to the Washington area. One evening he hopped a cab and showed up at the Iranian interests section of the Pakistani embassy, a few hundred yards from the edge of the vice president's residence. He declared that he wanted to return to Iran. When I called over to the embassy to ask if Amiri would agree to be interviewed before he left the country, the Pakistani who answered the phone hung up. Amiri did, however, give an interview to Iran's Press TV describing how he had been captured: he was drugged in Saudi Arabia, he said, and woke up on a military plane to the United States.

"During my stay there I was never free," Amiri said. "I was not allowed to use the Internet or any communication device, which is the first definition of freedom."[9]

On July 15, 2010, Amiri landed in Tehran. The Iranians created a heartwarming scene: He was greeted at the airport by his seven-year-old son and dozens of journalists and government officials, who laid a wreath of flowers around his neck. At a press conference, he claimed the United States had offered him millions to tell the press that he was a political refugee and knew the ins and outs of Iran's nuclear program. "I think that anyone in my position would not be ready to sacrifice their honor for material concerns," Amiri said.[10]

He staged an impressive piece of political theater. But even as Iran was rolling out the red carpet, there were clues that the hero's welcome would not last long. During a trip to Portugal, Iran's foreign minister, Manouchehr Mottaki, was asked whether Amiri could be regarded as a national hero. "We will see what has happened over these past two years, and afterwards we will see if he will be considered a hero," Mottaki said.[11] US officials also publicly countered Amiri's claims about having been tortured. "His safety depends on him sticking to that fairy tale about pressure and torture," one official said. "His challenge is to try to convince the Iranian security forces that he never cooperated with the United States."[12]

Amiri made one last appearance on Iranian television, giving an extensive interview on his ordeal. He maintained that he had no specific nuclear knowledge and had never even been inside the facilities at Qom or Natanz. (American officials think this statement was accurate.) The Americans, he said, suffered from bad intelligence and had mistaken him for an expert on Iran's activities. "My familiarity with nuclear sites in Iran may even be less than that of an ordinary person," Amiri said, his face shiny with sweat.[13] He seemed short of breath and sounded nervous.

Within days, he disappeared. Isolated reports have emerged from sites run by the Iranian opposition reporting his arrest and torture on charges of revealing state secrets. American officials say they would be surprised if they ever see or hear from him again.

NOT ONLY WERE the CIA, the NSA, and the Mossad doing their best to undermine the nuclear program, but the VOA—the Voice of America—did its best to undercut the entire Khamenei regime.

No one actually thought they were up to it. America's own government-funded broadcaster still operates from the same fortress-like headquarters on the Washington Mall where it fought Cold War censorship. If you were to walk into the lobby, in fact, you would be forgiven for thinking that the era of Mao and Stalin never ended. The hallways are long, gray, and uninviting. Pictures on the walls recall the glory days of VOA, when the oppressed masses in the Soviet Union, Eastern Europe, and Communist corners of Asia surreptitiously gathered around their radios, figuring that if they had to choose between local propaganda and Washington's view of the world, they would prefer Washington's. Long after the Berlin Wall had fallen and parents had to explain to their children what Communists were, VOA programming could be sleep-inducing, with a lot of emphasis on what farming life was like in small-town Iowa. And while VOA has modernized many of its studios, and has gotten pretty savvy about the Web, there are still pieces of broadcasting equipment hanging around that look like they are awaiting shipment to the Smithsonian a few blocks down the street. It's worth remembering that when VOA was in its heyday, subtly offering up a vision of life in the capitalist West, the founders of Twitter and Facebook were yet to be born.

But in recent times, perhaps VOA's biggest shortcoming was that its broadcasts were humorless and utterly lacking in irony. Despite the earnest efforts of many directors who were determined to yank it into the twenty-first century, the programming always sounded more Edward R. Murrow than Jon Stewart.

That was until two Iranian exiles, Kambiz Hosseini and Saman Arbabi, came up with the insight that there were no better subjects for rapier-like parody than two somewhat bumbling rivals: Iran's supreme leader and his nemesis, President Mahmoud Ahmadinejad.

Hosseini and Arbabi knew their audience: 70 percent of Iranians are American-obsessed youth, many of whom know their way around the Comedy Central website. Hosseini and Arbabi realized that the one attack the Iranian leadership would never be ready for is a Persian-language show that uses satire and audience engagement to cement the image of Iran's ossified leadership as a bunch of argumentative fools who would rather enrich uranium than enrich the economy.

And so, from a group of cubicles on Constitution Avenue, with a budget of well under a million dollars, they developed a satellite television show that arguably does more to undermine the Iranian leadership than billions of dollars in antimissile defenses, sanctions, and computer viruses ever could. Thus was born *Parazit* (which translates as "static")—the Persian answer to *The Daily Show*.

It would be wonderful to imagine that this stroke of brilliance arose from some ingenious thinking in the White House Situation Room or a conference over at the State Department. No such luck. It was entirely the brainchild of Hosseini and Arbabi, who do not exactly fit the VOA mold. Today, tens of thousands of people, sometimes hundreds of thousands, go to extraordinary lengths to watch the show—fine-tuning their satellite dishes and searching for Internet connections that the Iranian authorities have not yet found and disabled.

"We know it's been successful," David Ensor, the head of Voice of America, said to me late in 2011, "because the Iranians put such enormous effort into trying to block it."

No wonder. The running theme of the shows is the endless war between the supreme leader and his president, which plays out each week in Tehran in the form of petty insults, political humiliations, and the periodic arrest of Ahmadinejad loyalists. The intricacies of this palace intrigue, which Iranians know about in fanatical detail, provide the kind of grist for *Parazit* that the battles between the traditional Republican Party and the Tea Party provide for *The Daily Show*. It helps that Hosseini and Arbabi have an intimate understanding of the Iranian psyche—and of the fact that nothing is more dangerous to the supreme leader than the sense that his country is laughing at him.

"With Iran we have almost nothing else," said Ramin Asgard, who was the director of the Persian News Network, VOA's Persian-language channel. It was actually like the old Cold War days, when there was so little two-way communication between the United States and the target country of its broadcasts that the broadcasts themselves are the primary way to send a message. In the case of *Parazit,* the message is clear: your nation is being run by a bunch of crazies who can't figure out what's in their own best interests.

KAMBIZ HOSSEINI CAME to the United States only twelve years ago, from Rasht, in northwest Iran, a city known for the intellectual bent of its residents. As a teenager during the Iran-Iraq War, he starred in an early-morning children's radio program, *Flower Buds of the Islamic Revolution,* in which he acted out skits imbued with the Shi'a Islamic ideal of martyrdom. "They made me say things that I don't believe right now," Hosseini told me during a visit to VOA's studios.[14] But he loved the atmosphere and the freedom it hinted at. In college he worked under a New Wave filmmaker, studied experimental theater, and became a fan of Woody Allen and Harold Pinter. When Hosseini arrived in the United States in 2000, one of his plays was being performed in Tehran's most famous theater. But he pumped gas for his first job in the United States. "I didn't know a word of English," he recalled, which disqualified him for many things except a full-time job at VOA's Persian service, so he joined in 2005.

He became the host of *Shabahang*, a cultural program that was about as dull as a VOA broadcast can be. "I wasn't in charge, and the people who were in charge, they didn't know what they were doing," he complained.

Saman Arbabi, in his late thirties, is taller than Hosseini by several inches and gives off the disheveled, laidback air of a guy who doesn't really want to show up for a day job. He has a seemingly endless supply of graphic T-shirts that he wears untucked. And during each *Parazit* episode, he stands off-camera; his job is to introduce wacky video clips with pithy one-liners. But his main role is as executive producer, in which he focuses on the emotional impact of the show—down to selecting the soundtrack of Iranian and American rock music. He knows them both well, as he lived in Iran until 1985 and had what you might call a nontraditional upbringing: his father was an atheist in a country dedicated to perpetual Islamic revolution, and his political views leaned toward those of Iran's Communist Party. When Saman was twelve, he moved to Rockville, Maryland, the heart of Washington suburbia. He describes himself as a "horrible student" and a class clown; as a young man, he worked the grill at a local Hooters to pay his tuition. His goofy antics won the attention of a producer for a local television affiliate, who gave him an internship, and he was quickly hooked. In 2004, he got a call from VOA, which was expanding its Persian service, and soon he traveled to Afghanistan and the Middle East.

Hosseini and Arbabi knew each other socially, and they started griping at a bar one night that the broadcast had nothing that would speak to Iran's young people in their own cynical, sarcastic language. "We were bored and tired," Hosseini recalled. So the two typed up their fledgling idea for a show and presented it to Alex Belida, the director of the Persian News Network at the time. Astoundingly, he did not say no. "He knew this was a breath of fresh air. He knew at the very least this could entertain kids in Iran," Arbabi said.

Belida suggested they begin with ten-minute segments, which Arbabi described as "very fast-paced mini-documentaries." The first episodes aired in late spring of 2009, just after Obama took office and several months before the Iranian presidential elections.

The show gained more and more popularity when the rigged 2009 presidential elections in Iran led to street protests. Then, suddenly, a largely apolitical entertainment show became intensely political, as its hosts readily admit. "To do anything else at the time would have been ridiculous for the Iranian audience," he emphasized. "We found our niche and said, 'This is why we're here, to cover this.' We went a hundred and twenty percent political with Iranian news."

With so much else blacked out, viewers inside the country turned to Hosseini and Arbabi, who beamed back to them images of the protestors, bloodied and wearing green, marching to rock and rap music while being beaten by police. "People picked us up from that point on and we had to just follow them," Hosseini said. "They couldn't identify with anyone else in the media at the time." VOA eventually figured out what it had and gave the two their own half-hour, weekly prime-time slot.

The brilliance of the show is that it makes its point by avoiding most direct politics and instead focuses on the ridiculous, like the time Ahmadinejad boasted of Iran's launch of a satellite and declared that "God willing, we will send a second, bigger satellite into space that will be there for one year. Once we send a satellite more than one thousand kilometers, we can, with that same missile, reach thirty-five thousand kilometers. There, the direction is all downhill."

The camera cuts to Hosseini, who leans forward in his seat, incredulous and eyebrows arched. "It's downhill? In space? You go a thousand kilometers . . . and then it's downhill? Really, thank you, you're making us all proud."

Then, there was the moment that the commander of the much-feared Islamic Revolutionary Guard Corps, which Hillary Clinton had declared was responsible for Iran's slide into military dictatorship, offered to send the corps to the Gulf of Mexico to help clean up the BP oil spill.

"The IRGC is going to go to the Gulf of Mexico to clean up the oil?" Hosseini asked. "Do you even know what goes on in the Gulf of Mexico? Mexican music, everyone's naked, they're all dancing, love and good times, tequila.

"Mr. Qasemi," Hosseini continued, as mariachi music played, "if you come here to the Gulf of Mexico, you'll put the principles of the revolution in danger. You'll have to work with your eyes shut, and you can't clean up anything with eyes shut."

Even Shahram Amiri, the Iranian nuclear spy who returned to an uncertain fate, was a source of parody. While the CIA played down the embarrassment of losing a major asset who had provided information about Iran's secret programs, a routine on *Parazit*—funded by the same government that brought Amiri here—portrayed him as "The Man with Three Thousand Faces." Their own Amiri character was a portly, mustachioed man huddled over his laptop, making video-tapes while obviously being coached by an off-camera character.

"This chubbiness that you see," their Amiri character says, explaining his weight gain when he hit American shores, was an occupational hazard. "I was in the past thin," he said, "but during imprisonment and torture I became like this."

The most daring segments take on the supreme leader himself, always dangerous business. They recently played one tape of Khamenei declaring, "According to principles, I am not going to interfere in government affairs and decisions. Except in the case that"—and here Khamenei's eyebrows rise and he points his index finger—"I feel the best interests of the people are being harmed."

"Yes," Hosseini cut in. "We have laws, *except in the case that* Mr. Khamenei feels differently."[15]

Inevitably, Hosseini says, there were threats to his family back in Iran. His relatives, he said, were told, "Tell him you can do whatever you want and we won't touch your family if you stay away from Khamenei." With evident bravado, Hosseini said his response was to make fun of Khamenei for the full half hour on the next show.

It is difficult to measure the effect of satire, just as it is tricky to assess lasting damage done by computer worms. But as Arbabi said, "What we've done is something the US government has not been able to do in thirty-two years. We have these governments who don't talk to each other." At least now, there is a way of communicating, even if it involves putting in the knife and twisting it a bit.

MEIR DAGAN IS built like a fireplug. Short and bald, he rarely smiles, and he speaks in the sharp, declarative sentences of a warrior who has survived life in a tough neighborhood and appreciates the need for occasional ruthlessness. In conversation, he is quite emphatic about how the world works and views those who question the certainties of the Middle East with a slight cock of his head and an expression that seems to say, "You must have grown up someplace else." He also speaks with the discretion of a man who grew up protecting the deepest secrets of the Mossad, which he ran until he was forced into retirement in 2011, after a long, festering argument with the two men at the head of the government: Prime Minister Benjamin Netanyahu and Defense Minister Ehud Barak. Both made clear to Dagan that they intended to solve the Iran nuclear problem, permanently, on their watch. And both saw Dagan as an obstacle.

If Dagan is bitter about anything these days, it is about the way he was treated at the end of his term—when Netanyahu and Barak refused to reappoint him as the head of the Mossad. He wasn't alone: they also eased out the heads of three other security services, all of whom had roughly agreed with Dagan's assessment that Israel still had sufficient time to deal with the Iran problem. On his way out the door, Dagan had told the Knesset, Israel's parliament, that Iran's "technological difficulties"—a phrase that meant to encompass the cyberattacks—could delay the country's ability to build a bomb until 2015. Netanyahu and Barak believed this assessment, while consistent with the view of American intelligence agencies, was not only optimistic—it was dangerous. The world would not gather to confront a threat it thought might be distant.

By firing Dagan, Netanyahu created a permanent, highly cred- ible opposition figure, who until recently had daily access to the same intelligence that the prime minister himself did. And so after a few months of nursing his wounds, Dagan began publicly voicing his view: not only was Iran a few years from a real weapon, he said, but a direct, obvious "attack on Iran's nuclear reactors would be foolish."

It was not that Dagan was willing to let Iran get a weapon; far from it. He was just certain, as were the Americans, that a military attack was the surest way to guarantee that, in the fullness of time, Iran would become a nuclear weapons state. Iran would emerge from an attack more unified than ever, and more determined to build a bomb. And that debate—within Israel and between Israel and the Obama administration—became the animating argument of 2011 and 2012, pushing aside all other issues in the relationship, including peace with the Palestinians.

In that argument, Dagan has extraordinary standing. Over the course of forty years, he had shown he was more than willing to kill, sabotage, and attack on Israel's behalf. Talk to him for ten minutes, and you hear the voice of an unabashed hawk.

His mentor in the Israeli establishment had been Ariel Sharon, who appointed him to head the Mossad in the summer of 2002. Sharon and Dagan had known each other for decades, and in the early 1970s, Sharon, then a top commander in the Israeli Defense Force, assigned Dagan the grisly task of assassinating key Palestinian Liberation Organization militia in the Gaza. He took to the job with considerable enthusiasm. Sharon's assessment of Dagan quickly became legend: "Dagan's specialty is separating an Arab from his head."[16]

In 2007, it was Dagan who showed up in Stephen Hadley's West Wing office and threw down on his coffee table a portfolio of pictures of a nuclear reactor under construction in Syria, based on a North Korean design. You must destroy this facility, Dagan said, or my government will. President Bush declined to bomb it, after his aides feared that risking a war in yet another Islamic nation would put Bush in a category no American president wants to be in. (Vice President Dick Cheney, by his own account, was the only one in the Bush administration who argued in favor of the United States destroying the Syrian reactor, partly as a warning to Iran that it could be next.) In September 2007, the Israelis sent bombers over Syria that did the job. Today, that incident is used by advocates of an airstrike on Natanz and Qom as an example of a successful preemptive strike, though against a far closer, far easier target.

It was Dagan who ordered what became known, derisively, as the "Dubai Job," the killing, in a hotel room in Dubai, of a Hamas leader named Mahmoud al-Mabhouh. While the operation succeeded, it was done with an astounding absence of good tradecraft by young Mossad officers who were caught on camera entering and exiting the hotel where the assassination took place. That led to an unraveling of how they operated, including forging passports from countries allied with Israel. Diplomatic demarches and much embarrassment followed.

The mismanaged killing in Dubai was a rare blemish on Dagan's career, and it helped create a pretext for the decision not to extend his tenure. Dagan believes he and Israel's other intelligence chiefs were replaced because they had pushed back so hard against Netanyahu's determination to terminate the Iranian program with an overt strike.

"He's convinced that Netanyahu wanted to surround himself with his own team, loyalists who will not push back if the order goes out to launch a full attack on the nuclear sites," one of President Obama's senior advisers told me in the fall of 2011. "And we think that's probably the right analysis, and it's changed the dynamic inside the Israeli government."[17]

But when Dagan kept up his criticism of the military-attack option, he found himself in an open war with Netanyahu's government. His diplomatic passport was pulled. Barak, the defense minister, shot back on Israeli radio that Dagan was harming "Israel's ability to deter" the Iranians.[18]

There was considerable irony to that line of attack. Just a year before, no one inside the Israeli government spent more of their days thinking about new ways to sabotage the Iranian program than Dagan himself. Many of the early assassinations of Iranian scientists occurred on his watch, and it reminded some Israelis of Dagan's earlier days running an elite assassination squad against Hamas leaders. When the first discussions of cyberattacks on Iran took place, Dagan periodically sat in on the secure video conferences between Jerusalem and Washington, planning out the operations. He was not involved day-to-day, several officials told me, but checked in regularly to see that the cyberattacks were on track.

The cyberattacks' success did not dazzle the rest of the Israeli establishment. Netanyahu and Barak argued to the Americans that they were kidding themselves if they thought computer worms and sanctions would do any more than delay the inevitable. At some point, Iran would make enough progress that its capability to build a bomb would be unstoppable.

For a country like Israel, dedicated to never allowing a Holocaust to happen again, letting that situation fester was simply unacceptable. Netanyahu and Barak often pointed to the attack on the Osirak reactor in Iraq in 1981 and the attack on the Syrian reactor in 2007 as models for the kind of preemptive strike that Israel was poised to conduct in Iran. In fact, when Netanyahu came to Washington in March 2012 with talk of war in the air, he echoed the words of Menachem Begin, Israel's prime minister during the Iraq raid thirty years before. "We chose this moment, now, not later, because later may be too late," Begin had said in the days after the 1981 raid. "And if we stood by idly, two, three years, at the most four years, Saddam Hussein would have produced his three, four, five bombs."

Dagan had no patience for such talk. He shot back that Iran was a different case. Saddam had put all his eggs into one, lightly guarded basket; so had the Syrians. Iran had learned from those mistakes. Iraq's key target was aboveground; Iran's are deep below. Iraq's nuclear infrastructure was pretty well understood; much of Iran's remains a mystery.

What's more, Dagan appeared convinced by the American argument that Iran had suspended much of its nuclear weapons research in 2003, and has only resumed it sporadically. "I haven't yet seen any decision to cross the line and obtain a nuclear weapons capability," he said, breaking with the official Israeli view. "I see an approach to shorten the distance" to a bomb.

Dagan argued that exploiting Iran's many internal divisions would be the wisest strategy. Iran's fractured religious groups don't all accept the supreme leader, and he is not considered a particularly strong religious authority. The clerics in Qom—the side of town that worried about the future of Shi'ism, not the future of centrifuges—

were particularly critical of him. There were other divisions between moderates in the urban centers and more rabid conservatives in the rural areas. The military was divided too, between ordinary forces and the Islamic Revolutionary Guard Corps. And within the Revolutionary Guard, many were worried that sanctions were cutting into their most profitable businesses.

A smart policy would focus on worsening these rifts, Dagan contended, urging Israeli and American officials alike to "go directly against the regime itself. There is real division there." Bombing would have the opposite effect, unifying the country behind the mullahs, giving Iran the excuse to throw out inspectors and take the program deep underground.

"What Dagan believes is that the key element to building a bomb is the knowledge, and you can't bomb knowledge," one American who dealt with him often said. "In a few years, we'd be dealing with this all over again." To Netanyahu and Barak, this was woolly-headed thinking: regime change in Iran would be nice—but nothing Israel can bank on. Its timing is unpredictable and a successor government may be no less committed to a nuclear weapons option. Going after the capability, not the government, would be the only real guarantee, they said.

But Dagan's arguments, even after he was forced out, blew the long-simmering debate out of Israel's cabinet rooms and into the open. In the fractious, always overheated world of Israeli politics, many joined in, including former chiefs of staff of the Israeli Defense Force and the former leaders of Shin Bet (the internal security service) and other intelligence agencies. Israeli journalists told me that the Mossad itself, heavily invested in both Dagan and the sabotage efforts it had executed, was actively leaking word that many of its own top officers were worried about the huge risks of blowback from an overt strike.

"We are in a strange world," one senior Israeli official said to me, "where the defense minister and to a lesser degree the prime minister are focused intently on the military option, and the intelligence services and the military, with some exceptions, are deeply doubtful." Partly that was because of turf battles: the Mossad believes its campaign of sabotage and assassinations has successfully set back the Iranians for years, and with a few more explosions like the one that wiped out the giant missile development base, they could buy more time.

But in a debate like this, the Iranians also get a vote. As Israel argued, Iran focused more and more on uranium enrichment—and bringing to life that huge underground installation at Qom, under rock so deep the Israelis could not strike it.

Both were potential game-changers, and by the spring of 2012, Washington and Jerusalem talked ceaselessly of impending war.

Chapter 9
"The Land of Lousy Options"

ON A FRIDAY IN EARLY MARCH 2012, TWO DAYS BEFORE ISRAELI prime minister Benjamin Netanyahu was scheduled to arrive in Washington for a showdown meeting over whether, and when, Israel might strike Iran, President Obama gathered his national security team at the White House.

With Hillary Clinton, Leon Panetta, and the recently installed CIA chief, Gen. David Petraeus, all positioned around the table, Obama began describing the huge political challenge that accompanied Netanyahu's arrival.

War talk had gotten out of hand; for more than a month, there were stories appearing about Israeli contingency planning for a broad strike on Iran's nuclear facilities. Much of this was clearly being fueled by Israel's own top officials, including their minister of defense, Ehud Barak.

"I accept that Iran has other reasons for developing nuclear bombs, apart from its desire to destroy Israel, but we cannot ignore the risk," Barak told Ronen Bergman, a well-known Israeli writer on national security, for an article published in the *New York Times Magazine* just a month before Netanyahu arrived. "An Iranian bomb would ensure the survival of the current regime, which otherwise would not make it to its 40th anniversary in light of the admiration that the young generation in Iran has displayed for the West. With a bomb, it would be very hard to budge the administration."[1]

The defense minister knew his audience, and he was a master

at striking the note that would make Washington jump. "The moment Iran goes nuclear, other countries in the region will feel compelled to do the same. The Saudi Arabians have told the Americans as much, and one can think of both Turkey and Egypt in this context, not to mention the danger that weapons-grade materials will leak out to terror groups."

In short, every nuclear nightmare Obama talked about during the 2008 campaign—the world's worst weapons in the world's most volatile places—would be sped along by a weapons-capable Iran. The Israelis were basically making the case that if they had to attack Iran, it wouldn't be just in national self-interest—it would be to preserve stability in the Middle East.

Obama was "appalled" at the lack of discipline as one Israeli official after another offered up briefings on what it would take to wipe out Iran's nuclear capability, one of his aides told me. Inside the White House, debate broke out about whether the Israelis were truly serious about mounting an attack in months, or whether this was all a carefully planned media campaign, designed to turn the screws on Washington for even stricter sanctions, and a declaration from Obama that, if needed, the United States would join Israel in military action.

"The president was being jammed by the Israelis ahead of Netanyahu's trip, and he knew it," one participant in that Friday National Security Council meeting said. "But what else was new? This is the land of lousy options."

There was no love lost between the American president and the Israeli prime minister, and it was no secret. Unaware that reporters could overhear them, President Nicolas Sarkozy of France told Obama during a November 2011 summit, "I cannot bear Netanyahu; he's a liar." Obama's retort, caught on a long-range microphone, said it all: "You are fed up with him, but I have to deal with him even more often than you."[2]

Obama told his national security team that Netanyahu's visit had to be a success. The biggest risk to the American strategy to stop Iran's nuclear program, he told them, was a divisive split with Netanyahu that the Iranians could exploit. But the only way to quiet the beating of the drums, Obama said, was to declare outright that the United States did not believe a classic containment policy would work. In other words, what had succeeded with the Soviet Union for so many decades was not a credible option in this case.

Starting from a different place from the one Barak did, Obama came out in the same place: if Iran got a nuclear weapon, it would lead to a domino effect. A cascade of proliferation would follow. It could start in Saudi Arabia—which may have bombs in reserve in Pakistan. But Egypt would be tempted, if it could ever get its act together—and so would Turkey and the United Arab Emirates. If that happened, everything that John F. Kennedy had warned about a world of nuclear-armed states would come true—albeit four decades after Kennedy believed it was about to happen.

But there was a political calculus as well. If Netanyahu thought Obama was headed toward a containment strategy—in other words, that he was not truly willing to stop Iran from getting the bomb—then the Israeli leadership would conclude there was no choice but to go ahead with an attack. So Obama was caught in the classic paradox: to stop a war from happening, he had to declare he was willing, as a last resort, to help the Israelis take out Iran's facilities. "The question," said one former Israeli official, was, "Could he do it and have everyone believe him?"

THE OBAMA WHITE House had been at work trying to bridge the differences with the Israelis for months. In December 2011, Wendy Sherman, a former aide to Madeleine Albright, had taken her first trip to Israel as the new undersecretary of state for political affairs, the country's third-ranking diplomat. She came back pretty shocked at what she heard; one official after another had sounded the alarm on the advances Iran was making. They had complained that even after the International Atomic Energy Agency had finally, after years of internal debate, published summaries of the evidence that Iran was working on "possible military dimensions" of a nuclear program, from nuclear triggers to warheads, there had been muted international reaction.

Sherman drafted a memorandum for Hillary Clinton, hoping to keep the report of her concerns off the system of cables that had leaked so famously the year before. But it was only a matter of days before reports of her private memorandum also circulated in Washington. "We couldn't tell if the Israeli tone had changed or if Wendy was just new to this," one senior administration official who had read her report told me. "Or both."

It turned out to be both. So in February 2012, in preparation for Netanyahu's visit, Tom Donilon, Obama's national security adviser, took a large delegation of American officials to Israel for one of the most comprehensive joint reviews of the intelligence ever conducted. He wanted to make sure that when Obama and Netanyahu met, they weren't differing on the intelligence assessments.

Donilon's team spent five hours wading through the intelligence with the Israelis in the basement of the prime minister's residence. There were PowerPoint presentations on the state of the enrichment program, on the effectiveness of Olympic Games, on the Iranian progress toward weaponization. At around lunchtime, Netanyahu came in, looked at the group, and laughed at the number of Americans in the room. "We counted three American airplanes on the tarmac at Ben Gurion," he told Donilon.

Each side had its own agenda. The Israelis wanted to convey a sense of urgency—there would come a definite time, not imminent but soon, when they would have to make a decision about whether to strike before Iran was fully inside the "zone of immunity." The Americans wanted it clear there were options—more sanctions, more iterations of Olympic Games, more pressure. And the core of the American argument was simple: attack Iran, and you set the program back a few years, but you solve nothing.

"We wanted to make it abundantly clear that an attack would just drive the program more underground," one of the key participants in the talks that day told me later. "The inspectors would be thrown out. The Iranians would rebuild, more determined than ever. And eventually, they would achieve their objective."

As Netanyahu flew to Washington, Obama stepped into the vastness of the Washington Convention Center to make his case in front of a huge crowd of 13,000 people—all gathered for the annual meeting of the American Israel Public Affairs Committee. The committee is the most powerful of the pro-Israel lobbying groups in the United States, but it is also the one most likely to simply repeat the talking points of whatever Israeli government is in power at the time.

There weren't many Obama supporters in the audience; they had split with him when Obama pressured Netanyahu to stop the creation of new settlements in the West Bank that were, in Obama's mind, a huge impediment to getting an Israeli–Palestinian peace deal. There was no more highly charged issue, and eventually Obama had backed down, the beginning of his abandonment, at least for his first term, of any serious effort to press for a negotiated settlement.

And less than a year before, in May 2011, AIPAC's officials had backed Netanyahu when he went in front of Congress and pointedly rejected the use of the 1967 borders as a starting point for negotiating with the Palestinians—only days after Obama had called for doing exactly that.[3]

So it was no surprise that this Sunday morning, the group's biggest cheers—and biggest checks—were reserved for the like-minded. Before Obama entered the hall, Liz Cheney, the former vice president's daughter, had gotten a huge cheer when she ripped into the president for failing to back Israel with sufficient enthusiasm.

But once Obama arrived on the stage, glad-handing the group's leadership, he got right to the point: on his watch, he assured the group, Iran would not get the bomb.

"My policy here is not going to be one of containment," Obama announced. "My policy is prevention of Iran obtaining nuclear weapons." As if to make sure nobody misunderstood his point, he added, "When I say all options are on the table, I mean it."[4]

Netanyahu arrived at the White House the next morning, on his best behavior. When the cameras went on, he praised Obama and noted the president's more hard-line tone on Iran: "He stated clearly that all options are on the table, and that American policy is not containment."

What happened for the next few hours is difficult to know with any precision. The two men certainly talked about the covert program, and what they planned to do next. Obama, presumably, stressed that when he promised the United States would prevent Iran from getting to the final step, he meant it. Netanyahu told Obama that no decision on an attack had been made. But he warned that no matter what the Americans thought about the determination of Iranian leaders to wipe out Israel, Netanyahu took it seriously. "They mean it," he said. "If this will be resolved by diplomacy, great. But we have to prepare for the worst-case scenario." Time, he said, "is getting short." Of course, the Israelis said that three years ago.

Curiously, when Netanyahu—after giving a rousing speech to AIPAC—got back home, his tone had changed a bit.

"We're not standing with a stopwatch in hand," Netanyahu said a few days after seeing Obama. "It's not a matter of days or weeks, but also not of years. The result must be removal of the threat of nuclear weapons in Iran's hands."

The message, one of Obama's top aides told me, was that "we've bought a little time." Soon, the first negotiations with Iran in more than two and a half years were arranged. It was, Obama said publicly, the "last chance."

GEN. JAMES MATTIS is no one to be trifled with. The burly head of CENTCOM spent the last year bolstering defenses in case war breaks out with Iran. He has placed antimissile batteries around the region, gathered the equipment needed to sweep mines out of the Strait of Hormuz, and identified how the United States would take out Iran's air defenses and command-and-control if it needed to do so. He's also spent a lot of time thinking about the "and then what?" questions—as in, "Israel strikes . . . and then what?"

Mattis sought the answer in a war game that was under way while Netanyahu was visiting. Called "Internal Look," and described to my colleagues Mark Mazzetti and Thom Shanker, the two-week-long exercise ended the way all such exercises do: with the United States sucked into the war.

Mattis's exercise was classified, but in the account published in the *Times,* the Israeli attack set the Iranian program back by about a year. But at some point early in the exercise, the Iranians took a shot at a US Navy warship and killed about two hundred Americans. "A ridiculously high number," one former Israeli official told me. Maybe so, but every other simulation I've ever seen didn't turn out much better.

The simulations all start with the same premise: the Israelis believe that knocking back the Iranian program even for a short time is worth it. After all, in 1981, when Israeli pilots were about to take off to destroy Iraq's nuclear reactor at Osirak, they were told it might only delay Saddam Hussein two or three years—and the pilots were unlikely to get home alive. It turned out Saddam's nuclear ambitions never recovered. In 2007 the Israelis took out a North Korean-built reactor in Syria. The Syrians are now preoccupied with bigger problems.

POTENTIAL AIRSTRIKES ON IRAN

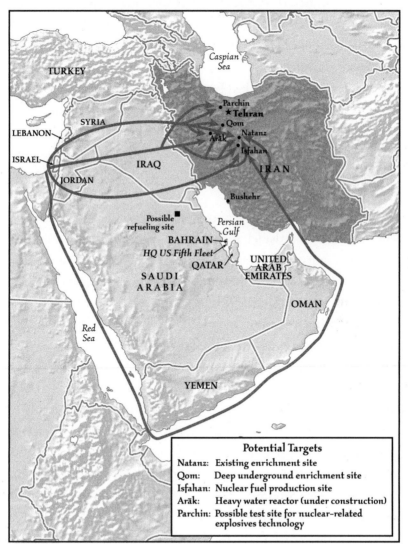

Potential Targets	
Natanz:	Existing enrichment site
Qom:	Deep underground enrichment site
Isfahan:	Nuclear fuel production site
Arāk:	Heavy water reactor (under construction)
Parchin:	Possible test site for nuclear-related explosives technology

At a 2009 simulation at the Brookings Institution, former top American policymakers and intelligence officials played the roles of the president and his top advisers; the Israeli prime minister and cabinet; and Iranian leaders. Great care was taken to preserve some verisimilitude, and that started when the Israelis attacked without telling the United States in advance. They hit six of Iran's most critical nuclear facilities, using a refueling base hastily set up in the Saudi Arabian desert. (Based on what we know about the Saudis' view of Iran, it hardly seems fanciful that the Saudis would take the local goat-herders off for an evening of entertainment while the Israeli planes landed.)

Washington was shocked but not surprised—and immediately demanded that Israel cease its attacks, even though many in the US government cheered on the effort. Then, even while calling for restraint on all sides, the United States deployed more Patriot anti-missile batteries and Aegis cruisers around the region, as a warning to Iran not to retaliate.

In the simulation, the Iranians don't abide by such warnings. They fire missiles at Israel, including its nuclear weapons complex at Dimona, but damage and casualties are minimal. Meanwhile, two of Iran's proxies, Hezbollah and Hamas, launch attacks in Israel and fire rockets into the country. Israel, wisely, barely responds.

But in this simulation, as in others, the Iranians try to use the event to unify their people, and to roll over opposition parties. Iran mounts a series of low-level attacks on Israel and portrays the United States as a paper tiger—unable to control its ally and unwilling to respond to Iran.

Then Iran fires missiles at the Saudi oil-export processing center at Abqaiq, and tries to incite Sh'ia Muslims in eastern Saudi Arabia to attack the Saudi regime. There are terror attacks against European targets, in hopes that governments there would turn on Israel and the United States.

Strife breaks out in Israel as the economy comes to a halt and a hundred rockets a day land in the northern part of the country, some aimed at Haifa and some at Tel Aviv. Hundreds of thousands flee.

Eventually, Israel wins Washington's acquiescence to retaliate against Hezbollah. It orders a forty-eight-hour campaign by air and special forces against Lebanon and begins to prepare a much larger air and ground operation. The Iranians, though, are not sitting still: They start lobbing missiles at Dhahran, an oil-industry center in Saudi Arabia. And they mine the Strait of Hormuz.

That's when the United States is unable to sit it out any longer. Oil supplies to the United States are threatened. Eventually the United States begins a massive military reinforcement. As the Brookings simulation ended, the Iranian forces were about to suffer a major defeat.

"All these simulations start differently and have different details," one senior military official told me. "But they all end the same, with deep American participation."

And they end with a few lessons: By attacking without Washington's advance knowledge, Israel has the benefit of surprise and momentum—not only over the Iranians, but over its American allies—and for the first day or two, they run circles around White House crisis managers. Soon, the battle sucks the region in, and then Washington. The war shifts to defending Saudi oil facilities against Iranian attacks, and Iran's use of proxies means that other regional players quickly become involved.

And in the end, no one wins. Facilities are bombed, but scientific knowledge remains. The Israelis declare the operation a success; in Washington, most officials conclude that setting back the Iranians by only a few years is not worth the cost. The Israelis say the Iranian regime is humiliated, and claim the attack might speed its demise. The Americans say that's a pipe dream.

IN THE DEPTHS of the Cold War, in 1983, a senior at Columbia University wrote in a campus news magazine, *Sundial,* about the vision of "a nuclear free world."

The student was Barack Obama. In the piece, he denounced "the twisted logic of which we are a part today" and praised student efforts to realize "the possibility of a decent world." But his article, "Breaking the War Mentality," which was rediscovered shortly before his election, said little about how to achieve the utopian dream.[5]

At critical junctures in Obama's career, the subject of nuclear disarmament would keep reappearing. After the *Sundial* article, Obama went silent on nuclear issues for the next two decades. Yet that phrase—a "nuclear-free world," which was Obama's paraphrase—would reemerge decades later as the signature item of his nuclear agenda.

When he became a senator in January 2005, Obama rekindled his interest in arms control, an issue that had little traction in the Republican-controlled Senate. Obama found a mentor in Senator Richard G. Lugar, the Indiana Republican, who was then chairman of the Senate Foreign Relations Committee and a longtime champion of nuclear nonproliferation efforts. The committee was the place where a young senator could demonstrate some seriousness on global issues, and later that year, Obama asked to join Lugar on a trip to monitor Russian efforts to scrap nuclear arms and secure atomic materials from theft or diversion—and he was photographed walking around on decommissioned missile parts. It added some credibility to his campaign arguments for vastly reducing the size of the American arsenal, though it later came to haunt Senator Lugar, who had to fight charges at home that he had become an "Obama Republican."

The question inside the White House once Obama was elected

Watching a direct feed from a stealth RQ-170 drone over Abbottabad, Obama and his national security team anxiously monitor the bin Laden raid. "The minutes passed like days," John Brennan, Obama's counterterrorism chief, said later. Pakistan's failure to detect the drone fed its paranoia that the United States could seize its nuclear arsenal. *(Official White House photo by Pete Souza)*

In the early months of Obama's presidency, Gen. David Petraeus, in the Situation Room next to Gen. James Cartwright, urged a reluctant Obama to "surge" into Afghanistan. The president agreed, but then withdrew significantly faster than Petraeus thought wise. *(Official White House photo by Pete Souza)*

Afghan president Hamid Karzai and Pakistani president Asif Ali Zardari at the White House. Obama's team debated which of the two was weaker, or tolerated more corruption, and tried to harness both into a negotiated political settlement with the Taliban. *(Official White House photo by Pete Souza)*

Gen. Ashraf Kayani, Pakistan's top military commander, takes Adm. Mike Mullen, then chairman of the Joint Chiefs of Staff, on a ride. Mullen invested deeply in his relationship with Kayani, but in his last days on the job denounced the ISI, which Kayani once ran, declaring the Haqqani network, which attacked the US embassy in Kabul, a "veritable arm" of the intelligence agency. *(Chairman of the Joint Chiefs of Staff)*

Richard Holbrooke, the diplomat who forged the Dayton Accords that ended the war in the Balkans, attempted to replicate his successes in Afghanistan and Pakistan as the State Department's special representative. He had a compelling vision, but often angered Obama and battled with Karzai. He died suddenly in December 2010. *(Paula Bronstein/Getty Images)*

Kambiz Hosseini (left) and Saman Arbabi on the set of their show *Parazit*—the Persian equivalent of *The Daily Show*—which the Voice of America beams into Iran to parody and undermine the country's leadership. *(VOA Public Relations)*

Iranian president Mahmoud Ahmadinejad at the Natanz uranium enrichment plant, the target of "Olympic Games," America's secret cyberwar operation to sabotage Iran's nuclear ambitions. Mostafa Ahmadi Roshan, pictured behind and slightly to the right of Ahmadinejad, was later assassinated—presumably by Israel. *(Office of the Presidency of the Islamic Republic of Iran)*

Satellite view of the Qom uranium enrichment site, built into a mountain so deep the Israelis feared they could not destroy it. *(GeoEye Satellite Image/Reuters)*

Thomas Donilon, just before his appointment as national security adviser, meets with Chinese president Hu Jintao at the Great Hall of the People in September 2010. Donilon took on "rebalancing" American power toward Asia as a personal mission. *(Feng Li/Agence France-Presse—Getty Images)*

Vice President Xi Jinping of China visits a farm near Maxwell, Iowa, in February 2012. It was an effort to give a populist touch to his rise in the Chinese hierarchy by returning to where he had first visited America as a young man. *(Steve Pope/Office of the Governor of Iowa)*

Kim Jong-il inspects a video company in Pyongyang, North Korea, with his youngest son, Kim Jong-un, who succeeded him when Kim Jong-il died in December 2011. *(Korea Central News Agency/Korea News Service)*

Secretary of Defense Robert Gates and China's minister of national defense Gen. Liang Guanglie inspect the honor guard at a welcoming ceremony in Beijing in January 2011. To make a point to Gates, who had questioned the quality of China's military hardware, the Chinese tested a stealth fighter during the trip. *(Reuters/Andy Wong/Pool)*

Obama went to Egypt in 2009, eighteen months before the Arab Spring, and declared a "new beginning" in America's relationship with a Muslim world that was about to be plunged into an era of uprisings. *(Official White House photo by Pete Souza)*

Hosni Mubarak meets with Obama in the Oval Office, only three months before the new American president called to tell him the only way to end the protests in Tahrir Square was to quickly get out of office. *(Official White House photo by Pete Souza)*

NATO's intervention in Libya led to a lengthy, bloody stalemate before rebels, seen here taking Surt, routed Qaddafi's forces and then executed the "King of Kings." *(Mauricio Lima/ New York Times/ Redux)*

Four Arab dictators, just months from being ousted in uprisings they never saw coming, during a visit to Libya. From left: Tunisian president Zine el-Abidine Ben Ali, Yemeni president Ali Abdullah Saleh, Libyan colonel Muammar Qaddafi, and Egyptian president Hosni Mubarak. *(Sabri Elmehedwi/European Pressphoto Agency)*

Hillary Rodham Clinton arrives in Tripoli for the first time since Qaddafi's ouster. Qaddafi was killed by rebels soon after she left. *(Kevin Lamarque/Agence France-Presse—Getty Images)*

Pakistanis protest drone strikes, which tripled during the Obama administration. While they debilitated al-Qaeda in the region, they also contributed to the deterioration in US–Pakistani relations. *(K. Pervez/Reuters)*

Members of Iran's Revolutionary Guard show off a stealth RQ-170 drone, picked up near the town of Kashmar, approximately 140 miles from the border with Afghanistan. An electronic problem brought it down, and Obama decided not to risk sending a team to recover it. *(Iranian Revolutionary Guard)*

A Predator drone firing a Hellfire missile. The White House tied itself in knots trying to explain in public the legal justification for a covert program that it could not acknowledge exists. *(United States Air Force)*

John Brennan, Obama's counterterrorism chief, pushed for a rapid withdrawal from Afghanistan and argued that America could protect its interests by keeping 10,000 to 15,000 troops on bases where they could launch drone strikes into Pakistan and prevent Kabul from falling to the Taliban. *(Official White House photo by Pete Souza)*

was how hard to push for his nuclear agenda. It had none of the electoral appeal of health care, or energy, or climate change. Still, he had a passion on this issue that was evident to my colleague Bill Broad and me when we interviewed the president about the origins of his thinking on this issue.

"It's naïve for us to think," he told us, "that we can grow our nuclear stockpiles, the Russians continue to grow their nuclear stockpiles, and our allies grow their nuclear stockpiles, and that in that environment we're going to be able to pressure countries like Iran and North Korea not to pursue nuclear weapons themselves."

Twenty-six years after he wrote his article in the *Sundial,* and just a few months into his presidency, in the spring of 2009, Obama appeared before a cheering throng in Prague to "state clearly and with conviction America's commitment to seek the peace and security of a world without nuclear weapons.

"I'm not naïve," he continued. "This goal will not be reached quickly—perhaps not in my lifetime. It will take patience and persistence."[6]

There were few initiatives that opened Obama to more charges that he was a lefty, that somehow he was stuck in some idealistic vision of a nuclear-free world. The facts did not support that: Obama was going step-by-step, perhaps too cautiously, and the US arsenal remains so overwhelming, it is hard to imagine challenging it. But since Prague, he has rarely discussed the topic. He has had other things on his agenda—the recession, the Arab Spring, the Iranian crisis. And once the Democrats lost control of the House in 2010, and lost seats in the Senate, Obama's hopes concerning the next step—finally winning passage of the Comprehensive Test Ban Treaty, which failed to pass on Bill Clinton's watch—were put on hold. Pakistan blocked his effort to even begin negotiations on the Fissile Material Cut-off Treaty, which would have largely ended the production of new nuclear material. The Pakistanis see it as a threat to their last line of defense.

Obama did score a win after successfully negotiating the new Strategic Arms Reduction Treaty (START) with the Russians at the end of 2010. But the treaty was modest at best, leaving each side with about 1,500 deployed weapons, but thousands more in inactive stockpiles. In late March 2012, he told reporters during the Nuclear Security Summit in Seoul that "we can already say with confidence that we have more nuclear weapons than we need."[7] But it was a fight he was not ready to start.

BY THE SPRING OF 2012, with sanctions beginning to hurt badly, the Iranians suddenly showed interest in talking about the future of their nuclear program. It may well prove the defining negotiation of Obama's presidency. For the first time since they came to office, senior members of the administration and even top intelligence officials said they thought they detected a change in Iran's attitude. The combination of sanctions and covert action, they said, may be beginning to change the mullahs' calculus. The Israelis did not share that optimism.

Yet if, after what Obama calls Iran's "last chance" at a settlement, the issue remains unresolved and Tehran appears openly or surreptitiously on its way to gaining a weapons capability, Obama's hopes of getting consensus on major reductions in the American arsenal will be shattered. As critics of his plans often note, the hardest part of reducing the American nuclear arsenal comes when the country is down to under one thousand deployed weapons. Then the United States faces the tyranny of small numbers. It would have an arsenal small enough that China, India, and Pakistan could aspire to match its size. And as soon as numerical superiority is lost, the opposition to Obama's goal—already virulent among some conservatives—will grow more forceful.

Obama and his team have anticipated this opposition, but in the first term they have avoided the hardest steps. They have not pressed the Pakistanis to stop expanding their stockpile. They have not pressed the Israelis to talk openly about their arsenal, or to address the obvious concern that it is going to be hard to get everyone else in the Middle East to talk about keeping the region nuclear-free if Israel does not acknowledge its one hundred or so weapons. In Asia, the Chinese and Indians, locked in a missile and nuclear race of their own, have to join the process. Yet the president never broached those subjects, at least in public. He may have let too much time pass: all those programs are racing forward.

For the next few years, all those questions may be overshadowed by the showdown with Tehran. When Obama declared that a nuclear Iran could not be contained, he appeared to be committing himself to military action if negotiations failed. He chose his words carefully. "They debated how to word this for quite some time," one witness to the conversation told me. "He rejected several other formulations. And, of course, he left some ambiguity, to keep the Iranians guessing."

In fact, one central issue hung in the air: while the president said an Iran with a nuclear weapon could not be contained, the more likely scenario over the next few years is an Iran that is simply nuclear-capable—capable of building a weapon but careful enough to stay one step short of doing so. That may well have been Iran's game plan all along—to become a "virtual" nuclear state able to remain just barely within the Nuclear Nonproliferaton Treaty. As one of Obama's top advisers said, "This is why the issue of 'Have Iran's leaders made a decision?' isn't the right question. They could be *avoiding* a decision."

Obama has never said whether a nuclear-capable Iran could be contained. Nor has anyone defined how close to a bomb is too close. For example, it is possible to imagine a deal in which the West agrees to allow Iran limited enrichment of uranium, at reactor-grade levels, with around-the-clock inspection. (Going into the negotiations, the United States said Iran must give up all of its

20-percent-enriched uranium, because it was simply too close to bomb-grade.) It all comes down to confidence—confidence that if Iran raced for a bomb, we would know. Before he left Washington, Defense Secretary Robert Gates had his doubts. "If their policy is to go to the threshold but not assemble a nuclear weapon, how do you tell that they have not assembled?" he asked. "I don't actually know how you would verify that."

Iran's record of nuclear hide-and-seek does not bode well for a strategy that relies on knowing when the country has taken the last step. But that may be the only choice. In the end, the decisions in Jerusalem and Washington and Tehran about how this ends—in negotiation or war—depend on how they define what, exactly, a nuclear-capable Iran looks like.

PART III
DRONES AND CYBER

THE REMOTE-CONTROL WAR

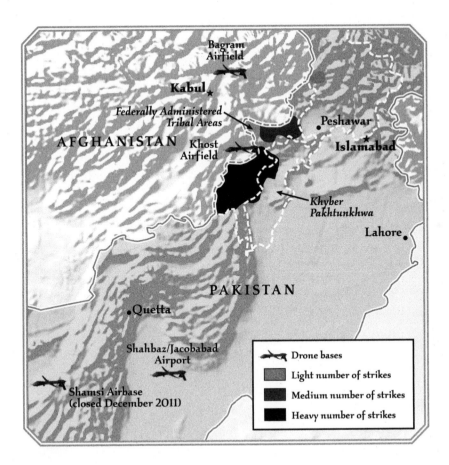

Chapter 10

The Dark Side of the Light Footprint

Barack Obama was not the first president to use drones to hunt down terrorists. Nor was he the first to employ cyberweapons to slow a nuclear program. As part of the post-9/11 search for new tools that would maximize the United States' technological advantage, George W. Bush launched the first drone attacks in hostile territory where American troops were denied access, and the first cyberattacks to undermine the ambitions of outlier states seeking the world's most powerful weapons.

Yet President Obama will go down in history as the man who dramatically expanded the use of those new weapons. Quietly, he is attempting to fit them into a new concept of how the United States can ensure its military predominance around the globe without resorting to the lengthy, expensive, and unpopular wars and occupations that dominated the past decade. They are the perfect tools for an age of austerity—far cheaper than landing troops in remote deserts and mountains, and often more precise. Obama's aides, when persuaded to talk about the subject, are the first to volunteer that these new tools are exactly that—*tools,* useful in some situations, useless in others.

"These are the keys to a 'light-footprint strategy,' and who wouldn't want a light footprint after the past ten years?" one senior American intelligence official who has been instrumental in making use of both weapons said to me early in 2012, as the late-winter sun streamed through his office. "What's different about this era? We have a keener awareness than ever of what it costs, in blood and treasure, to go into a country on the ground, and how difficult it is to extract yourself once you are there.

"But there are two big ways we can make mistakes," he added. "One is to forget that sometimes a light footprint can cost you more in the long run than going into a place with a much more decisive force—that was the lesson of Afghanistan. And the second is to fall in love with a whiz-bang new technology, because it's easy to justify relying on it more and more. And that's when a tactical weapon can begin defining your strategy."

In fact, the expansion of drone and cyber technology has dramatically transformed Obama's strategy in ways that few—perhaps including Obama himself—expected when he was elected president. Without the use of drones, Obama and his aides are convinced, al-Qaeda would not be near strategic defeat in Pakistan. Without the development of cyberweapons, they believe, Iran would be years closer to the capability to build an atomic bomb. Taken together with the greater reliance on Special Operations Forces—not just for the bin Laden operation but for the ten to fifteen raids they now run every night—these new weapons dramatically expanded the president's ability to wage nonstop, low-level conflict, something just short of war, every day of the year.

At this writing the Obama administration has ordered roughly 265 covert drone strikes, compared to just over 40 for George W. Bush's entire administration (when, to be fair, drones were in short supply).[1] The overwhelming majority of those attacks have taken place in North and South Waziristan, the tribal districts that have been a safe haven for both al-Qaeda and the Taliban.

Obama's embrace of drone technology—of remote, targeted killing with a technology that puts American forces at virtually no risk—surprised many of his supporters. They had focused during the campaign on his talk of hope and change, and missed his endorsement of drones, just as they missed his vow to step up the American commitment to Afghanistan.

Until recently, his administration was loath to discuss the logic under which the president was using drones to conduct a nearly constant, clandestine conflict. Not until it was forced to lay out a rationale—partly because Pakistan threatened to revoke its permission to use drones over its territory, and partly because a drone was used to kill an American citizen who had become a key member of al-Qaeda—did Obama's team begin to provide a public explanation for relying so heavily on armed drones.

It is a question Obama himself has clearly debated. Talk to people who have sat in the Situation Room as the former law professor grappled with these decisions, and they describe a thorough, probing examination of the tradeoffs. They portray Obama as certain that the growing precision of the drones means America does not have to put Special Operations Forces into no-go zones in Pakistan and Yemen, and hopeful that cyberweapons can forestall a shooting war with Iran.

But rather than explain his thinking in public, Obama has left the matter for others to argue about, and has often hidden behind the secrecy surrounding both programs. In doing so, he has left a hole in the middle of the Obama Doctrine and lost an opportunity to explain why America acts the way it does around the globe.

What is the difference—legally and morally—between a sticky bomb the Israelis place on the side of an Iranian scientist's car and a Hellfire missile the United States launches at a car in Yemen from thirty thousand feet in the air? How is one an "assassination"—condemned by the United States—and the other an "insurgent strike"? What is the difference between attacking a country's weapons-making machinery through a laptop computer or through bunker-busters? What happens when other states catch up with American technology—some already have—and turn these weapons on targets inside the United States or American troops abroad, arguing that it was Washington that set the precedent for their use? These are all questions the Obama team discusses chiefly in classified briefings, not public debates.

And as the White House gets more comfortable with the technology—because it mixes, in the words of one of Obama's national security aides, "precision, economy, and deniability"—what are the implications of relying on them so frequently as a permanent expression of American power?

This is hardly the first time the US government has faced these kinds of questions. At the Air and Space Museum on the Mall in Washington, every day tourists take their kids to watch silent movies of the Wright Brothers showing off the airplane to Army generals on a muddy field near the Capitol. Walk across the street to the lobby of the Energy Department, and there are sketches on display of the first atomic bombs—exactly the kind of first-generation bombs that we now worry are all too easy for terror groups to fabricate.

It took years to think through how to use these weapons, and most of the judgments were made on the fly: Would Gen. Douglas MacArthur be granted the permission he so desperately wanted to use nuclear weapons against the Chinese during the Korean War? (President Truman said no, but the very fact that it was considered sped China's decision to get a bomb of its own in the '60s, followed by North Korea four decades later.) Would the United States make good on its vow to use small, tactical nuclear weapons, if necessary, to stop any Soviet invasion across the Fulda Gap northeast of Frankfurt? (Probably yes, though fortunately the proposition was never tested.) Could an American threat to conduct preemptive cyberattacks against a country whose programmers are getting ready to mess with America's banking systems or electric power generators be credible? Maybe—but it requires a rethinking of deterrence.

All analogies have their flaws, and these are no exceptions. Drones can monitor their target for hours before they hit with deadly precision, making them far more accurate than a weapon dropped by a B-2 bomber. Cyberattacks, unlike nuclear missiles, are so stealthy that they offer the opportunity to wreak damage that may take an adversary months to detect and years to repair. In the case of drones, both Obama and his officials have been forced to speak out in recent times to explain at least in general terms both their strategy and their legal rationale. It's a compelling case, summarized by Ben Rhodes, the president's adviser and speechwriter, as "the use of force in the most precise way possible to deal with direct threats to the United States."

But in the case of offensive cyberweapons, the White House has said almost nothing. The administration has only recently acknowledged that the country is now spending hundreds of millions of dollars every year developing, refining, and—in the case of Iran—employing those weapons. It has said almost nothing about a strategic doctrine for using them. Instead, when the subject of cyber comes up, Obama and his advisers almost always turn the conversation to cyber *defense*—how to harden and protect America's power grid, its banking system, and the rest of its critical infrastructure. But if history is any guide, eventually it will be in America's own interest to explain its offensive capability, if for no other reason than because the Cold War taught us that a strong offense is the critical element of a good defense.

EXACTLY A MONTH after the siege of the American embassy in Kabul—an attack launched by the Haqqani network—the CIA had some of its biggest successes in the history of the drone wars in Pakistan. Over the course of forty-eight hours, starting October 13, 2011, it wiped out four of the most-wanted insurgents on the CIA hit list.

The dead included Janbaz Zadran, a subcommander for the Haqqani network who, the CIA contends, had planned numerous attacks on coalition forces. That same day another drone strike got Ahmed Sayfullah, an al-Qaeda paramilitary commander who was the son of the famous "Blind Sheik," Omar Abdel-Rahman, now serving a life sentence in North Carolina for conspiracy charges that grew out of the 1993 bombing of the World Trade Center—the predecessor attack to 9/11. The next day drones struck two al-Qaeda planners: Abu Miqdad al-Masri and Abd al-Rahman al-Yemeni. In the control rooms at the CIA's headquarters in Langley, Virginia, where many of the drones are piloted by remote control, there were cheers all around; no one could remember another time, one official recalled, "where we hit so many in so short a time. For a while, we were running out of targets."

Although drones—technically Unmanned Aerial Vehicles, or UAVs—come in many shapes and sizes, it is the ominous-sounding Predator and its far larger cousin, the Reaper, that have received the most attention. The Predator, a twenty-seven-foot-long misshapen plane, can spend a full day in the air, so high it cannot be seen.[2] The Reaper, a larger, more powerful, and deadlier version of the Predator, can fly up to 50,000 feet.[3] They are outfitted with cameras and radar that allow them to spy on suspicious groups and home in on targets.[4] While the Predator is armed with two laser-guided Hellfire missiles, the Reaper carries four, and two 500-pound "smart" bombs that guide their way to a target.[5] Apart from the strange beelike sound permeating the air from the drones flying high above, there is little warning for the sudden explosion as a missile or bomb launched from the drone reaches its unfortunate victim, leaving behind only scattered body parts.

The drones fly out of bases dispersed throughout the world, but are heavily concentrated in Afghanistan, where they are used against al-Qaeda and the Taliban—and regularly fly over the border into Pakistan. (A longtime base inside Pakistan withered after the bin Laden raid and was closed in November 2011, after the border incident that killed twenty-four Pakistani soldiers in a mistaken

American strike.) In Djibouti, the Seychelles, and Ethiopia, other bases are used to run drones over Somalia and Yemen, in pursuit of al-Qaeda affiliates.[6] Some of the bases are little more than desolate airstrips that have been upgraded by the CIA and the Air Force.[7] American mechanics and ground crews tend to the drones at the bases, but the pilots are far away, operating the Predators and Reapers with joysticks while viewing live images beamed back from the drones' sophisticated camera systems.[8]

Today the Air Force has more drone pilots in training than pilots for fighters and bombers combined, a testament to how quickly the culture of the Air Force has changed. A decade ago, drone pilots were regarded as the Air Force's geeks, and flying a Predator from a cubicle was no route to battle decorations. Today the drone pilots hunker down wearing flight suits at Air Force bases from the Nevada desert to the Virginia coast, while their counterparts at the CIA operate their fleet of drones separately.[9] All told, at least sixty military and CIA bases, including the bases from which pilots operate upwards of four hundred Predators and Reapers, make up the vast expanse of the drone program.[10] And a decade ago, almost none of that existed.

The effort and the infrastructure of the drone campaign have become so sprawling that the official refusal to discuss the subject has become ludicrous—and has begun to hurt Obama's own arguments about why this is a preferable way to hunt down terrorists with minimal casualties. The elimination of those four al-Qaeda and Haqqani leaders was apparently accomplished with no civilian casualties, yet the precision of the operations was never announced. And because word of the strikes leaks out piecemeal from the tribal areas, few outside the US government have a sense of how successful the program is or the degree to which civilian casualties have been reduced. The New America Foundation, which maintains a database of drone strikes in Pakistan, estimates that approximately 17 percent of all fatalities from drone strikes hit civilians or others who could not reasonably be called militants.[11]

That is a very different story from the one that John Brennan, Obama's counterterrorism chief, told in June 2011 when he said that for the previous year "there hasn't been a single collateral death because of the exceptional proficiency, precision of the capabilities we have been able to develop."[12] Brennan later backtracked, saying there had not been "credible evidence of collateral deaths." It is hard to believe that no civilians have been killed, and Brennan's argument may not be of much solace to anyone living upstairs or downstairs from the room where a terror suspect was standing when the Hellfire missile arrived.

Yet it seems clear the civilian casualties have now dropped dramatically, thanks to more precision weaponry and greater care—and the casualties are far lower than if conventional bombs were dropped on suspected al-Qaeda sanctuaries. "Every time I've looked into a report of numerous civilian deaths, it tracked back to a Pakistani F-16 strike, or something similar," one senior intelligence official told me. But the United States cannot explain its strategy. That silence is part of the unspoken deal with Pakistan, which wants to hide its episodic participation in the drone program because of fear of what its cooperation with the United States would look like to the Pakistani public. And if a strike goes bad and civilians are killed, the Pakistani government can deny it ever knew about it.

No one is more frustrated by this silence than American diplomats in Islamabad. They argue—on background, of course, because they are taking on the White House—that Obama's refusal to move at least some of the program out into the open is making it impossible to answer critics of the strikes who appear on Pakistani television several nights a week, charging that a strike has killed children or other civilians. Oftentimes, the diplomats tell me, those charges are just wrong. "We are doing ourselves a disservice," one senior American diplomat said to me. The secrecy prevents Americans from explaining who was hit, why they were on the list, and whether there was any collateral damage—and to admit to mistakes when they happen. The result is that the Taliban wins the propaganda war, fueling the argument inside Pakistan that culminated in the April 2012 vote in the Pakistani parliament to ban all drone strikes.

Clearly the limits of talking about drones are frustrating for Obama as well. Early in 2012, at an election event, the president joined the high-tech equivalent of a Town Hall meeting. He sat down for a Google+ "Hangout," a question-and-answer session with six young inquisitors who submitted questions on the White House's YouTube page.

The questions were wide ranging, covering the economy, jobs, and the wars. As always, Obama appeared relaxed in this setting, playfully trading jokes with the participants as he was served up a mix of largely earnest and predictable queries. Then in a taped question played for Obama to answer, a young questioner, referring to the civilian toll from the drone strikes, asked Obama—politely—to explain why the program helps the country, and whether the strikes are worth it.

By the rules Obama himself set, he was supposed to give a bland recitation of American combat rules, without ever acknowledging that the CIA uses drones to mount attacks. Instead, Obama threw the playbook aside and rejected the premise of the question—that drones caused high civilian casualties—and then launched into a broad defense of the program.

"I want to make sure that people understand, actually, drones have not caused a huge number of civilian casualties," he argued. "For the most part they have been very precise precision strikes against al-Qaeda and their affiliates. And we are very careful in terms of how it's been applied. . . . This is a targeted, focused effort at people who are on a list of active terrorists."

But Obama didn't leave it at that. He continued to defend the program, answering a question that was not asked. "It is important for everybody to understand that this thing is kept on a very tight leash. It's not a bunch of folks in a room somewhere just making decisions, and it is also part and parcel of our overall authority when it comes to battling al-Qaeda."[13]

His answer left White House aides shaking their heads; the next day they would return to stock answers, refusing to utter the word "drones" while seeking to explain the president's comments. (It must have been an instinctual response. As one of Obama's top intelligence officials put it to me later, "When the president decides to say it, it's suddenly declassified.")

What Obama had done, in non-legalese, was summarize the administration's best case—and there is a compelling case to be made. It should have been no surprise that he would turn to the use of force: when accepting his Nobel Peace Prize, he had declared that there will be times when nations "will find the use of force not only necessary but morally justified."[14]

Hunting terrorists who had struck American forces, and were planning to do so again, would seem to fit that definition. By all accounts, the program does operate on what Obama called a "tight leash," though the rules of engagement themselves have never been made clear to the outside world. What was surprising about Obama's answer was his embrace—without quite using the word— of a modified version of Bush's preemption doctrine.

Not preemption against a state, which was the logic of the Iraq invasion, though the reasoning was based on flawed evidence. Obama's preemption argument was significantly different. He wasn't making the case for an invasion or multibillion-dollar occupation. But he was making the case for narrow, preemptive strikes against terrorists who had struck before or who, intelligence showed, were suspected of planning attacks. As in the case of Iraq, the logic is only as good as the evidence—which is another reason the administration needs to be clearer about how it makes these life-and-death decisions.

So when Obama spoke of a "targeted, focused effort at people who are on a list of active terrorists," he was venturing into new territory. He also seemed to be making a case for targeted assassination, from thirty thousand feet. He did not use that phrase, of course. But it is essentially assassination, because the linkage to the attacks of September 11, 2001, more than a decade ago, has been strained by the passage of time. And looking back, it's hard to say exactly when the old rules suddenly no longer applied.

More than thirty-five years ago, the Church Committee, named for Sen. Frank Church of Idaho, had tilled similar ground when it was charged with investigating CIA abuses and plots to kill foreign leaders. It condemned assassinations as an instrument of American policy. Church's findings spurred many changes, including President Gerald Ford's executive order prohibiting assassinations.

That order remains in force today.[15] And so does Washington's policy of condemning the use of assassination as a political tool. In January 2012, Secretary Clinton took the unusual step of denouncing the sticky-bomb killing of Mostafa Ahmadi Roshan, a nuclear scientist at the Natanz facility in Iran. "I want to categorically deny any United States involvement in any kind of act of violence inside Iran," she said.[16] Intelligence and military officials insisted to me during interviews that the United States was very careful, in its dealings with Israel, to avoid providing information about Iranian scientists that would aid any targeted assassination plan. But they also admitted Israel hardly needed the help.

Obama's critics make a compelling case that it is something akin to legal sophistry to contend the drones are not simply another form of targeted assassination.[17] The question that Obama and his national security and legal team have danced around over the past three years comes down to this: What makes drone strikes different? Why is launching from high over the skies of Pakistan or Yemen or Somalia—aimed at a specific individual—different from taking out

Castro with an exploding cigar (one of the CIA's wilder, but never-executed strikes from fifty years ago) or a nuclear scientist on his way to the office to design a next-generation Iranian centrifuge?

The question is not only a legal one, however. It goes to America's image, something Obama promised to fix. Like the tank and the atomic bomb in past eras, the drone is now a permanent part of the nation's arsenal. It is also, as my former colleague David Rohde has written, "a potent, unnerving symbol of unchecked American power."[18]

Rohde saw this from both sides. He covered the wars in Afghanistan and Pakistan, and emerged, as I have, with a strong belief that drone technology is largely responsible for the success against al-Qaeda. When Obama came to office, it was hard to imagine that only three years into his presidency, not only would bin Laden be dead, but the fabric of his network would be torn to ribbons. When Rohde was kidnapped by the Taliban in 2008, an anguish that went on for seven months, he frequently heard the sound of American drones circling overhead at the camp where he was captive. He got a sense of the dread they created—not only among the insurgents, which is fine, but among villagers caught in the crosshairs, who suffer nightmares that the missile aiming for an al-Qaeda fighter in their midst might also take out their kids.

It is a subject I have discussed at length with many different officials inside the government—from policymakers to intelligence officials to the lawyers who work on the elaborate legal rationales for what can be struck, and what cannot. And in the administration's own deliberations on the policy, you can detect a distinct unease, because they know that while the weapon is far more accurate than it once was, they have become far more dependent on it—some say addicted to it—than ever before.

"Overdependent, in my mind," one current official involved in the debate said to me late in 2011. "Let's face it: These days, it's our only way into Pakistan. We can't put Special Forces on the ground—it was hard before the bin Laden raid, and it's just about impossible now." Impossible because the Pakistanis have thrown out most of the American trainers who helped Pakistani forces focus on insurgents, and Pakistan has denied visas for many CIA operatives. So, as the official said, "The only option, when you have actionable intelligence, is to send in a Predator and conduct the strike as accurately as you can. I think that's wise policy." But he also acknowledged that "it's hard to distinguish this, in a practical sense, from targeted assassination."

By early 2010—a year after Obama had ordered a major increase in the pace of drone strikes in Pakistan, and as the success of that program in eliminating al-Qaeda's middle management was becoming clear—the lawyers were given the job of coming up with an acceptable public justification for the strategy. The task fell to Harold Koh, the jovial liberal former dean of Yale Law School who was now the State Department's top lawyer. If the administration was going to have a prayer of convincing Obama's liberal base that the drone program had a justifiable legal basis, Koh was the man to make the argument. His impassioned writings and speeches while still at Yale made him one of the left's intellectual heroes, and one of their favorites for a Supreme Court appointment someday.

It was an assignment that Koh welcomed. "Almost as soon as I came in I raised the issue about why we hadn't clarified what our standards are," Koh told me one day in his State Department office. For weeks, Koh met with his counterparts from other government agencies to hash out the legal basis for targeted killings using drones, including the case for targeting US citizens. As one might expect, the discussion got pretty abstruse.

There was no question that drones were legal in Afghanistan; that was an internationally recognized armed conflict, and drones were like any other weapon—permissible as long as care was taken to avoid civilian casualties. Neither was there much argument within the administration that the United States could go after high-level al-Qaeda members in Pakistan, the headquarters of al-Qaeda itself, under the right to self-defense and the 2001 Authorization for Use of Military Force, which was passed overwhelmingly by Congress in the days just after the September 11 attacks. But what about low-level foot soldiers who were not plotting against the United States but wanted to control some piece of ungoverned land in Somalia or Yemen? The CIA, naturally, wanted the maximum latitude to go after everyone, everywhere. So did John Brennan, the White House counterterrorism adviser who pressed the case for the judicious use of drones anyplace where al-Qaeda and its associates travel. His view carried considerable weight, because it was often Brennan who made the final call on authorizing specific drone strikes, from his cramped office in the basement of the West Wing.

Koh picked the most rarified of audiences to make his case—a meeting in March 2010 of the American Society of International Law. While Koh started off making the case that part of his job was to act as the "conscience" of the administration, to assure that the United States was "following universal standards, not double standards," it was hardly the kind of audience that would get into an impassioned argument about the morality of a weapon of war. This was an audience focused on the narrowest of legal arguments. And Koh gave them exactly that, putting drone strikes—he never used the "D-word," of course—into the context of a strategy of "smart power" that makes "intelligent use of all means at our disposal."

Koh made the case that "US targeting practices, including legal operations conducted with unmanned aerial vehicles, comply with all applicable law, including the laws of war." Al-Qaeda, he said, "has not abandoned its intent to attack the United States, and indeed continues to attack us." That reality, he argued, meant it was wrong to insist that the United States provide suspected terrorists "with legal process" before using lethal force, from the ground or from the air.[19]

Koh was hinting at the core argument the Obama administration has settled on to justify the strikes—one that distinguishes between "lawful extrajudicial killing" and "unlawful extrajudicial killing." A "lawful" extrajudicial killing, in this construct, is the result of a careful study to determine that the target is an active combatant who is fighting American forces or planning attacks. An "unlawful" killing takes place without the benefit of such careful determinations. Of course, these judgments are made by the US government, with no hearings and no opportunity for the person in the drone's gunsights to present exculpatory evidence.

To Koh's mind, there was one other argument: all war involves killing, and all countries make horrific mistakes when fighting. But Koh makes a compelling case that while you can make mistakes with drones, you can make bigger mistakes with big bombers, which take out whole neighborhoods. The drone is a precision instrument. A B-2 pilot has no idea who he is hitting; a drone pilot should know exactly who he is targeting.

Koh returned to this theme when I asked him about the concern that a PlayStation mentality inevitably creeps into the minds of drone operators, who are sitting thousands of miles away from their targets and can come to view what they see on their computer screens as just another videogame.

"I actually talked to operators, and they were so offended by this," Koh recalled. "One operator told me, 'I used to drop bombs from a flying airplane. I could not see the faces of the people. . . . I am much, much more aware of the human concerns in these situations." In fact, drone pilots—whose numbers are burgeoning—have told me that they feel they almost know too much about their targets. They watch them for days before a strike and have often seen them play with their children or drop them at school. "It freaks you out," one former drone operator said. "You feel less like a pilot than a sniper."

The Obama review of the policy over how to use drones also included another big caveat: the United States could not assert a right to use drones to kill just anywhere. A country must expressly invite the United States to use drones to strike targets inside its territory—which was the case in Pakistan until the traumas of 2011 led to demands that the strikes cease—or they must be employed in a country that is "unwilling or unable to suppress the threat," in the words of one official who is involved in the program. (These rules apply only to armed drones, of course; as the drone crash in Iran showed, surveillance drones, the lower-altitude equivalent of the old U-2 spy planes of Cold War lore, go many places where they are not invited.)

A senior intelligence officer who is responsible for overseeing the program insists that the United States sticks to those rules. "If a country has a functioning government, we use them only with the permission of the host country," he said when I pressed for details on how the day-to-day, strike-or-no-strike decisions are made. "If they don't want it, we usually don't do it," he said, unless "it was an urgent issue of force protection."

"But if there is no functioning government . . ." His voice trailed off, and it was clear that the rest of the sentence would have been along the lines of "we do what we have to do." And that is exactly what the United States has done in Somalia, where there has never been a functioning government, at least in a Western sense. And it may one day be the excuse for further action in Pakistan.

In practice, of course, the delicate dance between Washington and leaders around the world about the use of drones is never quite as neat—or the permissions as clear-cut—as one might think if one were to listen to American officials. The State Department cables published through WikiLeaks gave a more accurate picture of the strange give-and-take over using these weapons. In January 2008, it was Gen. Ashraf Kayani, the Pakistani Army chief of staff, who asked a visiting American admiral, William J. Fallon, for "continuous Predator coverage" over Waziristan, the home of al-Qaeda. Fallon couldn't offer it—he didn't have that many drones available, he said.[20]

Six months later it was the Pakistani prime minister, Yousuf Raza Gilani, who was overriding objections from his own interior minister about Predator attacks in the tribal areas against militants, telling the American ambassador, Anne Patterson, "I don't care if they do it as long as they get the right people."[21] Of course, as soon as the cables became public, and certainly after the bin Laden operation, many of those same Pakistani officials demanded a halt to all Predator strikes inside their country, declaring them an unconscionable violation of the country's sovereignty.

The same was true in Yemen, the broken nation that was a sideshow in American policy until a young Nigerian who had been trained and equipped on Yemeni soil attempted to blow up an airliner approaching Detroit by igniting a bomb in his underwear— leading only to some pretty severe and painful burns. Then President Ali Abdullah Saleh decided the moment was ripe to sell Washington what it most needed: access to his country for drone operations.

Meeting with Gen. David Petraeus, now the head of the CIA, Saleh said the Americans could use all kinds of weapons against al-Qaeda camps in the country, as long as he could claim credit for doing the strikes himself, with Yemeni aircraft. "We'll continue saying the bombs are ours, not yours," Saleh said. Then Saleh's deputy prime minister joked that he had just come back from the parliament, where he had lied about the real source of the strikes.[22] This cover story, while slim, was useful to both sides. The Americans could keep running strikes—from Predators and from piloted aircraft. And Saleh could continue his own local battles, although a deal was eventually brokered in 2012 to force him out of office, in return for giving him medical treatment in the United States.

THE LEGAL ARGUMENTS for pursuing terrorists around the globe with Predators will never satisfy critics who see this all as a bizarre, typically American justification for a huge expansion of presidential power—essentially, the power to order executions. But the bigger risk of the current drone strategy is a geopolitical one. As the WikiLeaks cables make clear, much of the collateral damage from overusing drones comes in the form of political backlash against the United States. Every strike creates more and more public anger. America's stony silence only keeps the wound open.

The most convincing case for ending the destructive secrecy is made by Adm. Dennis Blair, the former director of national intelligence, who never fit well in the tight-knit world of Obama's administration, and was fired in May 2010, only sixteen months into the job. "Covert action that goes on for years doesn't generally stay covert," Blair told me in 2011. If the program was put in the hands of the military, the criteria for strikes could be published, along with information about who makes these life-and-death decisions. The administration could be held to account if it made mistakes. Blair has also argued for "jointly controlled drone strikes" with Pakistani participation.[23] He is right about the need to make the program far more public. But joint operations with the Pakistanis, particularly in the current political climate, seem bound to fail—even in better times, the ISI was notifying the targets that it was a good time to take that long-delayed holiday.

THE ADMINISTRATION'S PENCHANT for secrecy on the drone program has gotten it in trouble on another front: its unwillingness to produce a particular secret legal memorandum, first revealed by my colleague Charlie Savage, making the case for killing a US citizen abroad.

The citizen at the center of it all was Anwar al-Awlaki, a radical cleric with an unusual pedigree: born in New Mexico, he attended school in America and later became the most articulate English-speaking spokesman for al-Qaeda. Killing foreign combatants from afar was one thing, but the Justice Department knew it would need a better legal rationale for taking out Awlaki. After all, while Koh argued that terrorists on the battlefield don't merit due process, it is a much harder case to say the government can target, and execute, a US citizen.

The core of the memo was that Awlaki could be legally assassinated if he posed an imminent threat of attack on the United States, if it was not possible to capture him, and if he had willingly become a combatant on the wrong side of the war.[24] The memo was written sometime in 2010; by that summer, Leon Panetta, then still running the CIA, made it clear that if Awlaki was found, no one would hesitate to finish him off. Awlaki eventually ended up on the wrong end of a Hellfire missile in September 2011, along with another American, Samir Khan, who produced a magazine for al-Qaeda in the Arabian Peninsula.

As of this writing, the administration has refused to fully reveal whatever logic lies in the secret memo beyond what officials like Koh or the attorney general, Eric Holder, have said in their speeches. Of course, the secrecy only whets the appetites of many—including those in Congress—who want to read it. Sen. Patrick Leahy of Vermont told Holder at a hearing on Capitol Hill that he knew the release of the memorandum was "a matter of some debate within the administration." There was knowing laughter in the hearing room, and Holder merely replied, "That would be true."[25]

The laughter reflected the fact, as Holder knew well, that these legal justifications cannot remain secret for long. No American president is going to be given the unchecked power to kill without some more public airing of the rules of engagement. If the use of drones is going to be preserved as a major weapon in America's arsenal, the weapon will have to be employed selectively—and each time a public case will have to be made for why it was necessary.

◆

THE SENATORS, INVITED by the White House, filed into a secure briefing room on Capitol Hill in March 2012 for a demonstration that was designed to scare the hell out of them.

For roughly half an hour, on screens set up in the room, the senators got a vivid demonstration of what it might look like if a dedicated hacker—or enemy state—decided to turn off the lights in New York City.

In the simulation, the attack was hardly the most sophisticated. A worker for the power utility in New York received an e-mail from what appeared to be a trusted friend. From his office computer, he clicked on a link. It was a classic "spear phishing" attack, designed to dupe an authorized user into letting the cyber invaders into the computer systems that run New York's electric grid. It was not long before a few electrical circuits were tripped, then a few more, and eventually the entire city was plunged into darkness. Naturally, there was a heat wave on, so it took hours for the utility operators to realize this was not an ordinary blackout—and no one could figure out where the trouble had originated, the first step to restoring power. Temperatures rose, and so did tempers. Later, presumably, might come panic, looting, chaos, and deaths.

The purpose of the demonstration was nakedly political: the White House was pressing Congress to move ahead with a bill, long delayed, that would require the companies that operate the nation's critical infrastructure—power stations, telecommunications networks, financial markets—to bend to national standards, and national supervision, to secure their networks. Among those who came to make the case at the demonstration were Gen. Keith Alexander, who runs the National Security Agency and the new US Cyber Command, and President Obama's counterterrorism chief, John Brennan.

Alexander is one of the most important figures in Washington that no one ever heard of. His dual post over the NSA—which scoops up the transmissions of voice and data traffic around the world—and over the new Cyber Command means that he plays a critical role running both America's cyber offense and its cyber defense. There is nothing quite like the Cyber Command elsewhere in the government: it is a hybrid organization run by the Pentagon and the NSA from NSA headquarters, overseeing a staff of nearly 13,000. The idea was to end the infighting over cyber in the US government and combine the capabilities of the NSA with those of the Air Force and Navy.

In short, Alexander had to run the Iran cyber invasion while warning against similar invasions at home. In the rare moments he talks in public, senators say, General Alexander is pretty soft-spoken about America's vulnerability to such attacks—perhaps for fear of inviting hostile countries or terrorists to test the quality of America's defenses. "In a classified setting like the one the other day, it's very different," one senator commented to me later. "They lay out a very different set of facts—one in which we've done a pretty good job securing our military assets, and a pretty terrible one securing the nonmilitary infrastructure that we use every day."

Corporate America has gotten that message. The attack on Google in December 2009—which took some time to trace back to China—became something of a wake-up call to Washington and to corporations across the country, who were astounded that the most technically savvy company in Silicon Valley was penetrated so thoroughly. The Chinese attackers, whose connections to the government, if any, remain a mystery, got into Gmail accounts, including those of human-rights activists and a few government officials. But a second, less discussed element of the attack also stole source code—the heart of Google's business. It was an incident that revealed, as one senior intelligence official put it to me, "how this constant barrage of attacks has become the daily battle of our times." (It also led to nasty exchanges with the Chinese, who asserted that the United States was pursuing "hegemonic domination" in cyberspace.)

The blackout demonstration in Congress was classified partly because the administration wanted to read off a list of other companies that had been attacked, including RSA, the firm that makes the small electronic devices that companies and the government issue to employees to provide a secure "tunnel" into corporate databases and e-mail. Those tunnels have stymied both governments and corporate spies, making RSA a huge target.

Of course, the kind of attack demonstrated to the senators that day, on New York's infrastructure, bore a startling resemblance to what the United States was doing to Iran with Olympic Games. And the scenario they saw that day, bringing down a power grid, is something that the intelligence community proposed to President Bush when he looked for options on Iran in 2008, and presumably is being held in reserve today. Those facts were known to a few members of the Senate Intelligence Committee who were in the room, and to General Alexander and John Brennan. But most of the senators were clueless. They assumed the United States had cyber capabilities of its own, but asked few questions about it.

Already the Pentagon spends $3.4 billion a year on cyber defense and cyber offense, though it does not break down how the money is divided between the two. The new Cyber Command at Fort Meade has a budget of only $182 million—less than a shiny new fighter jet costs. But the Pentagon is now investing heavily in new weapons that attack computer systems in real time—not over a number of months, the way the attack on Iran played out. "It's an entirely different kind of approach when you need instant results," one former official with deep knowledge of the problem noted to me. The Pentagon is seeking weapons that would disable communications and satellites, freeze bank accounts, and turn off air-defense systems, even those not connected to the Internet.

"We learned a lot from the Libya experience," one senior officer told me, referring to the brief consideration of disrupting Muammar Qaddafi's air defenses with a cyberattack before the bombing of

Benghazi and Tripoli began. "And what we learned is that we don't know how to do this effectively enough, and fast enough."

And the United States is not alone in the race. A report written for a somewhat hawkish—and occasionally alarmist—congressionally created commission on China described recently a hypothetical scenario in which cyberweapons could disrupt the refueling of American fighter jets during a conflict over Taiwan. But the company that prepared the report—Northrop Grumman—also had an interest in sweeping up contracts in one of the few growing areas of the defense budget: cyber defense.[26]

RELUCTANT AS THE White House is to discuss drones—save for that one surprise presidential defense of their use—it is absolutely allergic to talking about our cyber-offense capabilities. Obama has not even acknowledged in public that the capability exists, though he has spoken frequently about the need to harden the country's computer networks, both public and private, against outside attack.

His fear, as he told his aides during the discussion of the cyberattack on Iran, is that any American acknowledgment that it is making use of cyberweapons—even under the most careful and limited circumstances—would create a pretext for other countries, terrorists, or teenage hackers to justify their own attacks. Obama's concern is a real one. But it leaves the world wondering about the American strategy—and about the constraints under which the United States would use cyberweapons. And while the United States attempted, in 2010 and 2011, to have some quiet conversations with the Chinese about cyberweaponry and limits on their use—an effort that did not get very far—the administration has so far resisted all talk of negotiating treaties that would restrain the use of cyberweapons.[27] In part this is because the weapons are in the hands of non-state actors—groups like Anonymous or perhaps, at some point in the future, terrorists—that don't sign treaties. But partly it is because the United States still holds a commanding lead in the technology.

"The first treaty to limit nuclear testing came nearly twenty years after the invention of the bomb," one administration official said to me when I asked about the White House's reluctance to discuss such treaties. "You don't get into a negotiation like that until others have pretty much the same capability."

Of course, with no treaties, there are no clear international rules. President Obama may insist, as he did when deciding to attack Iran's nuclear facilities, that a cyberweapon must be a precision instrument, aimed, for example, at those centrifuges but not at a power grid connected to a hospital or a school. Other countries— and certainly terrorists and hackers—are unlikely to be similarly conscientious. And not even the United States has, at least publicly, ever declared where and under what circumstances it will employ cyberweapons. "You do that with drones, because you are flying into someone's sovereign territory," said one official with authority over both drone and cyber weaponry. "But there are no boundaries when it comes to cyber."

Not only are there no boundaries, it is often hard to figure out where an attack comes from. In the nuclear age, a missile launch from the Soviet Union would light up a big screen in a mountain in Colorado. If there was an equivalent way to show where a cyberattack was coming from, the data would still not be able to tell the whole story with certainty. An attack launched from China could well be routed through a computer server in Romania, then bounced through Canada on the way to its target in the United States. It could take weeks or months to figure out where such a "false flag" attack actually originated. (This is why military planners don't talk about battlefields when it comes to cyberwar. They use the term "battlespace.")

All this makes retaliation pretty complicated. "The question," said Harold Koh, when he spoke out in defense of the administration's drones policy, "is if someone sitting in a room in one country types something into a keyboard and something happens elsewhere, is it subject to the laws of armed conflict?"

Then he half-answered his own question: "To the extent that we have articulated principles, we have made it clear that we think that the laws of armed conflict in fact apply to cyber operations in war and we have to do a translation exercise of how they apply," he told me. "But this translation exercise is really at a nascent stage."

On a Monday morning in January 2010, the top leadership of the Pentagon gathered to figure out that "translation exercise." The nation's senior commanders participated in a simulation of how they might respond to a sophisticated cyberattack—one far more complex than the one played out for the members of the Senate two years later. In the Pentagon's war game, a series of coordinated attacks was aimed at paralyzing America's power grids, its communications systems, and its financial networks.[28]

The results were dispiriting. The enemy had all the advantages: stealth, anonymity, and unpredictability. No one could pinpoint where the attack came from, so deterring a follow-on attack was nearly impossible. What's more, the military commanders noted that they lacked the legal authority to respond—especially because it was never clear if the attack was an act of vandalism, an attempt at commercial theft, or a state-sponsored effort to cripple the United States, perhaps as a prelude to a conventional war.

The simulation underscored how cyber offense has outpaced the search for a deterrent, something roughly equivalent to the Cold War–era concept of mutually assured destruction—if you take New York, I take Moscow. In fact, for years now an intense debate has broken out, inside the government and beyond, about what kind of deterrent the United States could construct. "It has to be credible," Joseph Nye, the Harvard professor and strategist, noted to me in the spring of 2012. "If an attack from China gets inside the American government's computer systems, we're not likely to turn off the lights in Beijing, or wipe out their command-and-control systems," he said. He compares this moment to the early 1950s, after the Soviets got the bomb. American strategists were groping for a way to create what Nye calls "a high cost" for an attacker.

Nye argues that one innovative possibility is to name and shame the country where the attack originated. The price could be higher than it sounds: a country that engages in such attacks might be regarded as a risky place to do business, to invest, to keep one's money. But making that kind of subtle deterrence work requires a much better ability to attribute an attack to a specific nation, and maybe to specific actors inside that nation. Secretary Clinton walked to the edge of doing that after the Google attacks. But she did not go the whole way because the United States could not establish a public case against who in China was responsible. "It's the nature of these attacks that the forensics are difficult," one senior administration official said at the time.

What the war game in 2010 established was that the old concept of defense, a "firewall" against attacks, is already outmoded. William Lynn III, the former deputy secretary of defense, who oversaw the simulation, said it reminded him of one of the great failed defensive concepts in history: the French effort to build an impenetrable Maginot Line ahead of World War II.

"A fortress mentality will not work in cyber," he told my colleagues and me after the war game. "We cannot retreat behind a Maginot Line of firewalls. We must also keep maneuvering."

So while the White House has said that "deterrence has been a fundamental part of the administration's cybersecurity efforts from the start," it has had a hard time deciding how to threaten retaliatory strikes. The Pentagon edged toward that kind of approach in the summer of 2011, declaring that a computer attack from a foreign nation would be considered an act of war that may result in a military response.[29] But it deliberately left unclear what the response would be. Economic sanctions? Retaliatory cyberattacks? A conventional military strike?

One of the creators of the government's offensive cyber strategy, Gen. James Cartwright, makes a compelling case that the secrecy may be working against American interests. "You can't have something that's a secret be a deterrent," he argued shortly after leaving his post as vice chairman of the Joint Chiefs of Staff. "Because if you don't know it's there, it doesn't scare you."[30]

A senior intelligence official disagreed: "Everyone who needs to know what we can do, knows," he said. "The Chinese know." And the Iranians, he added, "are probably figuring it out."

THE FUTURE OF President Obama's "light footprint" strategy is being developed these days at places redolent in American technological history, starting with the Wright-Patterson Air Force Base in Ohio. Just over a hundred years ago, in a cow pasture nearby, Orville and Wilbur Wright tested the first manned aircraft. Today Wright-Patterson is part museum—the Air Force One that took John F. Kennedy to Dallas is parked there—and part research-and-development testing ground for the future. In its "microaviary," the next generation of unmanned drones is buzzing around. They bear no resemblance to the Predator and Reaper engaging in attacks in Pakistan. Instead, they look like hawks and moths and bugs—if one of them went down in Iran, as that stealth drone did at the end of 2011, no one would notice.[31]

What is unfolding at Wright Patterson is already having an effect out in the field. Orders recently went out for a new type of drone called the Switchblade—a "kamikaze" drone that soldiers can deploy to scout and strike targets. Launched from a tube carried in a soldier's backpack, it sends a video feed back to the soldier, who can then direct it to dive at a target.[32]

It is fairly easy to imagine how these drones may remake battle-field strategy. It is a bit more difficult to imagine how cyberweapons will be mixed with traditional warfare. But it is clear that over the next few years, the American president is not going to be able to avoid discussing how the United States can use both weapons to its advantage, without violating its values. In its first three years, the Obama administration has shown ingenuity, admirable restraint, and some consistent principles in making use of these weapons. But it has done a far poorer job of explaining its thinking.

That is a lost opportunity. Precisely because drones and cyberwarfare have the potential to change the way we fight the wars of the future, the legal and moral questions raised by these weapons need to be part of the public conversation, and an international one. The world's concern is that the United States will use its technological advantage to create a new form of unilateralism. Unless properly managed, that simply invites a new form of arms race, just as President Obama attempts to undo the damage from arms races of the past.

PART IV
ARAB SPRING

THE REVOLTS, AND THE RISE OF
THE BROTHERHOOD

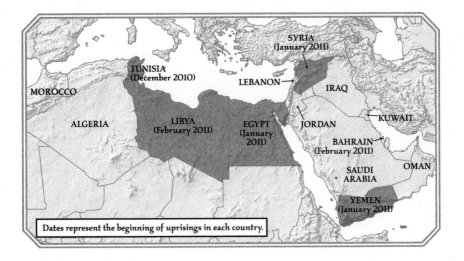

Dates represent the beginning of uprisings in each country.

Chapter 11
"You Sold Out the Revolution"

Cairo, January 25, 2012

A YEAR TO THE DAY AFTER THE EGYPTIAN PEOPLE BEGAN POURING into Tahrir Square to oust a dictator, Hosni Mubarak sat rotting in a cage, on trial for his life. But the unity that had inspired Egypt's youth—and then so many others, from unemployed college graduates to neighborhood elders to young women in *hijab*—had dissipated months before. As the foreign television networks departed and the revolution fell off the front page, Egypt was left between authoritarianism and an abyss. The popular aspirations for dignity, justice, and freedom remained. Yet out of the ruins of dictatorship, the country reverted to predictable competing factions, each one concerned with securing its own position in the new Egypt.

On the first-year anniversary, they came by the tens of thousands once again to Tahrir Square, streaming through the narrow side streets, past the burned-out, blackened hulk of Mubarak's old political party headquarters, and around the fence of the famed Egyptian Museum, now devoid of tourists. They surged into the square, the iconic heart of Cairo, some wearing T-shirts with an up-raised fist, sold in the markets weeks ahead of time to mark the first anniversary of a revolution no one saw coming.

But as they massed at the giant traffic circle, the unified shouts of "Down with Mubarak!" that had resonated across the square a year ago were already a distant memory. It did not take long for the square to mirror Egypt's new polarization, and the events that day explained a lot about why the Egyptians who lit the torch of revolution had been incapable of carrying it.

As day broke, Muslim Brotherhood volunteers took charge. Locking arms around the perimeter, they checked the IDs of people who entered, asserting control over what they hoped would be a day of great festivity. After decades of repression, they had much to celebrate: the previously banned Islamist organization had just won nearly half the seats in a new Egyptian parliament. The Muslim Brotherhood's huge soundstage, which dominated the best strategic position in Tahrir, underscored the Brothers' ascendance, drowning out competing calls of those demanding still greater change.

Mixed in among the Brotherhood loyalists was a smattering of beards belonging to the deeply conservative Salafis, who were out to show they were a force to be reckoned with, too—not just in the countryside where they got their strength but in teeming Cairo. The biggest shock of all—to the Muslim Brotherhood, to the Americans and the Israelis, and certainly to the secular Egyptians—was that the Salafis' far-right Islamist al-Nour Party had come in second in the elections with about 25 percent of the seats.[1] But as one former Mubarak adviser told me, "If you haven't held real elections in decades, you shouldn't be surprised that you get surprised."

If the Islamists were akin to a disciplined army, the liberals were the irregulars. Unlike the Muslim Brotherhood and the Salafis, the liberal bloc, more an anti-Islamist coalition than a pro–something else, had disintegrated into bickering, incompetent factions. As they straggled into Tahrir Square from a number of disparate smaller marches throughout the city, the liberals were more somber, concerned that their goals had been thwarted. They scattered across the square, armed only with tiny loudspeakers to rally the crowd, finding they were marginalized at their own anniversary. Just beneath the quasi-celebratory mood in Tahrir that day was the sense that, having broken the dam of the Mubarak dictatorship, they were now being swept away in a deluge that they could no longer control.

Something had changed. The young, largely secular Egyptians—whose brilliant organizing power through Facebook and Twitter had made this moment possible twelve months before—now realized that their revolution had blasted open the door for the emergence of a state in which the military old guard was hanging on and the rise of the Islamists. The veterans of Tahrir Square 2011 were still trying to figure out what had gone wrong. Clearly, they were skilled at tearing down autocrats. But they hadn't translated that into figuring out how to build a new country. As one student central to the movement told me at a gathering of friends in an apartment not far from the square, "We lost control." But when asked about their plan to regain it, he shrugged, and explained that the vast majority of those who had brought about the revolution were "not political," and had chosen not to run for office.

As the triumphant euphoria of revolution dimmed, Egyptians woke up to another stark reality: their transitional government was a decidedly undemocratic military council. The Supreme Council of the Armed Forces (SCAF)—a vestige of Mubarak's hated system—had taken over after Mubarak left and still controlled the country, at least for a while. Although Egyptians were grateful that the military stood with them during the revolution, a year later they were tired of being ruled by emergency laws and opaque decision-making. In the square, the liberals' chant of "Down with the Military Regime!" was accompanied by a question for their Islamist brothers and sisters: How can you celebrate when the revolution isn't over? A chant resounded in one corner of the square: "You sold out the revolution!"[2]

The military had the wisdom to stay out of the way. In fact, in the days just before the anniversary, the Supreme Council of the Armed Forces, still the closest thing Egypt had to a working government, had handed out some preemptive gifts—pardoning more than a thousand prisoners and promising to ease up on the notorious state-of-emergency laws that Mubarak had used to suppress all dissent.

The strategy seemed to work, at least temporarily. Everyone— protestors and partiers alike—showed up to make their statements, and then went home. By ten p.m., many Egyptians had turned off the news and tuned in to a local soccer match. As one American from Texas, living in a conservative neighborhood of ancient Alexandria, about three hours north of Cairo, noted the next day, "In general, everyone was more proud of what they had accomplished than distressed by what they hadn't."

The symbol of that accomplishment was Mubarak's trial, taking place behind the high walls of what used to be known as the Mubarak Police Academy. At age eighty-three, frail and resigned, Mubarak had gone from living in spectacular exile in his palace by the sea in the resort town of Sharm el-Sheikh, to what amounted to a hospital jail-cell near Cairo. Just days before the anniversary, Mubarak had been taken into the courthouse in a wheelchair as his lawyers tried to answer to charges that, in the desperate last days of his almost thirty-year rule, Mubarak had ordered the shooting of protestors. The newspaper headlines echoed the prosecution's call for the death penalty.

Mubarak wore a blank expression as he listened to his lawyer spinning out a dubious defense, in a soliloquy that the Egyptian media did not bother to report in its entirety. (Television stations had long since been barred from showing the drawn-out deliberations of Mubarak's court trial; the judge was sick of the lawyers pandering to the cameras. Instead, they aired the fresh drama of the opening sessions of parliament.) "In accordance with the constitution," Mubarak's lawyer told the court, "he is still the president until this day."[3] Whatever the legal merits of his argument, it ignored the reality that the country had moved beyond the Mubarak era.

The real question was: Moved to where?

Chapter 12
Searching for the
"Right Side of History"

Eighteen months before revolution came to Tahrir Square, Barack Obama stood in the grand auditorium at Cairo University and offered the traditional Muslim greeting, *assalaamu alaykum.* Then, in a gesture that his political advisers must have known would only fuel the "birthers" in their endless quest to impugn Obama's citizenship, he spoke of his roots in "a Kenyan family that includes generations of Muslims," and the wonder, as a young boy growing up in Jakarta, of hearing "the call of the *azaan* at the break of dawn and the fall of dusk" as the call to prayer emanated from every minaret. None of the forty-three presidents who had come before could have connected with a Muslim audience in that way. Contributing to the campaign-rally feel of the event, some in the enthusiastic crowd sporadically cried out, "I love you!"

Obama's Cairo speech was perhaps one of the most finely crafted and memorable of his first year in office, but also one of the most self-conscious. Through it, Obama came back to a two-year-old promise, from the early days of his campaign, to deliver a major policy speech in the heart of the Arab world. He used the speech to clear the air, and to declare that America was under new management.[1] He called Iraq a "war of choice"—a deadly accurate phrase that riled both George W. Bush and members of the military who balked at the suggestion that they had been pawns in an exercise in military adventurism. He reserved some of his bluntest words for Israel, and openly sympathized with the Palestinians, talking of the "daily humiliations, large and small, that come with occupation." After years of heavy-handed talk by President Bush of a "war on terror"—and, in Bush's worst choice of words, a battle against "Islamofascism"—Obama deliberately avoided using the words "terrorism" or "terrorist." Instead, he spoke in uncompromising terms about the fight against al-Qaeda and urged the Arab world to join the battle against violent extremism.

This was the honeymoon phase of a new presidency, of course, when Obama still had the glow of "hope and change" around him, and before the Arab world began questioning whether he, like presidents before him, was putting American interests ahead of their aspirations. But even then it was clear that Obama was tiptoeing around the issue that would soon captivate the region: the future of the Arab world's dictatorships. Acutely aware that he was Egyptian president Hosni Mubarak's guest, he spoke only in general terms about the need for "governments that reflect the will of the people" and that offer "the freedom to live as you choose." But he never directly addressed what was happening just outside the doors of Cairo University: the stepped-up repression of political parties that challenged Mubarak's own, the jailing of critics of the regime, the corrupt funneling of profitable businesses to Mubarak's family and inner-circle cronies.

It was a delicate balancing act, as Hillary Clinton acknowledged to me when we talked about the speech in light of the Arab Spring. "One of the reasons that the president went to Cairo was to go to a place that needed change and to do it in a way that wasn't calling out Mubarak," she said later, "but was calling out that the United States was going to be on the side of change in a hopefully responsible, sustainable way."

If he could have known that the region would soon burst apart, Obama would have given a somewhat different speech; his discussion of the need to promote democracy for the region was underwhelming. Obama rightly distinguished himself from Bush by assuring the Arab world he was not interested in imposing any particular system of governance on anyone, an important reminder after the United States tried, with limited success, to put its fingers on the scale in Baghdad and Kabul. While embracing the need for fair elections, accountability, and respect for human rights and particularly women's rights, Obama was intent on striking a nonimperialist chord. So he sidestepped the question of whether he believed a country could enjoy the benefits of full partnership with Washington while still preserving its authoritarian grip at home. There seemed to be an implicit assurance to the Mubaraks of the world: we'll applaud you for embracing change, but don't worry about paying a price for maintaining your dictatorship. (As one senior American official put it to me recently, "We deal with China every day," so any such warning to the Arab kings and dictators might seem wholly hypocritical.)

Obama concluded with a long list of pledges, including a new fund to support technological development in the region, centers for "scientific excellence," expanded exchange programs for students, and a new "corps of business volunteers to partner with counterparts in Muslim-majority countries."

He received a rousing standing ovation, but even Obama later conceded that the speech was longer on promises than on deliverables: a year later, when he asked for an assessment of how well the administration had implemented the ideas he announced in Cairo, he was, in the words of one aide, "deeply disappointed in how little got done."

WHEN REVOLUTION BROKE out a year and a half later, the White House quickly intimated to reporters that, while the CIA and most experts failed to predict even the possibility of the region erupting, the new president had, in fact, seen it coming. It sounded like the worst kind of spin, as if press aides had been told to take a surprise angle and declare that only a president who had grown up in the tumult of 1960s Indonesia would recognize the tremors. But it turns out that for Obama, that claim had more than an element of truth.

From the beginning of his term, Obama had been unhappy with the quality of the analyses he was getting about the long-term stability of the region. He suspected that the CIA assessments he received each week were biased toward straight-line projections that assumed if an authoritarian regime has been in place for a long time, odds are that it will stay in place. (Leon Panetta, in his last days as CIA director, asked for a study of why his agency so often missed evidence of when the "triggers" of political upheaval were about to be pulled. It's never been made public.) Further disappointed that little had been done to follow up on his Cairo speech, in August 2010 Obama ordered a "Presidential Study Directive" to analyze the stability of the Arab countries—friends and foes alike.

The result was an eighteen-page report, most of which remains classified to this day. The administration kept the document secret for an obvious reason: Obama didn't want Egypt's Hosni Mubarak or Saudi Arabia's King Abdullah, or his royal friends in Bahrain and Kuwait, to pick up the morning paper and read that the White House staff was actively debating how ripe their nations were for popular revolt. But that was exactly the debate that was occurring, in the weekly meetings run by Dennis Ross, who was Obama's top Mideast expert, and Samantha Power, who had written a Pulitzer Prize–winning book about the horrors of the genocide in Rwanda. According to several participants, the process was plagued by a gnawing recognition that just as it is impossible to predict when revolutions will come, it is also hard to anticipate or prevent the sectarian tensions and old-fashioned score settling that often accompany them.

The topic of Egypt's future came up frequently. "There's no

question Egypt was very much on the mind of the president," said one official who helped draft the report. "You had all the unknowns created by Egypt's succession picture—and Egypt is the anchor of the region."

At the time the report was being put together, it seemed likely that Mubarak would dig in to stay in office, at least until he could engineer a way for his son, Gamal, to succeed him. This was at a moment when Egyptian bloggers were still being thrown in jail and Mubarak was struggling to deal with the return home of Mohamed ElBaradei, the former chief of the International Atomic Energy Agency, who had become the de facto leader of a still-toothless opposition movement.[2]

The study was hardly just an academic exercise: eighteen months in office had demonstrated to Obama that his government had only begun to grapple with how to balance American strategic interests—especially with friendly dictators in critical places like Cairo and Riyadh—with the democratic values he embraced in his Cairo speech. Soon Michael McFaul, a Stanford professor and Russia expert who was directing Russia policy at the National Security Council, was pulled into the conversation: regime change was his specialty.

McFaul had spent years compiling data about what triggers regimes to fall and how the process is managed, and he started pacing many in the White House through stripped-down versions of his academic research. It turned out that even in the rarefied world of the NSC, they didn't want numbers; they wanted "historical metaphors and case studies." So he gave it to them, in a blitz of e-mails and PowerPoints. There was Russia, where engagement with the regime allowed the United States to push along democratization. Indonesia, the president's favorite example from his youth, was a country that took two decades to finally figure out democracy. There was the economic miracle of South Korea, where wealth preceded democratic change. And the Philippines, which has never fully gotten its economic act together but made a democratic transition anyway.

"That was the start of the 'Nerd Directorate,'" McFaul told me with a laugh one day in his office, shortly before he headed off to become the next American ambassador to Russia. That was the self-mocking moniker he and Ross had given the effort, which did come to resemble a graduate school class in comparative democratic revolutions, taught in the dreary conference rooms of the Old Executive Office Building.

"There are many different factors involved in the cases we have looked at: economic crises, aging authoritarians, negotiated transitions between elites," McFaul told me. "There is not one story line or a single model," he added. "There are many paths to democratic transition," but the one common thread was that "most of them are messy."[3] He argued that through "true engagement with the regime—not just, you know, closing our eyes and not just fostering regime change," the United States could find a middle path and "help to, in an evolutionary way, push things along."

The ultimate conclusion of the study that was given to Obama was startlingly obvious: whenever modest efforts toward democratization began in the Middle East and North Africa, they usually stalled. If unrest heated up, the study predicted, most regimes in the region were more likely to "opt for repression rather than reform to manage domestic dissent."

But even the president's own team underestimated how ripe the region was for change. Their study was largely about "lessons learned" from the past; it did little to prepare them for the future. In fact, the presidential study concluded that if a revolution were to occur in the Arab world, it would probably be in a place peripheral to American interests, such as Morocco—whose regime to this day remains among the most resilient. No one thought Tunisia was headed for trouble, so it was barely examined. Instead, the report concluded that the most likely scenario suggested that the older generation of strong-arm leaders would have to die off before the region could experience any significant political opening.

McFaul was not happy with the final product. It was far too timid in its conclusions, he thought, and too hands-off in its prescriptions for how the United States should encourage political transition. "The impulse of any government is to get back to the status quo—but that's always where we make our biggest mistakes," he told me later. What's more, everyone was sidestepping the hardest questions: If a country like Egypt went up in flames, should the United States engage whatever rose out of the ashes? What does the United States say the day after a freely conducted election in which hard-line Islamists emerge victorious? What if the new leaders were fundamentalists who hate the idea of peace with Israel, who want to roll back women's rights or close down newspapers? Does Washington keep supplying foreign aid to an elected government that ignores or rejects American interests? (The Bush administration had faced the same issue when Hamas succeeded in the Palestinian elections in 2006.)

All great questions, but the Obama White House never really had time to debate them before the region imploded in protest.[4] History was about to overtake Obama's study, and its authors would spend most of 2011 and beyond making those calls largely on the fly.

WHEN THE FIRST news of the WikiLeaks disclosures broke, in November 2010, Sami Ben Gharbia, a Tunisian activist with a quick wit and a well-defined sense of injustice, knew he had to read the cables written by the American diplomats based in Tunis. Ben Gharbia had cofounded a net activist group called Nawaat and had launched an independent opposition blog seven years earlier. Now he was anxious to see what the cables would reveal about the object of his activism: Tunisian president Zine El Abidine Ben Ali.

President Ben Ali was an American ally, sporadically cooperative in counterterrorism initiatives. But cooperation came at a high cost: Americans had to look the other way when it came to Ben Ali's habit of throwing challengers in jail and giving his family the first crack at his favorite sport, looting the national economy. Since Ben Ali had been in power for twenty-three years, Ben Gharbia figured the cables would be rich with anecdotes of excess. He was not disappointed. WikiLeaks yielded a gold mine—mostly about stolen gold.

None of the American or European newspapers, including the *New York Times*, published the Tunisian cables.* Nawaat, however, quickly created its own miniature WikiLeaks series, called "TuniLeaks." Ben Gharbia and his colleagues translated and posted seventeen of the cables describing Ben Ali's most outrageous behavior. More would follow.

TuniLeaks made it clear that behind the high walls of the American embassy, diplomats had long been disgusted by Ben Ali's corrupt regime. In a June 2008 cable wonderfully entitled "What's Yours Is Mine" (Who said diplomats have no sense of humor?), the American ambassador at the time, Robert Godec, wrote, "Whether it's cash, services, land, property, or yes, even your yacht, President Ben Ali's family is rumored to covet it and reportedly gets what it wants."[5] He wasn't kidding about the yacht: Ben Ali's nephews had, in fact, expropriated the beautiful pleasure craft of a French businessman.

The cables showed that, years before the Arab uprisings, signs of discontent with Ben Ali were well known. "It is the excesses of President Ben Ali's family that inspire outrage among Tunisians," Godec wrote. "With Tunisians facing rising inflation and high unemployment, the conspicuous displays of wealth and persistent ru-

---

* On this, I plead guilty. As I began reading through the cables for the *Times* in September 2010, Tunisia was hardly on my mind. Cables on the Iranian nuclear program and Chinese espionage seemed to rank far higher on the scale of strategic importance.

mors of corruption have added fuel to the fire. . . . This government has based its legitimacy on its ability to deliver economic growth, but a growing number of Tunisians believe those at the top are keeping the benefits for themselves."[6]

Even zoo animals were being plucked up by the dictator's family. Godec described, in the summer of 2009, a visit to one of Ben Ali's daughters, who kept a pet tiger named Pasha on the premises that "consumes four chickens a day." (It reminded Godec of Saddam Hussein's son, Uday, who owned lions.) While Pasha kept to his poultry diet, the family served its guests ostentatious dinners that included yogurt and ice cream flown in from the French Riviera.

Not surprisingly, the published cables began to strike a chord among the country's shopkeepers and intellectuals alike.[7] Ben Ali quickly attempted to ban the TuniLeaks site, but critics of his regime maneuvered via social networking, and the hashtag "#tunileaks" was created to share cables and other state secrets via individuals' Twitter feeds.

In the summer of 2011, Ben Gharbia told me that "translating the cables [was] crucial to us," not because they revealed anything new, but because they confirmed the country's worst suspicions. "Tunisians knew the basic information in the cables, of course," he said. "It was obvious. But they didn't know the Americans knew it too. And when they read the cables, they no longer believed the Americans supported the regime. It brought the middle class out, and then others who are wealthy. They thought that without the United States, Ben Ali was very vulnerable."

TuniLeaks had been up for two and a half weeks when a policewoman confiscated the vegetable cart of Mohamed Bouazizi. The twenty-six-year-old Tunisian street vendor protested the humiliation by pouring gasoline over his body and self-immolating in front of a local municipal building.[8] Bouazizi's desperate act spawned a series of protests in his town that quickly spread across the country. In the popular telling of the tale, Bouazizi was the spark that lit the whole region afire. After less than a month of impressive, peaceful demonstrations, Ben Ali fled the country.

Some, including Hillary Clinton, suspect that the prevalence of social media, including WikiLeaks, served as the accelerant. "I'm not sure the vegetable vendor killing himself all by itself would have been enough," Clinton told me later. "I think the openness of the social media, I think WikiLeaks, in great detail, describing the lavishness of the Ben Ali family and cronies was a big douse of gasoline on the smoldering fire."

Given how furious Clinton had been at the publication of the State Department cables—an understandable reaction, given the huge breach of secrecy, the embarrassing phone calls she had to make explaining the leak to world leaders, and the expulsion of a handful of her ambassadors—it was a surprising statement. When American diplomats had raised the issue of WikiLeaks to me, it was usually to chew out the *Times* for risking American national security. (Clinton expressed her displeasure to me too, as we prepared the publication in November 2010 of "State's Secrets," the *Times'* series drawn from the WikiLeaks revelations.) But with the passage of time, she had finally found a leak she liked—an obscure set of her own department's cables that, by revealing the excesses of a brutal and corrupt dictator, may have helped ignite the most massive democracy movement in the Middle East in anyone's memory.

NOT ONE EXPERT, activist, politician, or spy had predicted Ben Ali's rapid overthrow. They then proceeded to compound the error by insisting it was a unique circumstance, unlikely to spread.

That problem started at the top, at President Obama's daily briefings. According to the accounts of two officials, after Ben Ali fled, Obama asked whether it might inspire a domino effect against neighboring dictators. "The answer was 'Very unlikely, sir,' or something to that effect," one witness to the exchange reported later. The risk to Egypt, in particular, they estimated was less than 20 percent.[9] Obama's intelligence briefer was not alone: an Israeli official later told me that the estimates on the likelihood that Tunisia's problems would spill over the border were "about the same."

Not surprisingly, leaders throughout the region were trying to convince themselves that they, too, were safe. And so they were particularly angry when Secretary Clinton, traveling to Doha for a conference just as Tunisia was heating up, warned that "the region's foundations are sinking into the sand."[10] She received an immediate response from the Middle East's top leaders.

There were "a lot of very personally emotional arguments— from Egyptians, the Emirates, Saudis—to a lesser extent Kuwaitis," she recalled later. The angriest of all was "the foreign minister of Egypt, who just was so upset with me." Didn't she understand that the Egyptian relationship with the United States was built on stability, and the stability was built on Mubarak's rule?

Many in Washington thought that Mubarak's rule was likely coming to an end anyway. He had left Egypt for medical treatment several times, and the American assessment was that he suffered from a rare, slow-moving bile-duct cancer. The assumption was that Mubarak would rig the transition, North Korea–style, for his corrupt son, Gamal, who, through private investment, his consulting firm, and convenient promotion as "partner" in multiple businesses in Egypt, had become a multimillionaire. Already, the elder Mubarak had appointed Gamal to the post of deputy secretary-general for the ruling National Democratic Party: the power shift had already begun.[11]

Washington openly challenged what was happening in Egypt only once, and after the trouble it caused, such attempts were never tried again. In 2005, in her first year as secretary of state, Condoleezza Rice gave a speech at the American University in Cairo in

which she assailed Mubarak's government for locking up protestors and political challengers, and called for free elections. "For
sixty years, my country, the United States, pursued stability at the
expense of democracy in this region here in the Middle East, and
we achieved neither," she declared.[12] The crowd of six hundred or
so was surprised; those opposed to Mubarak's rule were heartened;
many others were skeptical of America's intentions. The government's supporters were outright insulted. Mubarak made his displeasure clear: he never came to Washington again while George W.
Bush was in office. Bush tacked back to the middle, never daring to
repeat Rice's critique.

When Obama took office, Mubarak saw an opportunity to
repair the relationship with a new, inexperienced president who
prided himself on pragmatism, and he immediately made plans to
visit the White House. (The trip was canceled at the last minute
when his grandson died.) When Obama arrived in Egypt for the
Cairo speech, a few weeks later, Mubarak lost no time casting himself as the protector of the Egyptian peace treaty with Israel, and
America's closest ally in the Arab world. Mubarak's apparatchiks
took note that Obama did not directly call for fair elections, and
they kept pointing to one line in the speech acknowledging that
"there is no straight line" to the kind of free and open system Americans advocate.

From the accounts of Americans who dealt with Mubarak later,
the aging Egyptian leader realized that Obama had a lot else on his
mind as he struggled to manage an economic crisis and two wars.
"I think he concluded that Obama wasn't going to challenge him,"
one of Obama's aides who witnessed the conversations between the
two men said.

It turned out that Mubarak was misreading Obama, but that
error paled in comparison to the other misjudgments the Egyptian
leader was about to make.

❖

THE UNRAVELING IN Egypt started eleven days after Ben Ali fled Tunisia, but its roots went back further. Because Mubarak had a record of cracking down brutally on street protestors, the blogosphere had become a much safer place to try to undermine his regime.

The Egyptian opposition's most successful online effort had been a Facebook group called We Are All Khaled Said, started a year and a half earlier. Two policemen had grabbed twenty-eight-year-old Said from a local Alexandria cybercafé in June 2010 and beat him to death in the street. The official story line that he was a drug dealer rang false; in fact, the beating was likely retribution for his posting of a video online that documented police corruption. Started by a young Google marketing executive, Wael Ghonim, to protest the brutal police killing, the Facebook group spurred some of Egypt's biggest protests in years. The Egyptian government was unmoved.[13] Then, after Ben Ali fell, everything changed.

The spark came when an activist group called the April 6 Youth Movement* decided to expand the small annual "Police Day" protest on January 25, which commemorates a 1952 Egyptian police revolt against the British. (In one of those wonderful ironies of history, Mubarak had made it a national holiday in 2009, never guessing that day would be the harbinger of his downfall.) Several groups signed on to an expanded rally, including Ghonim's We Are All Khaled Said, along with other, primarily liberal groups, and even the Muslim Brotherhood's youth wing. While the popular image is that this was a "Twitter revolution," the reality was more prosaic: cell phones and eye-catching posters, and plain old word of mouth more effectively

---

* The April 6 Youth Movement began in 2008 as a Facebook group expressing solidarity with striking workers in the industrial city of al-Mahalla al-Kubra. Although April 6 evolved into an online political movement with over 100,000 members, it failed to result in any meaningful change over the next three years.

spread the message throughout the dusty, winding streets of dense Cairo.

The flood of protestors started flowing into Tahrir Square on January 25. As television images began beaming around the country—largely thanks to Al Jazeera—the crowds, the excitement, and the sense of foreboding grew. Egyptians wondered if, this time, revolution might work. People rapidly began mobilizing in other cities throughout the country—Alexandria, Suez, Mansoura, and elsewhere. Parents came to look for their kids and stayed to protest. Young women showed up, as did the Coptic Christian community. Sectarian differences set aside, they were unified by one thought: Mubarak had to go.

The protest escalated three days later, on January 28, into the "Day of Rage," with a long battle between police and protestors on the Kasr al-Nil Bridge, which links several of Cairo's neighborhoods. The protestors won, and the next day, they set afire the immense gray headquarters of Mubarak's ruling National Democratic Party on the edge of Tahrir Square. The message to Mubarak seemed clear: leave, or the regime will burn.

"When I looked around me and I saw all these unfamiliar faces in the protests, and they were more brave than us—I knew that this was it for the regime," Ahmed Maher, a founder of the April 6 Youth Movement, said to me a few days before the first anniversary of the protest.[14] Walid Rachid, another April 6 founder, recalled that in the lead-up to the protest, the rallying cry was "In the name of Allah, the answer is Tunisia." By the end of the day on January 25, the new slogan was "In the name of Allah, the answer has become Egypt."[15]

THE INITIAL US responses to the escalating Egyptian protests were hesitant and confused. When the first demonstrators appeared in Tahrir Square, Secretary of State Hillary Clinton worked from the traditional American script. "Our assessment is that the Egyptian government is stable and is looking for ways to respond to the legitimate needs and interests of the Egyptian people," she said. That conclusion quickly proved to be backward.

Two days later, Vice President Joe Biden argued that he "would not refer to [Mubarak] as a dictator."[16] (He said later he regretted the comment as soon as it was out of his mouth.) Ironically, the administration had prepared for this day with the Presidential Study Directive, but fell right into the trap McFaul had warned the "Nerd Directorate" about. Obama's team initially assumed that the status quo was the best option, especially when it came to backing a strategically vital ally.

Mubarak's clueless, then brutal reaction to the protests triggered the beginning of a division inside the White House that only magnified as the images from Tahrir were projected on the big flat-screen television displays in the Situation Room. The younger advisers who had come up through the campaign—Denis McDonough, the sharp-tongued deputy national security adviser; and Ben Rhodes, who wrote the 2009 Cairo address—could imagine themselves in that square. Along with Samantha Power, they took the view that the worst place Obama could end up was on the wrong side of history. Clinton, Gates, and others who had risen in the traditional foreign-policy establishment were thinking back to revolutions that once seemed promising but had gone awry— Iran in 1979—and the implications of years of chaotic transition in Egypt that could threaten core American interests, especially the peace treaty with Israel. Over the next few days, Mubarak himself resolved this dispute for Obama by pushing him into the camp of his younger advisers.

That process started moments after Mubarak appeared on Egyptian television on January 28, haughtily addressing his nation in formal Arabic, and giving little ground. He announced that his government ministers would resign, but he would not: like the pharaohs, he cast himself as protector of the state. The speech was utterly defiant and unmoving—enraging the very people in the square it was meant to appease.

As soon as it aired, Obama called Mubarak for a thirty-minute conversation, urging him to listen to the protestors and heed their demands for change. But while he exerted pressure for Mubarak to act, and act quickly, he was careful to avoid suggesting that the Egyptian president had lost American support. Obama's natural caution was kicking in—he was not prepared to burn any bridges just yet.

"Mubarak was even more defiant on the phone than he was on TV," one of Obama's advisers later told me. The protests, Mubarak asserted, were instigated by outside interference. Other Egyptian leaders had faced worse than what was happening now on the street, and had overcome it, he insisted. "Give me ten days," Mubarak told Obama. "Nasser put down something like this. So can I. Just give me ten days."

Obama hung up the phone and told his staff he thought Mubarak had been in power so many years—living a cosseted life on a military base not far from the Cairo airport—that he had lost the ability to recognize the significance of the uprising. He saw everything in the light of past protests and convinced himself that they could be put down by classic police-state tactics. Moreover, he couldn't imagine an Egypt that he wasn't running. Mubarak "couldn't get his head around what we were asking him to do," Clinton reflected later. "He had a lot of voices around him who were quite dire. He was hearing people in his government," she added, who were warning him, "'You know, if you go, Egypt collapses, Islamists take over.'"

What's more, Mubarak seemed convinced that Obama would easily back down. After all, he had dealt with six American presidents, been dined and complimented by all, and he seemed to have the formula down for keeping them well leashed: remind them he is America's one true ally in the region, the one standing between Washington and a chaotic, Islamist future. But with the passage of each new day of protests—and the prospect that his regime might crumble anyway—that line sounded less and less compelling.

Obama decided to turn up the heat by going in front of the cameras and describing—in the most limited way—his unsatisfying phone call. "When President Mubarak addressed the Egyptian people tonight, he pledged a better democracy and greater economic opportunity. I just spoke to him after his speech. And I told him he has a responsibility to give meaning to those words, to take concrete steps and actions that deliver on that promise."[17]

Obama's careful approach pleased no one. To Egyptians in Tahrir Square, it was wishy-washy. One activist I spoke with later balked at the notion that the US government had been supportive, and asserted, "We got no solidarity with Obama." To other leaders in the region, however, Obama's decision to pressure Mubarak at all was a sign of weakness, and perhaps a troubling indication that the president would willingly abandon a longtime ally.

The phone calls started coming in. King Abdullah of Saudi Arabia was insistent that Obama needed to stick with Mubarak, even if he started shooting protestors in the streets. The Saudis clearly saw what was happening in Cairo and imagined it spreading to Riyadh. The Israelis were similarly apocalyptic. "I don't think Obama understands what he's getting into," one senior Israeli official fumed to me as the protests built. Prime Minister Benjamin Netanyahu told Obama he needed to stay in firm support of Mubarak, no matter what.

Secretary Clinton made the argument that the right path was to pressure Mubarak for change—with as many threats as necessary—but not to pull the rug out from beneath him. The issue, as some in the administration portrayed it, was less about Mubarak and more about the message that the United States sent to the rest of its allies.

As one official explained, "Because if you are willing to turn on someone who you have used and relied on for so many years, then what is the basis of the relationships and the loyalty going forward for someone else?"

ONE WEEK INTO the protests, Obama barged in, unannounced, to a 3:30 p.m. Situation Room meeting of his national security team. He had crashed meetings before, but it was clear to everyone in the room that he was getting increasingly frustrated with the widespread perception that the United States was behind the curve on events in Egypt. Despite the fact that Obama "had kept pressing us to be more aggressive," Ben Rhodes recalled, the advisers were still focused on debating meager steps—whether Obama should make a second call to Mubarak, or whether it was time to issue another statement. The debate was timid and narrow.

Obama took the seat Tom Donilon, the national security adviser, had occupied at the head of the table and made the case, one participant recalled, that "he believed that a number of the regimes in the region were vulnerable to the same kind of popular uprising." No one disputed that; the question was how to effectively manage the US reaction to protect its interests and position in the region. Clinton, in particular, expressed concern that, tempting as it was to celebrate the democratic passions of the Tahrir moment, risks abounded. The aftermath of revolution was often ugly, she warned.

"We were all trying to assess a fast-moving present situation and then draw conclusions about what the future would look like," she told me later. "And there were a lot of cautious voices and there were some in the White House—not just the Cabinet—who were saying, 'Wait a minute, what's on the other side of this and how do we get there in the most peaceful way that is more likely to produce a democratic outcome?'"

The question at the meeting wasn't whether to throw Mubarak under the bus—he had thrown himself under it. Instead, Obama's advisers had to ask whether it made sense to try to extract him, or if, at this point, it was too late. For all their fears of what would come next in Egypt, the good news about the upheaval was that it ran counter to the extremist narrative—a point Donilon kept making. The students on the street were not yelling "Death to America!" or even chanting anti-Israel slogans. There were no homages to bin Laden, or al-Qaeda. The grievances were all directed at Mubarak, himself, for his oppressive iron rule, gross economic mismanagement, corruption, and failure to pay attention to the crumbling infrastructure of his country.

Obama, Donilon later told me, thought it was a futile effort to try to save Mubarak; all the indications suggested that the military would not shoot protestors on a large scale, which meant that, sooner or later, Mubarak was doomed. "History was moving here," Donilon recalled Obama saying, "and we needed to be on the right side of history."

Then, in the middle of the meeting, everyone paused. Mubarak was about to give another speech. Perhaps the rumors that had circulated in Washington—and that Leon Panetta had repeated in front of Congress—were true, and Mubarak was about to submit his resignation.

Mubarak's speech lasted only five minutes, but it was so disorganized that no one was quite sure what he said. Rather than announce he would step down, he vowed that he would not run again for president after his term expired. Lest this concession be perceived as weakness, he added, "I say in all honesty and regardless of the current situation that I did not intend to nominate myself for a new presidential term. I have spent enough years of my life in the service of Egypt and its people."[18]

Shouts of outrage and frustration in the square began immediately. In the Situation Room, Obama told his advisers the speech was insufficient. He had to give Mubarak a push in the right direction, and he had to do it fast, before the violence worsened. "He personally basically overrode just about his entire government," said one official in the room, noting that Gates and Clinton were still actively opposed.

"Look, this is what I'm going to do," Obama said, according to notes of the meeting. "I'm going to call [Mubarak] now and then I'm going to go out and make a statement saying there needs to be a transition." Immediately, staff began scrambling to prepare, but Obama called them off. "I don't even need that many talking points for that call."

"That was it," another official said. "That was the end of the discussion." For Obama, the turning point had arrived. As Reagan had done with Philippine president Ferdinand Marcos, Obama decided to tell a longtime American ally that it was over. The real question, though, was whether Mubarak would listen—or care.

The phone call evolved into the harshest conversation between the two men—and, as it turned out, almost certainly their last. Obama told the Egyptian president that his speech was completely inadequate. "If this transition process drags out for months," he said, according to a transcript of the call, "the protests will, too."[19]

Mubarak, oblivious to the stark reality on the ground, declared that the protests would end in a few days. "Egypt is not Tunisia. These protests will be over soon. I know my people. I respect your opinion, but I'm better informed."

Obama walked up to the line of using the word "resign," but pulled back just short of it. "I think it's important that you seize this opportunity. The protests continue to build. I think it's very important for you to explore over the next twenty-four to forty-eight hours a means by which you can move this transition forward on a more timely basis."

Mubarak refused to give way. He told Obama that he would circle back to him that weekend—but he was clearly trying to buy some time, and his words suggested he wanted to get Obama off his back. "Let's talk in the next three or four days and not before that," Mubarak said.

Obama, however, did not let him have the last word. "I reserve the right, Mr. President, if things are not settling down, I'll call you before that." Then Obama gave a final appeal: "Mr. President, I always respect my elders. You've been in politics for a very long time. But there are moments in history when just because things have been the same in the past doesn't mean they'll be the same way in the future. You've served your country well for over thirty years. But I want to make sure that you seize this historic moment."

Donilon called the conversation "as poignant and direct a conversation between two heads of government that I was familiar with" in thirty years, since Ronald Reagan and Menachem Begin spoke during the invasion of Lebanon. But when this conversation was over, Mubarak remained in place—and the question became whether his own military, the linchpin of his regime, would abandon him.

As the battle in Egypt raged on, Mike McFaul saw President Obama and asked the obvious question: "What do you think is going to happen?"

"What do I want to happen, or what do I think?" Obama asked. "What I want is for the kids in the square to win and that Google guy to be president. What I think is we're going to be in for a long, protracted transition."[20]

A DAY AFTER the phone call between Mubarak and Obama, Tahrir Square erupted into the epic "Battle of Camels," with Mubarak's loyalists galloping in on camels and horses, presumably the very same animals used to take tourists around the pyramids, just on the edge of the city. It looked surreally like a scene from *Lawrence of Arabia*: camels, rocks, swords, screams, and makeshift explosives.

The fight that ensued unified the secular protestors and the Muslim Brotherhood, whose top leadership eventually issued an order for all able-bodied men to join in the liberation of Tahrir Square. As the battle reached full pitch, the military finally intervened—on the side of the protestors. Egyptian soldiers, who had been quietly watching behind the iron gates of the museum, fired warning shots at the pro-Mubarak thugs, forcing them out of the square.

That key moment shifted the balance of power—and truly marked the end of the Mubarak era. For days, Egyptian officers had been receiving e-mails from Americans they had once trained with at American bases—as part of the security cooperation between the two countries—cautioning them against firing on the protestors. "You could almost hear them making the calculations in their heads," recalled one senior American official. "Did they want to stick with an aging, sick leader whose likely successor was his own son, who the military didn't trust? And we just kept repeating the mantra, 'Don't break the bond you have with your own people.'"[21] Now, faced with a stark choice, the Egyptian military heeded the warning.

JUST AS OBAMA'S decision to side openly with the Egyptian people looked like it might pay off, his attempts were complicated by his own messenger.

The envoy was Frank Wisner, a retired legendary American diplomat who had served everywhere, and knew everyone—including Hosni Mubarak. Wisner had been the American ambassador in Cairo during happier times in the US–Egyptian relationship. Clinton and one of her top deputies, Bill Burns, knew that Mubarak would see Wisner, and the two could talk honestly. Wisner was an old-school, barrel-chested diplomat who knew how to get through to an old-school, dug-in dictator. His mission was to fly to Cairo armed with a letter to Mubarak and instructions from Obama to "err on the side of bold here, on the side of pushing these guys."

But if Obama thought the only solution was for Mubarak to get out of the way instantly, Wisner did not. He pointed out that the Egyptian constitution would have thrown the question of succession to the parliament—a corrupt institution dominated by Mubarak's cronies. "You needed something orderly, and that means you needed something to change the rules," Wisner said. Threading through that middle, murky space was part of how Wisner interpreted his mission.

The day after Obama's last call with Mubarak, Wisner arrived in Cairo and was whisked right to the presidential palace. Even with the president of the United States and now his own military telling him it was time to move on, Mubarak clearly still did not get it. During the course of several hours, Mubarak delivered a lecture, chewing over the same old line: if this place is taken over by the Muslim Brotherhood, you know what it will look like. He portrayed himself as the last man standing between an Egypt that America could deal with and one that looked like Iran.

Obama was too young, too green to know the real dangers—that seemed to be the unspoken subtext of Mubarak's message. The Egyptian leader pointed out he had agreed to step down after the elections—what else did you Americans want? "He was determined to prove that he was in charge, of course; in his mind anything else would have showed weakness," Wisner later told me. "So while he was prepared to receive me and talk to me, it was also to convey how he saw things—and he saw himself at the center." Believing he had done the best he could, Wisner sent a report back to Washington, saw a few old friends, and returned home.

On February 5, a few days after President Obama had taken a stand in favor of transition, Wisner made what in Washington amounts to a terrible gaffe: he said what he thought in public. At a conference in Munich, Wisner announced that "President

Mubarak's continued leadership is critical—it's his opportunity to write his own legacy." He went on to say that, with so much change afoot, Mubarak "must stay in office in order to steer those changes through." Of course, this was the exact opposite of Obama's admonition to Mubarak to step down immediately.

The normally cool Obama read Wisner's comments and was outraged. "This was about as pissed as I've ever seen him," said one official when he read the text of Wisner's comments. Naturally, Wisner's words made front-page news the following day, and, as one White House official put it, "It looked like Frank was giving cover to Mubarak to stay on." (Before the gaffe, there had been talk of bringing Wisner back to a senior job at the State Department later in Obama's term; the possibility evaporated that afternoon.)

Making matters worse, Secretary Clinton warned that any transition would take time. (On that, she turned out to be more accurate than she knew.) Other American officials had suggested Mubarak might formally stay in office until his term ended the following September. The mixed messages were confusing and embarrassing. Obama reacted by demanding that they "pull the messaging on [Egypt] into the White House."

"This is what happens when you get caught by surprise," one senior American official told me as the White House scrambled to clean up after Wisner. "We've had endless strategy sessions for the past two years on Mideast peace, on containing Iran. And how many of them factored in the possibility that Egypt," and the dominoes that would soon follow it, "moves away from stability to turmoil? None."[22]

The Wisner episode exposed a continuing rift in the administration over how to balance America's values and interests in the Middle East. Obama was angry because Wisner's call for caution—an instinct shared by Clinton and Gates—made it appear that the administration wanted to protect a dictator rather than side with protestors in the square. But the fact was that Obama, too, seemed torn between idealism and pragmatism. While he had sided with the younger staff who thought it more important to stand with protestors seeking democracy and freedom, he knew that Gates and Clinton were right to be concerned that without Mubarak, the country could head into an abyss. "I told him I thought this would probably turn out all right," Clinton later told me, "but it would take twenty-five years."

The break came on Thursday, February 10, when Vice President Biden got on the phone with Omar Suleiman, Mubarak's newly appointed vice president and longtime intelligence chief. This was the third time the two men had spoken in a week, and the airwaves were filled with rumors that Mubarak was stepping down. Suleiman told Biden that he was preparing to assume Mubarak's powers, but also indicated that "certain powers" would remain with Mubarak, including the power to dissolve the parliament and fire the cabinet. "The message from Suleiman was that [Mubarak] would be the de facto president," one person involved with the call said, but it was close enough to a resignation that it might work.

Yet when Mubarak addressed the Tahrir crowds that night, the speech he gave drastically differed from what Suleiman had communicated to Biden. According to Egyptian cabinet members, the elder Mubarak had been persuaded by his son, Gamal, to rewrite his remarks to instead reaffirm his increasingly tenuous hold on power.[23] Delivered in the unbowed tone of a father of the country, the speech scarcely mentioned a delegation of powers. Rather, he promised to continue guiding Egypt through a transition until the following September.

It was that rambling, convoluted address that proved the final straw for the Egyptian military, now fairly certain that it would have Washington's backing if it moved against Mubarak. Egypt's top officers seemed to have come to the same conclusion that South Korea's did in the 1980s and Indonesia's did in the 1990s: the country's leader had changed from an asset to a liability.

The next day, with his own military abandoning him and tens of thousands still amassed in Tahrir Square, Mubarak quietly left for his home in the resort town of Sharm el-Sheikh. As Omar Suleiman broke the news that the Egyptian strongman had officially resigned, the cheers of jubilation went up in Tahrir. They had done it. After less than three weeks of mostly peaceful protests, they had brought down a dictator.

WHAT DID WE learn about Obama from the fall of an American ally? One way to read his actions is that he is far less concerned about preserving longtime American alliances just because diplomatic orthodoxy said that the United States could not live without them. Under this interpretation, Obama takes some significant risks, and possesses a willingness to reshuffle the established order. This was Israel's interpretation, and Saudi Arabia's. "We probably have as strained a relationship with the Saudis after this as we have had in forty years," one senior administration official told me. "We're still rebuilding it."

But the other interpretation is that Obama recognized that it made little difference whether the United States pushed Mubarak or tried to save him—he was a goner either way. After his last, strained conversation with Mubarak, Obama told his aides he wasn't going to back a dying dictator with the faint hope of buying a few more years of stability. That would only perpetuate, he said, a failed American approach, one that left Egyptians understandably bitter.

Yet the message that the United States chose to be on the side of the protestors was not clearly conveyed, particularly in Egypt. In Cairo in the days leading up to the first anniversary of the uprising, many young Egyptians told me that Obama was a fair-weather friend who did not declare clearly enough that Mubarak had to go. "Obama changed his decisions," one activist told me. "Once he knew the revolution would win, he sided with the revolution. I don't trust a man like that."

It was a strange reaction—for years Egyptians have complained about Americans meddling in their politics; this time they complained about not enough meddling. But it was a reminder that this revolution was about Egypt, not about America. And Obama did not want to own it any more than he wanted to own Iraq and Afghanistan.

CHAPTER 13
THE RIDDLE OF THE BROTHERHOOD

IN A SUNNIER ERA OF EGYPT'S RELATIONS WITH THE UNITED STATES, Jacqueline Kennedy persuaded Congress to spend millions of dollars to save one of Egypt's great monuments: the temples of Abu Simbel, built during the glory days of Rameses II as a symbol of Egyptian power. Fifty years after she intervened, and a year after the revolution that was supposed to change everything in Egypt, it is safe to say that Congress is in no mood to spend taxpayer dollars on preserving Egypt's past or investing in its future. And without question, the newest power center in Egypt—the Muslim Brotherhood's political headquarters in a dilapidated apartment block on Roda Island in the middle of the Nile River—will never show up alongside Abu Simbel on a list of World Heritage Sites.

The apartment block is technically home to the "Freedom and Justice Party," the political arm of the Brotherhood. Trash is everywhere in the lobby. To reach the conference room on the second floor—where some of the most important discussions on Egypt's future are happening—you have to first ascend a narrow, dank staircase. And in the first weeks of 2012, delegation after delegation ventured up that dark stairway, anxious to meet the people who would soon be running Egypt, or might be, if the Brothers can successfully negotiate or wrestle power away from the ruling military council.

Anne Patterson, the American ambassador to Egypt, made the trek as soon as it became clear that the Brotherhood would win the largest bloc of seats in the new Egyptian parliament. Given Washington's aversion to the Islamic group that had launched Ayman al-Zawahiri, the Egyptian-born chief disciple of Osama bin Laden and now head of al-Qaeda, such a pilgrimage would have been unthinkable a year before. Patterson wasn't the only one who came to pay her respects. The British flew in a high-powered delegation, and the Russians and the Chinese followed, bearing the promise of future gifts.

After more than eighty years of keeping one step ahead of the secret police, organizing in quasi-secrecy, facing imprisonment, repression, and occasional torture, the Brotherhood's moment had finally come. Islamist parties such as the Freedom and Justice Party had not only won in Egypt; they were newly empowered in Morocco, Tunisia, Libya, and even Jordan, where King Abdullah was reluctantly allowing them more leeway. But the historical antipathy between old Arab leaders and the Islamists would be difficult to overcome. When Abdullah came to Washington in early 2012, he warned everyone of the dangers of allowing the group to gain too much influence. The Saudi interior minister once called the Brotherhood "the source of all troubles in the Arab world."[1]

And even in the State Department, Hillary Clinton and her top aides questioned which faction of the Muslim Brotherhood would ultimately prevail. The one that rose as a secret society led by Hassan al-Banna in the 1930s, who proposed creating a caliphate across the Middle East? Or the one that was telling Ambassador Patterson that the party today is composed of pragmatists, who worried about attracting investors?

The answer would not be simple; the Brotherhood itself is far from monolithic, and the faction that won the early battles may not win the later ones. One intelligence report circulating widely in the US government early in 2012 suggested that a far more ideological strain of Islamists occupied many critical positions in the mid-ranks of the Egyptian military, and could be biding their time, waiting for Mubarak's former cronies to retire.

"In five years, the very secular military we are dealing with today could take on an entirely different character," one senior member of President Obama's team said to me. "But we have to work with what we've got."

What the Muslim Brotherhood got, when the dust settled, was just about 47 percent of the seats in the new lower house of parliament. Its exact powers were unclear, because Egypt had taken the hurried step of holding elections before anyone got around to writing the new constitution. The fact that most of the Brotherhood members who got elected had never before served in public office, and didn't have a clue how to write or pass a bill, only added to the haze of what was coming next. But inside the Freedom and Justice Party headquarters, the only thing that mattered in the opening days of 2012 was that they had achieved what Mubarak swore he would never permit: a significant voice in how Egypt would be run. It was even possible that the new Islamist parliamentarians could soon be overseeing the same security forces that once threw them into Cairo's dungeons.

Now the party leaders were out to cast themselves as the moderate voice of political Islam. Compared to the other big winners of the election—the fundamentalist Salafi Al-Nour Party, which won about a quarter of the parliamentary seats—the Brotherhood looked like a bunch of Berkeley liberals, something no one would have characterized them as previously.

Winning an election, however, would not guarantee they could exercise the responsibilities they earned. Power would first have to be ceded to them by the aged group of military leaders who currently ran the place through the Supreme Council of the Armed Forces. Old and never really political, they were too burned out to truly govern—but they were not anxious to see the military's privileged status end. All those years while the Muslim Brotherhood was underground, Egypt's military was flying high, controlling much of the economy, including resorts, gas stations, pharmaceutical facili-

ties, and fish farms, and receiving a steady $1.3 billion annual mili-
tary aid package from the United States. (The military built up such
a cushion, in fact, that when the Egyptian government was burning
through more cash than it had in early 2012, the Egyptian military
lent the government a cool $1 billion.) With their own perks, prop-
erty, and revenue streams on the line, it wasn't certain how willingly the military would turn over control to the new Islamist-led
parliament.

Back in Washington, no one knew which was more worrisome:
an Egypt run by Mubarak's old military apparatchiks or one run
by the Brothers. And no one knew how to deal with the surge of
Salafis and the blatant ineptitude of the liberal factions. The prospects for a US-friendly democracy were looking less promising every day. "Now we're waiting to see what it means," Clinton said to
me about a month after the election. "And I don't think anyone
sitting in Washington today can tell you exactly what it does mean."

THE JOB OF calming the Americans and convincing them that the
Muslim Brotherhood was not about to turn Egypt into the next
Iran fell to Essam el-Erian, a jovial senior leader of the Freedom and
Justice Party. He was already practicing his lines for the influx of
American diplomats who he knew would be trudging up the same
stairway that two of my colleagues, Tom Friedman and David Kirk-
patrick, and I took to get to his sparse receiving room one Sunday
afternoon.

"This is the first time Egypt had a fair and free election," el-
Erian told us. This was the dawning of a brand-new era of Egyptian
politics, and he knew the whole language of representative democracy by heart. El-Erian's involvement with the Islamist movement
runs deep. A doctor by training, he was now an elected member of
parliament, but the memory of years spent running from one basement to the next to avoid the security forces on his tail remained

fresh. Still, he bore few obvious scars from his many stints in jail over the years, and he was clearly warming to his new role. A few months after one jail spell, el-Erian emerged declaring, "In Egypt, prison is like death. It comes suddenly and goes just as quickly."

Yet el-Erian had sat out the revolution in Tahrir Square in January 2011. He is in his late fifties, and like other members of his generation in the Muslim Brotherhood, the uprising just seemed to him like one more futile demonstration that would end up with broken heads and protestors led off to jail.

But the revolution he had refused to participate in quickly turned into the opportunity of a lifetime. When elections came around, the liberals proved to be astoundingly incompetent campaigners. They spent their time obsessed with procedural minutiae—how to divide voting districts, in what order to draft the constitution and hold presidential elections—while the Brotherhood got busy mobilizing their eighty-year-old grassroots network into an effective electoral machine. By the time we saw him, el-Erian and his colleagues had emerged with something they had never dreamed of before: a real electoral mandate. Now they were trying to figure out what to do with it.

Should they demand that the military government step down immediately? Ally with the hard-line Islamic fundamentalists or the secular liberals, both groups that he found about equally distasteful? Bide their time, so the Brothers could get their act together? For years, out of power, they had the luxury of maintaining their ideological purity. They could argue that Egypt's problem was not only Mubarak's dictatorship but also his insistence on a secular state, one that played by the West's rules. Now Mubarak was gone and the Brotherhood had to come up with real solutions to the country's many problems.

The answer, el-Erian said, was that he and his fellow Brothers were going to move cautiously. He insisted there was no advantage to pushing the military government out of power immediately.

(With an economic crisis looming, this was no great concession: who wants to come into power just as you are forced to slash the budget?) There was no need to seize the presidency—complete with all the lofty hopes and expectations of the people—immediately. "It will be enough to be in parliament," he said. There was no need to renounce the peace treaty with Israel, at least not anytime soon. The treaty with Israel "is a commitment of the state, not a group or a party, and this we respect." But, he added, Israel had to understand that the Arab Spring was "the biggest change in the Arab world's history," and the enhanced freedom of speech would give voice to Arab anger over the Israeli occupation of the Palestinian territories.

Even if the hard-line Salafis, whom el-Erian talked about with some disdain, called for banning booze and bikinis, the Muslim Brotherhood would not be diverted from focusing on economic issues, he insisted. "Inclusion in the political process was good for the Muslim Brotherhood, and we hope it will be good for the Salafis, too," el-Erian argued. "When you meet the facts on the ground, you develop new tools; you learn."

We pressed on the alcohol-and-bikinis question, because it went to the heart of Egypt's collapsing tourism economy. "Are you sure that is very important?" el-Erian said. "We are keen to discuss the major issues," starting with writing a new constitution. "To have a democracy in the Arab world, to make compatibility between our Arab Islamic culture and democratic values, democratic principles," he said with a sigh, "this is our huge burden."

The Brotherhood needed some time to formulate strategy, he offered. And, of course, to enjoy the experience of being courted by American officials who, just a few months before, would have sooner drunk the Cairo tap water than appear in pictures sipping tea with representatives of the Muslim Brotherhood.

El-Erian clearly relished the turning of the tables. "We hope the officials, the American people, welcome the result and deal with a new Egypt and a new world," he said with a smile.

Of course, he reminded us as we left, there would be a lot more people coming up those stairs. "Everyone wants to see us," he said. "The Chinese were here, the Russians were here." He assured us, "We'll talk to everyone."

AT LEAST EL-ERIAN talked willingly. That wasn't true of everyone who came out of the Tahrir uprising.

Two months after Mubarak was ousted, in March 2011, Secretary of State Hillary Clinton arrived in Cairo to take the pulse of the new Egypt. The excitement of the revolution was still hanging in the air and, by and large, the population was hopeful. Clinton knew she needed to walk a fine line between supporting the emerging democracy and getting caught up in the inevitable domestic power struggles, lest the United States be accused of interference in Egyptian affairs.

First, she had to deal with the ruling military council, which served as Egypt's transitional government. Almost by default, Field Marshal Mohamed Hussein Tantawi, well into his eighties, emerged as the closest thing the country had to a leader. His official role was head of the Supreme Council of the Armed Forces. Tantawi was singularly unsuited for the broader task of running a country in such political and economic upheaval, and he made no secret of the fact that it was a job he never wanted. "He's out of gas" was the summary judgment of an American official who dealt with him often. Under the circumstances, that may have been a blessing.

Very little in Tantawi's past had prepared him for this role—a 2008 State Department cable revealed by WikiLeaks labeled him "aged and change-resistant," which summed him up pretty well. He was schooled by the Soviets, during the heyday of centrally run economies. He spent decades in service to Mubarak, and his only other known loyalty was to the military itself. By his own admission, Tantawi knew virtually nothing about how to get the Egyptian economy rolling again; one of his first acts was to reject help from the International Monetary Fund, which had a bad history with Egypt. Egypt would accept no conditions, the field marshal said, because it smacked of colonialism and foreign interference. The economy deteriorated rapidly.

On her first trip to Cairo after the uprising, Clinton's biggest frustration lay not with the military but with the amorphous groups of young liberals. In public, it was all hugs: Clinton, standing out in her bright-red suit jacket, was escorted through cheering crowds in Tahrir Square, flanked by bodyguards. "To see where this revolution happened and all that it has meant to the world is extraordinary for me," Clinton said with emotion. "It's just a great reminder of the power of the human spirit and universal desire for human rights and democracy."[2]

In private, though, the youth of Tahrir were unimpressed with Clinton's commitment to their cause—and she was unimpressed with their inability to pull together even the most rudimentary political organization.

While the Obama administration had moved at a surprisingly rapid speed, at least by Washington's standards, to ease Mubarak out the door, the youth of Tahrir felt disappointed by Obama. The president they had cheered during his Cairo University speech, in their mind, had been far too cautious when the uprising began. As Lisa Anderson, the president of the American University in Cairo, put it to me, "Obama came too late here. He didn't get any points for dismissing Mubarak."[3]

So when Clinton invited various youth groups to engage her in a "dialogue" during her visit in March 2011—a Cairo listening tour—some of them snubbed her. The January 25 Revolution Youth Coalition, an umbrella of half a dozen youth groups, posted—on Facebook, of course—their decision to forgo the meeting with

Clinton. They wrote that "based on her negative position from the beginning of the revolution and the position of the US administration in the Middle East, we reject this invitation."[4]

In the end, Clinton did meet with a group of young liberals, though other activists pointed out to me that most were from US-funded organizations. (The implication was that these folks were not "true Egyptians"—a theme that would emerge again in Egypt's post-uprising politics, far more ferociously, in just a few months.)

Clinton was typically direct and, it turned out, prescient. She told the activists that she met, "If you don't organize, if you don't pick candidates, if you don't participate in the process, the Islamists are going to win." Where was their slate of candidates? Where was their platform for Egypt's future?

The activists, however, were unimpressed. They "blew her off," one participant in the conversation recalled, saying it was a new age for Egypt and there was really nothing to worry about. The liberal ideals that had roused the country on January 25, they insisted, would surely translate into a new political order.

The Americans were shocked by the naïveté of the young protestors. "One thing that most progressive political activists have in common, whether it was the McGovern campaign or Occupy Wall Street, is they don't really like politics and they somehow think that if they just show up and speak eternal truths, people will agree with them," said one senior American official. "They don't organize; they don't run candidates well."

EGYPT HAD SCORNED the United States for not sufficiently supporting the revolution, but as the year wore on, the Obama administration increasingly found itself in a Catch-22: Money or even advice from nongovernmental pro-democracy groups was cast as interference, an effort by Washington to quietly manipulate events from afar. Then again, if the United States gave nothing, it risked seeming coldhearted, unwilling to support a democracy movement it claimed it welcomed.

Hillary Clinton complained to me that "any time we tell our story, we're accused of interfering or somehow denying their right to chart their own future." So, while US representatives made their presence known every day, they were careful to stay on the sidelines.

In short, Americans had watched the revolution on television, cheered, and then went about their lives. And Egyptians had overthrown a dictator, then failed to finish the job. Many woke up a year later to discover that far less had changed than they had hoped, and they feared the revolution was in danger of being extinguished. Neither the Americans nor the Egyptians had figured out how to strike the right balance, how exactly to talk to each other as the messy transition played out. President Obama did not want to show up in Cairo until he knew whom he would be shaking hands with at the airport. As Clinton later explained, "One of our problems is we don't really have an Egyptian government to have a conversation with."[5]

By May, with Egypt calming down, and Syria, Libya, Yemen, and Bahrain in the throes of their own struggles, Obama decided to deliver a long-delayed Arab Spring speech—his chance to declare a broader American approach to the uprisings spreading across the region. In the run-up, his staff desperately looked for programs he could announce that would require only a minimum amount of new money: "It was like trying to turn copper into gold," one top official told me as he waited for Obama to speak, "and about as successful."

The speech itself was a rousing call for backing democracy movements around the world, but, fortunately, without the missionary zeal of George W. Bush's second inaugural address. "We have the chance to show that America values the dignity of the street vendor in Tunisia more than the raw power of the dictator," President Obama said. "There must be no doubt that the United States of America welcomes change that advances self-determination and opportunity," he affirmed, to allay the doubts he knew existed on the streets of Cairo, Tunis, and other capitals.[6]

The tone was pitch-perfect; the follow-through, disappointing. Obama held out the possibility of $1 billion in debt forgiveness, but Egypt's external debts were in the tens of billions. There was another $1 billion in loan guarantees, and the promise of some relatively unambitious initiatives to create an enterprise fund and start a trade and investment partnership in the region. None got any traction in Congress.

The United States just did not have the money to give, or the will to give it. "The worst would have been to create expectations, in Egypt and throughout the region, that we couldn't fulfill," one senior economic official in the administration said to me, somewhat sheepishly. A White House official later put it to me in vivid comparative terms: "The Marshall Plan was $150 billion in today's dollars," he said. In contrast, the "Middle East Fund" that Obama planned to announce in his next budget to support reforms throughout the region would be "less than $1 billion." And no one had any illusions that the Europeans, in a deep crisis of their own, would do much better.

The easy answer to why Obama failed to fund something approaching a Marshall Plan for the Arab world is that the uprisings happened at a time of tremendous budget austerity. But as some senior officials conceded, that was as much an excuse as an explanation. There was, in fact, a change of policy behind it as well—rather than use nation-building funds to help guide countries to democracy, Obama's team was determined to hang back until a clear direction, and an agreeable leader, emerged. "I've been thinking about this question a lot, which is that—if we were unconstrained in Egypt, would we give them $10 billion?" one senior official involved in those discussions said to me one afternoon, pacing the floor of his ornate office. "Let's say they were a year into the transition and the government wasn't systematically working against the US, and they had a huge economic imperative. Would we give them $10 billion now? No. Is that because we're tight on money? No. It's because we are confident that the World Bank and the International Monetary Fund can do a significant chunk and we can get the Gulf States to do the rest."

In short, America would talk about democracy promotion. But it would no longer be democracy's venture capitalist.

By the end of 2011, much of what Clinton had warned about during the debate over whether to push Mubarak out had come true. The country seemed adrift. Egypt burned through its financial reserves at an alarming rate, and the political moderates were being squeezed, on one side by Mubarak-era generals clinging to power and on the other by Islamist parties on the rise.

Clinton succinctly described the problem one weekend late in 2011, after she had just returned from yet another meeting to manage the Egyptian situation. If she shows up in Egypt in a year, she said, and finds herself sitting opposite a bunch of generals who are still running the country, the revolution will have failed. And if she is sitting opposite a new Islamist government that is prosecuting the Coptic Christian minority, forcing women to take virginity tests or walking away from the peace treaty with Israel, that will also be a failure.

If, on the other hand, she said, she's in a place with a big, cacophonous democracy in which everyone is yelling at everyone else and it's unclear who is running the place, well, that may be the best we can hope for.

BY THE BEGINNING of 2012, the American officials arriving at Cairo International Airport could sense the decades-old alliance with Egypt slipping out of their grasp.

They were whisked past the entrance to the air force base where Mubarak used to live, often the first stop for visiting senior Americans in the old days. Back then, they had to endure Mubarak's lectures, of course, which had grown increasingly shrill in the years before his ouster. He would declare that post-Saddam Iraq needed a strongman to keep them in order—someone like Mubarak himself. He would lament the Islamist turn in Pakistan, and explain that the region needed more secular states—more like the one he ran.

"He is a tried-and-true realist, innately cautious and conservative, and has little time for idealistic goals," Margaret Scobey, the US ambassador in 2009, reported back in one cable revealed by WikiLeaks. "Mubarak viewed President Bush as naïve, controlled by subordinates and totally unprepared for dealing with post-Saddam Iraq, especially the rise of Iran's regional influence."

It was a tiresome routine, but when ambassadors and deputy secretaries came, at least they knew who they were dealing with. "There is no question it was easier when Mubarak was around," one longtime American official told me. "All you had to do was make one phone call. Now you have to make one hundred."

In Mubarak's absence, there was no common cause, no grand project between the two countries. And there were competitors. One report circulating through the US government in early 2012 stated that the Chinese had designs on the Suez Canal, and were making noises about building a modern terminal for distributing Chinese-made goods, right at one of the most strategic shipping points in the world. The details were suspiciously vague. But even if it was more talk than action, it was more than the United States was talking about. It would cost billions of dollars, a small price for the Chinese to pay. Meanwhile the United States tried to scrape together a couple hundred million dollars to announce an "Arab Spring" initiative—at a moment when the Egyptians were spending $2 billion a month just keeping their currency from collapsing.

Still, in January 2012, there was something wonderfully dignified in seeing Egyptians pour into the polling places in the grimiest

Cairo neighborhoods for the first real election of their lives (not counting Mubarak's staged elections, in which few bothered to vote). I was hard-pressed to find an Egyptian who was not thrilled about the elections, even if they ticked off a litany of other fears about the economy, security, and the potential for real democracy. Whatever the imperfections of the hastily thrown together electoral process, the act of casting a real vote was so novel that the Egyptians turned out in droves—and ran a pretty good election.

On the second-to-last day of voting for the lower house of parliament, I took a stroll through Rod El Farag, an overcrowded neighborhood that seemed a world away from the boutiques and coffeehouses of Cairo's city central. Here there are narrow, winding streets that residents identify by landmarks rather than by name. Dense, dusty, and teeming with community life, it was quintessentially Egyptian.

In the middle of the neighborhood, a down-and-out school served as the polling station. It was surrounded by young security officers huddled together at the entranceway, casually slinging AK-47s over their chests. They kept a close eye on the steady trickle of people still passing through at this point in the late afternoon. But they did not seem to be excluding anyone. Bustling women in headscarves, who had never known a free election in their lifetimes, pushed past them. They brought little children, to whom they wanted to introduce the new idea that a ballot might actually mean something. While no one talked openly about it, Egypt had done something even more important than topple a dictator; it had ended an era of passivity.

On every stucco or stone wall there were campaign posters and banners advertising the scores of new political parties that did not exist only a few months before. It wasn't as if they had distinctive platforms; this election was all about people who the neighbors knew or trusted or thought would be more likely to improve their lives. Because a large portion of the population is illiterate, each party adopted its own symbol—a cactus, a soccer ball, a piano, even a toothbrush. And so Egyptians lined up, leaflets in hand, to check off the box for the soccer-ball party or cast their ballot for the toothbrush guy.

But as I wandered around, it became clear that much of the organization and efficiency of the elections was thanks to the Muslim Brotherhood volunteers. Throughout the elections, young members sat in neighborhoods like Rod El Farag with laptop computers open, providing assistance to anyone who stopped by to ask about voting. Voters were given little maps to direct them where they needed to go. Turning the paper over, they would notice the Freedom and Justice Party's logo on the back. The strategy was fairly subtle—the logo was all it took.

The Brotherhood's professionalism during the elections impressed everyone—from Jimmy Carter, who, naturally, had come to monitor the historic proceedings, to the American diplomats who fanned out to watch the process, to the liberals who could only look on in reluctant admiration as the Brotherhood accomplished what they could not.

"I'm amazed at the party organization, the rigor, and discipline of the Muslim Brotherhood," one senior American diplomat told me. "They will be a major political party for years to come."

Even many of the liberals gave them credit. I spoke with Ahmed Safyeldin—a self-described agnostic and active participant in liberal causes. Tall and lanky, he had perfected his English after a few years studying at the Virginia Military Institute. Despite his liberal leanings, he described without even a hint of bitterness how his family had come to rely on the Brotherhood. Growing up in the poor, agricultural region of Beni Suef, he said, "The Muslim Brotherhood came into my village, and brought lorries of fruits and vegetables," selling them at discounted prices. "They supported medical clinics"—and, through doing so, won the hearts and minds of the people they served.

The irony is that Mubarak, who spent so much time warning Washington that he was the only one who could keep Egypt from falling under the Brotherhood's sway, actually ended up fueling the movement's rise. By leaving his citizens without a social safety net, by failing to invest in the country's crumbling infrastructure, by never addressing its astounding illiteracy rates, he paved the way for the Brotherhood's success, neighborhood by neighborhood. In a land where the state delivers so little, even the smallest clinic will win respect and loyalty. So when it came time to vote, most Egyptians decided to cast their ballots for candidates they knew could provide something—Islamist or not, it almost didn't matter—rather than a disparate group of unknowns. For Ahmed and many others, it wasn't surprising that the organization that had dug deep roots in Egypt's neighborhoods for so long would walk away with a near majority.

OVER TIME, the Obama administration adjusted to the new reality. When the deputy secretary of state, Bill Burns, one of the United States' most experienced diplomats in the Middle East, showed up in Cairo in January 2012, he stopped first at the military headquarters and then headed straight to the Muslim Brotherhood offices.

"Our interest is not in which political party wins or loses in an election, it is whether democracy wins or loses," he told the Egyptian press.[7] But as Burns later acknowledged, there was nothing else he could say. It was too early to tell if the Brotherhood believed its own rhetoric about focusing on the economy or whether it was feeding a line to the foreigners who were streaming in. After all, the same Muslim Brotherhood that was talking about maintaining the peace treaty with Israel also kept praising an attack a few months earlier on the Israeli embassy in Cairo on its website. Which party had just gotten elected?

The answer, in Burns's mind, was that both realities could be true at once. The Muslim Brotherhood was full of technocrats and small businessmen, but it also had hard-liners in its ranks. Which wing would dominate? We simply don't know, Burns told me, just as we don't know in Tunisia, where Islamists also won. And to some degree, it wouldn't make a difference if we did know. The elections were credible. If Washington didn't like the results—well, the days of calling over to the CIA to put a friendly dictator in power were long gone.

But there was one lurking fear: the rise of the Salafis, the true fundamentalists. Everyone had "missed the Salafi groundswell," one senior American diplomat told me. The Salafis were strongest in the rural areas, among Egypt's poorest, and had attained about a quarter of the parliamentary seats. They thrived in places where even the Muslim Brotherhood didn't have much of a presence. But no poll had predicted their rise. Even the Muslim Brotherhood leadership was surprised by the ultra-Islamists' strength at the polls. At the gleaming new Muslim Brotherhood headquarters not far from Tahrir Square (the Brotherhood got the splendid building, while the party got the dump), they talked about the Salafis as a kind of crazy neighbor who lived down the street, constantly spewing religious doctrine rather than worrying about whether someone was fixing the schools and picking up the garbage. As an American diplomat said to me in Cairo, it made you wonder, "What else are we missing?"

The Salafis' influence is the big mystery in the new Egypt. By themselves, they cannot accomplish much. But since the Muslim Brotherhood garnered less than a majority, it will have to draw together support from somewhere to get anything done. Although the Freedom and Justice Party leaders claimed that their ruling coalition would not include the Salafis, the major concern, as one of Secretary Clinton's aides put it, is that even if they aren't part of a formal coalition, "the Salafists are going to pull the Muslim Brotherhood to the right."

Everyone recognized that the results at the polls produced a titanic shift, but no one could quite say whether it would be good for Egypt—much less for the rest of the Arab world or for the United States. "Anyone who tells you that they understand what is about to happen here is either lying or doesn't know what they are talking about," one senior American official told me. "We're making it up every day."

A RIGHTWARD TUG was not the only problem on the road to democracy. In the months after Mubarak fell, an unsettling pattern had emerged. Nabil Fahmy, former Egyptian ambassador to the United States, and now dean of the school of public affairs at the American University in Cairo, described those days with a touch of satire. Fahmy recalled arriving back in Egypt in 2011 in a jet-lagged haze. He had fallen asleep, he said, and woke up the next morning uncertain what day it was. But to orient himself, he told me, he simply had to listen to the news. If there were big demonstrations, it had to be a Friday. If the protestors were making demands, it was the weekend. By Monday, there would be a standoff between the military council and the protestors. By Wednesday, the stalemate ended as the military conceded on some small point or another—and promised to lift some aspect of the emergency laws or fund some project. By Thursday, protestors would be getting ready to repeat the cycle.

In reality, the liberals and other groups who kept returning to the streets had a lot to complain about. More than eighty people had died in protests in the year since Mubarak had been ousted, most at the hands of security forces who, out of fear or incompetence, overreacted when the streets filled again with young people charging that too little had changed. As many as twelve thousand others were awaiting trial by military tribunals for infractions that ranged from the serious to the inane. Bloggers who criticized the military were being jailed. Then there came the case of Naguib

Sawiris, a Coptic Christian telecommunications executive and leader of the Free Egyptians Party. He was charged with "contempt of religion" for retweeting a Mickey Mouse image that showed the Disney character in Islamic robes with a full beard. (Minnie Mouse was in a full-face veil.)[8] Emergency laws still reigned, and the effect was disquieting.

At the most basic level, the streets of Cairo were less safe than ever before, and the Copts felt it the worst of all. In the face of increased sectarian tensions, thousands of them had packed their bags and left the country.[9] "Under Mubarak," a Coptic friend remarked, "at least I had been able to walk the streets at night without fear. Now every time I leave my house, it's a calculated decision."

As the one-year anniversary of the uprising approached, the police started erecting giant stone walls across the narrow streets around Tahrir Square to stop new waves of protests from tearing apart the Interior Ministry and other government institutions that demonstrators claimed still reeked of the old regime. The barriers gave the place the faint feel of Berlin, circa 1961. So did the graffiti. On the walls of the downtown campus of the American University in Cairo, workers were whitewashing walls that had an English-language acronym sprayed everywhere: ACAB— "All Cops Are Bastards."

I went to meet the very people who, if they weren't the ones carrying around the cans of spray paint, were probably the first to utter the viral slogans that made their way to the walls of Cairo. Rania Salah Seddik, a fiery and fast-talking activist, had organized a gathering for us to meet several of her friends, all of whom had been on the front lines on January 25. Rania's brother Ahmed Salah Seddik greeted my research assistants and me, and ushered us into an open, largely empty apartment with vaulted ceilings. Several activists gathered around a small table, eager to tell us about their experiences bringing down a dictator and their hopes for keeping the spirit of Tahrir alive.

The protests they ignited almost a year earlier had broken down a wall of fear that had existed in Egyptians before, they told us, and they claimed they would face bullets and blood to ensure the revolution was completed. Here were the engineers of the revolution, but it was clear they were now sidelined. A mixed tone of hope and resignation permeated the room. They recognized that the time horizon for success would be stretched out much further than they had originally anticipated. This would take a very long time—"maybe twenty to thirty years," Ahmed suggested determinedly. They were committed to the long haul. What they got most excited about—the focus of their strategy sessions—was going back into the streets and exerting more pressure with protests and sit-ins, all of the techniques with which the youth had demonstrated their competitive advantage.

But when elections came around, they had been divided on the question of whether to participate. Rania argued for boycotting the vote; so had others in the room. The hastily drafted electoral procedures were unfair, she said. The parties were corrupt or too weak. The results would be unrepresentative.

Several of her friends disagreed: for most Egyptians, the activists acknowledged, voting was the only tangible benefit they had seen out of the uprising. They certainly weren't finding new jobs or making more money. No one in the room had voted for the Muslim Brotherhood, but most said they were willing to give them a try. "It's the will of the people," Abdelrahman Jad, another animated activist with unwavering convictions, conceded.

On one issue, they did all agree: the United States, they thought, was part of Egypt's problem—even with Mubarak gone. "I believe I'm fighting the US," Rania said. "The military is US-made. Mubarak was US-made. The US money just doesn't go to the people." While she couldn't tell me basic facts about the Egyptian economy, she knew that the United States gave $1.3 billion in annual aid to the military and she was convinced that the bullets and tear gas canisters used against her and her friends a year ago could have come from only one source. It wasn't that she thought Americans were by and large bad—she had traveled to the United States many times before, loved Los Angeles, and had many American friends. But when it came to politics and policy, any talk of common values and shared interests between the two countries was only a convenient cover for Washington's coldly strategic national interests, she insisted.

A few days later, I sat down with Ahmed Maher, one of the founders of the April 6 Youth Movement that had helped launch the uprising. He had a calming presence and a soft voice. He, too, however, expressed disdain for entering organized politics. The military had offered him an appointed position in parliament, he said, apparently to buy him off—or wrap him up in the system. He immediately refused. How could he agree to be a puppet of the military? He felt he could get more done outside the government anyway. Maher was probably right. Even those liberals who did make it into parliament seemed more interested in using their seats as a forum for continued protest than as a place to change Mubarak-era laws or attempt job-creating initiatives. At one of the first sessions of parliament, as they were holding elections for committee chairs, the liberals stormed out, complaining that the Freedom and Justice Party was dominating the session. The result: the passionate revolutionaries got no chairmanships. They were masters of Facebook and flash mobs, but were paralyzed by the sharp elbows of daily politics.

It wasn't just the students who were edged out. So was the man who had returned to Egypt to lead the revolutionaries to victory. When Mohamed ElBaradei left his post as the director general of the International Atomic Energy Agency at the end of 2009, he stopped jousting with the Iranians and took on Mubarak. His return to Cairo was a major turning point for the opposition: Mubarak might jail a member of the Muslim Brotherhood, but he couldn't arrest Egypt's most famous citizen, winner of the Nobel Peace Prize. From his quiet villa in a gated neighborhood far outside Cairo, ElBaradei's constant stream of critiques ate away at Mubarak's legitimacy. Many protestors made him a symbolic leader—a member of the establishment who had signed on with Egypt's youth. When they ousted Mubarak, they excitedly mobbed ElBaradei in the square. For a while it looked like the Nobel laureate could end up occupying the presidential palace.

But once Mubarak was gone, it became obvious ElBaradei had little connection with ordinary Egyptians. He had spent much of his professional life outside the country. He was too secular, too Western. He had an apartment in Vienna and a country home in the south of France.

By January, when I dropped by ElBaradei's villa in a posh neighborhood outside Cairo to catch up with him for the first time since he had left the IAEA, he had all but given up. Over coffee in his living room, he told me that if he ran for president, it would cripple his effectiveness: he would be caught between a stubborn military and the Islamist majority in parliament. Worse yet, it seemed the Muslim Brotherhood and Tantawi's Supreme Council of the Armed Forces were in the process of working out their own agreement for sharing power—roughly that the military would handle all military affairs and some foreign relations, and leave the rest up to the Islamists. How, ElBaradei asked, would a liberal president be able to cut through all that? Instead, he wanted to turn to his base—the liberal, revolutionary youth—and focus his efforts on training them to be more prepared for the next electoral round. The American officials who met ElBaradei heard his explanation—and walked away, shaking their heads.

Beyond protests and politicking, another even more dangerous threat was escalating: the foundering economy. Egypt was spending billions just to keep its currency afloat. With tourism completely dried up and financial reserves critically low, the country was on the verge of becoming the Greece of North Africa. And like the Greeks, the Egyptians approached the subject with varying degrees of denial or panic.

Essam el-Erian, the Muslim Brotherhood official, settled on a strategy of optimism. "After building a democratic system, the money will flow back in," he insisted during that visit to the Freedom and Justice Party. "Many Arab investors want to invest in Egypt," he said. But the evidence was scarce. American and European money was holding on the sidelines, while they tried to figure out what the Islamist victory actually meant. The Saudis and other oil-rich countries in the Gulf—aghast at the treatment of former president Mubarak on trial, lying on a stretcher in a cage—had promised aid and investment, but delivered almost nothing.

Unemployment had been high before the revolution; it went higher after Mubarak was ousted. Building projects halted and the outskirts of Cairo were dotted with the shells of unfinished apartment complexes. No one could find work, and young people could not afford to get married. Meanwhile, the military council had no discernible economic plan.

Worst of all, the tourism sector lay in ruins. Layers of dust had accumulated on the floors of the Egyptian Museum, largely undisturbed by the scuffling feet of tourists. When I walked through the museum with my two research assistants one afternoon, it was us and the mummies—we were the only Americans there. The same was true at the Pyramids of Giza, where Egyptians offering guided tours and trinkets outnumbered us by at least ten to one.

In a series of calls to the leadership at the end of 2011, Hillary Clinton told the Egyptians they now had no choice: they had to let the IMF, whose offers had been rejected in May, back into the country. She sent her deputy Bill Burns and Robert D. Hormats, the undersecretary of state for economic, energy, and agricultural affairs, to explain to the Egyptians why their choice was to either sign up with the IMF or try to navigate a crippling economic crisis alone while the government was still in transition. "It's exactly the position you don't want to be in," Hormats said, "where a new parliament is asked to cut services." While a few billion dollars in IMF loans might have done the trick back in May of 2011, Egypt's finance minister cried out in early 2012 that the country would now need $11 billion or more.[10]

But the liberal activists I spoke with, along with many other political players, hated the idea of taking any foreign aid. Ahmed Salah Seddik, one of the Tahrir youth I met with, told me, "The revolution was against Mubarak—it's our revolution. No other country should interfere. We don't want US money." (Of course, the IMF is not part of the United States, but to Ahmed and his friends, they all seemed the same.)

The military wasn't much better. Any outside interference, its top officers feared, could reveal embarrassing details of the military's investments, or the corruption that has feathered so many nests. What's more, the officers running the interim government had never seen anyone from the IMF before. "To them," one senior American official said after a meeting with the military council, "there's not much difference between an IMF and a Martian."

"Actually," he added, "they probably know more about Martians."

The only ones taking a more pragmatic approach seemed to be the Muslim Brotherhood. After decades spent railing against Western imperialism, they had nonetheless openly recognized the need to manage the impending economic crisis and shown a willingness to negotiate if the conditions were acceptable.

El-Erian said the Muslim Brotherhood understood the conflict that was coming, but he was not sure its Salafi partners did. "We hope that we can pull the Salafists—not that they pull us—and that both of us will be pulled by the people's needs."

In short, those in power in Egypt were playing a highly

dangerous game—deciding whether to fear the markets or the newly empowered voters more. Stick to your principles and wait too long, and the country's economy could spiral out of control as foreign reserves dwindle. Take an aid package from the notoriously unpopular lenders of last resort, and the subsequent austerity measures imposed on the people could quickly turn into a political death sentence.

THE REAL PROBLEMS for Washington started around lunchtime on December 29, 2011. Julie Hughes, the Egypt country director of the National Democratic Institute (NDI), a democracy-promotion group funded by the United States and linked to the Democratic Party, was working in her office when a troop of Egyptian officers barged in unannounced. They gave no names, no identification, and claimed they needed no warrant. As Hughes tried to place a call to the embassy, they confiscated her phone—and since the men were waving around AK-47s, she decided not to argue with them. For the next five and a half hours, she and about two dozen other employees stood helplessly by as the men grabbed computers, collected files, and demanded Internet server passwords.

Groups like NDI had been grudgingly tolerated during the years in Egypt under Mubarak, though they were kept on edge because the government almost never gave them formal licenses. (They remained perpetually "pending.") Hughes, a loud and witty international-development professional who enjoyed telling tales of bureaucratic idiocy, was accustomed to operating in this sort of quasi-legal limbo. The expectation, of course, had been that the revolution—followed by real elections and presumably more democratic structures—would create a new age of openness. This should have been the moment for NDI and its Republican equivalent across town, the International Republican Institute, to thrive.

Instead, they were quashed. By the end of the day, Egyptian

forces had raided seventeen mostly US-funded organizations, including Freedom House, the International Republican Institute, and the International Center for Journalists. When the American embassy tried to uncover the reasons behind the raids, the answers they received were vague and unsatisfactory.

It marked an ugly turn in the evolution of the new Egypt. With the economy going down in flames, common criminals running amok, and protests over the military's rule continuing, Mubarak's successors needed an enemy on whom they could heap the blame. Who better than the foreigners who could easily be caricatured as trying to undermine Egypt's sovereignty? It was an old, and usually successful, Egyptian political ploy.

It began with military officers warning darkly of nefarious foreign "influences." Then the Egyptian press began to fill up with stories of how hundreds of millions of dollars were secretly being funneled in to control the outcome of Egypt's first election. ("As if we had hundreds of millions of dollars!" Ms. Hughes said, laughing, one evening over coffee.) But the reports were successfullly fueling anti-American sentiments.

The raids turned out to be the work of one of Egypt's most ambitious politicians, Fayza Abul Naga, minister of the wonderfully named Ministry of Planning and International Cooperation. She was a Mubarak-era holdout and crony of the former first lady, Suzanne Mubarak. In the vacuum left by Mubarak's ouster and trial, Abul Naga was elbowing her way to power in this new transitional government, opposing Western pressure for economic reforms and declaring her outrage that $65 million in grants for pro-democracy training was being sent from the United States directly to the democracy groups—rather than through her ministry.[11]

When the skeleton holiday staff in the State Department first learned of the coordinated raids, they were a bit dumbfounded. To their minds, the United States had painstakingly avoided the appearance of involvement in Egyptian politics, so what could this possibly be about? President Obama called Field Marshal Tantawi, urging him to solve the problem. But he was probably calling the wrong guy; despite having encouraged the nationalistic paranoia, the military had also been taken by surprise by Abul Naga's bold move.

But the accusations only turned nastier: American pushback on the raids was characterized as further evidence of "interference" in a domestic Egyptian judicial investigation. Egyptian officials began to describe the raided organizations as tools of the CIA and "Israeli interests," hitting every hot button in Egyptian politics. Abul Naga did not quite come out and say that the protestors who brought down Mubarak were working for Washington, but that was the implication. By February 2012, formal criminal charges were issued for forty-three employees of the pro-democracy groups. By that time, most of the accused Americans had left the country; a small group, including Sam LaHood, the son of Obama's transportation secretary, was not so lucky. They took refuge in the US embassy. The charges looked like something out of a Borat movie: the democracy groups were inciting "religious tensions between Muslims and Copts" and were intent on "bringing down the ruling regime in Egypt, no matter what it is," on behalf of "Jewish lobbyists."

In fact, American law forbade the groups from seeking to influence elections; they could only offer how-to trainings for political campaigns. Even the Muslim Brotherhood and the Salafis had participated. "If anyone was trying to throw the election in our direction," one American diplomat quipped to me, "they sure did a crappy job of it." But facts meant little. Soon, a trial began, with the Americans *in absentia*.

Naturally, Congress and the State Department reacted by warning that Egypt's $1.5 billion in annual aid was at stake. After all, Clinton told the Egyptians, how could she certify that Egypt was transitioning to civilian, democratic rule when the old guard was holding show trials? But the Egyptians sensed the threat to cut off the money was an empty one: Egypt's military aid, by far the biggest part of the package, was essentially an annual payment for maintaining the Egypt-Israel peace treaty. If Congress killed the cash, the Egyptians could kill the treaty.

So Abul Naga declared that if the United States wanted to play tough, Egypt would turn to others for support. Iran, she suggested, might be a good option, knowing that would hit a particular neuralgia in Washington. The Egyptian prime minister played to the crowds, declaring, "Egypt will not kneel," language that conjured up the master-and-servant relationship Egyptians despised.[12]

For weeks, it seemed, no one had the power to step in and exercise some common sense. In the end, the US struck a deal that freed the Americans trapped in the embassy for a bond of $300,000 each, essentially ransom money to bundle them out of the country. The Egyptians could go ahead with the trial, with the Americans safely beyond their reach. Days later Clinton waived the conditions on sending aid to Egypt, enabling the $1.5 billion to flow, based on US "national security interests."[13] Even though the Egyptians told pollsters, quite overwhelmingly, that they did not want their country to rely on American aid,[14] it didn't seem smart to burn any bridges in the midst of a transition of power. Egypt was heading in an unpredictable direction, and the United States needed to preserve all the leverage it could get.

It was a rough way to mark the first anniversary of the revolution. What had begun with such promise—with hope that Egypt would emerge as a new model of democracy in the heart of the Arab world—had devolved into threats and mistrust.

At the root of this concocted debate over "American meddling" seemed to be an attempt at counterrevolution, under the guise of defending Egypt's independence and national dignity. After a year of keeping a low profile, Mubarak's old cronies—except the few token officials who ended up purged and jailed for corruption—were stepping once again into the spotlight. The hyped charges against the Americans were exquisitely designed to touch the latent but familiar chord of xenophobia, an effective tactic through which long-serving officials tried to reassert their role as protectors of the state.

So, despite Obama's best efforts, the United States had been sucked into the new politics of Egypt. Obama would have to either support the military by assuring them of unconditional American aid or risk a messy, public break. Thirty-three years after Anwar Sadat signed the historic deal with Israel, this was no time to be exploring trial separations.

AT THE BEGINNING of April 2012, a delegation of the Freedom and Justice Party came to Washington on what could only be described as the Muslim Brotherhood's charm offensive. With slick Power-Points, the group whose very name inspired fear and loathing on Capitol Hill glossed over the hardest question—how they would rule Egypt—and focused on an optimistic message that a new era had arrived. At Georgetown University, in a packed auditorim, one articulate, young female representative of the party—who also oversaw the Brotherhood's Twitter feed—made a rousing pitch that the group was "here to start building bridges of understanding with the United States."[15]

The Muslim Brotherhood had reason to look for allies in Washington. Mubarak's old circle of elites was becoming more assertive: two of the fallen president's old apparatchiks, including Omar Suleiman, the onetime intelligence chief who was on the phone with Joe Biden during Tahrir Square—were running for president.

Only four months before, Essam el-Erian, the enthusiastic party official, had reassured me that his group had no need to field a presidential candidate. Now they had reconsidered. They nominated Khairat el-Shater, a multimillionaire business tycoon and Brotherhood leader, to become the first civilian president. The

Brotherhood even had a back-up plan: if el-Shater proved ineligible (he had served in jail during Mubarak's rule for money laundering and his association with the Brotherhood), other candidates were in the wings. The message was clear: the Brotherhood wasn't going to let its chance go by.

But if the Brotherhood surprised Egyptians by reneging on their promise to keep out of the presidential race, the bigger surprise came when, a month before the elections, three of the country's leading presidential contenders (and seven others) were declared ineligible to run. El-Shater, the Muslim Brotherhood's leading candidate, was among them—for a supposed past criminal conviction. The leading contender for the ultra-Islamist party was also disqualified because his mother had been an American citizen. Even Omar Suleiman, Mubarak's former vice president and intelligence chief, was struck from the ballot. Conspiracy theories proliferated, but these seemed like the growing pains of a proto-democracy without rules. Ultimately, the electoral chaos said much about the challenge Obama and his successors will face in dealing with the most important political force in the Arab world.

The next few years will be a constant tug of war between fundamentalists and democracy-builders. The old guard will be pitted against the Islamist parties, with aspirations of changing the nature of the state and against those who led the revolution in the square. No doubt Americans will recoil at some of the laws that are passed, as Egyptians weave conspiracy theories about how Americans are seeking to meddle. But even among the ranks of leadership, there seem to be more Egyptians who want to build a real democracy than join a cause. Obama is betting that they will win the argument, and that maintaining ideological purity is hard in a country that has virtually no oil revenue, that has an economy in free-fall, and that needs the world's help.

The difficulty, of course, is how best to provide that help—and thus promote Egypt's democratic advancement—while not appearing to interfere with its choices. That is never easy: Congress will react to provocations with more threats to turn off the enormous military-aid package, and perhaps the ridiculously small civilian-aid package. Whether Obama can alter that ratio—$1.3 billion for the military, $250 million for civilian aid—and make civilian support primary, may be a test of his fidelity to his own declarations about supporting the most important uprising in the Arab Spring.

In Egypt, politicians seeking headlines will find ways to blame Washington for whatever ails the Egyptian polity. It will take years for a political culture to take root, and there is no assurance that that culture will protect the rights of the Copts, or build a functional democracy, or apply international standards of justice. But it is not as if anyone in Washington "lost" Egypt; Mubarak was going to go, and in retrospect he went more gently than might have been expected.

The Egyptian regime's fall had another, more disturbing implication. After seeing Mubarak's quick removal—and his reappearance in a courtroom cage—the leaders of neighboring countries vowed they would not let the same fate befall them. The result has been more blood spilled and a far more murky prognosis for democracy and stability in the Middle East. When the world looks back at how the United States responded to upheaval in the Middle East, Egypt may turn out to have been the easy case.

CHAPTER 14

WHAT WORKS ONCE DOESN'T ALWAYS WORK TWICE

Any future defense secretary who advises the president to again send a big American land army into Asia or into the Middle East or Africa should "have his head examined," as General MacArthur so delicately put it.

—*Secretary of Defense Robert M. Gates, at West Point, NY, February 25, 2011*[1]

TUNISIA AND EGYPT WERE THRILLING UPRISINGS, AND THEY MADE for mesmerizing television. They fed a narrative Americans love: long-suffering people—under the yoke of corrupt, ossified dictators—take to the streets to regain control of their own lives and their own countries. That is, of course, the story of the American Revolution.

And after a decade of fear in the West that the Arab world was falling into the hands of al-Qaeda and other Islamic extremists, the images flowing out of Tahrir Square suggested a very different picture. There were no posters or T-shirts glorifying Osama bin Laden or his deputy, Ayman al-Zawahiri, the Egyptian who had been radicalized on those same Cairo streets. The young protestors had accomplished, in under three weeks, what al-Qaeda was unable to engineer in two decades. The messy part—the chafing at continued military rule, the rise of the Muslim Brotherhood and other Islamist parties—all came later.

For President Obama, Egypt and Tunisia turned out to be the easy revolutions.

Less than a week after Mubarak stepped down in early February 2011, protests began rumbling in Yemen, Bahrain, Jordan, Algeria, Oman, and Morocco. Each posed Obama with a very different kind of challenge—and in many cases, an excruciatingly painful balancing act between America's values and its interests.

But two uprisings in particular—Libya and Syria—put what the White House steadfastly refused to call the emerging Obama Doctrine to the test. As Libya fell and the pictures leaking out of Syria grew more and more horrific, the questions about Obama's consistency grew more urgent, around the world and in Washington.

Many Arabs asked, How could the US president, much less *this* president, justify joining his allies in using force to protect Libyans from being slaughtered in Benghazi, but shrink back when Assad did the same, or worse, in Homs? How could he declare that it is America's moral responsibility to aid people who are being killed by their own governments, but only if it can be done without putting American lives at risk, and without American boots on the ground? Isn't that just halfway in? And how could he denounce Muammar Qaddafi and Bashar al-Assad for how they abused their own people, and yet fall silent when Bahrain's royal family—host to the US Navy's Fifth Fleet, the most important single facility for keeping Iran at bay in the Strait of Hormuz—presides over security forces that beat protestors and arrest the doctors who cared for the wounded?

"I could lay out a perfectly reasonable rationale for each decision we made, in isolation," one senior State Department official conceded to me early in 2012. "But the fact of the matter is, our interests never line up perfectly with our values, and they never have. So we're haunted by those same questions every day."

THE FIRST TEST came in Libya, where Col. Muammar Qaddafi had spent most of the past decade trying to reinvent himself as the dictator who, late in life, decided to rejoin the rest of the world.

For the previous three decades, he had been the worst kind of American adversary. Ronald Reagan called him the "mad dog of the Middle East," a phrase that stuck. President Anwar el-Sadat of Egypt probably was closer to the truth when he termed his neighbor "the crazy Libyan." Qaddafi had become almost a parody of a crazed megalomaniac, with his phalanx of buxom female guards trained in martial arts, his music video and photo albums dedicated to Condoleezza Rice, and his fear of elevators, which led him to demand to be allowed to pitch a tent camp in Central Park during the United Nations General Assembly. (New York said no.) The Brother Leader, as he called himself, was so bizarre that it was easy to forget he was also a deadly terrorist, as the world discovered when, in 1988, Libyan agents blew up Pan Am Flight 103 over the Scottish town of Lockerbie, killing 259 people aboard and 11 on the ground.

But in 2003, either because of sanctions or fear of invasion, Qaddafi gave up his nascent effort to build nuclear weapons. In truth, the venture had gotten him nowhere; he had not even unpacked most of the boxes that A. Q. Kahn sent with Pakistani-style centrifuges. For the next eight years, the West veered between accepting him back into the world community and holding him at bay, fearful that the new Qaddafi might really be the old Qaddafi.

What most people in the West missed was that Qaddafi's own people despised him. The depth of that hatred became clear after several lawyers began protesting the imprisonment of a colleague on the evening of February 15, 2011. Clearly inspired by the Egyptians and the Tunisians, the protests swelled into a demonstration of hundreds. In Tripoli, a battle started between civilians throwing stones and policemen spraying water cannons. Then, six days after Mubarak had been forced to leave Cairo, a ragtag collection of security forces loyal to Qaddafi and hired mercenaries—among them Chinese, Africans, and Bangladeshis—opened fire with machine guns into unarmed crowds. The attack, while brutal, did not have the intended effect. From Benghazi to Tripoli, hundreds of thousands of people braved the bullets and joined the protests. Qaddafi veered between brutal repression and transparently false efforts at accommodation: "Take down your Facebook pages," he snapped at Khalid Saih, a lawyer and activist, "and your demands will be met."[2]

The peaceful protestors decided to change course; they began arming themselves. What had started with Facebook calls for nonviolent action, like in Tunisia and Egypt, quickly escalated into a much bloodier scene.[3] As newly formed rebel groups began to consolidate control over Benghazi, the opposition stronghold to the east of Tripoli, American spy satellites showed Qaddafi's forces heading toward the city. Inside the White House, Obama's aides knew that the president would have to make a decision they had been spared in the previous uprisings: whether to intervene militarily on behalf of the rebels.

"I CAN'T BELIEVE we were about to debate taking military action in another Islamic nation," one senior member of Obama's national security team said to me one night over a beer, not far from the White House. Here was an American president, elected to extract the country from conflicts that had spun off in unforeseen directions, contemplating using his executive authority to start a new one. Obama had no plans to consult with Congress, save in a cursory way; like all modern presidents, he saw the issue of using military force as a critical executive prerogative.

It soon became clear, however, that Obama's national security team had rarely been so divided—and the divisions went to the heart of a vital question: What is the purpose of American power? Was it to protect those around the world who could not protect themselves? Or to be used only in the defense of critical American national security interests—a test that Libya clearly would not pass?

Some, like Susan Rice, one of Obama's earliest and closest advisers on foreign policy, were determined to see American warplanes join NATO forces to defend Benghazi and end Muammar Qaddafi's forty-year rule. Samantha Power, who won a Pulitzer for her analysis of the genocides of the past century—including the Clinton administration's failure to respond in Rwanda—also pressed the case from inside the National Security Council. Power had taken time off from her academic career to advise Obama during his campaign for president, and had schooled him in the "Responsibility to Protect"—the emerging concept that the international community has a responsibility to intervene to prevent mass atrocity. Now Obama was facing a much more dire test than the one he confronted with Mubarak. Could he stand by while Qaddafi destroyed his second-largest city, killing untold thousands simply to stay in power?

"There was this group [within the NSC] that was haunted by Rwanda," one participant in the meeting told me later. "They all walked into that session determined not to make the same mistake a second time."

But others were haunted by a far more recent mistake: Iraq. Before the meeting, Defense Secretary Robert Gates had been outspoken in warning the world that intervening in Libya, even simply with air power, would not be clean and easy. Gates knew he was leaving soon, so he was more willing than usual to speak his mind—even if it put him at odds with others in the administration.

"There's a lot of, frankly, loose talk about some of these military actions," he said, trying to make everyone think twice about pulling the trigger. "Let's just call a spade a spade. A no-fly zone begins with an attack on Libya to destroy the air defenses. That's the way you do a no-fly zone. And then you can fly planes around the country and not worry about the other guys being shot down. But that's the way it starts. So it's a big operation in a big country."[4]

This was classic Gates. He had overseen two wars in the last five years, costing over a trillion dollars and thousands of American lives. He paved the way out of Iraq, which he once privately termed a "dumb war," and was trying to find a way out of Afghanistan. Now he was attempting to prevent a president, twenty years his junior, from attacking yet another Muslim country—and, more important in Gates's mind, a country in which America had no significant national interests.[5] While no one in the administration or Congress argued for using ground troops in Libya, Gates sensed that his civilian counterparts didn't understand the potential scope and complexity of less aggressive actions. Gates knew what he was up against; he had to find a way for the president to live up to his moral commitments, but without taking huge risks or setting precedents Obama would regret if the United States got sucked into a longer, messier war.[6]

In private, Gates had been even more forceful to Donilon on the issue: a no-fly zone at this point wouldn't be enough to stop Qaddafi's forces from besieging Benghazi. They would need to be able to strike more broadly at forces loyal to Qaddafi. The fragmented, leaderless rebel forces would also need training and arms.

But this ran the risk of mission creep, the disease that had struck both Iraq and Afghanistan. The story was a familiar one by now: what begins as a narrow task soon becomes something larger, more expensive, and bloodier. In a tribal country like Libya, which suffered under years of ironclad rule and had no history of democracy, Gates made it clear that this could be a bad sequel to the tragic play America had been stuck in for a decade.

Susan Rice joined the Situation Room meeting through a video link from the US mission to the United Nations in New York City. Rice was always blunt-spoken; despite the fact that she was fairly petite, she was a basketball player, and all elbows. A Stanford graduate, a Rhodes Scholar, and the daughter of a Cornell professor and Brookings Institution scholar, Rice felt perfectly at home in the high-testosterone Sit Room atmosphere. She also knew this subject well; she had served as the director of international organizations and peacekeeping for the NSC during the Clinton administration—a post she held during the Rwandan genocide. She visited Rwanda after the killings were over and recalled, "I swore to myself that if I ever faced such a crisis again, I would come down on the side of dramatic action, going down in flames if required."[7]

Although Libya wasn't even approaching genocide levels, the parallels were clear. Qaddafi was delusional, erratic, and had a history of brutality. He had already killed more than a thousand people, and there was no question he would continue slaughtering his opposition unless he was stopped. And time was running out: every new satellite pass overhead showed more troops moving in on Benghazi.

While Gates urged caution, and Rice advocated strongly for intervention, Clinton initially fell somewhere in between. She had a complex history with respect to the use of military force. She had watched as her husband did nothing to prevent the massacre of 800,000 Rwandans in the mid-'90s, which he later came to regret as the greatest mistake of his presidency. On the campaign trail, she renounced her early support for the decision to go to war in Iraq, but in 2009 she again aligned herself with the defense establishment— Gates, Mullen, and McChrystal—and supported the surge in Afghanistan.

After some uncertainty, she decided to split from Gates. Qaddafi was vowing to hunt down the insurgents in Benghazi "like rats," declaring he would go "house by house and alley by alley."*

---

* It was a sign of how much respect Qaddafi had lost that the line was turned into an auto-tuned parody called "Zenga Zenga"—the unusual Libyan word for "alley." In no time, the YouTube video had gone viral.

Clinton argued that Obama could not sit idly by and watch that massacre.

Clinton flew to Paris to meet with the Libyan opposition and test the true extent of Arab support. She was surprised at what she found. Usually the Arab League was spineless. But this time, the league coalesced toward action, helped along by the fact that so many members despised Qaddafi. It called on the United Nations "to shoulder its responsibility to impose a no-fly zone over the movement of Libyan military planes and to create safe zones in the places vulnerable to airstrikes." How, she asked her colleagues at the White House, could the United States refuse a request from Arab neighbors who had never before put limits on one of their own? More important, she knew America's unique leverage would be essential to stop the impending massacre.

But for Obama, the critical question was whether the Arab states would do more than just ask for someone else to solve the problem—they had to participate, something most were loath to do. Qatar and the United Arab Emirates—tiny Arab powers—said they would consider sending planes to enforce the no-fly zone. This was crucial; it meant that the West would not be seen as unilaterally bombing another Arab country.

With Qaddafi moving toward an imminent attack and the international community aligned against him, Clinton was fully convinced; she joined ranks with Rice and Power in support of another intervention. So did a younger generation of advisers: Ben Rhodes, who had written much of Obama's Nobel speech on the use of force, argued that the Libya case fit Obama's own criteria for humanitarian intervention. Tony Blinken, Vice President Biden's national security adviser, differed with his boss and said the United States could not be perceived as sitting this one out. The question, though, was whether Obama could convince the countries with the most at stake to take the greatest risks and lead the charge. Soon the president was on the phone with Arab leaders, making it clear that for the US to participate, the Arab states had to have their planes in the air, too.

AS THE MEETING of the NSC convened on the afternoon of March 15, Obama was presented with satellite photos and other intelligence that Qaddafi's forces had already reached the town of Ajdabiya, the final stop on the way to Benghazi. It would be days, if not hours, before the Libyan military would launch an assault that could result in the massacre of thousands. But the only options presented to Obama involved doing nothing or enforcing a no-fly zone—which was close to doing nothing.

"What are we discussing at the UN? A no-fly zone?" Obama asked, turning to Adm. Mike Mullen, then the chairman of the Joint Chiefs of Staff. "Mike, is a no-fly zone going to stop anything we just heard about from happening?"

Mullen shook his head. "No sir."

"Well, then what are we even discussing here? Why are we even having this meeting?" Obama snapped, according to participants in the session. "If you're telling me that this guy is tearing through his country, about to overrun this city of seven hundred thousand people, and potentially kill thousands of people—why is the option I'm looking at one that will do nothing to stop that scenario?"

Nobody in the room knew what to say.

"This meeting is not worth having," Obama said, irritated. "I'm going to go to dinner with the Combatant Commanders"—an annual event with the four-star generals and admirals who run the biggest geographical commands around the world—"and by the time I come back, I want some real options." As soon as Obama left the Situation Room, the national security staff quickly began looking at options that would directly attack the approaching Libyan troops. One side-discussion, revealed only much later, involved whether to attempt a cyberattack on Libya's air defenses, in the hopes of bringing them down without firing a shot. It would have been an innovative use of a new weapon, paving the way for bombing runs, but also a risky one.

"Our problem was mostly technical," said one senior military official who was involved in the planning. "We just didn't have much time, and to do a successful cyber operation you need to know everything about the other side's computer infrastructure."

But there were other considerations as well. A debate broke out within the White House legal team about whether the president had the authority, under the War Powers Act, to order a cyberattack as part of a broader military operation without first consulting Congress. Others worried that a cyberattack would create a justification for other countries to hit the United States—the same concern Obama had expressed when he was debating the covert cyberattack on Iran.

Ultimately, the debate underscored the limits of cyber's effectiveness; unlike a bombing raid, accurate cyber operations take a lot of time to coordinate. "These cyber capabilities are still like the Ferrari that you keep in the garage and only take out for the big race and not just for a run around town, unless nothing else can get you there," one Obama administration official told my *Times* colleagues Thom Shanker and Eric Schmitt.[8]

But on the broader question of what to do about Benghazi, Obama's choices essentially came down to two: don't go in at all, or go in with something far, far bigger than the no-fly zone favored by the Arab League. Going in bigger would mean that the intervention in Libya would have to be reframed and its goals more explicitly defined. The United Nations Security Council would need to authorize any action necessary to protect civilian lives. This would give the military the room it needed to conduct more expansive operations, including airstrikes against Qaddafi's forces to stop the siege on Benghazi.

Biden and Gates argued the risks were simply too high: it would be better not to go in at all than to get immersed in a battle between

Qaddafi and his own people. This wasn't America's war, they said. It was a civil war.

Rarely had the choices been so stark or a new president's war council so divided. Four hours later, Obama reconvened the meeting. He was presented with all options, including attacking the Libyan troops from the air and from afar. It carried risks, but it was clear from Obama's reaction that, to his mind, it was the only viable choice. With the Arab League calling for intervention, and with France and England pushing for immediate NATO action, doing nothing was not a credible option. "We can't play the role of a Russia or a China," Obama told the NSC, according to the notes of participants. "If we don't act, if we put brakes on this thing, it will have consequences for US credibility and leadership, consequences for the Arab Spring, and consequences for the international community." He then played out a worst-case scenario of US inaction: a mass slaughter would occur in Benghazi, claiming tens or hundreds of thousands of civilian lives. And despite a clear and distinct opportunity to stop that atrocity, and after all Obama's own rhetoric about supporting universal human rights, the United States would be viewed as standing back, frozen by its mistakes in Iraq and Afghanistan. It would not wash, Obama said. He would be held morally responsible for failing to prevent a preventable massacre.

"That's just not who we are," Obama concluded.

VIEWED A YEAR later—and in light of Obama's agonizing choices in Syria, where he was accused of doing far too little to stop a far larger slaughter—his decision about Libya was revealing. It was not based on America's vital national interests: He held no illusions about the lack of Libya's strategic importance. Its oil exports were relatively trivial. It no longer had a nuclear weapons program, though doubtless Qaddafi now regretted giving up the arsenal, because it might have been the only thing that could have protected him from the airstrikes. It was an American embrace, at least in this one case, of the concept of a "responsibility to protect," even though White House officials went to great lengths not to use that term, for fear that it might lock them into some future decision.

But Obama is also innately cautious, and that was evident as he drew one line he would not cross in this post-Iraq age. He was not going to send ground troops into a third conflict. "When you are on the ground, you own the result—and it's not long before you are resented by the local population," Donilon said to me later. "We knew we needed a better way."

Obama wanted to strike from the air; Gates, having already lost the bigger fight on non-intervention, then insisted that the operation be time-limited. At a moment when limited American resources were under stress in Iraq (where the United States still had 47,000 troops as this debate played out) and Afghanistan (another 100,000), a lengthy commitment was not sustainable. Obama's solution was to get UN approval for airstrikes, but then to tell the allies that Washington would take the lead only at the beginning, so it could contribute its unique technologies without adding significantly to the $2-billion-a-week bill for Afghanistan.

Obama instructed Rice to present the United States' assessment of the situation in Libya and new resolution at the UN to the members of the Security Council who were pressing for action. "I want you to call their bluff," he said, according to one aide who was there. If they really wanted to protect civilian lives in Libya, they'd have to explicitly approve military action. NATO and its allies weren't going into Libya as peacekeepers to referee a protracted stalemate between loyalist and rebel forces, and they couldn't pretend that that was their role. To solve the problem, Qaddafi had to go. The UN resolution had to allow enough room to make that the de facto goal.

"If they're willing to sign up to this," Obama told Rice, "then we'll move forward."

But even with a broader mandate, Obama was specific: America's involvement must be limited in scope and finite in time. NATO always complained, he told his staff, that they were never allowed to take the lead on anything. Well, he said, now's their chance.

IT TOOK RICE only two days to get the Security Council to pass a resolution authorizing "all necessary measures"—short of foreign occupation forces—to end attacks against civilians. China, usually reflexively hostile to interfering in the internal affairs of sovereign states, didn't use its veto—it would have been too embarrassing for Beijing to appear to be carrying water for Qaddafi. "The Chinese hate the whole idea," one administration official told me at the time, "but they hate being isolated even more."

The primary dissenting voice, it turned out, was not one of America's typical rivals—it was a friend. Expressing concerns about the likelihood of success in Libya and the lack of consensus about the mission's objectives, Germany broke from the NATO alliance and abstained from the vote. Inside the White House, officials were derisive of Angela Merkel, the German chancellor, for failing to side with the United States. (That did not stop Obama, however, from presenting her with the Medal of Freedom when she came to Washington a few weeks later for a state visit.)

When the resolution passed, Qaddafi pretended to be unimpressed, ranting, "If the world is crazy, we will be crazy too."[9]

TWO DAYS AFTER the Security Council resolution passed—and eight years to the day after the United States announced its invasion of Iraq—NATO began its defense of Benghazi. Spurred by low approval ratings, French president Nicolas Sarkozy ordered his troops to preempt the coalition, striking hours before NATO had planned.[10] Sarkozy's premature action shook up an already unsettled alliance. From the beginning there were cleavages between France, Italy, and

Turkey. Sarkozy wanted to assemble a coalition outside of NATO to lead the attack. The others insisted that NATO had to be in the lead. When Sarkozy jumped the gun and began bombing strikes on his own, it only deepened the others' suspicions that Sarkozy's motives had more to do with his reelection than his military judgment. Barely having fired off its first shots, the alliance was already bickering.

Washington had hoped its allies would take charge, but not like this. Obama, aboard Air Force One during a trip to South America, was on the phone with the leaders of Turkey, France, and Britain to insist on a NATO-led command. In a particularly curt call with Sarkozy, he said he needed a public signal "so that there is no futher delay of our efforts," according to an informal transcript of the conversation. Clinton was doing the same with her counterparts, and eventually all parties accepted NATO's leadership.[11]

As that problem settled, however, another quickly surfaced: the Arab states that had pledged to contribute militarily—Qatar, the UAE, and Jordan—were getting nervous. They were worried about their own restive streets, and the optics of appearing to join an American- and European-led overthrow of an Arab leader, even a crazed one. When the NATO campaign began in earnest, Jordan and the UAE backtracked on pledging humanitarian aid and Qatar's planes remained grounded.[12] Again there was a flurry of phone calls, and eventually all three nations flew sorties and provided F-16s and Mirages. Even Morocco contributed by opening up its airspace to help with the operation.[13] Militarily, the participation of non-NATO Arab states made little impact. Symbolically, it was huge. Soaring over the Mediterranean, the tiny Qatari Air Force was flying alongside the Americans, the British, the French, and the Italians in a battle against a man who once saw himself as the greatest leader of the Arab world—before he called himself the "King of Kings" in Africa.

Throughout the whole process Obama, as usual, said little in public and little to Congress. To many on the Hill—including some of Obama's closest allies—there was something that rang of Bush in Obama's declaration that he needed no congressional authorization to join a UN-authorized military operation. When he did meet members of Congress, the day after the Security Council resolution passed, he assured them that the United States would only be involved in heavy fighting for "days, not weeks," before shifting into a supporting role.[14] In short, everyone played to type: a Democratic president who had castigated Bush for exceeding his authority now took the position that the president could authorize this kind of action on his own authority. And the Congress, while sputtering about the War Powers Act and complaining about the cost, had no interest in taking responsibility for committing American forces.

It had been nine days since American jets had started dropping bombs on Libya. Now the president had to explain why. To justify the mission in Libya to the public, Obama chose one of Bush's favorite locales: the National Defense University. It was here that Bush would regularly go to announce a new strategy for what he termed "victory" in Afghanistan and Iraq, to reliably enthusiastic military crowds. Obama had a trickier task. He had to effectively counter both those who wanted him to stay out of Libya altogether and those who demanded that he go in all the way by taking the lead in NATO and declaring outright that the real goal was regime change. He had to explain a strategy that looked to much of the world to be summed up by the phrase "halfway in."

Obama charged Ben Rhodes, his talented young adviser and speechwriter on national security, with finding the words. Rhodes returned to the principles about the use of force that Obama had described when he accepted the Nobel Peace Prize.

At the National Defense University, Obama scanned his audience. They were mostly military—burdened by two long wars, multiple tours, extended deployments, and no clear victories. It was time to convince them that US involvement in Libya was necessary, but that it could also be sharply limited.

"Mindful of the risks and costs of military action, we are naturally reluctant to use force to solve the world's many challenges. But when our interests and values are at stake, we have a responsibility to act," the president told them solemnly.[15]

For the next half hour, Obama waxed on about the strength of the NATO alliance, the unusual nature of the Arab League's call for action, and the legitimacy of the UN mandate. He never used the exact phrase "responsibility to protect," but he justified US action based on that doctrine. He suggested that, under the circumstances, inaction would have been a betrayal to "our fellow human beings." Although Libya did not threaten Americans' safety, Obama made the case it threatened our values. "Ultimately, it is that faith—those ideals—that are the true measure of American leadership."[16]

But the subtext was an argument that the United States did not always have to be "all in," as the military—and Bush—often put it. Even though NATO and its Arab allies were bombing a Muslim country to pressure a tyrant to step down from power, he did not argue that the United States would do whatever it took to get the job done. Quite the opposite: Obama reiterated that the use of ground troops was not even under consideration and Libya would not be another Iraq. "Regime change there took eight years, thousands of American and Iraqi lives, and nearly a trillion dollars," he said. "That is not something we can afford to repeat in Libya."

It was the next part of Obama's speech, though, that would cause his staff to do backflips as the scope of the horror in Syria unfolded later that year and into 2012. "To brush aside America's responsibility as a leader—and more profoundly—our responsibility to our fellow human beings under such circumstances would have been a betrayal of who we are," Obama continued. "Some nations may be able to turn a blind eye to atrocities in other countries. The

United States of America is different. And as president, I refused to wait for the images of slaughter and mass graves before taking action."

He insisted he was not setting a precedent for future interventions. But of course, whenever a president uses military force, a precedent is exactly what he sets. And so months later, as a brutal crackdown in Syria sent the death toll over nine thousand in violence far worse than was seen in Libya, Obama's aides faced the uncomfortable question of why Libyans deserved to be saved on humanitarian grounds by the United States and NATO while Syrians did not. In public, they talked about the many differences between the two cases—chiefly, the Security Council never agreed on an intervention in Syria: Russia and China used their veto. In private, many agreed with their critics. "It's a painful argument to make," one senior State Department official conceded, "because the only reason that we're not doing the same for the Syrians is that it is hard"—hard to sell to the public, hard to win an international consensus, and much harder to execute from the air.

AT THE END of March, after just two weeks of helping to destroy Qaddafi's air defenses, the United States withdrew its bombers, fulfilling Obama's promise that the United States would contribute "unique capabilities at the front end of the mission to protect Libyan civilians" and then relinquish control of major operations to America's allies.[17] As the French and the British took charge of the air campaign, the handover seemed successful. And it was all pretty remarkable; in the sixty years of the US–European military alliance, this was the very first NATO operation in which the United States declined to be at the forefront.

"We did lead—we cleared the way for the allies," Tony Blinken, Biden's national security adviser, assured me shortly after the handover to NATO. "But real leadership is successfully encouraging others to step up to their responsibilities. We've talked for years about burden-sharing, and either we would not let other countries act or they wouldn't or couldn't do it. This time we did, and they did."

He was right; NATO needed the push. But almost as soon as the Americans left the front lines, it became abundantly clear that NATO was incapable of completing the mission alone. In May, during a visit to NATO headquarters, officials acknowledged to me that they did not have the firepower to finish the job. In a blistering assessment, Defense Secretary Gates, who was leaving office and thus had nothing to lose, told an audience in Brussels several weeks later, "The mightiest military alliance in history is only eleven weeks into an operation against a poorly armed regime in a sparsely populated country—yet many allies are beginning to run short of munitions."[18]

Once again, the United States was forced to step back in—contributing more aircraft than any other country, 75 percent of aerial refueling tankers, and the vast majority of the total intelligence, surveillance, and reconnaissance (what the military calls ISR) capabilities, including three unmanned Global Hawk surveillance drones. The United States also resupplied Europe's precision-guided munitions when they ran out three months into the campaign. It turned out to be good business: in total, the United States sold about $250 million in ammunition, spare parts, fuel, and other support.[19]

As the fighting moved into the cities, making accurate bombing increasingly difficult, President Obama agreed to yet another contribution of "unique capabilities": two armed Predator drones, fresh off the battlefields of Iraq and Afghanistan.

"There was incredible resistance inside the Pentagon," one senior White House official told me later. "We had to intervene just to free up time for two Predators."

The addition of the Predator drones to the battlefield went a long way to fill the gap in NATO's efforts—the effect on the ground was immediate. Coupled with the improving coordination between the United States, NATO, and rebel fighters, by August, the drones allowed for faster and more efficient rebel advances.

But as Gates noted, the Libya case illustrated that NATO is hardly the kind of fighting force it needs to be. "While every alliance member voted for [the] Libya mission, less than half have participated at all," Gates said, the sarcasm in his voice barely hidden, "and less than a third have been willing to participate in the strike mission." This, he said, did not necessarily reflect a lack of interest; rather, "The military capabilities simply aren't there."[20] For all the false modesty about how the United States wanted to "lead from behind the scenes," it quickly ended up being dragged back onto the stage.

As THE ARAB Spring slipped into a long, hot summer, Qaddafi's dominion over Libya narrowed and narrowed. He or one of his infamous sons would show up on TV every once in a while, taunting the rebels and NATO to find them. "I tell the coward crusaders: I live in a place you can't get me," Qaddafi declared at one point. "I live in the hearts of millions."[21] In fact he lived in borrowed houses and tents. His argument that the uprising was the work of foreigners wore a little thin. "The people of Libya, the true Libyans, will never accept invasion or colonization," he declared in one of his last diatribes over Libyan television, before he lost control of the broadcasting facilities. "We will fight for our freedom, and we will sacrifice ourselves."[22]

By the summer, no matter what the UN resolution said, it was pretty clear that the mission was all about regime change, and more specifically a manhunt for Qaddafi himself. American officials grew a little testy at the notion that they had surreptitiously shifted the goal: Secretary of State Clinton later contended that Qaddafi was a legitimate target, even when on the run, because he remained a threat to his own people. That was certainly true in the spring of

2011, but the case was much harder to make as city after city fell to the rebels.

Qaddafi's end finally came in October, just two days after Clinton had visited Tripoli to congratulate the Libyan rebels on their uprising—and to urge them not to blow it. For a dictator who had gone essentially unchallenged since he took power in a coup in 1969, it was a pretty ugly ending. Qaddafi's convoy was near the city of Surt when it was struck by a missile—launched from one of those Predator drones that the White House had a difficult time extracting from the Pentagon. Qaddafi survived the strike, and jumped into a drainage pipe to hide.[23] The rebels pursued him and, after a brief battle with his guards, dragged him out, a Kalashnikov in one hand, a pistol in the other.[24] The exact circumstances of the Brother Leader's final moments are a bit murky, but within about an hour he had been shot in the head, and his body was put on display. It was not exactly due process, but neither the Americans nor the Europeans complained, at least openly. Exhausted, they were interested in declaring victory and getting out.

The administration quickly argued the intervention demonstrated that there was an alternative approach to the kind of land wars and occupations that had marked the long decade after 9/11. Washington had insisted, by its own account, that the countries with the strongest interest in the outcome needed to make the biggest contribution to the effort. American officials made no effort to hide the fact that American power—and tolerance—was limited by commitments elsewhere. The message to Europe and the Arab states was clear: This is your neighborhood, your refugee crisis, and primarily your problem. Call if we can help.

It was a philosophy that seemed to match the national mood. Viewed in those terms, Libya was an enormous success. The United States had mobilized the UN Security Council to pass a resolution with teeth, and the allies began enforcing it within days. While all the talk about "leading from behind" was wildly overdrawn, Obama proved his point that the world could not expect the United States to play the world's policeman alone, especially when American interests were not directly at stake. For the first time, the Arab states also took their "responsibility to protect" a population from its own murderous leadership seriously. Libya was never going to be another Rwanda, but it was also no Iraq, where the Arab neighbors remained missing in action.

In the end, Libya was something of a perfect revolutionary storm. The conditions for international intervention—from the politics to the geography—are unlikely to be replicated. It worked because the NATO allies saw a way to topple Qaddafi without putting boots on the ground (save for some British special forces who were critical in making the initial call for airstrikes), without spending much money, and without taking many casualties. It was intervention on the cheap.

But America's far more limited role once the shooting stopped also abrogates, for good or ill, any responsibility for what follows. Like Iraq after Saddam, Libya after Qaddafi was left a hollowed-out state; for forty years Qaddafi had underinvested in infrastructure, and all of Libya's institutions had withered under one-man rule. Like Iraq, it has oil revenue of its own to fix the problem. Yet unlike Iraq, it is going to have to solve those problems without an outside force to keep a lid on old tribal rivalries. This time there will be no army of American advisers and contractors, no briefcases full of cash to buy acquiescence from tribal leaders.

"That means we're not around on the ground, where we breed resentment," one of Obama's national security aides said. "It's up to the Libyans."

That is exactly why Obama rejected the Pentagon's request late in 2011 for 100,000 American troops who would be permanently on call for "stability operations." After Iraq and Afghanistan, Obama was determined to get the United States out of the nation-building business. A new realism has set in about the limits and costs of American influence in remaking societies.

But there is risk, too, in overlearning this lesson.

The security and rebuilding role we played in Europe in the forties, South Korea and the rest of Asia in the fifties and sixties, and the newly freed former Soviet Republics in the nineties proved critical to both security and prosperity. And it is easy to forget that dropping bombs and walking away is fraught with hard-to-predict dangers as well, as we learned in Afghanistan after 1989. As a nation, we lost interest in Afghanistan for a dozen years, and regained it one September morning after 3,000 people were dead in Manhattan, Washington, and a field in Pennsylvania. It was only then we realized the price of complete disengagement. Since then, we've spent $3.3 trillion and thousands of American lives overcompensating.[25] Somewhere there exists a happy medium between permitting degeneration into explosive instability and occupying broken states. So far, despite many experiments in how to mix diplomacy, aid, and counterterrorism, we haven't quite found the formula.

MUAMMAR QADDAFI WAS overthrown in eight months because the allies were unified, because the Libyan military was incompetent, and because Obama and other world leaders combined patience with good luck.

But what works once doesn't always work twice. In Syria, as of this writing, it is all playing out differently. After a year of increasingly brutal violence—far greater than anything seen in the rest of the Arab uprisings—Syria has become what one top military commander described to me as "a laboratory experiment in the limits of our power to intervene." It is, he added, "the un-Libya."

The irony, of course, is that the United States has far more at stake in the outcome in Syria than it ever did in Libya. As the tensions with Iran ratcheted up early in 2012, American officials came to believe that nothing would rattle the Iranian regime more than losing its one ally in the Arab world. If Syria cracked, Iran's ability to funnel weapons to Hezbollah and Hamas would be badly damaged—and its influence would wither accordingly. It would presumably no longer be safe territory for Iran's Qods Force to run operations and for Iranian bankers, oil traders, and nuclear scientists to evade sanctions. The fall of Bashar al-Assad would not only remove a tyrant who had already killed upwards of 9,000 of his own people in the year since protests began; it would also likely leave Iran more isolated than at any time in the past three decades. There were risks, including that a more militant Islamist regime would eventually take Assad's place. But that was a long-term concern, and meanwhile the people of Homs and Dara'a were dying every day.

But Syria was also a case in which Washington was once again taken by surprise. Until the uprisings, Assad was viewed as a gawky, British-educated ophthalmologist, a rational if ruthless player who might, over time, be peeled away from Iran with some combination of promised foreign investments and an end to sanctions. He seemed more predictable, more savvy, and less brutal than his father, Hafez al-Assad, who in 1982 killed thousands in the Hama massacre. It turned out that this assessment was dead wrong; facing the reality that his regime was under mortal threat, the younger Assad proved to be just as brutal as his father, but more cunning in how he dealt with the outside world. He also learned from Qaddafi's mistakes.

While Qaddafi went on the air to liken the people of Benghazi to "rats" who would be exterminated—giving the outside world the rationale for a quick, decisive strike—Assad made up an elaborate tale that the thousands killed in Syria's populous neighborhoods were the victims of "terrorist armed groups." It was a ridiculous pretense, as were his sham offers of political reform. But the pretense helped sustain the rift between Russia and China and the rest of the UN Security Council—and assure that any resolution authorizing force would be vetoed. Rather than announce that he would hunt down protestors house by house, room by room, and murder them in their closets, Assad professed to know nothing about the escalating killings, the round-ups of civilians, the bodies set on fire. "I don't own [the military]," he told Barbara Walters in an interview in which he presented himself as the picture of civilized calm, in an impeccable black suit. "I am president. I don't own the country, so they are not my forces." The UN report that documented rape, torture, and the targeting of children? "As long as we don't see the documents and the evidences, we cannot say yes, that's normal."[26]

As in Tunisia and Egypt, it is all but impossible to figure out what, exactly, triggered the 2011 uprising in Syria.

Perhaps it was the brutal beating of very peaceful protestors in Damascus, who planned their own "Day of Rage" a little more than a month after Mubarak was ousted. More likely, it was the images of Hamza Ali al-Khateeb, a thirteen-year-old boy whose only mistake was to attend a protest in the southern city of Saida in April.

The protest was against the treatment of a group of teenagers, who had been detained after scrawling Arab Spring slogans on their school building. When they were finally released, they had been beaten and burned and had their fingernails pulled out. Hamza had gone to the Saida protest with friends and family, but got separated from them when the Syrian army began firing rounds of ammunition.[27]

Two weeks later, Hamza was delivered to his parents wrapped in plastic sheeting and a blanket. His father pulled the covers back, and saw how his son had been mutilated: burned head to toe, with deep cuts, a broken neck, and shattered kneecaps. His genitals were missing.[28] Someone turned on a camera and started slowly filming every wound on Hamza's body. The images took off on the Internet and Al Jazeera. Facebook pages in remembrance of Hamza drew tens of thousands of members. Assad vehemently denied the facts, saying that a special investigating committee had determined "there was no torture."[29]

As protests escalated, the casualties mounted from the hundreds to the thousands, and peaceful protestors were driven to take up arms. At first, the White House tried to simply humiliate Assad into halting the violence. In July 2011, it sent American ambassador Robert Ford to Hama, the scene of the huge massacre thirty years before, to talk with people on the street. "My team and I see it as an integral part of our mission to give these people an ear and a voice," he said from Hama, "to amplify their hopes and legitimate grievances so that the international community and most importantly the Syrian regime pays attention."[30] It was a valiant effort, closely coordinated by the White House, but it ended up underscoring how few tools Washington possessed. Assad had clearly decided that when it came to slaughtering the people of Hama, his dad had the right idea. "If Assad views this as life-or-death for him, and it is, then no amount of diplomacy is likely to persuade him," one of Obama's top advisers told me soon after the Ford mission. Ford and his small team were recalled twice for safety reasons; the second time, in February 2012, they locked the embassy door behind them. The situation deteriorated rapidly—even the CIA station pulled out.

Assad bought more time by periodically allowing in observers from the Arab League or Kofi Annan as the envoy from the United Nations, carefully restricting their access, vaguely promising talks for some kind of political settlement, then ratcheting up the killing. At one point he agreed to a peace plan, then stepped up attacks—a move that finally got Syria ejected from the Arab League. Even the Russians and the Chinese were recipients of Assad's coy games. Until intrepid and fearless reporters hired smugglers to get inside Syria—

including Marie Colvin and my colleague Anthony Shadid, both of whom died bearing witness to the horrifying scenes—Assad kept the worst of the images off the international airwaves.

Assad also enjoyed three great advantages that eluded Qaddafi.

First of all, his country was hard to bomb: Libya was more accessible from the sea, and the Libyan forces massing to attack Benghazi were gathered in a large deserted region that was easy to hit. In Syria the fighting was in crowded neighborhoods, and any air attack would kill hundreds of the civilians that the Arab League and West were trying to protect.

Unlike Qaddafi, Assad commanded a real military, well trained and well armed. Over the years, he had invested in tanks and heavy artillery, and he was perfectly willing to turn that firepower on restive neighborhoods. While there were significant defections from the military, the officer corps was dominated by the Alawites, Assad's sect, a small minority in a country that is overwhelmingly Sunni Muslim. Those officers knew that this was an all-or-nothing battle: if the government fell, their life expectancies would be measured in days and weeks. Unlike the troops in Egypt, the Syrian military did not hesitate to open fire on protestors.

Finally, the opposition to Assad was reduced to a fractious group of political rivals, exiles, and armed militants, who were so deeply divided they could not agree on even the rudiments of a strategy to topple the dictator. So when the predictable cry went up in Congress—"Arm the Syrian rebels!"—Obama wisely ignored it.

The "Free Syrian Army" that fought Assad was barely an army at all—it was really just a ragtag group of free-form militias. Some members came from the tribes; others were linked to the fight by regional or ethnic bonds. There was some evidence that elements were linked to al-Qaeda and had participated in ethnic killings. These weren't exactly the Syrian equivalent of Egypt's idealistic students. So, tempting as it was to hand off weapons and wish the Free Army good luck in toppling Assad, many in the White House recalled how the United States came to rue the day it armed lo-cal groups in Afghanistan during the war with the Soviets. Those weapons, of course, had been pointed back at American troops for a decade.

But the United States could not forget the Syrians—strategi-cally, the country was far more important than Libya. A compromise was struck: $12 million for satellite-communications equipment and night-vision goggles.[31] At least the rebels could see their way through the dark streets as Assad's army chased them down.

But Gates's assessment when Syria imploded in 2011—"I see no appetite" for military action, he said—remained true in the spring of 2012. "Don't kid yourself," a senior American commander who had been examining options for Obama and Defense Secretary Leon Panetta told me. "There is no way to do this other than a full-scale war." Panetta himself argued that an intervention could speed up a civil war and that, in the post–Iraq War world, "there are limi-tations of military force, especially with US boots on the ground."[32]

By then it was clear that whatever diplomatic magic Hillary Clinton and Susan Rice were able to muster when they won backing for the Libya intervention was failing them when it came to Syria.

"We had a well-developed understanding of what we were try-ing to achieve," Clinton insisted in a conversation in mid-February 2012. "Push forward the Arab League, which we spent a lot of time doing—helping them think through what they could constructively do and overcome the internal division that affected their think-ing." There was the usual round of late-night phone calls and hand-holding of Arab politicians who were worried about the reaction on their own streets if their government joined in ousting Assad. Clinton dispatched Bill Burns, the deputy secretary of state and longtime Mideast negotiator and former ambassador to Russia, to help the Arab League find a way to confront Assad.

Burns's work looked like it was paying off when the Arab League decided to send observers to investigate the situation in Syria—until the man designated to lead the mission turned out to be Lt. Gen. Muhammad Ahmed al-Dabi, a man who is best known for running Sudan's notorious military intelligence agency, and long accused of overseeing—or at least overlooking—human rights violations. As thousands of protestors gathered to receive the Arab League monitors, bullets were flying. Even the monitors were sent packing, seemingly paralyzed by the violence that continued unabated.

At the United Nations, Clinton and Rice ran into a wall of opposition, and Burns hit a speed bump: Russia. In public, the Russians argued that they had been deceived by Obama and NATO about the real purpose of the Libya resolution months before. What had begun as a humanitarian intervention, they said with some accuracy, had morphed into an excuse for regime change. But the Russians were not exactly upset by the outcome: in an aside to Obama during a summit meeting in France in May 2011, Medvedev whispered, "All that said, I agree with you; Qaddafi has got to go."

Syria, though, was a different story. Russia had both economic and geostrategic interests: Syria purchases millions of dollars in Russian arms annually and is host to a vital Russian military base—the only one outside the former Soviet Union.[33] The Russians were not about to move to oust Assad any more than Obama would have moved to oust the king of Bahrain, host to a vital American base.

So Clinton and Rice drafted a resolution that, as Clinton told me in frustration in mid-February 2012, "had no wiggle room" for any military action, no sanctions, and no arms embargo. This wasn't Libya-Lite; it was toothless.

Clinton went to the UN to sell the resolution herself. "Now, I know some members here may be concerned that the Security Council could be headed toward another Libya," she asserted. "That is a false analogy." Pointing to an Arab League proposal for political transition that Assad was fighting, she argued that "spurning the Arab League, abandoning the Syrian people, emboldening the dictator . . . would mark a failure of our shared responsibility and shake the credibility of the United Nations Security Council."

Everyone agreed—except, of course, the Russians and Chinese. Sergey Lavrov, the prickly Russian foreign minister, dodged Clinton's calls, then pushed for more time, then asked for substantive changes in the language of the resolution. Clinton decided to call his bluff and force them to veto the measure. They did. Although the resolution got thirteen votes in favor, the two vetoes killed it.

"Bottom line," Clinton said with more than a hint of annoyance in her voice, "no compromise, no agreement."

By mid-spring, with nine thousand Syrians already dead by the UN's estimate, even the Russians and the Chinese realized Assad's legitimacy was shot. But still there was little the Security Council was willing—or able—to do to cut short Assad's war of attrition against his own people. Clinton gathered her counterparts from Turkey, Syria, Saudi Arabia, Qatar, and elsewhere at "Friends of Syria" conferences; they offered verbal encouragement for the opposition and little else.

In April 2012, the entire UN Security Council finally threw its support behind former secretary general Kofi Annan's peace plan, which called (yet again) for a cease-fire and deployment of UN monitors. Assad agreed to the plan—but by then any remaining trust in his word had evaporated. So while obituaries for Assad's regime were being written, the commitment to working in coalitions meant that no actions were taken to actually remove him from power. It seemed the Security Council wanted to let nature take its course. Meanwhile, the Syrians were dying.

◈

A YEAR INTO the uprising in Syria, there is plenty of reason to believe that Assad is mortally wounded. The demographics of the country are against him. The insurgents are highly motivated. The other Arab states will not throw him a lifeline. But with the world so divided on how to deal with his brutality, the countdown to his departure will be measured in corpses.

Obama's reaction to the Libyan and Syrian uprisings—and his management of less violent revolutions in the region—gave the world their first hard look at what the Obama Doctrine looks like on the ground.

Obama has shown he will not hesitate to use military force in defense of America's direct interests—the bin Laden raid is the boldest example—but that he will use it in the most sparing way when those interests are indirect. Libya fit into the doctrine because Obama concluded American technology could make a decisive difference, because he was confident he could impose time limits on the American involvement, and because the risk of casualties was so low. It may be a long time before we see that unique alignment of the stars again.

Yet for all its successes, the Libya intervention also provides some cautionary tales, both for President Obama and for his successors.

When the United States assisted in ousting Qaddafi, it sent a strong unintended message to other dictators: think twice about giving up your nuclear weapons.

In an interview in April 2010 in which he talked of his hopes of luring "outlier" states back into the fold, President Obama told my colleague, Peter Baker, and me that Libya was a vivid example of the benefits that can flow to a country when it chooses to give up its weapons. "Qaddafi decided the costs outweigh the benefits," the president said. "I should point out that every country that's made that decision I think looks back and says that was the right decision to make. And we're hoping that at some point Iran and North Korea will come to that same conclusion."[34]

A year later, when Qaddafi was on the run, the Iranians and

the North Koreans came to the opposite conclusion. Both North Korea's leaders and the official Iranian press questioned whether NATO would have launched its attack if Qaddafi had held on to his nuclear program. When they saw Qaddafi's bloody corpse, they must have surmised that the West's offers to bring "outlier" states back into the fold in return for giving up their weapons are not worth much when the street uprisings begin. In Libya, the United States and its allies were given a chance to finish off a weakened, long-time adversary—and they took it. A nuclear-empowered Qaddafi might well be in power today, overseeing a steady slaughter of civilians.

Regrets of a different kind may arise depending on what kind of state emerges in Libya—if a state emerges at all. The light-footprint approach is superb for knocking out and kicking down dictators. But just as the liberals learned a year after Tahrir Square, bringing down a regime doesn't mean the job is done; you still need to build something up in its place or risk a successor who is hostile to your interests. If Libya reverts to tribal chaos, it will raise the question of whether the United States and its allies, overreacting to the staggering costs of occupations in Iraq and Afghanistan, may have let the pendulum swing too far in the other direction.

Those questions will be of interest to historians, looking back at uprisings that took the world by surprise. Washington, though, will likely be transfixed by what is to come: the rise of a dizzying variety of Islamist states, each one of which will pose a different challenge to the United States. The lesson of the past five decades in the Middle East is that any effort to pull back from the region is bound to fail. We simply have too many oil interests, too many terrorism apprehensions, too many concerns about Iran, and too many important alliances—chiefly with Israel—to simply pretend that the United States is not a central player in the reshaping of the region.

Eighteen months after the uprisings began, the Obama administration is still struggling with two competing instincts. One is to keep America's involvement to a bare minimum, to repeat the president's maxim that the change sweeping the Arab states is about them, not about us. The other is to make full use of whatever leverage America still has in the region, to steer the emerging governments onto a path that is democratic, keeps the oil flowing, and is run by leaders willing to take the president's phone calls. So far, no one has found the right blend of strategic patience and targeted engagement.

The years ahead will be messy for the nascent governments forming in the wake of the Arab uprisings. The lack of jobs—particularly for young people—will inevitably lead to more protests, and it will be easy, once again, to blame the West—for either its meddling or its stinginess. It will be tempting for Obama and the presidents of the future to stay largely on the sidelines as these countries experience their growing pains. But history suggests that whenever America thinks it can extricate itself from the Middle East, it will inevitably get sucked back in.

PART V
CHINA AND NORTH KOREA

THE REBALANCING

China's claimed territorial waters

CHAPTER 15
RESTRAINING THE TIGER,
CONTAINING THE KIMS

How do you deal toughly with your banker?

—*Secretary of State Hillary Rodham Clinton, newly in office, in a question over lunch to Australia's prime minister, Kevin Rudd, March 2009, as reported in a leaked State Department cable*[1]

ON A BITTERLY COLD BEIJING DAY IN JANUARY 2011, BOB GATES was as livid as his aides could ever remember seeing him.

For the last two days, the American defense secretary had sped around Beijing's massive six-lane boulevards in a highly public, orchestrated effort to end the deep chill between the Pentagon and China's fast-growing and increasingly confident military.

For Gates, the only member of Obama's cabinet who had played a day-to-day role managing the Cold War standoffs with the Soviet Union, the tit-for-tat nastiness he witnessed almost daily between the United States and China was familiar. "Gates talked about China as a modern-day Soviet Union," one of his former colleagues recalled. That assessment may have been too harsh: Gates understood, better than most, the fault lines inside the Chinese government, and the degree to which decision-making was dispersed. And he was quick to join Obama in insisting the US was not out to contain China the way it had the Soviets.

For a year, Beijing and Washington had been snarling at each other, judging every perceived slight as symbolic of a brewing, if rarely explicit, strategic confrontation. The Chinese thought the United States was interfering with its dealings with Tibet and Taiwan, and secretly planning to contain its rise. They had cut off exchanges with the US military and stepped up testing of new, high-tech arms designed to blind American satellites and interfere with their communications. The Americans, meanwhile, looked at the wave of cyberattacks aimed at the United States—from the hacking of Gates's own office at the Pentagon, to Google and Boeing, even the 2008 Obama presidential campaign—and they saw China's hand. Normally such diplomatic and electronic power plays would never faze Gates, who from his days at the CIA knew how superpowers needled each other. But on this particular morning in Beijing, the challenge was about to get even more pronounced.

Hours before Gates's motorcade was supposed to pull up to the Great Hall of the People on Tiananmen Square for a meeting with President Hu Jintao, aides told Gates that the Chinese military had just conducted its first test of China's new J-20 Stealth Fighter jet in the city of Chengdu 1,200 miles away. The jet was designed to avoid American detection and to close the huge technology gap between China's air force and the far more advanced capability in the United States. Perhaps it was just a coincidence that this new weapon the Chinese had worked on for years—a sleek, twin-engine craft (using the signature tailfins of the Pentagon's F-22 Raptor)—happened to be ready for its test flight just as Gates was visiting. But Gates wasn't a big believer in coincidences.

As soon as they got word of the test, Gates's aides huddled to try to figure out what message the Chinese were sending. The first interpretation, one senior aide later told me, was that it was "a giant screw-you to Gates and Obama—a reminder that anything we can build, they can build cheaper." The Chinese had noticed when Gates expressed doubts about whether China's rapid military expansion would catch up to American technology anytime soon. And on his way to Beijing that very trip, he told reporters there was still "some question about just how stealthy" any new Chinese stealth jets really were.[2] Who knows, Gates had said, when they'll actually be operational?

He got his answer on the trip—and was left debating how to handle this symbolic show of force. Leaving the country in a huff was not an option. After all, President Hu was coming to Washington in just weeks for a state visit that had been postponed during a particularly contentious turn in US–Chinese relations. Making sure this trip went off successfully was a major priority for the White House. But if there was a lesson in Obama's early outreach to China, it was this: what Obama's team viewed as extending a cooperative hand —welcoming them as equals in managing world affairs—was viewed by some factions in Beijing as weakness. Gates was not about to pretend the test had not happened.

Gates walked up the broad steps of the Great Hall, his back to the square where pro-democracy protestors were violently shot down twenty-two years before. As he entered the formal reception rooms—there is no such thing as an informal chat with Chinese leaders—he decided to acknowledge the elephant in the room. "So I asked President Hu straight up," he told me later that day. But Hu's face turned quizzical when Gates mentioned the test.

"Hu turned to the guy next to him and asked if he knew what I was talking about," Gates said. "That guy shook his head no and moved down the line." The pattern continued until they hit the first officer in uniform. He knew all about it. The test, it was reported, had been rescheduled from an earlier date because of a minor equipment malfunction.

When I asked Gates later that night whether Hu could really have been in the dark about such an important development, the onetime spymaster paused for a moment. "I take President Hu at his word." Then he flashed that trademark grin that made me think that Gates, who at sixty-nine had been around for all of China's many modern incarnations, might have harbored his own doubts. So did other Americans on the trip. One senior American diplomat who was in Beijing that day—though not at the meeting—told me later that Hu probably knew exactly what was going on, and might well have been playing a crafty game with the about-to-retire Gates.

But one of Gates's senior aides offered a second, very different, interpretation of the day: the stealth test, he said, was "a giant screw-you to President Hu" from his own military. Hu Jintao, he noted, had ordered the Chinese military to try to smooth over its rocky relations with the Pentagon—the reason for Gates's visit—and the more nationalistic generals were perhaps looking to undermine that command.

"There is a remarkable amount of chaos in the system, more than you ever saw dealing with the Chinese twenty years ago," Brent Scowcroft, Gates's mentor and the former national security adviser for two Republican presidents, observed shortly after the stealth test. "The military doesn't participate in the system the way it once did. They are more autonomous—and so are a lot of others."

WHAT SCOWCROFT CALLS "chaos in the system" may be America's greatest challenge dealing with the world's emerging superpower in the years ahead.

Out of habit, Americans tend to think about China as a monolithic power, one centrally commanded from the Zhong-nanhai leadership compound next to the Forbidden City. That's not an entirely outdated image. China still censors its media through a huge bureaucracy in Beijing; it still issues five-year economic plans (it recently published its twelfth), and it remains a one-party state. Timothy Geithner, Obama's treasury secretary and the one cabinet official with the longest and deepest ties to Asia, often notes, "we have no real precedent" in recent history for a world-class, competitive manufacturing nation that is also still "a fundamentally state-run economy," in which the state "sets the price of everything that matters—the exchange rate, energy, credit, capital, the price of land."

And yet, one of the great contradictions about modern-day China is that for a country obsessed with control, the Beijing leadership holds far fewer levers of power than Mao did in the mid-1960s. Back then Mao could—and did—order up the Cultural Revolution, and send the intellectual elite out to the countryside to harvest rice for their "reeducation." When he recognized the economic disaster he had triggered, he ordered the country to reverse course.

But that China disappeared with the remarkable era of economic opening ushered in by Deng Xiaoping, the president who set the country on a path of "market socialism" that created today's $5 trillion colossus. Deng allowed some economic experimentation at the local and provincial level, which meant pulling back the central government's hand far more than most Westerners realized at the time. Once started, it was a process that proved difficult to stop.

As Gates discovered that January day in Beijing, President Hu and his neighbors at Zhongnanhai were possessed of neither Mao's authority nor Deng's vision. This group of Chinese leaders could not engineer a sweeping change in the country's direction from the top, even if one came to mind. Hu spent his time settling disputes among factions in the government, putting down protests in Tibet, making sure North Korea neither imploded nor exploded, and negotiating with the collective leadership—which he never seemed to control. China may be far wealthier and more influential than at any time in history, but its leadership is at its weakest since the beginning of the revolution that swept in the Communists.

Hu's encounter with Gates was only the most vivid case in which the Obama administration found itself dealing with a leadership boxed in, or circumvented, by rival power centers. It was hardly the first time. Obama's first three years in office were spent trying to convince Hu to revalue China's currency, pressure Iran to rein in nuclear North Korea, cease claiming exclusive territory in the South China Sea, and crack down on the daily raid on American technology. At some moments Hu and his fellow technocrats edged toward addressing those concerns. At others, they backtracked. It took a while for the new American administration to appreciate the degree to which the Chinese leadership was at the mercy of nationalist admirals, greedy ministers, and big corporate interests who have more clout, and less deference, than at any time since Mao emerged from the caves and created the People's Republic.[3] Ultimately, this required Obama to take quite a different approach to dealing with the Chinese—one in which he abandoned his initial accommodation and set up what amounted to an "electric fence" around key parts of Asia that would zap the Chinese if they claimed too much "exclusive" territory or harassed foreign fishermen and oil explorers.

It was not just the military pursuing its own path in Beijing. Many of China's companies, both state-owned and independent, did as well. The catchphrase for these new economic power brokers in the Chinese press is "vested interests"—and although the private sector's growing influence over policy has been hotly debated in China, that influence can also give Beijing some great excuses.[4] "The Chinese admit this, almost proudly," one former Obama official who dealt often with China told me. "Someone goes into Google's computers, and the answer we get is 'We have 1.3 billion people and a quarter of them want to be entrepreneurs. How are we supposed to police what they are doing on the Internet?'" (In reality, whenever Chinese authorities decide to shut down the Internet to squelch political protests, they are extremely effective.)

China's internal divisions have made it far harder to strike the kind of deals that made it possible for the two countries to open up diplomatic relations decades ago or get China entry into the World

Trade Organization. If Nixon were going to open China today, the Interior Ministry would probably get into an argument with the Chinese president's office about whether to let Air Force One land, and then demand the plane's antimissile technology as the price for refueling.

"The broader debate we have been having for three years in the administration internally," one of Obama's key China strategists told me, "is how can we make it compelling for the Chinese to move more aggressively to try to accommodate our concerns? They've been moving, and when they think it is completely in their interests, they're moving with alacrity. But where they may have some sympathy for our view but there are huge internal fights, they are doing only as much as they need to buy some peace."

In fact, a few months before Obama traveled to Asia in 2011 to announce the American "pivot" toward the Pacific—a poorly chosen term because the Europeans thought they were going to be ignored—the president told his staff, "I need leverage!"

It was an admission most American politicians—especially those running for reelection—do not want to make: recent American presidents have had diminishing influence on China, for all the obvious reasons. Just look at the headlines for the past three years—from both US and Chinese papers—and the source of Obama's frustration becomes obvious. When Hu and his prime minister often said they would let China's currency gradually rise, so that their goods would not be underpriced on world markets, their own commerce ministry promptly labeled that move a "catastrophe" for the Chinese economy. Hu often said the Chinese market would remain open for foreigners. Yet talk to business leaders and you will hear a cascade of complaints about regulators who have made it nearly impossible for foreign energy, communications, and banking firms to compete with China's state-backed favorites. Oftentimes, American firms can invest in China only if they are willing to turn over their proprietary technology, which is why so many auto and high-tech companies have balked.

Yet as one senior administration official noted to me, "People who blithely say that we'd win a trade war because China obviously couldn't sustain the damage caused by cutting off their goods are just naïve and silly." Any significant trade restrictions the United States imposed on China would swiftly lead to an equally harmful retaliation on the United States. That is why the most effective lobbyists against tariffs on Chinese goods are American companies that buy from China, do business in China, or have ventures with Chinese firms. So as Obama's outburst underscored, the form of leverage threatened most often by Washington politicians looking for an easy applause line actually offers little leverage at all.

Barack Obama is the first American president to have grown up in the Pacific Basin. Many of his earliest childhood memories are from his days in Indonesia, his stepfather's home. His memoirs are filled with remembrances of Jakarta's sights and smells. He spent his teen-age years in Hawaii, a state that thinks a lot more about Asia than it does about Europe. It doesn't take much insight to see that Asian cultures run through Obama; Europe runs around him. Even his legendary self-control—the absence of Bill Clinton's outbursts, or George Bush's with-us-or-against-us pronouncements—makes him seem like a politician from a more buttoned-down, controlled Asian environment.

So it was no surprise that Obama was determined not to make the mistake Clinton made, denouncing the "butchers of Beijing" in the 1992 campaign—just three years after the Tiananmen Square massacre—only to reverse course and usher China into the World Trade Organization. Nor was he going to make the mistake Bush made, calling the Chinese a "strategic competitor" and letting his aides talk about containment strategies—only switching to "strategic partner" when Bush needed the Chinese to embrace his counterterrorism strategy.

Instead, Obama made almost the opposite error, one that many on his staff now talk about openly. He made so many accommodations to Chinese sensitivities that the leaders in Beijing thought they smelled weakness. And their reaction ultimately forced Obama to take a harder line.

In that first year in office, Obama did everything he could think of to convince the Chinese he was ready to recognize that their size and influence had given them a far bigger voice in the world.

One of the administration's first decisions was not to spend a lot of time dwelling on human rights issues—in short, not to repeat the mistake Bill Clinton made in 1993. During his presidential campaign, Clinton had threatened to link China's trading status to its treatment of its own people. The killings at Tiananmen Square were still at the forefront of everyone's memory, and the line drew big cheers. Then he discovered that such efforts always boomerang on the United States; no one gets hurt more than the American companies relying on Chinese suppliers, or doing business there. He ended up completely separating trade and human rights.

So when Hillary Clinton took her first trip to China as secretary of state, she said little about the crackdown on dissidents—which was, it turned out, about to get a lot worse. "We pretty much know what they're going to say," she quipped in her first month on the job.[5] In other words, why waste your breath—and leverage—when you know Beijing will give no ground? Jeffrey Bader, Obama's chief Asia adviser, who was along on that trip, later described the backlash: "She got roasted," he said with a wry smile. "Although anyone who's been in the US government for thirty years knows exactly what she meant, because that is the character of those discussions."[6]

Clinton's comments set a tone of accommodation to the Chinese, which was amplified as Obama went out of his way to show Beijing that he regarded them as among the most critical economic players in the world—an admission the Europeans had long resisted. The effort, as Obama's aides put it pretty bluntly, was "to usher them to a seat at a table that until now has been occupied mostly by white European men." That's a slight overstatement: the Japanese had been at the table at Group of Eight economic summits for years. But when Obama decided, eight months into office, to go beyond the ossified G8 as the primary club of nations that managed the global economy, it was a signal that the world had changed in significant ways. China, India, Brazil, and other rising powers needed an equal voice.

"We told them, 'We want you to be part of the system and we're willing to give you a stake in shaping the rules of the game that's commensurate with being a rising economic power,'" one of the president's senior advisers told me.

Most Americans are rightly tuned out of the politics of big annual economic summit meetings—after all, the purpose of these summits is almost always to bury differences in feel-good communiqués that are forgotten within an instant of their publication. But the symbolism of this move—diluting Europe's influence, and Japan's—was hard to miss, and only an American president could have led the way. It led to a tremor of fear through Europe, which always worries, with some justification, that the United States is far more fixated on the fast-growing markets of the world than on what Donald Rumsfeld undiplomatically but accurately called "old Europe."

When Obama met Hu Jintao for the first time at an economic summit in London in 2009 to deal with the global economic crisis, headlines appeared suggesting that from now on, big decisions would be made by a "G2"—in other words, the world's largest economy was teaming up with the soon-to-become second largest, and the rest of the world would have to fall in line. Obama himself never used the phrase, but others did. David Miliband, the British foreign secretary, warned that Europe risked becoming "spectators in a G2 world shaped by the U.S. and China" if they didn't get their act together, and fast.[7] The Italians said Europe was on its way to being "irrelevant"—"bypassed" by the Chinese-American marriage.[8] That was never the idea. But it sure looked like it was after Obama and Hu, at the summit, embraced a common strategy—big economic stimulus plans to kick their economies into gear—while the Europeans largely headed in the other direction, opposing new spending and cutting budgets.

But the hype soon outpaced the reality. The problem with the "G2" concept was that it presumed a level of common interests and trust that simply does not exist between the United States and China. It would be hard enough for a rising power and the preeminent superpower to work so closely in any conditions. But China and the United States have huge differences on trade rules, on military intervention, and on interfering in the internal politics of other nations. The Chinese premier, Wen Jiabao, dismissed the G2 buzz—he probably suspected any perception that the Chinese had hitched themselves to Washington would incite a nationalist outcry. And Obama himself understood the risks of seeming to offer to share the title of number-one world power. Eventually, Hillary Clinton sunk the concept for good: "Distrust lingers on both sides," she said early in 2011. "There is no such thing as a G2."[9]

It was only a matter of time before Obama and Hu Jintao came to an impasse over how to handle the one country that drove both leaders to distraction: Kim Jong-il's North Korea.

For starving hermits, the North Koreans had a pretty good decade. Despite predictions of their imminent demise, they survived. Kim Jong-il, son of the country's founder, didn't seem fazed by the spoofs of him in the West as a goofy dictator in big sunglasses and platform shoes. He stuffed the country's gulags with suspected dissidents and built up an impressive corps of special forces who could run submarine raids into South Korean waters. He sniffed out South Korean spies with remarkable efficiency: according to American officials, of the roughly one hundred intelligence agents dispatched by Seoul over the years, only a handful returned. Most impressively, Kim regularly outmaneuvered George W. Bush, who had declared the North a charter member of the "axis of evil" in his first term. Bush then took the country off the list of state sponsors of terrorism in the second term—a reversal of strategy that sent his vice president, Dick Cheney, into public outbursts of anger. After all, Cheney made clear early in Bush's time that he would try to push the North off a cliff. It didn't work.

In fact, during Bush's tenure the North perfected a pretty good survival strategy. It thrived as the crazy neighbor, living in a run-down house in the middle of a very, very expensive neighborhood. Periodically it would very publicly wrap its dilapidated pile in explosives, threaten to blow up the neighborhood, and demand an endless supply of takeout food. Whenever anyone in the neighborhood balked, it would set off a few well-placed explosions. It was the equivalent of declaring, "Nice, expensive real estate you have here. Wouldn't it be a shame if it was so radioactive no one could live there?"

North Korea, in short, usually acted like an organized crime syndicate with a seat at the UN. It was linked to drug trafficking, currency counterfeiting, money laundering, the production of fake Viagra, insurance fraud, and the sale of endangered species.[10] But the Bush administration, like the Clinton administration before it, closed its eyes and pretended that if you sign enough agreements, one of them will stick.

In 2005, the United States—along with Japan, China, Russia, and South Korea—signed a deal in which the North agreed to eliminate, bit by bit, "all nuclear weapons and existing nuclear programs" and rejoin the Nuclear Nonproliferation Treaty. No one knows if Kim Jong-il actually thought about doing so, or was playing for time. But a few months later, Bush froze North Korean accounts at a bank in Macau, where Kim himself reportedly kept much of his cash. The freeze hurt, and in 2006 the North responded by launching a Taepodong-2 missile and, three months later, set off a nuclear device of its own for the first time.

The test was something of a dud, but Kim, the son of the country's founder, used it to full effect. It forced the United States into the first real negotiations with the North in years. That task was given to Christopher Hill, a veteran American diplomat brought in by Condoleezza Rice to undo the damage done in Bush's first term. Hill got further than anyone expected, negotiating a timetable for dismantlement. For visual effect, the North even brought down a cooling tower at its main nuclear site in Yongbyon—in front of CNN cameras, of course—to show it was headed into a new, cooperative era.[11]

Given Obama's explicit openness to further communication, one might have expected Kim Jong-il to send a congratulatory note after Obama's inauguration, saying that he looked forward to future talks. Instead, he sent a different kind of missive: another Taepodong-2 launch in April 2009, this time carrying what the North said was a satellite, so that Kim could deny that he'd launched a ballistic missile in violation of Security Council resolutions. (The satellite immediately fell into the sea, proving the adage that if the North Koreans launch an intercontinental missile at the United States, the safest place to stand is wherever they are aiming.)

That was when the Obama administration discovered how difficult it was to get in sync with the Chinese when it came to restraining the North Koreans. "The Chinese refrain was, 'We can't control these crazy Kims, but if you pressure them, they behave even worse,'" one administration official told me at the time. Along with the Russians, China opposed any truly tough sanctions against the North, or any real penalty. The compromise was a weak "president's statement" from the UN Security Council, with little binding force. The North then announced that, in retaliation for the UN action, it would once again expel all inspectors from the country's main nuclear site. Kim's government threatened a second nuclear test, and, for good measure, added that it was developing a new intercontinental ballistic missile designed to hit American cities. Even by North Korean standards, this was pretty extreme.

But at this point Obama still seemed hesitant about whether to draw a "red line" that the North Koreans would cross only at their peril. I had been struck by the fact that Obama had not repeated President Bush's warning, after the 2006 nuclear test, that the United States would hold North Korea responsible—in ways to be left to the imagination—if it sold its nuclear technology abroad. (As Cheney noted in his memoirs, Bush had violated his own threat when the North Koreans helped Syria build a nuclear reactor, which Israel ultimately destroyed.) Clearly there was a debate inside the Obama White House about whether a similar statement would be too provocative. Finally one day Denis McDonough, the deputy national security adviser, e-mailed me to say they had decided to let Gates make that threat—which he did, although without the presidential imprimatur it got little attention.

On May 25, 2009, the North exploded its second underground test in three years; this time, it was not a dud. While few in Washington were surprised, it affected Obama's diplomacy toward the North for years to come. "Starting on that day," Jeffrey Bader said to me later, "everyone in the White House became a North Korea hawk."

This latest provocation was so egregious that even the Chinese could not ignore it. At the UN they voted for an arms export embargo and new sanctions, including a legal mechanism for inspecting ships that were suspected of carrying weapons. And for a while that seemed to sting the North Koreans—especially after the United States tracked a ship that appeared to be headed to Myanmar and forced it to turn around. It was the first of several such incidents over the next few years.

But despite the UN vote, Obama was learning a hard truth about the Chinese. They did look down on the North Koreans as wayward, annoying neighbors. But when the neighborhood rumble began, they refused, time and again, to turn the screws. They did not cut off fuel or subsidized food, fearing instability in the desperately poor nation. In fact, Chinese investment in the North increased, as local provinces near the border began to look for raw materials in nearby North Korean territory. No one could blame them: if the North collapsed, refugees would have no place to go except China. They could not get past the mines at the DMZ between North and South, and it is a long swim to Japan.

And for all the talk in Washington about how the Chinese were the North's last protectors, and the only ones with influence over the Kim family and its band of generals, what the Chinese were telling the Americans in private was very different. Perhaps some of the most fascinating cables in the WikiLeaks collection involve the delicate dance between the United States and China over how to pressure the North Koreans.

Considering that only sixty years ago, American and Chinese forces faced off against each other in Korea, the fact that they were talking at all was positive. The cables are filled with Chinese officials laughing about the frustrations of dealing with their paranoid North Korean counterparts—and insisting their own leverage over the Kims was a lot more limited than the Americans believed.

In April 2009, days before the North's nuclear test, He Yafei, the Chinese vice foreign minister, told American officials at a lunch that North Korea wanted direct talks with the United States and to get them was acting like a "spoiled child" to attract the attention of the "adult."[12] (Secretary Clinton, wisely, was telling her aides to hold back on any enthusiasm for such talks—the constant reiteration of the need to sit down with North Korea and its neighbors had a whiff of desperation, she feared.)[13]

When James Steinberg, the deputy secretary of state, sat down in

September 2009 with China's powerful state councilor for foreign affairs, Dai Bingguo, Dai joked that in a recent visit to North Korea he "did not dare" to be too candid with Kim Jong-il, who was still suffering the effects of a stroke. Steinberg was told the North Korean still had a "sharp mind" and retained his reputation among Chinese officials as "quite a good drinker." (Mr. Kim apparently assured Mr. Dai during a two-hour conversation in Pyongyang, the capital, that his infirmities had not forced him to give up alcohol.)

But it turned out the Chinese knew more about Kim's drinking habits than his nuclear intentions. Dai admitted that the Chinese intelligence was "unsure" whether North Korean "threats of another nuclear test were serious." The test happened days later. Soon after, Chinese officials predicted that negotiations intended to pressure the North to disarm would be "shelved for a few months." They have never resumed, as of this writing.

"By the end of 2009, the Chinese got truly concerned that the North could collapse," Bader said later. "And their whole attitude changed: they would do nothing that they feared could create instability." Despite Obama's warning that a nuclear North Korea with long-range missiles in its arsenal would require the United States to bulk up its own presence in the Pacific—and might scare the Japanese into edging toward a nuclear weapon of their own— the Chinese would not cut the North's oil, money, or food. Obama called Hu Jintao to make his point about moving forces into Asia more explicitly.

It was "not a threat. It is simply reality," Obama told Bader.[14]

The Chinese were unmoved.

MEANWHILE, THE AMERICANS and the South Koreans were planning—perhaps a bit overoptimistically—for the day when North Korea might collapse.

In late February 2010, the American ambassador to South

Korea, Kathleen Stephens, met for lunch in Seoul with Chun Yung-woo. Chun was deputy foreign minister at the time; he was soon to become the country's national security adviser. He is an understated diplomat, with none of the fire of his conservative boss, President Lee Myung-bak. But at lunch that day he predicted that "two or three years" after the death of Kim Jong-il, the country's ailing leader, the North would collapse. And that would be the opportunity that South Korea and the United States have waited for since the armistice brought a halt to the Korean War in 1953.

In a cable classified "secret" that Stephens later sent to Washington, Chun predicted that a new, younger generation of Chinese leaders "would be comfortable with a reunited Korea controlled by Seoul and anchored to the United States in a benign alliance."

But Chun was a realist. If Seoul was destined to control the entire Korean Peninsula for the first time since the end of World War II, the Chinese would need to be placated—which is to say, bought off. He described a never publicly discussed plan within the South Korean government to assure Chinese companies that they would have ample commercial opportunities to mine the mineral-rich northern part of the peninsula. In short, he hoped that China's search for cheap, nearby raw material would trump the country's distress at losing the buffer that North Korea provided from American forces. It was a devil's bargain: lose an ally, gain its riches.

The main role for the United States, he said, would be to stay out of the way. That meant the United States would have to keep its military presence well south of the demilitarized zone, the heavily mined demarcation line that now divides the two Koreas. (Staying south of the DMZ is mostly a symbolic gesture; as the Chinese know, the United States could fly from their bases in South Korea to the Chinese border in minutes.) If Stephens offered an opinion about whether she thought this grand bargain would work, her cable back to the State Department did not let on. But it was a fascinating insight into how the South Koreans view the future, and what a central role China will play in the drama when North Korea's high-wire act ends.

Chun had his share of complaints about the Chinese. He told Stephens that he thought the six-nation talks intended to get North Korea to dismantle its nuclear arsenal were being treated by the Chinese as a giant game, meant to deflect pressure from both China and North Korea. The Chinese had just put the negotiations with the North in the hands of the "most incompetent official" in the Chinese pantheon, an arrogant, Marx-spouting former Red Guard who "knows nothing about North Korea, nothing about nonproliferation."[15]

The candor in these cables was refreshing, especially for reporters who are subjected daily to the pabulum of official diplomatic statements. Yet after nearly twenty years of covering North Korea, I was struck by several things while reading through the cable traffic between Seoul and Washington. The first was how long they were on educated guesses about what was going on in North Korea and how short they were on facts. In February 2009, the American consulate in Shanghai—a significant collection point for intelligence about North Korea—sent cables back to Washington reporting that the Chinese who knew North Korea best disbelieved the rumors that Kim Jong-un, Kim Jong-il's youngest son, was being groomed to run the country. Several Chinese scholars with good contacts in the North said they thought it was likely that "a group of high-level military officials" would take over, and that "at least for the moment none of KJI's three sons is likely to be tapped to succeed him." The eldest son was dismissed as "too much of a playboy," the middle son as "more interested in videogames" than governing. Kim Jong-un, they said, was too young and inexperienced.

Perhaps so, but when Kim Jong-il died in December 2011, that young, inexperienced son was named his successor. It was only one example of how North Korea's decision-making processes remained opaque to the United States and China.

The second striking element of the cables was how little influence over the North Koreans the Chinese seemed to have. They described efforts by the Chinese to tutor the North in how to execute financial reforms. Instead, the North Koreans consistently ignored them or screwed it up, setting off an economic crisis when the government tried, and failed, to revalue its worthless currency. (There's a reason the North is the most skilled counterfeiter of $100 bills.)

And the third striking point was the recognition by the South Koreans that, in the words of one South Korean diplomat quoted by Stephens, "unless China pushed North Korea to the 'brink of collapse,'" the North would refuse to take meaningful steps to give up its nuclear program. That seemed about right.

PETER ORSZAG, OBAMA'S first director of the Office of Management and Budget, was accustomed to answering detailed, impatient questions about the cost of Obama's health-care program from suspicious members of Congress. In the summer of 2009 he had a new experience: answering those questions from America's lenders, the Chinese.

On a blistering hot day, a large delegation of senior Chinese officials was in Washington for President Obama's first "Strategic and Economic Dialogue" with the Chinese. It was the hallmark of the Obama effort to upgrade the relationship: holding the kind of deep talks usually reserved for allies. (Now, of course, everyone wants a strategic dialogue—the Japanese and the Pakistanis, the British and the Indians . . . the list goes on.) For three days, top officials would meet in endless sessions on everything from how to avoid military conflicts at sea to the daily argument about the proper value of the yuan, China's currency. But Orzsag was surprised to be asked to tote over his PowerPoint on Obama's health-care proposals.[16]

The Chinese weren't particularly interested in whether Ameri-

cans used a single-payer option or insured every child in the land—
the arguments that were preoccupying the cable airwaves. The
Chinese had only one concern. "They wanted to know, in painstak-
ing detail, how the health-care plan would affect the deficit," one
participant in the conversation later recalled.[17] How, exactly, would
this fit into America's ability to manage its debt, pay its bills, and
keep its currency relatively stable?

Soon the luncheon took on the air of a Wall Street meeting
between prospective investors and a hedge-fund manager, rather
than a diplomatic engagement between two sovereign nations.

It was the kind of conversation that was unimaginable twenty
years ago, or even ten. No one buying treasury bills then would
likely have asked how much it would cost the United States to
invade and occupy Iraq. (Answer: more than Obamacare.) This
health-care conversation with the Chinese in 2009 revealed just how
tough it was to answer Hillary Clinton's rhetorical question to the
Australians: "How do you deal toughly with your banker?" Orszag's
presentation seemed to say: very carefully, and with lots of charts.

The unspoken message of China's interest in the issue was
clear: the United States was already bogged down in two wars, and
appeared, to Chinese analysts, "in decline or distracted or both."[18]
America's lenders in China wanted assurances that the US budget
deficits would not worsen, and neither would the chance that they
would be paid back. As one senior American treasury official told
me later in 2011, some of the biggest choices the House and Senate
make these days also have to pass muster, at least informally, in the
Great Hall of the People. "You know how the generals always say
that when it comes to our strategy in Afghanistan, the enemy has a
vote?" he asked. "Well, when it comes to America borrowing a few
trillion dollars, the Chinese have a vote too."[19] And it isn't just a
vote on how the United States spends its money; in the boardroom
of the World Bank, just down the street from the White House,
when the Chinese talk, people listen.

The nature of the Chinese "vote," though, is often deliberately mischaracterized, mostly by politicians arguing that America has sold its soul. It's not as if Beijing's financial wizards have a choice when it comes to buying treasury bills: if they want to keep their currency from appreciating too fast, they have to recycle their surpluses into dollars. The Chinese are not about to sell the several trillion dollars in assets they already hold; the last thing they want to do is devalue one of their own biggest assets.

But in ways that were inconceivable just a few years ago, the Chinese have used both formal and informal meetings with their American counterparts to explore whether Washington's plan for reducing its debt is credible—and to remind American officials that they have options to gradually shift their money, say, to oil wells in Africa or real estate in the Middle East.

The borrower-banker dynamic was pretty hard to hide by the time Obama made his first trip to China in late 2009. And the Chinese, while welcoming him fairly warmly, stage-managed the visuals. Obama had arranged for a "Town Hall meeting" with young Chinese in Shanghai—a format that, as Bader put it so well, "made Chinese officialdom nervous," turning every detail into "hand-to-hand combat."[20] They feared Obama would not sufficiently censor his own words about China's human rights record. So they refused the American request to broadcast the event on Chinese central television, which would have made it available to the whole country. (In the end, the speech went live on the website of China's main news agency and Shanghai television; while the White House claims there were fifty-five million hits by Chinese viewers, it was clearly a climb-down.) Then the Chinese banned questions at a press conference with President Hu, and censored an interview Obama conducted with a less well-known Chinese newspaper that the White House selected because it often challenged the country's power structure.

The substance of Obama's trip was fine. The optics of the trip were terrible: the narrative had taken hold of a superpower bending to China's will on issues large and small.

For a new president, this was dangerous territory.

◆

By 2010, all the inevitable, smoldering tensions between a rising power and an established one were beginning to burst out. Confrontations were brewing everywhere, from Washington to the South China Sea.

In Obama's first year, he had ducked two perpetual flashpoints with Beijing. One was the tradition of greeting the Dalai Lama of Tibet for a visit to the White House. The Chinese see this ritual as an endorsement of Tibet's desires to break free, even though every president carefully intones that Tibet is part of China but should have religious freedom and some autonomy. But back home, pressure was growing on Obama from the left to meet with the Dalai Lama, as a symbol of solidarity after a period of extraordinarily brutal crackdowns by the Chinese in Tibet. Then there was the long-delayed decision on arms sales to Taiwan, part of the fading American commitment to the island.

No matter how finely Obama calibrated these events, facts make no difference in China when the issues are Tibet and Taiwan. Even younger Chinese who chafe at their government's crackdown on Internet freedom become indignant at the idea of the United States interfering on questions they have been told, since elementary school, strike at China's sovereignty and the country's "core interests." In fact, both Taiwan and Tibet touch a deeper Chinese emotion. China's telling of its own history paints the one-hundred-odd years before 1949 as the country's "Century of Humiliation." Japan, Russia, Britain, and to a lesser degree the United States all tried to break up parts of China or control some of its most lucrative ports, under the infamous "unequal treaties" that treated China as a weak player and made foreigners living there legally untouchable. It is a period of history that most American students are never taught about; in contrast, every Chinese student can recite the litany of outside powers' offenses to national pride.

So when the Dalai Lama emerged from the West Wing and chatted with several correspondents about his long conversations with the president—Obama had given the Dalai Lama a copy of a letter Franklin Roosevelt had written to him when the Dalai Lama was seven years old—the Americans saw a kindly and gentle religious figure; the Chinese saw another effort to divide their land.

They reacted similarly when Obama finally gave the Taiwanese a modest package of arms (but none of the F-16s they wanted, which could strike back at the mainland). The reaction in Beijing amounted to a calculated, prolonged tantrum. Long-arranged visits between Chinese and American military units were canceled. When Jeffrey Bader and James Steinberg showed up in Beijing, they were dressed down—and then given a lengthy presentation about China's rights throughout the contested South China Sea. China said it would be a "national priority" to establish its rights in the 1,200-mile loop that runs from Hainan Island nearly down to Singapore—territory in which many countries in Asia lay claim. China's declaration of rights to the region, including a map it often uses to describe the seascape it says it should control, go back to the 1940s. That was long before exploration began in the region for new oil sources. Now it was clear to Bader and Steinberg that trouble was brewing a year into Obama's tenure.

OF ALL THE places wealthy Chinese tourists flock these days—Tiffany's in New York, the fashion shows in Paris, the beaches in Bali—the Paracel Islands are not high on the list. They are a pile of barren rocks in the middle of the South China Sea, covered with guano deposits. They can barely support plant life, much less casinos and restaurants. So it looked pretty odd when, in 2010, the Chinese government made a big show of setting up tourism offices there.

Beijing's plan for the islands, of course, were never about appearing in the pages of *Travel & Leisure* magazine. They were about Pacific strategy: Vietnam, the Philippines, and Brunei still hold competing claims on these islets, because whoever can credibly claim ownership has a much stronger case to make for virtual control of hundreds of miles of valuable surrounding water with abundant fish and undersea minerals. Exxon Mobil and Russia's Gazprom are also poking around for untapped oil and gas deposits, which they hope could rival Saudi Arabia's.[21]

With the tourism office, China was laying a much bolder claim. Then, Beijing began an active campaign to drive ships out of the waters around the islands. America got its first glimpse of the Chinese strategy in 2009, when the Chinese hassled an American surveillance ship in what the Pentagon maintained was international waters; one unarmed ship, the USNS *Impeccable,* had to spray water from the ship's fire hoses to "defend" itself from the circling Chinese vessels. As confrontations at sea go, this wasn't exactly the Battle of Trafalgar. But it left many in Washington worried; this is how superpowers and their rivals make mistakes. When the Pentagon protested, the PLA Navy compared the US presence in those waters to "a man with a criminal record wandering just outside the gate of a family home."[22]

By 2010 the Chinese were hassling and threatening surveillance crews from several Asian nations, far beyond the two-hundred-nautical-mile limit from Chinese shores. Vietnamese fishermen were being arrested. Then, far north of the South China Sea, a drunken Chinese fisherman started another incident—this time with Japan.

The fisherman had been operating his trawler off of the Senkaku Islands, which Japan administers but China still claims. When the Japanese Coast Guard tried to chase him away, he rammed one of their ships. When I lived as a correspondent in Tokyo in the late '80s and early '90s, there were several incidents like this, and after everyone involved sobered up and got a night's sleep, all was resolved. Not this time.

The fisherman was arrested. In China, historical memories of Japan's brutal occupation of the country are never far below the surface, and in 2010 the Chinese used that inflammatory history to dramatically escalate the incident. When the fisherman was not immediately released, the Chinese limited exports to Japan of "rare earths"—natural resources that Japan relies on for critical components in cell phones, wind turbines, fluorescent lightbulbs, and computer circuit boards. Rare earths are not all that rare, but China controls about 95 percent of the world market, so it knew it had leverage—the Japanese had nowhere else to turn. Japan's prime minister—barely holding on to power himself—called China's behavior after the trawler incident "fairly hysterical."[23] Later, the Chinese export limitations expanded to the Untied States and Europe—for what the Chinese claimed were environmental reasons.

The White House was awash in theories about what the Chinese were doing: appealing to the country's basest nationalistic instincts ahead of a leadership transition, playing out a dispute between bureaucratic factions, or just flexing their muscles. The good news was that countries around Asia were calling back to Washington, urging it to reassert its old role in Asia as power-balancer and peacekeeper. The Navy was eager to oblige. "We had people in the Pentagon telling us, 'We told you so,'" said one senior administration official. Perhaps they were worried about China's aggressiveness, he continued, or "perhaps they were making a case for not cutting the budget."

"Personally, I believe that the assertiveness that we saw from China during that year had nothing to do with a perception of 'Obama's weak,'" Jeffrey Bader later told a Harvard audience. "I think that's nonsense. I think it had to do in part with a belief in some quarters of China that the US was a declining power. That

China's on the rise, China's time had come. There was a drumbeat in the blogosphere that we need a more assertive foreign policy." In fact, visit any Chinese classroom these days and it isn't long before Chinese students ask you what you think of the launching of China's first-ever aircraft carrier. The "China's time for glory" story is pervasive.

So Obama's team began debating how to push back. As Bader later put it: "We had to tell them point-blank that we don't accept any of this."

THE TURNAROUND STARTED with Hillary Clinton. She had been invited as an "observer" at a regional summit of ten Southeast Asian nations in the summer of 2010. But she used the occasion to organize countries across the region to stand up and make the case against China's aggressive push. It was a little like organizing the neighborhood kids to stand up collectively to a bully; Clinton later said to me that she deliberately avoided having the United States take the lead, in hopes of avoiding a narrative of a superpower showdown.

"I was very intent upon us not looking like we were big-footing it, because that would, I thought, push people back to their corners," she said, as the Asians try to preserve good economic ties with China but look to the United States for protection.

When country after country referenced dissatisfaction with China's behavior in their statements—and when Clinton concluded a day of meetings with her own remarks advocating a cooperative international solution—China's foreign minister, Yang Jiechi, was furious. If there is one thing that drives Chinese officials to distraction, it is isolation. "We began to re-create a sense of parity, if you will," Clinton argued to me later. "China's going to have huge influence in the region, but we want to empower other countries by our presence." When Clinton herself spoke, she tried to wrap the Chinese, once again, in international rules that would bind its hands. "The United States, like every nation, has a national interest in freedom of navigation" and "would not tolerate the use or threat of force by any claimant." The United States maintained it was happy to "facilitate" a resolution of the territorial disputes to protect international freedom of navigation—an offer that sounds pretty benign in the United States, but not in China.

Within hours Clinton was denounced by her Chinese counterpart for launching an "attack on China."[24] The Chinese delegation warned her not to step into China's business with the rest of Asia, and millions of Chinese bloggers lit up in agreement.[25] The gist was that the United States had crossed an important and dangerous line in terms of Chinese authority in the region.[26] But several Asian leaders regarded this as a moment of turnaround—a declaration that a country that had been obsessed with containing Pakistan and Iran, and extracting itself from Iraq and Afghanistan, might be edging back to the role it played from the end of World War II to the end of Vietnam.

In fact, the Chinese had done something Obama could not have accomplished himself: they drove their neighbors into America's arms. Bader recalls that at the end of 2010 he had a blunt exchange with his Chinese counterparts: "I told them, you know, you've had a great year: your relations with India, Vietnam, Indonesia, Japan, and South Korea are substantially worse than they were a year ago. But your relations with North Korea are better. So that's your report card."[27]

BY THE END of the year, the Chinese leadership apparently came to the same conclusion. One day toward the end of 2010, I stepped into Tom Donilon's office in the West Wing to discuss a recent trip he and the president's departing economic adviser, Larry Summers, had taken to China to try to reset the relationship.

"Have you seen this?" he asked. He was reading a translation from one of the Chinese Communist Party's dullest, driest publications. The article was entitled "Adhere to the Path of Peaceful Development," and at first I thought it would be another hollow recitation of a now-familiar Chinese mantra to foreign powers: don't worry, be happy; we just want to make a buck, but don't care much for global hegemony.*

But the author was Dai Bingguo, who holds the wonderfully vague title of "state councilor." A young-looking seventy, Dai seems like he ought to be a member of the old guard. But he only entered government service after the Cultural Revolution had passed its peak. He gets sent to the hot spots—among them North Korea and the ethnic rioting in China's far western regions.

Now something of an elder statesman, he was essentially Donilon's counterpart in the Chinese system but also ran critical offices inside the Communist Party's central committee, where the real work gets done. And it was Dai's job to end the battles inside China over how to handle the Americans.

Donilon was particularly fascinated by Dai's article because he had been conducting a series of quiet sessions with Dai—over dinners, sometimes lasting hours—as part of an effort to understand the thinking of the Chinese leadership. As Donilon and I looked over a translation, it was clear that the article appeared to be a sharp rebuke of the year of South China Sea provocations—and a warning to hawks, including those in China's military, to back off. It quoted,

---

* The article reads, in part, "It is reiterated in the part on external relations that China stands firmly for peace, development, and cooperation; pursues the independent foreign policy of peace; sticks to the path of peaceful development and the win-win strategy of opening up; safeguards China's sovereignty, security, and development interests; and is ready to work with other countries to build a harmonious world of lasting peace and common prosperity. This explains fully China's external stance, its path of development, its goal, and the way to achieve the goal. Therefore, it has great relevance and far-reaching significance to China's diplomacy under the new circumstances."

repeatedly, Deng Xiaoping's principles of sticking to China's problems at home and avoiding trouble abroad: "As Comrade Deng Xiaoping once said, if one day China tries to seek hegemony in the world, people of the world should expose, oppose and overthrow it. The international community can hold us to account. Some say China wants to replace the United States and dominate the world. That is simply a myth."[28]

Donilon's staff and much of the intelligence community was poring over the document, and had concluded it was intended as a way for the country's leadership to strike back at the more nationalistic forces, including retired military who seemed to be speaking for current officers. Dai was clearly speaking for Hu Jintao. To Donilon's eye, the article did not appear intended as propaganda for easily impressionable foreigners.

"We didn't know the Dai Bingguo article was coming," Bader recalled after leaving the administration.[29] "I had spoken to a number of Chinese think-tankers in the course of the previous year, virtually baiting them to respond to some of the more hypernationalistic venting we had seen from these retired admirals. And they in essence said to me, 'We can't, we're intimidated. I write something and I get ten million blog posts denouncing me as a traitor.'" Clearly, Dai intended to change that.

THE CHINESE SAW plenty of chaos—and weakness—in our system too, and they did not hesitate to take advantage of it.

Early in 2011, over lunch at the Central Party School outside Beijing—where the party's leadership goes to debate questions that are a bit too uncomfortable to air in public—a retired general in the People's Liberation Army settled into a seat next to me during a break in a conference we were both attending. It had been one of those long mornings where officials on both sides had exchanged set-piece statements, extolling a new era of "mutual cooperation." The Chinese talked about "peaceful rise" and the Americans urged "transparency." It was all a little sleep-inducing. Lunch offered the only opportunity for truly unscripted, unmonitored exchanges, and the former general looked at me quizzically and asked, in essence, what we had been doing for the past decade. "I sat through many meetings [inside the PLA] in the '80s and '90s where we tried to imagine what your military forces would look like in ten or twenty years," he told me. They spent months examining America's advantage in submarines and satellites, the fearsome global strike capability to have a plane lift off in Missouri, drop a bomb over the Balkans—hitting, say, the Chinese embassy—and come home in time for dinner. They assessed America's investments in new military technologies and compared them to their own. Keeping up with the American military budget, they concluded, was more than the Chinese economy could afford.

"But frankly, we never thought that you would spend trillions of dollars and so much time tied down in Afghanistan and the Middle East," he said. "We never imagined that is a choice you would make."

Not so secretly, the Chinese were delighted by the Bush-era wars. The longer the United States was bogged down trying to build democracies in foreign lands, the less capable it was of competing in China's backyard.

But now that America was emerging from a lost decade in the Middle East, the Chinese began to ask: How should China respond? With cooperation, confrontation, or something in between?

That was the central question at the beginning of 2012 as China entered a rocky period of leadership change. American intelligence agencies reported that there were three competing schools of thought developing in China.

One was to listen to Dai Bingguo's advice: focus on domestic issues, keep creating jobs, and bide China's time. A second, smaller group argued that China was big enough to work with the United States on problems like climate change, combating international piracy, and protecting intellectual property. All were areas where China and the United States had some overlapping interests, even while openly competing for influence in Asia, Latin America, and Africa. And the third school—largely in the military—argued that this is China's time, and the country should not be tethered to a set of Western-written rules meant to keep China down. In the analysis of the US intelligence community, the first and the second schools had won most of the fights. But the third school had all the energy. It was not hard to whip up nationalist sentiment.

"There will be deep areas of rivalry between the US and China," said Kurt Campbell, the assistant secretary of state for Asia. He relentlessly—and quite successfully—traveled throughout the continent to entice countries like Myanmar out of China's orbit and back into America's through Obama's first term. "But there is a difference between rivalry and open antagonism."

Jon Huntsman was in his last days as American ambassador to China when he slipped into a black leather jacket and sunglasses, dispensed with the limousine, and headed as inconspicuously as possible to the jammed Wangfujing shopping district in Beijing.

In his younger days—when he was a Mormon missionary in China, not an ambassador weighing what still seemed like a plausible run for the presidency—Huntsman might have blended in around the iconic McDonald's that dominates the pedestrian shopping area. Back then he was just another twentysomething who had come to explore China, and change it. It was then that he learned Mandarin, and his way around the back streets of a Beijing that, save for a few sections, no longer exists today.

But by 2011 he was too well known to escape attention. Video from onlookers' camera phones shows him closely trailed by a

Marine guard. Later, the American embassy in Beijing would say that Huntsman was out with his family shopping, and just happened to encounter a crowd out on a winter's day. No one believed that—especially not the Chinese leadership.

What worried those leaders the most that Sunday morning on February 20, 2011, was that the Arab Spring could leap the Pacific and reignite forces that the previous generation of Chinese leaders thought they had satisfactorily extinguished in Tiananmen Square twenty-two years before. Huntsman had spent his entire ambassadorship pressing the Chinese to open up their political system, and on the local level there were now more than a few real elections. But the Chinese had no intention of doing the same at the regional or national level, fearing anything that could threaten the party leadership. When Tibetans began protests in 2008, the crackdown was harsh.

Around one p.m. that Sunday, plainclothes police flooded the area, alerted by postings on blogs and on Twitter that an antigovernment protest might gather steam. There would be no mass gathering in Tiananmen; the disaffected knew that would be too provocative. Instead, the bloggers were calling for just a walk-by of the shopping street near the McDonald's, and maybe a few low-key expressions of discontent.

Video of what actually unfolded suggests the protestors never achieved anything close to an organized presence. A few dozen people showed up outside McDonald's for what was supposed to be "China's own Jasmine Revolution," as described by one of the expatriate dissidents calling for democratic reforms. The protestors ranged from stylish young students to hunchbacked old women, but the diversity was more impressive than the message.

Police pushed onlookers away from the scene and confiscated cameras. Protestors who shouted or resisted were quickly stuffed into vans, some to be released moments later. A man who placed jasmine flowers in one of the planters outside McDonald's was surrounded and seized, although he was released when reporters got too close.[30] In the end, only three people were arrested in Beijing, and about the same in Shanghai.

Huntsman quietly left the scene, but not before the Chinese noticed him and issued a demarche to Washington. "They went batshit," one senior administration official later told me. "They didn't quite accuse the US of starting these protests, but that was the implication."

In fact, when images of the revolutions under way in Tunisia and Egypt first hit China, Hu Jintao scrambled to call an emergency "study group" among his top advisers to get their bearings. Like the Saudis and the Israelis, the Chinese—through state-approved editorials—criticized the United States for abandoning their loyal friend Mubarak in his great hour of need. Americans were portrayed as "shifty and capricious."[31]

There were countless news stories across China about Egyptians and Tunisians who had lost family members in riots, or who saw their livelihoods destroyed. The message to Chinese readers was clear: protesting against your government leads to chaos, misery, and fear. "Normal life is no longer possible" for Egyptians and Tunisians, warned a Xinhua special report.[32]

And then, when this tiny so-called Jasmine protest took place on Chinese soil, Beijing proclaimed they would nip any kind of Chinese Spring in the bud. Zhou Yongkang, a politburo member responsible for security issues, said the core lesson of the Arab Spring for China was this: China must "strive to defuse conflicts and disputes while they are still embryonic."[33]

The crackdown spread. The government reverted to terror-inducing tactics from a past era: widespread disappearances, thugs beating up activists. "They're worried, and they are trying to stop history, which is a fool's errand," Hillary Clinton said of the

Chinese. "They cannot do it. But they're going to hold it off as long as possible."[34]

By the end of 2011, Richard Haass, a former senior State Department official who now runs the Council on Foreign Relations, put the Chinese dilemma succinctly: "The irony is inescapable: political leaders in the US and Asia are busy debating how best to meet what they see as the threat from China; political leaders in China are debating how best to meet the many threats they perceive to China. Most of the threats the Chinese see to their country come from within."[35]

WHILE THE CHINESE were preoccupied, Obama faced a more dangerous challenge from the North Koreans, and by 2011 it was only getting worse.

The North was preparing for its own leadership change, and no one seemed quite certain how much longer Kim Jong-il could hang on. He had visited China three times since recovering from his stroke. But when American officials probed, gently, about his condition, "we got nothing of use," one senior official told me.

Eventually, it became clear that Kim was lining up his youngest son, Kim Jong-un, to be his successor. Yet the CIA knew so little about Kim Jong-un that until he finally appeared by his father's side, their only picture of him had been taken a decade ago at a Swiss boarding school that he had attended under an assumed name. "It was astounding how little we understood about what he had done, how he thinks, even what the military thought about him," one intelligence official who had been tasked to put together a full profile of him told me.

"The only thing we knew for certain is that he bore a scary resemblance to his grandfather," North Korea's founder, Kim Il-sung.

But there was evidence that the youngest Kim had been involved, at least peripherally, in planning attacks on South Korea that could give him some credibility with the North Korean military leadership, which could not have been happy about having an experience-free youngster placed at the country's helm. American and South Korean intelligence officials believe he'd had some role in the March 2010 sinking of the *Cheonan,* a South Korean corvette that was torpedoed near the sea demarcation line that separates the North and South. Forty-six sailors died. At first, many speculated the ship had hit an old mine. But an international panel of investigators later found a torpedo shell near the wreckage, along with explosive traces that made it clear the ship was hit by a torpedo launched from a mini-submarine. The North Koreans were the only reasonable suspects.

When the evidence was presented to the Chinese, they declined to accept the conclusion. "It was remarkable," President Lee Myung-bok, the South Korean leader, told me when we met in Seoul early in 2011. "The Chinese did not want to act, so they just ignored the evidence." Showing remarkable restraint, Lee did not counterattack on the submarine base where attacking ships had been launched. But the result was that the North paid little price for its action.

That reality led to a sharp, almost ugly exchange between Obama and Hu Jintao when they next met at an economic summit. Obama charged that by ignoring the evidence, Hu was giving the North Koreans a free pass to attack again. Hu responded that China was simply being evenhanded, siding with neither North nor South. Obama was so annoyed that he publicly charged the Chinese with "willful blindness" at a press conference.

By November, the North was at it again, as I discovered one day when I was asked to come by the White House for a briefing. I had already heard rumors that Siegfried Hecker, a Stanford nuclear scientist who once headed the Lawrence Livermore National Laboratory, had been invited to North Korea in recent days. There were rumors flying that he had been shown some evidence of a major nuclear advance by the North. But before I could reach him, a group of senior White House and State Department officials were filling me in on just what Hecker had seen: a complete uranium-enrichment facility, built at the nuclear site where inspectors had been thrown out eighteen months before.

For years there had been reports that the North was building such a facility, based on equipment it had bought from A. Q. Khan, who had also sold his centrifuges to Iran. But the enrichment plant Hecker saw had been built so quickly that it was almost certain the North had moved the equipment from another site. "I was stunned," Hecker told me when I called him after emerging from the White House that afternoon. He said he saw "hundreds and hundreds" of centrifuges that had just been installed, along with "an ultramodern control room."[36]

The White House was clearly sensitive about one aspect of the story. American intelligence agencies had somehow missed the construction of the facility, even though it was located on one of the most carefully monitored pieces of real estate on Earth: the Yongbyon nuclear site. Before I had stepped into the West Wing, one of my briefers later admitted, there had been a lengthy discussion about how to answer the question of whether this was an intelligence failure. They settled on an artful evasion: "The US intelligence community has been focused on a North Korean enrichment program for a long time." True, but so had everyone else familiar with North Korea's program. (I had written extensively about the suspicions starting in 2003.)

The administration officials who briefed me said they were then headed to talk to allies around Asia, and the Chinese, about how to respond to the discovery. That turned out to be a fruitless effort; there was little response. And then, just two weeks later, the North shelled a South Korean island—not far from where the *Cheonan* sank—after the South Korean military had conducted live-fire exercises. Again, there were reports that Kim Jong-un had been involved in the decision to attack the island, perhaps just an effort to burnish his image.

It seemed clear back in Washington that the North was attempting to repeat its oldest trick: stage an incident, let a crisis mentality set in, then open negotiations for food and aid. But as Robert Gates had declared early in Obama's tenure, "I don't want to buy the same horse a third time." The horse went unpurchased, but the North went unpunished.

A YEAR LATER, Kim Jong-il was dead. His demise apparently took the entire North Korean leadership by surprise; when American intelligence agencies later reran their tapes of satellite images from that late-December weekend in Pyongyang, they saw that his special train had pulled out of the station on a well-guarded trip. Then it stopped. Troops massed around it. And slowly, it reversed course and headed back to the capital. It was two days before a public announcement was made.

The funeral that followed was transfixing. For the first time in years, there were live images being beamed around the world from the cold, barren streets of Pyongyang. The hearses proceeded down the main boulevard—big, bulky black cars that looked like they came out of the 1960s. Several of them, it turned out, did. On the streets, the cameras showed people wailing uncontrollably. The inevitable debate broke out in the West: Were the North Koreans genuinely grieving? Were they brainwashed? Were they putting on a show for the West?

All three could have been true. But what was truly impressive was how quickly the country—and the military—seemed to rally behind Kim Jong-un. Within hours of the announcement of Kim Jong-il's death, the North Korean Workers Party called for the nation to unite "under the leadership of our comrade Kim Jong-un." But the young heir apparent did not have twenty years to build up support among the narrow North Korean elite. So the propaganda department swung into action: It broadcast a documentary on how the young Kim was a "military genius," and pictured him riding a white horse, as his father once did. Then came a photo that reminded some Americans of Michael Dukakis's failed presidential campaign, riding around in a tank.

That was just the beginning of the tough-guy imagery. The documentary claimed he oversaw the April 2009 test launch of the long-range rocket and quoted him saying, "I had determined to enter a war if the enemies dared to intercept" the rocket.

Why would the North Korean military accept this chubby-faced leader? It is not clear, but it is likely his ascendance was considered the path of least resistance. He was so inexperienced, so young (twenty-eight years old by some accounts, but no one knows for certain), that it was possible the military leadership had decided he would make a useful figurehead, while a regent—perhaps Kim Jong-il's brother-in-law—wielded the real power. Despite the country's image as a one-man dictatorship, the North in recent years seems to make decisions by putting different power centers in contention with one another. Obama himself seemed to be making this point in late March 2012, when he visited the DMZ. Once he got back to Seoul, he took the first poke at the young North Korean, saying, "It's not clear exactly who's calling the shots and what their long-term objectives are."[37]

The Chinese seemed equally mystified. A senior American official who went to Beijing to meet China's leadership shortly after Kim Jong-il's death reported back that "to their credit, they didn't go through and try to tell us what a great leader Kim Jong-un is." But Washington was still trying to figure out what the official referred to as "two goals in contradiction: the Chinese very much want these guys to survive but also haven't given them enough to live."

Obama made yet another effort to open negotiations with the North, and for two brief weeks in the spring of 2012 it seemed like it might be promising: the North agreed to suspend all missile and nuclear tests, and would allow nuclear inspectors back into the country. In return, it wanted food aid delivered—the same old cycle, the cycle of extortion Obama had vowed to break. Usually, the United States insists that it never links food aid to political negotiations, so that a starving populace does not suffer because it is ruled over by despots. But in the North's case it is impossible to separate food from politics: since the North insists on delivering the aid itself, the West worries that the food it delivers is immediately diverted to the North Korean military.

The deal did not last long. Within two weeks the North announced it would launch another "satellite" into orbit, in honor of the hundredth birthday of Kim Il-sung, the country's founder. The true purpose seemed to be to solidify a claim on power by his look-alike grandson. The American negotiators insist they had clearly warned the North that any space launch would be considered a thin guise for a missile test, and a violation of the accord. Much of the rest of the world chimed in with similar warnings. The North Koreans not only ignored the protests, they invited foreign reporters into the country to tour the test site and peer at the satellite, and they buried them in propaganda about the North's fearsome powers.

Days later the rocket lifted off—and turned into an instant humiliation. After a little more than a minute into flight, the rocket went wildly off track and broke up, dumping the satellite—derisively described by one American official as "a small refrigerator wrapped in tin foil"—into the sea. The United States canceled the food aid worth about $200 million. And with the collapse of the deal, the hope evaporated that inspectors might get into that new uranium-enrichment site and figure out whether the North was capable of producing a new kind of weapon.

The whole bizarre episode raised a host of questions about the young Kim Jung-un—and about the Obama strategy for dealing with the country.

Had Kim approved the deal and then been overridden by hard-liners in the military, who saw benefit in following the old strategy of periodically ratcheting up tension with the United States? In other words, did the incident reveal his tenuous hold on power? Or had he planned this two-step move—agreement and defiance—all along, in hopes of solidifying his rule by using one of the techniques his father had been famous for engineering? After all, despite the failed launch, Kim got promoted within hours, right on schedule, as head of the National Defense Commission, the one major title he had not yet assumed from his father.

The theory that the young Kim was behind the strategy seems compelling. As one senior American intelligence official told me, "Everything we've seen and heard out of the North suggests this was a product of careful calculation." Yet the differing theories may say as much about us as they do about the North. After decades of peering into the Hermit Kingdom, we are still missing the construction of new nuclear facilities, and we still understand little about how the country makes decisions.

By Western standards, the failed test was just an embarrassing fiasco. "The North Koreans have managed in a single stroke to not only defy the UN Security Council, the United States, and even their patron China, but also demonstrate ineptitude," Marcus Noland, one of the best of the North Korea watchers in Washington, told my *Times* colleagues after the failed space shot. "Some of the scientists and engineers associated with the launch are likely facing death or the gulag as scapegoats for this embarrassment."[38]

By the North's own terms, though, it may have been a partial success. Every provocation, even a failed one, plays to the Chinese fear of chaos in the region brilliantly. They keep the Chinese oil and investment flowing. The next nuclear test will probably do the same—it will lead the Chinese to call for yet more talks, another way of trying to preserve the status quo.

For Obama, the North has been an odd exception to his much-discussed "engagement" strategy. While he sent some secret letters to the North's leadership in the early weeks of his presidency, contacts were minimal—"limited engagement," one of his top North Korea advisers called it, as a synonym for nearly none. No American official has ever met Kim Jung-un. Obama, according to aides, reacts viscerally to the North Koreans and the abuses they visit on their people—just as George W. Bush did. Oddly, Obama so far has talked to the North Koreans a lot less than Bush did in his second term.

Today, Obama's best hope is that the modern world will catch up with the Kim dynasty, as it caught up with Ben Ali, Mubarak, Qaddafi, and Assad. But who knows when that could happen: every American president since Harry Truman has been hoping for the regime change that has never arrived. While there are no overt signs of restiveness in the country, the very fact that Kim Jung-un felt compelled to explain the rocket failure publicly reflected the fact that there are a million cell phones in the country today—and the Kim family's monopoly on information is eroding. That does not guarantee eventual collapse of the state. But it could speed it, and make it noisier, when the moment comes.

That could be a prosperous Asia's messiest moment. At an event just a day or so after the failed test, the youngest Kim watched a precision military parade—the one thing the North gets right, every time—and heard his soldiers yell.

"Kim Jung-un!" they shouted about a young man they barely knew. "Defend him to the death!"

ALL OF WASHINGTON's elite, it seemed, had poured into a cramped ballroom just before lunchtime one unseasonably warm day in February 2012 to listen to a man who was a complete cipher: Xi Jinping.

The only thing all of them knew about Xi was that at age fifty-eight he was the odds-on favorite to become the next president of China, and arguably the second most powerful leader in the world. The certainties ended there. Most of the senators, lobbyists, television anchors, and journalists stuffed into the Marriott in Woodley Park that morning had never heard of him just three years before. Even that day, only a handful had ever heard his voice. From the flurry of articles that preceded his introduction to Washington, they knew he visited Iowa in the mid-1980s, when he was still a local official more interested in the problems of what to feed farm animals than in whether China could keep up its breakneck growth. This was long before the Chinese elite entertained the thought that their country's economy might overtake the United States', at least by the crude measure of sheer size. Apart from the Iowa venture, Xi's exposure to the United States was scant. But he knew what America does best: provides the top college and graduate school education in the world. So like many of the Chinese leaders who have quietly engaged in an internal competition to get their children into the Ivy League, he enrolled his daughter at Harvard, under an assumed name.

Chinese knew Xi less for anything he said than for the fact that he was married to a well-known Chinese folk singer named Peng Liyuan, a popular figure among generations of Chinese who grew up hearing her sing about life in the countryside. And they knew he was a "princeling," a term for the sons of leaders of the Chinese revolution. But it was a complicated history: Xi Zhongxun, his father, had been a loyalist of Mao who got on the wrong side of the volatile founder of modern China. He was purged in 1962 and spent the better part of a decade and a half in virtual exile before he was formally "rehabilitated" two years after Mao's death. The elder Xi, who died a decade ago, is often talked about today in glowing terms, as the creator of one of China's first special economic zones and a critic of the crackdown on the Tiananmen Square protestors in 1989. His years in the wilderness clearly affected his son, who witnessed his father's arrest and moved with the family to work in the countryside. According to one report, the elder Xi was put in jail three times—a trauma for any teenager, and something that would make him particularly sensitive, one would think, about China's treatment of those perceived to be in opposition to state power.[39]

Yet on the critical issues between Washington and Beijing—the Chinese debate about whether and how soon to compete with the United States for global power, or Beijing's willingness to take on corruption, entrenched interests, and the military—the rising Chinese leader was impossible to read. "I've spent an hour or two with him, and I couldn't tell you," one senior American official said after emerging from talks with Xi. Many China experts whispered that they thought his family history and record as a local Communist Party leader suggested he would jump-start the economic reforms that petered out under the uninspired leadership of Hu Jintao. But that assessment appeared based more on guesswork than facts; a decade ago, people were saying the same of Hu.

Xi Jinping was in Washington to impress, and to show the leadership back home he could handle the Americans, or at least do no appreciable harm to his candidacy. He had already been hosted at a huge dinner at the White House, endured an election season-inspired critique of China's trade behavior from Joe Biden during a toast at the State Department, and faced a gauntlet of human rights protestors who would have been jailed, or worse, in Beijing. Now, in the hotel ballroom, he had to give the ritual policy speech about China's plans for the next few decades. He was determined to make no news, and he succeeded. After an introduction by Henry Kissinger that recalled Nixon's trip to China exactly four decades before, Xi cited a Chinese proverb: "When you drink the water, don't forget who dug the well." The aging well diggers in the audience nodded and smiled. Then came a series of other bromides: the Chinese-US relationship was "an unstoppable river that keeps surging ahead," and would thrive if proper care were given to "mutual cooperation." He called for more student exchanges—something no one could oppose—and offered a requisite paean to the Iowa family who put

him up in their teenager's bedroom, and showed him a side of
America he had never learned about as a schoolchild in China.

What was particularly striking, though, was what he did *not*
mention: President Obama's "pivot" to Asia—part of a long-brewing
move toward something that Tom Donilon had first talked about to
me in February 2009, during Obama's initial weeks in office. When
Obama had surveyed the world he was inheriting, Donilon said,
he and his aides had concluded American diplomacy and military
deployments were "underinvested in Asia," largely as a result of
years of post-9/11 focus on the Middle East. It took nearly three
years for the policy to unfold, and when it did, Donilon told me he
thought "it was as big a strategic move as the US has made in a long
time." On one level he was certainly right: during the Bush years,
a parade of Asian leaders complained publicly and privately that
the United States was only barely cognizant of the degree to which
China was filling the vacuum left by America's focus on the other
side of the world. "Ten years ago the first question any Southeast
Asian leader would ask is, 'How will this play in Washington?'" the
prime minister of one significant American ally said to me over a
dinner in DC in 2011. "For the past few years it's been, 'How will
this play in Beijing?'"

Obama's strategy was to make the American military presence
in Southeast Asia more obvious—starting with a small base in
Australia, far from China's shores, and then through similar ar-
rangements elsewhere in the region. And he established a new group
to tighten trade relationships—a "Trans-Pacific Partnership"—to
which China was invited, but only if it agreed to standards on
openness to investment and trading rules that clearly would drive
Chinese enterprises up the wall. The message was clear: China could
not have it both ways. It could not demand respect as a great rising
power but still insist that it be treated as a "developing economy"
that cannot be expected to play by the rules that govern established
economies. It would have to choose. "What the Chinese hate the

most is the sense that they are excluded or isolated," one of the strategists who put the plan together observed at the end of 2011. "That's their vulnerability, and this is aimed at making them decide between exclusion and their desire to set their own rules."

Whether any of this will work is still an open question. We likely won't know for several years; in the midst of a leadership transition, the big decisions are likely to be put off. But soon after Xi left Washington, the administration got a reminder that the big question in China—whether to take on the United States for global leadership—is hardly a settled one.

THE REMINDER CAME from Wang Jisi, an academic with close ties to the leadership and who is one of China's most influential writers on foreign affairs. In person, Wang is soft-spoken and inquisitive; when I saw him in 2011 he had insightful questions about how Obama saw the world, and the future of American power. But it was his writing about how a rising generation of Chinese leaders—Xi Jinping's generation—sees America that caught Washington's attention. Wang had published, through the Brookings Institution, an analysis that suggested that when the current generation of Chinese leaders retires over the next year, the bide-our-time, worry-about-problems-at-home mind-set may also be retired.[40]

"Chinese distrust of the United States has persisted ever since the founding of the People's Republic of China in 1949," Wang began. But in recent times—and during Obama's presidency—"it seems to have deepened."

China's leaders know, he wrote, that "their nation has ascended to be a first-class power in the world and should be treated as such." But they are also convinced that the United States is "a declining power over the long run," and "now this nation is no longer that awesome, nor is it trustworthy, and its example to the world and admonitions to China should therefore be much discounted."

Washington's real aim, he added, is "to prevent the emerging powers, in particular China, from achieving their goals and enhancing their stature."

Wang then went on to describe some paranoid thinking among Chinese leaders. They were convinced, he wrote, that the United States orchestrated the award of the 2010 Nobel Peace Prize to Liu Xiaobo, one of the country's most famous imprisoned dissidents. The Chinese government protested, and prohibited Liu, in jail for "inciting subversion," from receiving the prize.

Obama's "pivot" toward Asia, despite everything the president says, is "largely directed at constraining China," Wang contended. American "spy planes and ships are so close to Chinese borders that the PLA is seriously alarmed at operational levels." And Hillary Clinton's assertion of "freedom of navigation" in the South China Sea amounts to "meddling" in issues that are none of Washington's business. Even the pressure to get China aboard on clean-energy technologies is part of a "Western conspiracy" to sell low-carbon technology to China while restraining the rise of its industries, he argued.

And North Korea? "It is a widely held view in Beijing that the United States would like to see 'regime change' in Pyongyang and that American pressures on the North Korean government are aimed at undermining or overthrowing it at Chinese expense."

Raw as it sounds, Wang's characterization of the view of the Chinese leadership echoes sentiments Americans will confront frequently in coming years. If he is right—if this really is the prevalent view of Chinese leaders and the country's new power brokers outside Zhongnanhai, and not just chatter in the blogosphere—then China underappreciates the kind of resistance it is likely to face. Obama's aides have largely dismissed Wang's view that China's next generation of leaders will be increasingly nationalistic. They conveniently prefer Dai Binggou's school of thought that the peaceful rise is the only path. But no one really knows. And if Wang is right,

Washington has a problem: roughly 70 percent of China's leadership jobs will be turning over in 2012.

Just as the world watched with anticipation as Obama was ushered in to remake a new chapter in American international engagement, new Chinese leaders will have their moment over the course of the next year. If modern history tells us anything, the Chinese will be determined to maintain stability at all costs during the transition. But it may not be entirely in their control. Already fractures within the leadership are breaking out.

Just as Xi Jinping was visiting the United States, one of those fractures became public in the strange case of Bo Xilai, a wealthy populist politburo member and former minister of commerce. In the huge and influential city of Chongqing, Bo built a charismatic persona, acting more like a Western politician than the typical conformist politburo member.

Bo fought organized crime and portrayed himself as a promoter of egalitarian values. He also tried to create a bit of nostalgia around the values of the Cultural Revolution and openly lobbied for a post on China's highest ruling council. But the party abruptly dismissed him in March 2012, after his vice mayor fled to the American consulate in Chengdu, seeking asylum and bearing documents telling a story of internal turmoil in the politburo and divulging scandalous allegations of crime and corruption by Bo himself. The vice mayor's tales of political intrigue and infighting among the party members were a small treasure trove for American intelligence agencies. But the United States could not grant him asylum; getting him out of the country was just too tricky, with hundreds of Chinese security agents outside the consulate doors. Soon thereafter Bo's wife was arrested on charges of murdering a British businessman, and the downward spiral continued.

The lesson was clear: step outside the Party's way of doing business and you will regret it. Across Washington, China experts inside and outside the government were trying to read between the lines.

Was there a deep power struggle under way for control of the government? Did the breach suggest a broader struggle between those who wanted to choose the leadership the old-fashioned way and those seeking more open politics and insisting on greater rule of law? "We're still trying to figure it out," one of Obama's aides told me. "We don't understand it."

What Obama learned in his first three years in office is that the biggest check on Chinese power is China itself: every time Beijing overreaches, its neighbors get scared and seek deeper alliances with Washington.

There are two big risks ahead. The first is that the world could ultimately divide into two camps—an American camp and a Chinese camp, re-creating the dynamics of the Cold War. That seems unlikely, at least over the next decade.

The second risk—the bigger risk—is what Graham Allison, the Harvard strategist, calls "the Thucydides Trap." The phrase is drawn from the tome on the Peloponnesian War that has ruined many a freshman year in college. Thucydides concluded that as tensions escalated between a rising Athens and a Sparta that wanted to hold on to its preeminent role in the world, "what made the war inevitable was the growth of Athenian power and the fear which this caused Sparta."

We are seeing similar themes today: a fear in America of China's rise, fueled by America's concerns about its long-term economic fate, and a fear in China that America is determined to contain a competitor unlike any it has ever faced before. Those fears alone do not make conflict inevitable; they can be managed. But fear has driven many great powers to make bad decisions in the past, and just because we and the Chinese understand this history does not guarantee we will avoid the same mistake.

EPILOGUE

ON AN EARLY DECEMBER EVENING AT THE END OF 2011, PRESIDENT Obama gathered the Joint Chiefs of Staff and the nation's combatant commanders into the State Dining Room at the White House. It was an unusual setting for one of the most consequential conversations about the nation's military future: two giant, lavishly decorated Christmas trees flanked the portrait of a pensive-looking Abraham Lincoln. Beneath, a mix of top military brass and national security officials sat uncomfortably around a series of tables set up in a giant rectangle, with Obama directly beneath Lincoln. The mood seemed to mirror the Great Emancipator's expression in the uncertain moments of the Civil War.

"This was the end of an era," one of the commanders told me later. "And that was a hard concept for many in the room to accept." For a decade since 9/11, the Pentagon had possessed a virtual blank check to pursue any program that could be sold as necessary to protect against an array of new threats. The defense budget had grown by an astounding 67 percent over ten years in real terms, to levels 50 percent higher than it had been for an average year during the Cold War (adjusted for inflation).[1] "We're Americans," Adm. Dennis Blair, who served briefly as Obama's director of national intelligence, had said to me drolly. "If it's worth doing, it's worth overdoing."

The president's message to the military was that the spigot needed to begin closing: the United States was going to have to find a way to maintain its military dominance—and global leadership—while cutting $500 billion out of the defense budget over the next ten years.

Even Obama had been shocked, his aides said, by the cumulative cost of the nation's response to 9/11. An estimate my colleagues and I put together for the tenth anniversary of the attacks suggested that the United States had spent at least $3.3 trillion responding to the attacks over the course of the decade, securing the country, invading and attempting to rebuild two nations, and caring for the American wounded. Put another way, for every dollar al-Qaeda spent destroying the World Trade Center and attacking the Pentagon, America had spent $6.6 million in response.[2]

The annual Pentagon budget of $700 billion was equivalent to the *combined spending* of the next twenty largest military powers.[3] Diplomacy, development, and humanitarian assistance—what Obama had campaigned on increasing, to change America's image in the world—still amounted to less than a tenth of that amount. The world had come to expect that America would underwrite global security, regardless of the cost. Obama was determined to change that mind-set.

As part of a budget deal that reflected the bitterness and intractability of the country's partisan divides, Congress had already passed into law one approach to solving the sustainability problem: if Democrats and Republicans could not agree on other budget cuts, the defense budget would simply be cut across the board.

It was, as Obama had already said to his staff, the ultimate in legislative stupidity: that the United States would continue doing everything it has done in the world—just around 9 percent less.[4] It was the kind of budget-cutting thinking—hardly uncommon in Washington—that failed to set priorities and completely divorced resources from achieving objectives. There was no consideration of how to reshape American defenses to fit the kind of threats America is likely to face in coming years, no way to free up money to invest in new opportunities. Instead, every outdated weapons system, and every underutilized American base abroad, would survive. They would just shrink.

"That's not the way we are going to go," Obama told his staff one day as they considered their options, one of his national security aides recalled. He had previously pressed for a sped-up review of the country's defense posture and strategy. In Obama's mind, the weapons systems designed for a Cold War that ended nearly a quarter century ago finally had to die—no matter what the defense lobbyists had to say about it. So did the Pentagon's plan to keep 100,000 troops ready for "stability operations"—exactly the kind of operation the United States had just ended in Iraq, and that Obama had said would end in Afghanistan by December 2014. By scratching that off the proposed budget, Obama's message was clear: America was out of the occupation business.

"We knew we had to have a different approach," Tom Donilon told me after the meeting. "We've got a world driven by shifting threats, technological change, and remarkable new financial realities. These are the things of which strategy is made." And yet in the decade since 9/11, as the country raced to build higher defenses and pay for two wars whose human and financial costs were spiraling out of control, one strategy review after another had failed to fundamentally realign the world's biggest military budget with contemporary challenges. Like much of America, much of the military was running on autopilot.

It soon became clear to the Joint Chiefs and the four-stars in the room that the real purpose of the State Dining Room meeting was less to solicit their advice than to adjust them to a new reality. America could no longer afford to do everything, fight every war, remake every failed state.

Obama went around the room, asking whether the draft he had circulated of a new strategic review—an increased focus on Asia and on Special Operations Forces, as well as a sharp reduction in the size of the conventional force in the Middle East and Europe—would enable them to do their jobs. They each agreed they could—what other answer were they going to give the president about a strategy that would be announced in just a few weeks?

For Obama, this was the end of the first chapter of his presidency, of getting beyond his inheritance. Moving to the next step— finding a way to preserve and enhance American power in a new age of national austerity—would take a lot more than just resigned agreement among the chiefs and the commanders. That is the real challenge of the time he has left in office.

In his first term, Obama only began to redefine American interests and redirect American capabilities. He faced many obstacles— particularly the prolonged economic downturn—and a Congress permanently entrenched in partisan bickering. He spent a lot of political capital on health care and the stimulus. National security was the place where he had the most leeway—and where, as many of his critics conceded, he had performed far better than expected. But he had yet to really chart his own course and forge his own initiatives. Now he has to do so amidst an age of reckoning—a time when the checks his predecessors wrote are finally coming due.

But as he told the military leaders that day in the State Dining Room, the country could not just keep doing what it had always done, only on a smaller scale. Priorities have to be set; trade-offs have to be made, and he had begun the process already, without them. He chose to spend $1 trillion on health care, not on rebuilding Afghanistan.[5] But many of the hardest decisions—on America's global role, on energy, on climate change—had been deferred.

R. Nicholas Burns, who spent thirty years as a top diplomat before leaving the foreign service just as Obama came to office, makes the point that during the biggest decisions he participated in—from German unification to the war in the Balkans to NATO expansion—

"no one ever stopped and asked, 'How much will this cost?'" In the Bush years, those who did ask that question, like Lawrence Lindsay, the White House economist who warned the Iraq War could cost upwards of $100 billion, were forced out of their jobs. (Mr. Lindsay missed the mark: the cost was closer to $800 billion.)[6]

Today, the price tag is often the first question. Can we afford to remake the Navy a major presence in Asia? Can we afford to create an Arab Spring Marshall Plan the way we did for Europe? Can we afford to take on Iranian nuclear proliferation if it means the price of oil will skyrocket?

Obama fundamentally changed the mind-set in the White House during his first term by asking the can-we-afford-it question. (The egregious exception was his failure to embrace the recommendations of his debt commission.) He ended an open-ended commitment in Iraq, and sped a path for withdrawal in Afghanistan over the objections of his generals. He emblazoned in the American mind that we can no longer afford troop-heavy interventions, unless our national survival is at stake. He wisely kept the United States from spending money on the European economic crisis, though he was too cautious in supporting the rise of democratic institutions after the Arab Spring. Whether he has changed course because of the age of reckoning, or because he believes it's the right strategic path, or both, he has made the point that we need a smarter approach to America's global interventions.

IT IS TOO early to know if the emerging Obama Doctrine—a lighter footprint around the world, and a reliance on coalitions to deal with global problems that do not directly threaten American security— will prove a lasting formula. His effort at "rebalancing" away from the quagmires in the Middle East toward the continent of greatest promise in the future—Asia—was long overdue. But it is a change of emphasis more than a change of direction.

Obama proved he was adaptable to new realities, what James

Fallows rightly called "the main trait we can hope for in a president."[7] Afghanistan required the steepest learning curve. Obama had come into office talking about helping to remake the society, to leave Afghanistan a better place than the corrupt, fractured, undereducated, and deeply impoverished nation that had become the petri dish of terrorism. He was right to scale back an unrealistic project. But every time he narrowed America's goals, he gradually walked away from those commitments to the Afghans. Remarkably, scaling back the commitment seems to be the one point that most Republicans and Democrats can agree on; overestimating our power has resulted in a little humility.

The decision to pull back rapidly has come at some cost to America's reputation. Few in the State Department, or the White House, want to acknowledge that the gains for Afghan women, girls, and minorities over the past ten years may be lost as the Taliban regain parts of the country. "The hardest part for everyone is admitting the obvious: the difference we made is unlikely to be lasting," one of Obama's top strategists conceded. The best thing we can say about Obama's handling of Afghanistan is that it will conclude a chapter that both countries would rather forget. Afghanistan proved to be a war without winners, only losers.

Obama justified rolling back the American role in Afghanistan by making the case that nation-building begins at home. There is no question that ending the wars frees up resources to focus on problems far more critical to America's strategic future. The dismal economy, the huge fiscal deficit, the flagging public education system, and an aging infrastructure are all inextricably connected to the country's ability to be competitive around the world.

But there is a downside to the shrinking American presence as well: it has contributed to a perception around the world that the United States is in retreat, and even in decline. We look more and more like twentieth-century England, pulling back from overseas commitments we can no longer afford. The trick is avoiding

England's fate—sharply diminished influence around the world. Obama's challenge is to convince American allies and adversaries that his strategic shift will bolster American power.

Hillary Clinton began to make that case in a speech to the Naval Academy in April 2012. "While the geometry of global power may have changed, American leadership is as essential as ever," she said.[8] That's an expected line from American officials. But America's competitive advantage is that its approach to the world seems a bit less self-interested than, say, China's. Part of America's appeal today is that it still seems to stand for a search for opportunities, instead of a search for rare-earth metals. Obama has played that advantage well.

The big gamble of resizing America's global footprint is whether it will truly strike the balance between preserving American influence and convincing the rest of the world to step up and take responsibility for far greater contributions to global stability. Phase one was ditching the "with us or against us" talk of the Bush era, and the blind insistence that the rest of the world play by American rules. Obama seems perfectly comfortable in allowing other nations to take the lead, or at least the credit—which was the essence of the ill-thought-out phrase that America was "leading from behind." Underlying that impulse is the recognition that America may remain the first among equals for decades, perhaps centuries, but it cannot afford the burdens of being a sole superpower. Obama's willingness to recognize this reality has led to charges that he does not believe in "American exceptionalism." It is a wrongheaded critique: a country can be exceptional without having to pitch in every game.

Libya was the great example here. Obama deliberately sought to make sure the countries with the greatest direct interests in the outcome contributed the most resources. It was an effort to change the world's expectations. And while it was a success, its limits became clear during the failed effort, through 2011 and the beginning of 2012, to halt the carnage in Syria. By stepping back a bit, working to assemble an international consensus, the United States avoided the charge that it was once again shaping the Middle East for its own benefit. But all of Hillary Clinton's shuttling to the United Nations and the Arab League did not change the fact that thousands of people were being slaughtered by a ruthless dictator every month, with no real end in sight. The Syrian people have reason to wonder why, despite stirring orations on the need to protect human rights and dignity, the United States chose to protect the Libyan people but not them. The true answer is that intervening in Libya was relatively risk-free for Americans; intervening in Syria is not. But no one in the Obama administration wants to admit to that brutal calculus, at least in public.

Perhaps the most important legacy of Obama's first term in office and the best hint of what is to come lies in Obama's turn toward Asia. American presidents have been talking about steering east for decades, but Obama was the first to recommit the American military presence to the area of greatest opportunity. Ben Rhodes, the president's young deputy national security adviser, recalled the feeling of the president's trip to Asia in late 2011, when the "pivot" strategy was being discussed.

"I've never spent nine days dealing with issues that were so disconnected from, for lack of a better phrase, the inheritance. There was very little discussion of Afghanistan, the global financial crisis, or Middle East peace. This was the United States going to countries, talking about the things we wanted to talk about, pursuing initiatives, many of which we began in our administration." He paused for a moment and then added, "This is what foreign policy could look like after the wars are over."

It was in Asia that the administration's approach had changed in subtle but important ways. Attempts to reach out to the Chinese in Obama's first years—the classic "engagement" strategy—left the Chinese with the perception of American weakness. The United States appeared to be the supplicant, checking in with its banker. Subsequently, Obama and his staff scrambled to find negotiating leverage. And they succeeded by capitalizing on the fears that the Chinese had created when they overreached in the South China Sea, and by appealing to trading partners who had been intimidated by Chinese tactics. The announcement of a tiny base in Australia helped reestablish the sense that the United States remained committed to the region. "This was a coming of age of the Obama administration," Walter Russell Mead, the political scientist and historian, wrote later. It was part of an effort to allow China to rise while putting boundaries on its behavior; at every step, China has to choose between going its own way and being excluded or isolated. And what China hates most, the administration has concluded, is isolation.

Obama's new approach is hardly a silver bullet. Punishing China for breaking rules is harder than ever. American companies now depend on China as a producer, a supplier, and a market; they have become China's most effective lobbyists in Washington. That is why talk in Congress of raising tariffs or restricting Chinese imports to the United States rings hollow. The trick is to make it clear to China that it can no longer get away with the pretense that it is a "developing country," in need of special treatment, while it simultaneously seeks the privileges of a great power.

WHILE IT IS premature to know how historians will judge Obama's presidency a decade or two from now, we can make some preliminary assessments. By narrowing America's strategic objectives, by showing considerable patience and ingenuity in handling challenges like Iran's nuclear ambitions, by rethinking the management of China's new influence, and by insisting that other nations no longer take American intervention for granted, Obama created a foundation for a new direction for America's global role. But he has been slow in building on that foundation.

His biggest shortcomings have been in two areas. First, he has often walked away from priorities he described in his campaign as essential to American prosperity and power around the world: addressing climate change, remaking American energy policy, and reducing America's frightening debt. He needed to address those more forcefully when he had a majority in Congress; his chance may now be lost.

The second disappointment, though, came in an unexpected area: his communication of his long-term goals. Few presidents have ever given better set-piece speeches on everything from the use of military force to the need to support democracy in the Middle East. But after having given a speech, Obama does not consistently return to its themes, and oftentimes his message is lost. Apart from a recommitment to Asia and nation-building at home, Obama has not successfully explained an overarching strategy to maintain and enhance American leadership and power in the world. Perhaps that reflects his reading of the American public: they are war-weary, and Congress, of course, wants to refocus at home.

For who he is, for what he represents, Obama will certainly be a historic president. The question now is what else he will be remembered for—not just in a year, but for decades to come. Getting beyond the 9/11 era, while necessary to maneuver through the first years of his presidency, proved insufficient to his promise. Now that the nation is emerging from two bitter wars and a bruising recession, his challenge is to exploit this moment of opportunity and harness a sense of national purpose at a time of extraordinary partisan division. The global balance of power is at a critical inflection point. How the United States navigates the next few years will almost certainly determine whether the best we have to offer—opportunity, innovation, unparalleled universities, and the attractiveness of our freedoms—can transcend the decline in influence that inevitably accompanies the rise of so many competitors.

In three and a half years, Obama has used a new doctrine to narrow America's mission and focus on truly vital national interests, something we lost track of in the past decade. Yet the next step will be even harder. Drone strikes and precision cyberweapons can keep some threats at bay without going to war, and coalitions can help spread the cost of less-vital common enterprises. Obama's task now is to go well beyond those first steps, and to convince citizens, allies, and adversaries that a dramatic renewal of American power and leadership is at hand—and must be sustained into the future.

Acknowledgments

CONFRONT AND CONCEAL IS A BOOK OF REPORTING, INCLUDING on events few could have imagined when the project began as a follow-on volume to *The Inheritance* (Crown, 2009), an account of the national security challenges left to President Obama. And as the book grew in scope and ambition, so did my indebtedness to many for their help, research, and insights.

My thanks start at the *New York Times,* where I have reported and written from Washington and abroad for three decades. Jill Abramson, our executive editor and a wise friend, and Dean Baquet, who enlivened the Washington Bureau before taking his enthusiasm for great stories to New York, were good enough to give me a leave to pursue this project. Bill Keller, Jill's predecessor before he returned to column writing, was in on the start of this idea and shared thoughtful advice and provocative questions, as well as the benefit of his reporting on Pakistan and Iran, throughout the process.

When I set aside my daily reporting responsibilities to work on this book, Graham Allison, the director of the Belfer Center for Science and International Affairs at Harvard's John F. Kennedy School of Government, offered me a place to write, test ideas, and talk with the leaders, policymakers, intelligence professionals, and activists who come through the doors each week. I have been privileged to co-teach with Graham "Central Challenges in American National Security, Strategy and the Press," and its engaging mix of graduate students, military fellows, and undergraduates test out ideas, play out scenarios, and critique my thinking.

In Washington, the United States Institute of Peace gave me office space and peace and quiet to write, with a lovely view of the Lincoln Memorial to inspire. My thanks to the Hon. Richard H. Solomon, to Tara Sonenshine, and to Paul Hughes, who made my work possible.

The most crucial help of all came from an enterprising, hardworking team of research assistants who joined in many interviews, traveled the globe, gathered facts and anecdotes, sketched out the story, and corrected many of my faulty assumptions and analyses. Afreen Akhter and Natalie Black, both students in our Harvard course in the fall of 2010, launched the work on Afghanistan and Pakistan. Afreen, with her deep understanding of Afghanistan, was the glue that held the project together for a year and a half before she headed to the State Department. Natalie's knowledge of Pakistan and her British wit were invaluable. Yeganeh June Torbati, a Yale graduate and terrific reporter on the Middle East, was another early recruit, and she contributed her fluent Persian and understanding of Iran's inner workings to piece together the odd dance between the president and the mullahs.

Starting in the fall of 2011, Samantha Pitts-Kiefer and Jessica Harrison, also of the Kennedy School, brought their keen intellects and superior editing and writing skills to many sections of the book. Samantha delved into the secret drone program and nuclear policy, and Jessica constantly pressed for clear thinking on the broad themes of the Obama presidency, the Arab Spring, and the new era of diplomacy and conflict. Meghan Healy Luecke, a graduate student at Tufts specializing in China, unwrapped the fascinating tale of a new president dealing with an uncertain Chinese leadership. Tim Maurer, of the Center for Strategic and International Studies, helped decipher the new territory of cyber policy.

Our Washington office was held together by Lauren Barr, an American University graduate student, whose writing, enthusiasm,

Arabic skills, network of contacts, and impressive knowledge of the region also made it possible for us to navigate Cairo a year after the revolution.

I know I learned more from each of them than they learned from me; the book could not have been produced without their dedication and talent. Anyone worried that America is in decline would be disabused of the notion after a day of working with this assemblage of young intellect and energy.

Many journalistic colleagues answered questions, offered insights, and shared sources. At the *Times,* Eric Schmitt and Thom Shanker were constant sources of insight into the counterterrorism program. Peter Baker, David Brooks, Elisabeth Bumiller, Helene Cooper, Tom Friedman, Mark Landler, David Leonhardt, Annie Lowrey, Mark Mazzetti, Charlie Savage, Richard Stevenson, and Bobby Worth all helped me think through some of the hardest issues. In New York, Joe Kahn, Susan Chira, and Nick Kristof, friends for many years, always provided invigorating ideas. I am particularly grateful for the help of Bill Broad, my longtime colleague in covering Iran, North Korea, and all things nuclear. John Markoff, a great colleague and brilliant guide to Silicon Valley, was a partner in much of the early reporting on cyberwar and Stuxnet.

In Beijing, Michael Wines, Ed Wong, and Sharon LaFraniere guided me through the fascinating contradictions of the world's fastest-growing power. The incredibly talented David Kirkpatrick was a great guide, and great company, in post-Mubarak Cairo. All of us at the *Times* profoundly miss the conversations and deep insights of Anthony Shadid, one of the greatest of this generation of foreign correspondents, who died while covering the uprising in Syria.

At Harvard, many colleagues were generous with their time and insights, but none more than Meghan O'Sullivan, R. Nicholas Burns, Olli Heinonen, Matt Bunn, Steve Miller, Joseph Nye, and Will Tobey. The staff of the Belfer Center made everything possible;

my thanks to Patty Walsh, Kevin Ryan, Lovita Strain, Leah Knowles, Alison Hillegeist, and DeBrittany Mitchell.

The dean of Harvard's Kennedy School of Government, David Ellwood, and Harvard's president, Drew Faust, welcomed a daily journalist back to Cambridge. The historian Michael Beschloss read chapters and put this complex moment in the American story in the right historical frame.

Scores of officials, former officials, and other sources gave generously of their time and analysis. They are too numerous to name, and several would be horrified, or fired, if I named them here. But I am particularly in debt to Tommy Vietor, the spokesman of the National Security Council, and Ben Rhodes, the deputy national security adviser for strategic communications, for putting up with questions and setting up interviews at all levels of the White House staff. Mike Hammer and Ben Chang did the same at the State Department, and George Little and Cynthia Rapp at the CIA.

The Crown division of Random House never fails to impress with their savvy and their speed. This project began under the creative editorial eye of my friend John Glusman; when he moved up in the publishing world, Sean Desmond leaped in with enthusiasm, impeccable judgment, good humor, and great calm. Molly Stern, the publisher of Crown, was an enthusiastic supporter of this project from the start. Annie Chagnot, Stephanie Knapp, Tara Gilbride, Jay Sones, Lauren Dong, Christopher Brand, Linnea Knollmueller, Rachelle Mandik, and Mark Birkey made all the moving parts come together.

No author can survive in the new world of electronic and traditional publishing without a master guide, and I'm lucky that Michael Carlisle of Inkwell Management is both my agent and longtime friend. Richard Pine, also of Inkwell, knew when to intervene with an incisive insight and turn of phrase.

As always, the most important support came from family and

from home. My parents, Joan and Ken Sanger, have supported every endeavor, as have my sister, Ellin, and her husband, Mort Agress.

This book would not have been possible without the love and skilled eye of my wife, Sherill, who always gives 100 percent to everything she does. She encouraged this project even as she was taking up a demanding job teaching some of the neediest students in Washington. Our sons, Andrew and Ned, kept both of us laughing, and never failed to ask critical questions about a world they are now old enough to begin exploring on their own.

This is a work of current history, meaning that the facts are regularly overtaken by events and that judgments, by necessity, are unsettled. Nonetheless, the errors—in fact or interpretations—are my own.

David E. Sanger
Cambridge, Mass.
April 2012

A Note on Sources

Confront and Conceal is based on reporting that I have conducted since Barack Obama and his transition team began examining the world he would confront after his inauguration on January 20, 2009. As the endnotes indicate, I drew heavily on my own news stories, including many written with colleagues at the *New York Times*. I also made selective use of the archive of published State Department cables that the *Times* obtained from WikiLeaks via the *Guardian* of London. Those cables helped fill out the story of the early days of the administration, but the archive ends in February 2010, thirteen months after President Obama took office.

The bulk of the reporting in the book was gathered through interviews with senior administration officials, and dozens of their deputies and assistants, conducted after I took a leave from the *Times* in the summer of 2011. Almost every senior member of the president's national security team was generous enough to sit down and talk through their experiences, some more than once. Most insisted on speaking on background, meaning that they could not be quoted by name unless they specifically approved. Their level of candor varied, of course, and they were acutely aware that their comments could be used by President Obama's political opponents in the impending 2012 election. Nonetheless, most were willing to place at least some comments on the record.

The exception to this practice involved reporting on sensitive intelligence matters, and especially on Olympic Games, the covert program to undermine Iran's nuclear program. That project remains among the most highly classified inside the US and Israeli governments. On this subject, both American and foreign sources demanded complete anonymity.

Readers are understandably suspicious of anonymous sources. So am I. But nearly three decades of reporting, more than half of them in Washington, have convinced me that when it comes to intelligence issues, there is no other choice. As one would expect, I placed greater weight on the accounts of sources who have a long track record of accuracy.

Following the practice of the *Times* in reporting on national security, I discussed with senior government officials the potential risks of publication of sensitive information that touches ongoing intelligence operations. At the government's request, and in consultation with editors, I withheld a limited number of details that senior government officials said could jeopardize current or planned operations.

ENDNOTES

Where there are attributed quotes in text that are not cited in the notes, they derive from personal interviews.

Prologue

1   Though it is difficult to say with certainty, the first detailed report appears to have been written by Brian Krebs, in "Krebs on Security," available at http://krebsonsecurity.com/2010/07/experts-warn-of-new-windows-shortcut-flaw/. Ralph Langner, a computer security expert in Hamburg, was the first to identify that the worm was aimed at Iran, although at the beginning he mistakenly identified the target as a civilian nuclear power plant the Iranians were starting up with Russian help. He later came to realize the target was the Natanz centrifuges.

2   Charles Lane, "Obama's Year One: Medius," *World Affairs Journal,* January/February 2010, http://www.worldaffairsjournal.org/article/obamas-year-one-medius.

Chapter 1: Blowing Smoke

1   "77 US Troops Wounded in Attack on Afghan Base," MSNBC, September 11, 2011, http://www.msnbc.msn.com/id/44474315/ns/world_news-south_and_central_asia/t/us-troops-wounded-attack-afghan-base/#.T3dWm7-XT5g.

2   Jack Healy and Alissa J. Rubin, "US Blames Pakistani-Based Group for Attack on Embassy in Kabul," *New York Times,* September 14, 2011, http://www.nytimes.com/2011/09/15/world/asia/us-blames-kabul-assault-on-pakistan-based-group.html.

3   "US Admiral: 'Haqqani Is Veritable Arm of Pakistan's ISI," BBC News, September 22, 2011, http://www.bbc.co.uk/news/world-us-canada-15026909.

4   Joshua Partlow, "In Helping Afghanistan Build Up Its Security Forces, US Is Trimming the Frills," *Washington Post,* August 26, 2011, http://www.washingtonpost.com/world/asia-pacific/in-helping-afghanistan-build-up-its-security-forces-us-is-trimming-the-frills/2011/08/24/gIQAwYmhfJ_story.html.

Chapter 2: "Afghan Good Enough"

1 "Bush's Final Approval Rating: 22 Percent," CBS News, February 11, 2009, http://www.cbsnews.com/stories/2009/01/16/opinion/polls/main 4728399.shtml.

2 "Afghanistan's Marshall Plan," *New York Times,* April 19, 2002, http://www.nytimes.com/2002/04/19/opinion/afghanistan-s-marshall-plan .html.

3 Rachel Bronson, "When Soldiers Become Cops," *Foreign Affairs* (November/December 2002), 131.

4 The White House, Office of the Press Secretary, "Remarks by the President About a New Strategy for Afghanistan and Pakistan," March 27, 2009, http://www.whitehouse.gov/the_press_office/Remarks-by-the -President-on-a-New-Strategy-for-Afghanistan-and-Pakistan/.

5 "Press Release of Senator Lugar: Senate Unanimously Passes Kerry-Lugar Pakistan Aid Package," Website of Richard G. Lugar, United States Senator for Indiana, June 25, 2009, http://lugar.senate.gov/news/ record.cfm?id=315031&; Christi Parsons and David Cloud, "Obama Announces Drawdown of Forces from Afghanistan, Saying 'Tide of War Is Receding,'" *Los Angeles Times,* June 22, 2011, http://articles.latimes .com/2011/jun/22/news/la-pn-obama-speech-afghanistan-20110622.

6 Joe Klein, "General Stanley McChrystal," *Time,* December 16, 2009, http://www.time.com/time/specials/packages/article/0,28804,194637 5_1947252_1947255,00.html.

7 Parsons and Cloud, "Obama Announces Drawdown of Forces from Afghanistan, Saying 'Tide of War Is Receding.'"

8 State Department cable, dated April 3, 2009, from Ambassador Paul Simons, classified "secret," available at http://www.nytimes.com/ interactive/2010/11/28/world/20101128-cables-viewer.html#report/paki stan-09SANTIAGO324.

9 Parsons and Cloud, "Obama Announces Drawdown of Forces from Afghanistan, Saying 'Tide of War Is Receding.'"

10 State Department cable, dated July 16, 2009, from Ambassador Karl W. Eikenberry, classified "secret/noforn," available at http://www.ny times.com/interactive/2010/11/28/world/20101128-cables-viewer .html#report/karzai-09KABUL1892.

11 Sabrina Tavernise and Helene Cooper, "Afghan Leader Said to Accept Runoff After Election Audit," *New York Times,* October 19, 2009, http:// www.nytimes.com/2009/10/20/world/asia/20afghan.html.

12 Jonathan Karl, "Behind the Scenes: John Kerry and the Karzai Deal," ABC News, October 20, 2009, http://abcnews.go.com/blogs/headlines/ 2009/10/john-kerry-the-karzai-deal/.

13 Peter Baker, "Could Afghanistan Become Obama's Vietnam?" *New York Times,* August 22, 2009, http://www.nytimes.com/2009/08/23/weekin review/23baker.html.

14   The stories of the battling that took place during the surge review have been exhaustively detailed, including in Bob Woodward's useful and revealing *Obama's Wars* (New York: Simon and Schuster, 2010). I relied heavily on an account that a number of *New York Times* reporters gathered in the days right after the decision, and interviews in which administration officials opened up some of the notes from the meetings. See Peter Baker, "How Obama Came to Plan for 'Surge' in Afghanistan," *New York Times,* December 5, 2009, http://www.nytimes.com/2009/12/06/world/asia/06reconstruct.html.

15   Alex Spillius, "White House Angry at General Stanley McChrystal Speech on Afghanistan," *Telegraph,* October 5, 2009, http://www.telegraph.co.uk/news/worldnews/barackobama/6259582/White-House-angry-at-General-Stanley-McChrystal-speech-on-Afghanistan.html.

16   Eric Schmitt, "US Envoy's Cables Show Worries on Afghan Plans," *New York Times,* January 25, 2010, http://www.nytimes.com/2010/01/26/world/asia/26strategy.html.

17   Rod Nordland, "Taliban Hit Back in Marja with a Campaign of Intimidation," *New York Times,* March 17, 2010, http://www.nytimes.com/2010/03/18/world/asia/18afghan.html.

18   Joseph Berger, "US Commander Describes Marja as First Salvo in Afghan War," *New York Times,* February 21, 2010, http://www.nytimes.com/2010/02/22/world/asia/22petraeus.html.

19   Rajiv Chandrasekaran, "In Marja, It's War the Old-Fashioned Way," *Washington Post,* February 20, 2010, http://www.washingtonpost.com/wp-dyn/content/article/2010/02/19/AR2010021905294.html.

20   Dexter Filkins, "Afghan Offensive Is New War Model," *New York Times,* February 12, 2010, http://www.nytimes.com/2010/02/13/world/asia/13kabul.html.

21   Ibid.

22   "Karzai to Lawmakers: 'I Might Join the Taliban,'" MSNBC, April 5, 2010, http://www.msnbc.msn.com/id/36178710/ns/world_news-south_and_central_asia/t/karzai-lawmakers-i-might-join-taliban/.

23   Elisabeth Bumiller, "Some Skeptics Questioning Rosy Reports on War Zone," *New York Times,* November 7, 2010, http://www.nytimes.com/2010/11/08/world/asia/08military.html.

24   Ahmed Rashid, "The Afghan Enforcer I Knew," *New York Times,* July 13, 2011, http://www.nytimes.com/2011/07/13/opinion/13Rashid.html.

25   Alissa J. Rubin and Scott Shane, "Assassination in Afghanistan Creates a Void," *New York Times,* July 12, 2011, http://www.nytimes.com/2011/07/13/world/asia/13afghanistan.html.

26   Dexter Filkins, "Death of an Afghan Godfather," *New Yorker,* July 12, 2011, http://www.newyorker.com/online/blogs/newsdesk/2011/07/ahmed-wali-karzai-killed.html#ixzz1S0MWqgl7.

27   United Nations Assistance Mission in Afghanistan, "The Kabul Con-

ference," accessed February 22, 2012, http://unama.unmissions.org/Default.aspx?tabid=4482.

28 Atla Abawi, "Karzai at Kabul Conference: Security Handover by 2014," CNN World, July 20, 2010, http://afghanistan.blogs.cnn.com/2010/07/20/karzai-at-kabul-conference-security-handover-by-2014/.

29 "Conference Endorses Afghan Goal for Security Handover," BBC News, July 20, 2010, http://www.bbc.co.uk/news/world-south-asia-10687527.

30 State Department cable, dated July 16, 2009, from Ambassador Karl W. Eikenberry.

31 Elisabeth Bumiller, "Karzai's Response to Cables Relieves the US," *New York Times*, December 8, 2010, http://www.nytimes.com/2010/12/09/world/asia/09military.html.

32 Joshua Partlow, "More Afghan Soldiers Deserting the Army, NATO Statistics Show," *Washington Post*, September 2, 2011, http://www.washingtonpost.com/world/asia-pacific/more-afghan-soldiers-deserting-the-army/2011/08/31/gIQABxFTvJ_story.html.

33 Timothy Heritage, "NATO Aims to End Combat Mission in Afghanistan by 2015," Reuters, November 20, 2010, http://www.reuters.com/article/2010/11/20/us-nato-summit-idUSTRE6AI32P20101120.

34 *National Strategy for Counterterrorism*, The White House, June 28, 2011, http://www.whitehouse.gov/sites/default/files/counterterrorism_strategy.pdf.

35 "Karzai and NATO Agree on Afghanistan Exit Strategy," BBC News, November 20, 2010, http://www.bbc.co.uk/news/world-europe-11802121.

36 USAID, "Afghanistan: Facts & Figures," accessed April 23, 2012, http://afghanistan.usaid.gov/en/about/facts_figures.

37 Ibid.

38 Mark Mazzetti, Scott Shane, and Alissa J. Rubin, "A Brutal Afghan Clan Bedevils the US," *New York Times*, September 25, 2011, http://www.nytimes.com/2011/09/25/world/asia/brutal-haqqani-clan-bedevils-united-states-in-afghanistan.html.

39 Mark Mazzetti, Scott Shane, and Alissa J. Rubin, "Brutal Haqqani Crime Clan Bedevils US in Afghanistan," *New York Times*, September 24, 2011, http://www.nytimes.com/2011/09/25/world/asia/brutal-haqqani-clan-bedevils-united-states-in-afghanistan.html.

40 Joshua Partlow and Ernesto Londo, "Costly Coalition Plan to Recruit Thousands More Afghan Forces Draws Concerns," *Washington Post*, January 17, 2011, http://www.washingtonpost.com/wp-dyn/content/article/2011/01/17/AR2011011702058.html; CIA World Factbook, "Afghanistan Economy," accessed April 23, 2012, https://www.cia.gov/library/publications/the-world-factbook/geos/af.html.

41 Sally McNamara, "Training Afghanistan's Security Forces: NATO Has Made Solid Progress," Heritage Foundation, June 16, 2011, http://www

.heritage.org/research/reports/2011/06/natos-solid-progress-in-train
ing-afghanistans-security-forces.

42 CIA World Factbook, "Afghanistan Budget," accessed April 23, 2012,
https://www.cia.gov/library/publications/the-world-factbook/
fields/2056.html.

43 Dexter Filkins, "Petraeus Opposes a Rapid Pullout in Afghanistan,"
New York Times, August 15, 2010, http://www.nytimes.com/2010/08/16/
world/asia/16petraeus.html.

44 Rajiv Chandrasekaran, "Within Obama's War Cabinet, a Looming Battle
over Pace of Afghanistan Drawdown," *Washington Post,* March 31, 2011,
http://www.washingtonpost.com/world/within-obamas-war-cabinet
-a-looming-battle-over-pace-of-afghanistan-drawdown/2011/03/18/
AFvx955B_story.html.

45 Andrew Malcolm, "Obama, As Suspected, Disregarded the Afghan Troop
Drawdown Recommendations of General Petraeus," *Los Angeles Times,*
June 23, 2011, http://latimesblogs.latimes.com/washington/2011/06/
general-david-petraeusobama-afghan-troops.html.

46 "Text of President Obama's Speech on Afghanistan," *New York Times,*
June 22, 2011, http://www.nytimes.com/2011/06/23/world/asia/23
obama-afghanistan-speech-text.html.

Chapter 3: The Bomb Scare

1 This account of the Taliban bomb incident is based on interviews with
current and former White House officials, military officials, and intelligence officials who were involved in resolving the first significant
nuclear scare of the new administration. The details remain highly classified, and not all the participants had exactly the same memory of the
events. Few kept contemporaneous notes. Another account of the same
incident, which differs in some details from my reporting, appears in
Joby Warrick, *The Triple Agent* (New York: Doubleday, 2011), 62–65.

2 There is an extensive discussion of Pakistan's nuclear security in my book
The Inheritance (New York: Crown, 2009), which was published about five
months before the Pakistani scare. See also David E. Sanger, "Obama's
Worst Pakistan Nightmare," *New York Times Magazine,* January 8, 2009,
http://www.nytimes.com/2009/01/11/magazine/11pakistan-t.html.

3 David E. Sanger and William J. Broad, "US Secretly Aids Pakistan
in Guarding Nuclear Arms," *New York Times,* November 18, 2007,
http://www.nytimes.com/2007/11/18/washington/18nuke.html.

4 Jane Perlez, David E. Sanger, and Eric Schmitt, "Nuclear Fuel Memos
Expose Wary Dance with Pakistan," *New York Times,* November 30, 2010,
http://www.nytimes.com/2010/12/01/world/asia/01wikileaks-paki
stan.html.

5 "Transcript, President Obama's 100th-Day Press Briefing," *New York*

Times, April 29, 2009, http://www.nytimes.com/2009/04/29/us/politics
/29text-obama.html.

6   Perlez, Sanger, and Schmitt, "Nuclear Fuel Memos Expose Wary Dance
with Pakistan."

7   Ibid.

Chapter 4: Getting bin Laden, Losing Pakistan

1   Bob Woodward, "Death of Osama bin Laden," *Washington Post,* May 6,
2011, http://www.washingtonpost.com/world/national-security/death
-of-osama-bin-laden-phone-call-pointed-us-to-compound--and-to-the
-pacer/2011/05/06/AFnSVaCG_story.html. Woodward translates the
line as "May God facilitate."

2   Nicholas Schmidle, "Getting Bin Laden," *New Yorker,* August 8, 2011,
http://www.newyorker.com/reporting/2011/08/08/110808fa_fact
_schmidle.

3   Jill Abramson, "Mission Unfinished," *New York Times,* September 11,
2011, www.nytimes.com/2011/09/08/us/sept-11-reckoning/war.html.

4   Adrian Brown, "Osama Bin Laden's Death: How It Happened," BBC
News, June 7, 2011, http://www.bbc.co.uk/news/world-south-asia
-13257330.

5   Woodward, "Death of Osama bin Laden."

6   "Obama on bin Laden: The full '60 Minutes' Interview," CBS News,
May 8, 2011, http://www.cbsnews.com/8301-504803_162-20060530
-10391709.html.

7   Schmidle, "Getting Bin Laden."

8   Woodward, "Death of Osama bin Laden."

9   Mark Mazzetti, Helene Cooper, and Peter Baker, "Behind the Hunt for
Bin Laden," *New York Times,* May 2, 2011, www.nytimes.com/2011/05/03/
world/asia/03intel.html.

10 Salman Masood and Carlotta Gall, "Political Killing Adds to Turmoil
Within Pakistan," *New York Times,* January 6, 2011, http://www.nytimes
.com/2011/01/05/world/asia/05pakistan.html.

11 Shehrbano Taseer, "The Challenge of Religious Extremism in Pakistan,"
Discussion at the Atlantic Council, June 27, 2011.

12 Salman Masood and Carlotta Gall, "Political Killing Adds to Turmoil
Within Pakistan."

13 Author interview with Shehrbano Taseer at Atlantic Council, June 27,
2011.

14 Ibid.

15 David E. Sanger, *The Inheritance* (New York: Crown, 2009), 192–95.

16 Carlotta Gall, "Governor's Assassination Deepens the Divide in Pakistan," *New York Times,* January 6, 2011, http://www.nytimes.com/2011/
01/06/world/asia/06pakistan.html.

17 Jake Tapper, Sunlen Miller, and Tahman Bradley, "Obama Gives Order,

Bin Laden Is Killed: White House Time Line," ABC News, May 2, 2011, http://blogs.abcnews.com/politicalpunch/2011/05/obama-gives-order -bin-laden-is-killed-white-house-time-line.html.

18 Ibid.

19 "Obama on bin Laden: The Full '60 Minutes' Interview," CBS News, http://www.cbsnews.com/8301-504803_162-20060530-10391709 .html.

20 "Raymond Davis Interrogation by Punjab Police," YouTube video, accessed February 22, 2012, http://www.youtube.com/watch?v=NiNkKb 9Sxj4&feature=player_embedded.

21 Matthew Cole, Kirit Radia, and Lee Ferran, "American Official Involved in Pakistan Shooting Identified," ABC News, January 28, 2011, http:// abcnews.go.com/Blotter/lahore-shooting-raymond-davis-american -official-involved-shooting/story?id=12785027.

22 Waqar Gillani and Jane Perlez, "American Charged in Pakistan Killing," *New York Times,* January 28, 2011, www.nytimes.com/2011/01/29/ world/asia/29pakistan.html.

23 Arthur S. Brisbane, "An American in Pakistan," *New York Times*, February 26, 2011, http://www.nytimes.com/2011/02/27/opinion/27pubed .html.

24 Schmidle, "Getting Bin Laden."

25 Ibid.

26 Mazzetti, Cooper, and Baker, "Behind the Hunt for Bin Laden."

27 Jim Lehrer, "Interview with CIA Chief Panetta," *PBS NewsHour,* May 3, 2011, http://www.pbs.org/newshour/bb/terrorism/jan-june11/panetta _05-03.html.

28 Schmidle, "Getting Bin Laden."

29 Eric Schmitt, Thom Shanker, and David E. Sanger, "US Was Braced for Fight with Pakistanis in Bin Laden Raid," *New York Times,* May 9, 2011, www.nytimes.com/2011/05/10/world/asia/10intel.html.

30 "Counterterrorism: Past, Present, and Future," author interview with Michael Leiter, at Aspen Security Forum, July 28, 2011.

31 Ibid.

32 Ibid.

33 Mazzetti, Cooper, and Baker, "Behind the Hunt for Bin Laden."

34 Schmidle, "Getting Bin Laden."

35 Ibid.

36 Ibid.

37 Ibid.

38 Ibid.

39 Press Briefing by Press Secretary Jay Carney, May 3, 2011, http://m.white house.gov/the-press-office/2011/05/03/press-briefing-press-secretary -jay-carney-532011.

40 Schmidle, "Getting Bin Laden."

41   Mazzetti, Cooper, and Baker, "Behind the Hunt for Bin Laden."

42   "Bin Laden Raid Was Revealed on Twitter," BBC News, May 2, 2011, http://www.bbc.co.uk/news/technology-13257940.

43   Schmidle, "Getting Bin Laden."

44   Author interview with Michael Leiter.

45   Michael D. Shear, "Obama Fills a Gap in the Seals' Tool Kit," *New York Times,* May 9, 2011, http://thecaucus.blogs.nytimes.com/2011/05/09/obama-fills-a-gap-in-the-seals-tool-kit/.

46   Schmitt, Shanker, and Sanger, "US Was Braced for Fight with Pakistanis in Bin Laden Raid."

47   Schmidle, "Getting Bin Laden."

48   Ibid.

49   Press Briefing by Press Secretary Jay Carney, May 3, 2011.

50   Ibid.

51   Mark Landler and Helene Cooper, "New US Account Says Bin Laden Was Unarmed During Raid," *New York Times,* May 3, 2011, www.nytimes.com/2011/05/04/world/asia/04raid.html.

52   Press Briefing by Press Secretary Jay Carney, May 3, 2011.

53   Jane Perlez, "Denying Links to Militants, Pakistan's Spy Chief Denounces US Before Parliament," *New York Times,* May 13, 2011, www.nytimes.com/2011/05/14/world/asia/14pakistan.html.

54   Ibid.

55   Ibid.

56   Mariana Baabar, "Time to Press 'Reset' Button on Pak-US Ties: Kerry," *International News* (Pakistan), May 17, 2011, http://www.thenews.com.pk/Todays-News-13-6036-Time-to-press-'reset'-button-on-Pak-US-ties-Kerry.

57   Salman Masood and David E. Sanger, "Militants Attack Pakistani Naval Base in Karachi," *New York Times,* May 22, 2011, www.nytimes.com/2011/05/23/world/asia/23pakistan.html; Salman Masood and David E. Sanger, "Standoff on Pakistan Naval Base Ends," *New York Times,* May 23, 2011, www.nytimes.com/2011/05/24/world/asia/24pakistan.html.

58   Masood and Sanger, "Standoff on Pakistan Naval Base Ends."

59   Dexter Filkins, "Letter from Islamabad: The Journalist and the Spies," *New Yorker,* September 19, 2011, www.newyorker.com/reporting/2011/09/19/110919fa_fact_filkins; Elaine M. Grossman, "Mullen: Pakistani Nuclear Controls Should Avert Any Insider Threat," *National Journal,* July 8, 2011, http://www.nationaljournal.com/nationalsecurity/mullen-pakistani-nuclear-controls-should-avert-any-insider-threat-20110708.

60   Syed Saleem Shahzad, "Al-Qaeda Had Warned of Pakistan Strike," *Asia Times Online,* May 27, 2011, http://www.atimes.com/atimes/South_Asia/ME27Df06.html.

61   Filkins, "Letter from Islamabad."

62 Carlotta Gall, "Pakistani Journalist Who Covered Security and Terrorism Is Found Dead," *New York Times*, May 31, 2011, www.nytimes.com/2011/06/01/world/asia/01pakistan.html.

63 Jeffrey Goldberg, "Obama to Iran and Israel: 'As President of the United States, I Don't Bluff,' " *Atlantic*, March 2, 2012, http://www.theatlantic.com/international/archive/2012/03/obama-to-iran-and-israel-as-president-of-the-united-states-i-dont-bluff/253875/.

Chapter 5: The Long Game

1 Author interview with Vali Nasr, February 5, 2012.

2 Nicholas D. Kristof, "What Holbrooke Knew," *New York Times*, May 14, 2011, www.nytimes.com/2011/05/15/opinion/15kristof.html.

3 Author interview with Vali Nasr.

4 Jenny Schlesinger, "The Context of Ambassador Richard Holbrooke's Final Words," ABC News, December 14, 2010, http://abcnews.go.com/blogs/politics/2010/12/the-context-of-ambassador-richard-holbrookes-final-words

5 Steve Coll, "Looking for Mullah Omar," *New Yorker*, January 23, 2012, http://www.newyorker.com/reporting/2012/01/23/120123fa_fact_coll.

6 Ibid.

7 "Transcript of Siraj Haqqani's Interview," October 3, 2011, BBC News, http://www.bbc.co.uk/news/world-south-asia-15148488.

8 Coll, "Looking for Mullah Omar."

9 Ibid.

10 Keller describes the dilemma excellently in "The Pakistanis Have a Point," *New York Times Magazine*, December 14, 2011, http://www.nytimes.com/2011/12/18/magazine/bill-keller-pakistan.html.

11 "Outta Here: After a Decade in Afghanistan, the United States Rushes for the Exit," *Economist*, February 4, 2012, http://www.economist.com/node/21546046.

12 See Charlie Rose, "The Secretaries: Conversations on Diplomacy with Hillary Clinton and Henry Kissinger," April 20, 2011, http://www.charlierose.com/view/interview/11631.

13 Henry Kissinger made the statement in an address at the Woodrow Wilson International Center for Scholars on November 1, 2011, available at http://www.wilsoncenter.org/event/afghanistan-there-regional-endgame.

14 Robert Baer, "Taliban Imposter: The US Doesn't Know Its Enemy," *Time*, November 28, 2010, http://www.time.com/time/nation/article/0,8599,2033376,00.html.

15 Dexter Filkins and Carlotta Gall, "Taliban Leader in Secret Talks Was an Imposter," *New York Times*, November 22, 2010, http://www.nytimes.com/2010/11/23/world/asia/23kabul.html.

16 Alissa J. Rubin, "Assassination Deals Blow to Peace Process in Afghan-

istan," *New York Times,* September 20, 2011, http://www.nytimes.com/
2011/09/21/world/asia/Burhanuddin-Rabbani-afghan-peace-council
-leader-assassinated.html.

17   Ibid.

18   Ibid.

19   Alissa J. Rubin and Jack Healy, "Survivor Tells of Taliban Plot in Former
Afghan President's Assassination," *New York Times,* September 22, 2011,
http://www.nytimes.com/2011/09/23/world/asia/survivor-describes
-talibans-rabbani-assassination-plot.html.

20   Steven Lee Myers, Matthew Rosenberg, and Eric Schmitt, "Against
Odds, Path Opens Up for US–Taliban Talks," *New York Times,* January
11, 2012, http://www.nytimes.com/2012/01/12/world/asia/quest-for
-taliban-peace-talks-at-key-juncture.html.

21   Rod Nordland, "Talks with Taliban a Long Way Off, American Envoy
Says," *New York Times,* January 22, 2012, http://www.nytimes.com/
2012/01/23/world/asia/taliban-talks-a-long-way-off-us-envoy-says.html.

22   "Beginning of the End," *New York Times,* February 18, 2012.

23   Kristof, "What Holbrooke Knew."

24   "Pakistan Defends Lack of Action During NATO Attack," *Dawn,* December 2, 2011, http://www.dawn.com/2011/12/02/pakistan-defends
-lack-of-action-during-nato-attack.html.

25   "A Conversation with Ambassador Sherry Rehman," United States Institute of Peace, February 15, 2012, http://www.embassyofpakistanusa
.org/news500_02152012.php.

26   Keller, "The Pakistanis Have a Point."

27   Declan Walsh, "Pakistani Parliament Seeks End to US Drone Strikes,"
New York Times, March 20, 2012, http://www.nytimes.com/2012/03/21/
world/asia/pakistani-parliament-demands-end-to-us-drone-strikes
.html.

Chapter 6: The Secret War

1   Her Majesty's Treasury, "Consolidated List of Financial Sanctions Targets in the UK," accessed March 19, 2012, http://www.hm-treasury.gov
.uk/d/irannuclear.htm.

2   William Yong and Robert F. Worth, "Bombings Hit Atomic Experts in
Iran Streets," *New York Times,* November 29, 2010, http://www.nytimes
.com/2010/11/30/world/middleeast/30tehran.html.

3   "Israel's Agent Reveals Details," Press TV, January, 29, 2011, http://
www.presstv.ir/detail/162509.html.

4   For the best discussion of the OSS effort and its remarkable parallels
to the modern day, see William Tobey, "Nuclear Scientists as Assassination Targets," *Bulletin of the Atomic Scientist,* January 12, 2012, http://www
.thebulletin.org/web-edition/features/nuclear-scientists-assassination
-targets.

5   William J. Broad, "Iran Shielding Its Nuclear Efforts in Maze of Tunnels," *New York Times,* January 6, 2010, http://www.nytimes.com/2010/01/06/world/middleeast/06sanctions.html.

6   Parisa Hafezi, "Iran Stops Oil Sales to British and French Firms," Reuters, February 19, 2012, http://www.reuters.com/article/2012/02/19/us-iran-oil-europe-idUSTRE81I07W20120219.

Chapter 7: "Cut Off the Head of the Snake"

1   The White House, Office of the Press Secretary, "Videotaped Remarks by The President in Celebration of Nowruz," March 20, 2009, http://www.whitehouse.gov/the_press_office/Videotaped-Remarks-by-The-President-in-Celebration-of-Nowruz.

2   "Clinton: Obama Is 'Naive' on Foreign Policy," Associated Press, July 24, 2007, http://www.msnbc.msn.com/id/19933710/ns/politics-the_debates/t/clinton-obama-naive-foreign-policy/#.T2i-nlF9nww.

3   Bill Neely, "Barack Obama Greeted with Hatred and Quiet Hope in Iran," *Telegraph,* January 21, 2009, http://www.telegraph.co.uk/news/worldnews/barackobama/4306674/Barack-Obama-greeted-with-hatred-and-quiet-hope-in-Iran.html.

4   "Iran's Response to Obama's Nowruz Message," YouTube video, accessed February 23, 2012, http://www.youtube.com/watch?v=ZNg0A3PLdxQ.

5   State Department cable, dated April 20, 2008, from CDA Michael Gfoeller, classified "secret," available at http://www.nytimes.com/interactive/2010/11/28/world/20101128-cables-viewer.html#report/iran-08RIYADH649.

6   State Department cable, dated April 2, 2009, from Ambassador R. Stephen Beecroft, classified "secret," available at http://www.guardian.co.uk/world/us-embassy-cables-documents/200230.

7   Ibid.

8   Barbara Slavin, "US Contacted Iran's Ayatollah Before Election," *Washington Times,* June 24, 2009, http://www.washingtontimes.com/news/2009/jun/24/us-contacted-irans-ayatollah-before-election/.

9   The White House, Office of the Press Secretary, "Statement by the President on the Passage of the Kids Tobacco Legislation," June 12, 2009, http://www.whitehouse.gov/the_press_office/Statement-by-the-President-on-the-passage-of-the-kids-tobacco-legislation.

10 Nazila Fathi, "Iran President and Challenger Clash in Debate," *New York Times,* June 3, 2009, http://www.nytimes.com/2009/06/04/world/middleeast/04iran.html.

11 Robert F. Worth and Nazila Fathi, "Unrest Deepens As Critics Are Detained," *New York Times,* June 14, 2009, http://www.nytimes.com/2009/06/15/world/middleeast/15iran.html.

12 The White House, Office of the Press Secretary, "Remarks by President Obama and Prime Minister Berlusconi of Italy in Press Availability,"

June 15, 2009, http://www.whitehouse.gov/the_press_office/Remarks
-by-President-Obama-and-Prime-Minister-Berlusconi-in-press-avail
ability-6-15-09.

13   The White House, Office of the Press Secretary, "Remarks by President Obama and President Lee Myung-Bak of the Republic of Korea in
Joint Press Availability," June 16, 2009, http://www.whitehouse.gov/the
_press_office/Remarks-by-President-Obama-and-President-Lee-of-the
-Republic-of-Korea-in-Joint-Press-Availability.

14   Nazila Fathi, "In a Death Seen Around the World, A Symbol of Iranian Protests," *New York Times*, June 22, 2009, http://www.nytimes
.com/2009/06/23/world/middleeast/23neda.html.

15   Ibid.

16   The White House, Office of the Press Secretary, "Press Conference by the
President," June 23, 2009, http://www.whitehouse.gov/the-press-office/
press-conference-president-6-23-09.

17   Sue Pleming, "Obama Says Iranian Candidates Very Similar,"
Reuters, June 16, 2009, http://www.reuters.com/article/2009/06/16/
idUSN16284630.

18   State Department cable, dated December 3, 2010, from US Consulate
in Dubai, classified "confidential," available at http://www.enduring
america.com/home/2010/12/3/wikileaks-iran-special-us-diplomats
-assess-the-green-movemen.html.

19   Robert F. Worth, Sharon Otterman, and Alan Cowell, "Violence Grips
Tehran Amid Crackdown," *New York Times,* June 20, 2009, http://www
.nytimes.com/2009/06/21/world/middleeast/21iran. html.

20   Alireza Nader, "The Revolutionary Guards," in *The Iran Primer*, US Institute of Peace, 2010, available at http://iranprimer.usip.org/resource/
revolutionary-guards.

21   "Karroubi on Strengthening Basij," *Tehran Domestic Service in Persian,* November 26, 1989, Foreign Broadcast Information Service.

22   Neil MacFarquhar, "Layers of Armed Forces Wielding Power of Law,"
New York Times, June 23, 2009, http://www.nytimes.com/2009/06/23/
world/middleeast/23security.html.

23   Nazila Fathi, "A Recount Offer Fails to Silence Protests in Iran," *New
York Times*, June 17, 2009, www.nytimes.com/2009/06/17/world/
middleeast/17iran.html.

24   State Department cable, dated June 15, 2009, from Charge d'Affaires
Richard Miles, classified "confidential," available at http://www
.guardian.co.uk/world/us-embassy-cables-documents/212138.

25   Robert F. Worth, "Dissidents Mass in Tehran to Subvert Anti-US
Rally," *New York Times,* November 4, 2009, http://www.nytimes.com/
2009/11/05/world/middleeast/05iran.html.

26   I described Iran's troubles and early mistakes at length in *The Inheritance*

(New York: Crown, 2009), in a set of chapters called "The Mullahs' Manhattan Project."

27 Matthew Cole, "Iran Nuclear Scientist Defects to US in CIA 'Intelligence Coup,'" ABC News, March 30, 2010, http://abcnews.go.com/Blotter/exclusive-iran-nuclear-scientist-defects-us-cia-intelligence/story?id=10231729.

28 David E. Sanger, "Iranian's Saga Takes a U-Turn Toward Bizarre," *New York Times,* July 14, 2010, http://query.nytimes.com/gst/fullpage.html?res=9A04E4D8133AF937A25754C0A9669D8B63&pagewanted=all.

29 Julian Borger, "Iran: US Behind Missing Scientist," *Guardian*, October 7, 2009, http://www.guardian.co.uk/world/2009/oct/07/iran-usa.

30 William J. Broad, "UN Finds New Uranium Traces in Iran," *New York Times*, May 13, 2006, http://www.nytimes.com/2006/05/13/world/middleeast/13iran.html.

31 Mark Landler and David E. Sanger, "Clinton Speaks of Shielding Mideast from a Nuclear Iran," *New York Times,* July 22, 2009, http://www.nytimes.com/2009/07/23/world/asia/23diplo.html.

32 Ibid.

33 David E. Sanger and Eric Schmitt, "US Speeding Up Missile Defenses in Persian Gulf," *New York Times*, January 30, 2010, www.nytimes.com/2010/01/31/world/middleeast/31missile.html.

34 David E. Sanger, "Obama Wins UN Vote on Nuclear Arms," *New York Times*, September 24, 2009, http://www.nytimes.com/2009/09/25/world/25prexy.html.

35 David E. Sanger and William J. Broad, "US and Allies Warn Iran Over Nuclear 'Deception,'" *New York Times,* September 25, 2009, http://www.nytimes.com/2009/09/26/world/middleeast/26nuke.html.

36 "Iran Rejects Nuclear Deal, MP Says," Al Jazeera, November 7, 2009, http://www.aljazeera.com/news/middleeast/2009/11/2009117101516424577.html.

37 William J. Kole, "Ayatollah Khatami: Iran Protesters Will Be Punished 'Without Mercy,'" *Huffington Post*, June 27, 2009, http://www.huffingtonpost.com/2009/06/26/ayatollah-khatami-iran-pr_n_221307.html; "Iran Rejects Nuclear Deal, MP Says," Al Jazeera.

38 David E. Sanger and Thom Shanker, "Gates Says US Lacks a Policy to Thwart Iran," *New York Times,* April 17, 2010, http://www.nytimes.com/2010/04/18/world/middleeast/18iran.html.

Chapter 8: Olympic Games

1 The seminal story on the origin of what became known as Stuxnet appeared in January 2011: William J. Broad, John Markoff, and David E. Sanger, "Israeli Test on Worm Called Crucial in Iran Nuclear Delay,"

New York Times, January 15, 2011, http://www.nytimes.com/2011/01/16/world/middleeast/16stuxnet.html. This account builds on the reporting for that article and is based on interviews with numerous current and former officials, technical experts, diplomats, and weapons inspectors in several countries who have been involved in parts of the covert effort against Iran. Because the operation remains classified, none of them would speak on the record, and some American and Israeli officials who were directly involved in directing the effort refused to talk about it at all, noting that similar operations are ongoing. While their stories largely agreed on the details of how the world's largest state-sponsored covert cyberattack unfolded, some of them differed on specifics. Some undoubtedly had only partial access to the program. As a result, the account that appears here is as complete a picture as I was able to piece together, but it is almost certainly not a complete account. As one participant said to me, the effort to explain the cyberattacks now is a little like writing about the Manhattan Project in 1945; the fuller story will be filled in, likely in bits and pieces, in future years as elements of the program are declassified.

2   I describe the previous sabotage campaigns at greater length in *The Inheritance* (New York: Crown, 2009), 76–80. For accounts of earlier sabotage efforts, see James Risen, *State of War: The Secret History of the CIA and the Bush Administration* (New York: Free Press, 2006).

3   Other equipment that ran the centrifuges was Iranian-made, and was also subject to the attack.

4   David E. Sanger, "Iran Fights Malware Attacking Computers," *New York Times,* September 25, 2010, http://www.nytimes.com/2010/09/26/world/middleeast/26iran.html.

5   Matthew Cole, "Iranian Defector: I've Escaped from CIA," ABC News, June 30, 2010, http://abcnews.go.com/Blotter/iranian-defector-escaped-cia/story?id=11053597#.T47ktlp9nwx.

6   "Iran Scientist Shahram Amiri—Video Transcripts," BBC News, June 8, 2010, http://www.bbc.co.uk/news/10269255.

7   Cole, "Iranian Defector."

8   "Wife of Abducted Iranian Nuclear Scientist Shahram Amiri Speaks," YouTube video, accessed July 25, 2011, http://www.youtube.com/watch?v=otlfvNUq0pA.

9   Press TV, "Exclusive Interview with Shahram Amiri," July 14, 2010, YouTube video, accessed April 18, 2012, http://www.youtube.com/watch?v=Gk3F0sUUwq8. Since then, a few competing narratives of what happened to Amiri in Saudi Arabia have emerged, some suggesting he called a former Basij member in London for help defecting, others suggesting the trip was planned long in advance.

10   Tabnak, "Shahram Amiri: America Wanted to Transfer Me to Israel,"

July 24, 2012, http://www.tabnak.ir/fa/pages/?cid=108984 (article in Persian).

11 "Iran Waiting for Amiri's Side of Abduction Story: Minister," Agence France-Press, July 14, 2010, http://www.spacewar.com/afp/ 100714120815.a12dy7qf.html.

12 David E. Sanger and Mark Mazzetti, "US Says Scientist Aided CIA While Still in Iran," *New York Times,* July 15, 2010, http://www.nytimes .com/2010/07/16/world/middleeast/16iran.html.

13 "Shahram Amiri," July 18, 2010, YouTube video, accessed July 25, 2011, http://www.youtube.com/watch?v=TEgsYKQRmKg&feature=youtube.

14 This section is informed by interviews with Hosseini, Arbabi, and Asgard conducted in person and by phone on April 27, 2011, and June 10, 2011.

15 *Parazit,* season 3, episode 19, August 19, 2011, YouTube video, accessed September 17, 2011, http://youtube/xPst-EFQtLU.

16 Ronen Bergman, "Will Israel Attack Iran?" *New York Times Magazine,* January 25, 2012, http://www.nytimes.com/2012/01/29/magazine/will -israel-attack-iran.html.

17 Dagan and the other intelligence chiefs declined to speak to the author on the record about their tenure.

18 "Barak: Dagan's Comments on Iran Hurt Israel's Ability of Deterrence," *Haaretz,* June 6, 2011, http://www.haaretz.com/news/diplomacy -defense/barak-dagan-s-comments-on-iran-hurt-israel-s-ability-of -deterrence-1.366295.

Chapter 9: "The Land of Lousy Options"

1 Ronen Bergman, "Will Israel Attack Iran?" *New York Times Magazine,* January 25, 2012, http://www.nytimes.com/2012/01/29/magazine/will -israel-attack-iran.html.

2 Yann Le Guernigou, "Sarkozy Tells Obama Netanyahu Is a 'Liar,' " Reuters, November 8, 2011, http:// www.reuters.com/article/2011/11/08/us -mideast-netanyahu-sarkozy-idUSTRE7A720120111108; Isabel Kershner, "In Overheard Comments, Sarkozy Calls Netanyahu a 'Liar,' " *New York Times,* November 8, 2011, http://www.nytimes.com/2011/11/09/ world/middleeast/in-overheard-comments-nicolas-sarkozy-calls -benjamin-netanyahu-a-liar.html.

3 Helene Cooper and Ethan Bronner, "Netanyahu Gives No Ground in Congress Speech," *New York Times,* May 24, 2011, http://www.nytimes .com/2011/05/25/world/middleeast/25diplo.html.

4 Mark Landler, "Obama Presses Netanyahu to Resist Strikes on Iran," *New York Times,* March 5, 2012, http://www.nytimes.com/2012/03/06/ world/middleeast/obama-cites-window-for-diplomacy-on-iran-bomb .html.

5 Much of the characterization of Obama's attitude toward nuclear power is drawn from a piece I reported on with William Broad in 2009. See William J. Broad and David E. Sanger, "Obama's Youth Shaped His Nuclear-Free Vision," *New York Times,* July 4, 2009, http://www.nytimes .com/2009/07/05/world/05nuclear.html.

6 Ibid.

7 The White House, Office of the Press Secretary, "Remarks by President Obama at Hankuk University," March 26, 2012, http://www.whitehouse .gov/the-press-office/2012/03/26/remarks-president-obama-hankuk -university.

Chapter 10: The Dark Side of the Light Footprint

1 Declan Walsh, Eric Schmitt, and Ihsanullah Tipu Mehsud, "Drones at Issue as US Rebuilds Ties to Pakistan," *New York Times,* March 18, 2012, http://www.nytimes.com/2012/03/19/world/asia/drones-at-issue-as -pakistan-tries-to-mend-us-ties.html. Exact figures for drone strikes conducted by the CIA are difficult to amass, for obvious reasons. But based on reported strikes, documented in the *Long War Journal* and similar publications that track such reports, in Pakistan alone there were roughly 53 in 2009, 117 in 2010, 64 in 2011, and about 10 in the first few months of 2012.

2 Peter W. Singer, *Wired for War: The Robotics Revolution and Conflict in the 21st Century* (New York: The Penguin Press, 2009), 32–33.

3 Ibid., 116; Rob Evans and Richard Norton-Taylor, "Afghanistan War Logs: Reaper Drones Bring Remote Control Death," *Guardian,* July 25, 2010, http://www.guardian.co.uk/world/2010/jul/25/reaper-drone-mis sions-afghanistan-flights.

4 Singer, *Wired for War,* 33.

5 Associated Press, "Bomb-Laden 'Reaper' Drones Bound for Iraq," *USA Today,* July 15, 2007, http://www.usatoday.com/news/world/iraq/2007 -07-15-reaper_N.htm.

6 Greg Miller, "Secret Drone Bases: Avoiding Past Mistakes," *Washington Post,* September 21, 2011, http://www.washingtonpost.com/blogs/ checkpoint-washington/post/secret-drone-bases-avoiding-past-mis takes/2011/09/21/gIQAPaN0kK_blog.html; Nick Turse, "America's Se- cret Empire of Drone Bases: Its Full Extent Revealed for the First Time," *AlterNet,* October 16, 2011, http://www.alternet.org/world/152756/amer ica's_secret_empire_of_drone_bases%3A_its_full_extent_revealed_for_ the_first_time_/?page=entire.

7 Turse, "America's Secret Empire of Drone Bases: Its Full Extent Revealed for the First Time."

8 Singer, *Wired for War,* 33; Jane Mayer, "The Predator War," *New Yorker,* October 26, 2009, http://www.newyorker.com/reporting/2009/10/26/ 091026fa_fact_mayer.

9　Singer, *Wired for War*, 33; Charlie Savage, "UN Official to Ask US to End CIA Drone Strikes," *New York Times*, May 27, 2010, http://www.nytimes.com/2010/05/28/world/asia/28drones.html.

10　Turse, "America's Secret Empire of Drone Bases: Its Full Extent Revealed for the First Time"; Winslow Wheeler, "Keeping Track of the Drones," *Time*, March 1, 2012, http://battleland.blogs.time.com/2012/03/01/4 -keeping-track-of-the-drones/.

11　Peter Bergen and Jennifer Rowland, "CIA Drone War in Pakistan in Sharp Decline," CNN, March 28, 2012, http://edition.cnn.com/2012/03/27/ opinion/bergen-drone-decline/?hpt=hp_c3.

12　Scott Shane, "CIA Is Disputed on Civilian Toll in Drone Strikes," *New York Times*, August 11, 2011, http://www.nytimes.com/2011/08/12/ world/asia/12drones.html.

13　Video at Matt Compton, "President Obama Hangs Out with America," *White House Blog*, January 30, 2012, http://www.whitehouse.gov/ blog/2012/01/30/president-obama-hangs-out-america.

14　Barack Obama, Nobel Lecture given at Oslo City Hall, December 10, 2009, http://www.nobelprize.org/nobel_prizes/peace/laureates/2009/ obama-lecture_en.html.

15　Mark David Maxwell, "Targeted Killing, the Law, and Terrorists: Feeling Safe?" *Joint Force Quarterly* 64 (1st quarter, 2012), 124.

16　Alexander Marquardt, "US Denies Role in Iranian Nuclear Scientist's Assassination," ABC News, January 11, 2012, http://abcnews.go.com/ Blotter/iranian-nuclear-scientist-killed-amid-heightened-tensions/ story?id=15338086#.T3ufA1HmTFI.

17　John Sifton, "A Brief History of Drones," *The Nation*, February 7, 2012, http://www.thenation.com/article/166124/brief-history-drones.

18　David Rohde, "The Obama Doctrine," *Foreign Policy* (March/April 2012), http://www.foreignpolicy.com/articles/2012/02/27/the_obama_doc trine.

19　Harold Hongju Koh, speech given at the Annual Meeting of the American Society of International Law, March 25, 2010, http://www.state.gov/ s/l/releases/remarks/139119.htm.

20　State Department cable, dated February 11, 2008, from Ambassador Anne Patterson, classified "secret," available at http://dawn.com/2011/ 05/20/kayani-asked-for-continuous-predator-coverage/.

21　State Department cable, dated August 23, 2008, from Ambassador Anne Patterson, classified "confidential," available at http://www.guardian .co.uk/world/us-embassy-cables-documents/167125.

22　State Department cable, dated January 4, 2010, from Ambassador Stephen Seche, classified "secret," available at http://www.nytimes.com/ interactive/2010/11/28/world/20101128-cables-viewer.html#report/ yemen-10SANAA4.

23　Dennis C. Blair, "Drones Alone Are Not the Answer," *New York Times*,

August 14, 2011, http://www.nytimes.com/2011/08/15/opinion/drones-alone-are-not-the-answer.html.

24 Eric Holder, speech given at Northwestern University School of Law, March 5, 2012, http://www.justice.gov/iso/opa/ag/speeches/2012/ag-speech-1203051.html.

25 Charlie Savage, "A Not-Quite Confirmation of a Memo Approving Killing," *New York Times,* March 8, 2012, http://www.nytimes.com/2012/03/09/us/a-not-quite-confirmation-of-a-memo-approving-killing.html.

26 Bryan Krekel, Patton Adams, and George Bakos, "Occupying the Information High Ground: Chinese Capabilities for Computer Network Operations and Cyber Espionage," Report for the US-China Economic and Security Review Commission, March 7, 2012, http://www.uscc.gov/RFP/2012/USCC%20Report_Chinese_CapabilitiesforComputer_NetworkOperationsandCyberEspionage.pdf. Northrop Grumman received a $189 million contract in March 2012, to strengthen cyber security across the Department of Defense and for intelligence community networks. See Northrop Grumman, "Northrop Grumman Awarded $189 Million Contract by Defense Information Systems Agency to Strengthen Cybersecurity Across DoD, Intelligence Community Networks," news release, March 6, 2012, http://www.irconnect.com/noc/press/pages/news_releases.html?d=248290.

27 While it has opposed cyber arms control, the United States has been a driving force to crack down on cyber crime, including signing a global treaty. China and Russia have resisted so far.

28 This draws heavily from an article in the *Times* that I reported with two colleagues as part of a broader series on cyberwar. See John Markoff, David E. Sanger, and Thom Shanker, "In Digital Combat, US Finds No Easy Deterrent," *New York Times,* January 25, 2010, http://www.nytimes.com/2010/01/26/world/26cyber.html.

29 Siobhan Gorman and Julian E. Barnes, "Cyber Combat: Act of War: Pentagon Sets Stage for US to Respond to Computer Sabotage with Military Force," *Wall Street Journal,* May 30, 2011, http://online.wsj.com/article/SB10001424052702304563104576355623135782718.html.

30 Andrea Shalal-Esa, "Ex-US General Urges Frank Talk on Cyber Weapons," Reuters, November 6, 2011, http://www.reuters.com/article/2011/11/06/us-cyber-cartwright-idUSTRE7A514C20111106.

31 Elisabeth Bumiller and Thom Shanker, "War Evolves with Drones, Some Tiny as Bugs," *New York Times,* June 19, 2011, http://www.nytimes.com/2011/06/20/world/20drones.html.

32 John Villasenor, "Armchair Kamikaze: What the Latest Generation of Small Armed Drones Means for Antiterrorism," Brookings Institution, October 6, 2011, http://www.brookings.edu/opinions/2011/1006_switchblade_drones_villasenor.aspx.

Chapter 11: "You Sold Out the Revolution"

1 David D. Kirkpatrick, "Islamists Win 70% of Seats in the Egyptian Parliament," *New York Times*, January 21, 2012, http://www.nytimes .com/2012/01/22/world/middleeast/muslim-brotherhood-wins-47-of -egypt-assembly-seats.html.

2 Liam Stack and David D. Kirkpatrick, "Some in Egypt Turn Their Anger on Islamists, and the Syrian Embassy Is Attacked," *New York Times*, January 27, 2012, http://www.nytimes.com/2012/01/28/world/middleeast/ some-egyptian-protesters-turn-ire-on-muslim-brotherhood.html.

3 David D. Kirkpatrick, "Egypt Military Council Partly Curbs State of Emergency Law," *New York Times*, January 24, 2012, http://www.hrw.org/ news/2012/02/11/egypt-year-attacks-free-expression.

Chapter 12: Searching for the "Right Side of History"

1 Barack Obama, "A New Beginning," speech given at Cairo University, June 4, 2009, http://www.whitehouse.gov/the-press-office/remarks -president-cairo-university-6-04-09.

2 The best discussion of the Presidential Study Report is by my colleague Mark Landler in "Secret Report Ordered by Obama Identified Potential Uprisings," *New York Times*, February 16, 2011, http://www.nytimes .com/2011/02/17/world/middleeast/17diplomacy.html. Several members of the study group agreed to be interviewed for this book.

3 David E. Sanger, "When Armies Decide," *New York Times*, February 19, 2011, http://www.nytimes.com/2011/02/20/weekinreview/20military .html.

4 Ryan Lizza, "The Consequentialist," *New Yorker*, May 2, 2011, www .newyorker.com/reporting/2011/05/02/110502fa_fact_lizza.

5 Maha Azzam, "How WikiLeaks Helped Fuel Tunisian Revolution," CNN, January 18, 2011, http://articles.cnn.com/2011–01–18/opinion/ tunisia.wikileaks_1_tunisians-wikileaks-regime?_s=PM:OPINION; State Department cable, dated June 23, 2008, from Ambassador Robert Godec, classified "secret," available at http://www.nytimes.com/inter active/2010/11/28/world/20101128-cables-viewer.html#report/tunisia -08TUNIS679.

6 Scott Shane, "Cables from American Diplomats Portray US Ambivalence in Tunisia," *New York Times*, January 15, 2011, http://www.ny times.com/2011/01/16/world/africa/16cables.html; State Department cable, dated July 27, 2009, from Ambassador Robert Godec, classified "secret," available at http://www.nytimes.com/interactive/2010/11/28/ world/20101128-cables-viewer.html#report/tunisia-09TUNIS516.

7 Scott Shane, "Cables from American Diplomats Portray US Ambivalence in Tunisia"; State Department cable, dated July 27, 2009, from Ambassador Robert Godec.

8   Yasmine Ryan, "The Tragic Life of a Street Vendor," Al Jazeera, January 20, 2011, http://www.aljazeera.com/indepth/features/2011/01/201111684242518839.html.

9   David D. Kirkpatrick and David E. Sanger, "A Tunisian-Egyptian Link That Shook Arab History," *New York Times,* February 13, 2011, http://www.nytimes.com/2011/02/14/world/middleeast/14egypt-tunisia-protests.html.

10 Hillary Rodham Clinton, "Forum for the Future: Partnership Dialogue Panel Session with Q&A," January 13, 2011, http://www.state.gov/secretary/rm/2011/01/154635.htm.

11 Neil MacFarquhar, David Rohde, and Aram Roston, "Mubarak Family Riches Attract New Focus," *New York Times,* February 21, 2011, http://www.nytimes.com/2011/02/13/world/middleeast/13wealth.html; Philip Shenon, "The Hunt for Mubarak's Billions," *Daily Beast,* February 12, 2011, http://www.thedailybeast.com/articles/2011/02/12/the-hunt-for-fallen-egyptian-president-hosni-mubaraks-billions.html.

12 Helene Cooper, "With Egypt, Diplomatic Words Often Fail," *New York Times,* January 29, 2011, http://www.nytimes.com/2011/01/30/weekinreview/30cooper.html.

13 Kirkpatrick and Sanger, "A Tunisian-Egyptian Link That Shook Arab History"; Kareem Fahim, "Death in Police Encounter Stirs Calls for Change in Egypt," *New York Times,* July 18, 2010, http://www.nytimes.com/2010/07/19/world/middleeast/19abuse.html.

14 Kirkpatrick and Sanger, "A Tunisian-Egyptian Link That Shook Arab History."

15 Walid Rachid, speech given at American University, October 21, 2011.

16 "Biden: Mubarak Is Not a Dictator, But People Have a Right to Protest," *PBS NewsHour,* January 27, 2011, http://www.pbs.org/newshour/bb/politics/jan-june11/biden_01-27.html.

17 "Transcript: President Obama's Remarks on Egypt," *Time,* January 28, 2011, http://www.time.com/time/world/article/0,8599,2045085,00.html.

18 "Hosni Mubarak's Speech: Full Text," *Guardian,* February 1, 2011, http://www.guardian.co.uk/world/2011/feb/02/president-hosni-mubarak-egypt-speech.

19 Kirkpatrick and Sanger, "A Tunisian-Egyptian Link That Shook Arab History."

20 Author interview with Michael McFaul.

21 Sanger, "When Armies Decide."

22 David E. Sanger, "As Mubarak Digs In, US Policy in Egypt Is Complicated," *New York Times,* February 5, 2011, http://www.nytimes.com/2011/02/06/world/middleeast/06policy.html.

23 Associated Press, "Gamal Mubarak Behind Leader's Surprise Attempt to Retain Power," *The Australian,* February 13, 2011, http://www.the

australian.com.au/news/world/gamal-mubarak-behind-leaders-sur
prise-attempt-to-retain-power/story-e6frg6so-1226005194176.

Chapter 13: The Riddle of the Brotherhood

1   "The Arab Spring: A Long March," *Economist*, February 18, 2012, http://
www.economist.com/node/21547853.

2   Hillary Rodham Clinton, "Remarks in Tahrir Square," March 16, 2011,
http://www.state.gov/secretary/rm/2011/03/158409.htm.

3   Author interview with Lisa Anderson, January 9, 2012.

4   Amy Bingham, "Young Leaders of Egypt's Revolt Snub Clinton in
Cairo," ABC News, March 15, 2011, http://abcnews.go.com/blogs/poli
tics/2011/03/young-leaders-of-egypts-revolt-snub-clinton-in-cairo/.

5   David D. Kirkpatrick and Steven Lee Myers, "Egypt Says It Will Lift
Travel Ban, Allowing American Defendants to Leave," *New York Times*,
February 29, 2012, http://www.nytimes.com/2012/03/01/world/middle
east/egypt-says-it-will-lift-travel-ban-allowing-accused-americans-to
-leave.html.

6   The White House, Office of the Press Secretary, "Remarks by the President on the Middle East and North Africa," May 19, 2011, http://www
.whitehouse.gov/the-press-office/2011/05/19/remarks-president-middle
-east-and-north-africa.

7   William J. Burns, "Interview with Lamis el Hadidi, CBC TV," Cairo,
Egypt, January 11, 2012, http://www.state.gov/s/d/2012/180455.htm.

8   Thomas L. Friedman, "Trust, but Verify," *New York Times*, January 17,
2012, http://www.nytimes.com/2012/01/18/opinion/trust-but-verify
.html.

9   Emad Khalil, "NGO Report: 93,000 Copts Left Egypt Since March,"
Egypt Independent, September 25, 2011, http://www.egyptindependent
.com/news/ngo-report-93000-copts-left-egypt-march.

10 "Egypt Needs $11 Billion to Fund Economic Reforms: Finance Min-
ister," *Ahram Online*, February 10, 2012, http://english.ahram.org.eg/
NewsContent/3/12/34167/Business/Economy/Egypt-needs--billion-to
-fund-economic-reforms-Fina.aspx.

11 Kristen Chick, "Why Egypt Is Angry Over $65 Million in US Democracy
Grants," *Christian Science Monitor*, August 12, 2011, http://www.csmon
itor.com/World/Middle-East/2011/0812/Why-Egypt-is-angry-over-65
-million-in-US-democracy-grants.

12 David D. Kirkpatrick, "Egypt's Premier Vows Not to Yield in Prosecuting 19 Americans," *New York Times*, February 8, 2012, http://www
.nytimes.com/2012/02/09/world/middleeast/egypts-premier-vows-to
-prosecute-19-americans.html.

13 Susan Cornwell and Arshad Mohammed, "Clinton to Let Military Aid

to Egypt Continue: State Department Official," Reuters, March 22, 2012, http://www.reuters.com/article/2012/03/23/us-egypt-usa-aid-id USBRE82L13D20120323.

14 Mohamed Younis and Ahmed Younis, "Egyptian Opposition to US and Other Foreign Aid Increases," Gallup, March 29, 2012, http://www.gal lup.com/poll/153512/egyptian-opposition-foreign-aid-increases.aspx.

15 Sondos Asem, "A Discussion with Official Delegation of Egypt's Free-dom & Justice Party," Georgetown University, April 4, 2012.

Chapter 14: What Works Once Doesn't Always Work Twice

1   Robert Gates, speech given at the United States Military Academy, West Point, New York, February 25, 2011, http:// www.defense.gov/speeches/ speech.aspx?speechid=1539

2   Robert F. Worth, "On Libya's Revolutionary Road," *New York Times,* March 30, 2011, http://www.nytimes.com/2011/04/03/magazine/mag -03Libya-t.html.

3   Ibid.

4   Joseph Berger, "US Senators Call for No Flight Zone over Libya," *New York Times,* March 6, 2011, http://www.nytimes.com/2011/03/07/world/ middleeast/07nofly.html.

5   Jon Hilsenrath, "Gates Says Libya Not Vital National Interest," *Wall Street Journal,* March 27, 2011, http://online.wsj.com/article/SB1000142 405274870430890457622670426142 0430.html.

6   Gates, speech given at the United States Military Academy.

7   Massimo Calabresi, "Susan Rice: A Voice for Intervention," *Time*, March 24, 2011, http://www.time.com/time/magazine/article/0,9171,2061224, 00.html.

8   Eric Schmitt and Thom Shanker, "United States Debated Cyberwarfare in Attack Plan on Libya," *New York Times,* October 17, 2011, http://www .nytimes.com/2011/10/18/world/africa/cyber-warfare-against-libya -was-debated-by-us.html.

9   "UN Authorizes No-Fly Zone over Libya," Al Jazeera, March 18, 2011, http://www.aljazeera.com/news/africa/2011/03/201131720311168561 .html.

10 "Gunfire, Explosions Heard in Tripoli," CNN, March 19, 2011, http:// articles.cnn.com/2011-03-19/world/libya.civil.war_1_misrata-missiles -fighter-jets.

11 Joby Warrick, "Clinton Credited with Key Role in Success of NATO Airstrikes, Libyan Rebels," *Washington Post*, October 30, 2011, http:// www.washingtonpost.com/world/national-security/hillarys-war-how -conviction-replaced-skepticism-in-libya-intervention/2011/10/28/ gIQAhGS7WM_story.html.

12 Ibid.

13 Ivo Daalder, "Libya—A NATO Success Story," speech given at the Atlantic

Council, November 7, 2011, http://nato.usmission.gov/sp110711.html; Ivo Daalder, "Briefing on NATO Operations in Libya," October 21, 2011, http://www.state.gov/r/pa/prs/ps/2011/10/175980.htm.

14 Devin Dwyer, "Obama to Members of Congress: Action Versus Libya to Last 'Days Not Weeks,'" ABC News, March 18, 2011, http://abcnews.go .com/blogs/politics/2011/03/obama-to-members-of-congress-action -versus-libya-in-days-not-weeks/.

15 Barack Obama, speech given at the National Defense University, March 28, 2011, http://www.whitehouse.gov/the-press-office/2011/ 03/28/remarks-president-address-nation-libya.

16 Ibid.

17 Ibid.

18 Thom Shanker, "Defense Secretary Warns of 'Dim' Future," *New York Times*, June 10, 2011, http://www.nytimes.com/2011/06/11/world/ europe/11gates.html.

19 Lolita C. Baldor, "Officials Say US Drone Fired in Gadhafi Strike," *Guardian*, October 21, 2011, http://www.guardian.co.uk/world/feedarticle/ 9907510.

20 Robert Gates, speech on NATO's future, given in Brussels, Belgium, June 10, 2011.

21 Neil MacFarquhar, "An Erratic Leader, Brutal and Defiant to the End," *New York Times,* October 20, 2011, http://www.nytimes.com/2011/10/21/ world/africa/qaddafi-killed-as-hometown-falls-to-libyan-rebels.html.

22 Ibid.

23 Kareem Fahim, Anthony Shadid, and Rick Gladstone, "Violent End to an Era as Qaddafi Dies in Libya," *New York Times,* October 20, 2011, http://www.nytimes.com/2011/10/21/world/africa/qaddafi-is-killed -as-libyan-forces-take-surt.html.

24 Ibid.

25 While the precise costs will never be known, my *Times* colleagues and I put considerable effort into a tallying of the costs on the tenth anniversary of the September 11 attacks. See David E. Sanger, "The Price of Lost Chances," *New York Times,* September 11, 2011, http://www.nytimes .com/2011/09/08/us/sept-11-reckoning/cost.html.

26 Bashar al-Assad, interview by Barbara Walters, ABC News, December 7, 2011, transcript available at http://abcnews.go.com/International/ transcript-abcs-barbara-walters-interview-syrian-president-bashar/ story?id=15099152&page=2#.T1kU6VF9nww.

27 Hugh Macleod and Annasofie Flamand, "Tortured and Killed: Hamza al-Khateeb, Age 13," Al Jazeera, May 31, 2011, http://www.aljazeera .com/indepth/features/2011/05/201153185927813389.html.

28 Ibid.

29 Bashar al-Assad, interview by Barbara Walters, ABC News, December 7, 2011.

30　Statement of Robert Ford, ambassador to the Syrian Arab Republic, before the Senate Committee on Foreign Relations, August 2, 2011, available at http://foreign.senate.gov/imo/media/doc/Ford_Testimony2.pdf.

31　Robert Haddick, "This Week at War: Syria as Prologue," *Foreign Policy,* April 6, 2012, http://www.foreignpolicy.com/articles/2012/04/05/this _week_at_war_syria_as_prologue.

32　Elisabeth Bumiller, "US Defense Officials Say Obama Reviewing Military Options in Syria," *New York Times,* March 7, 2012, http://www .nytimes.com/2012/03/08/world/middleeast/united-states-defense -officials-stress-nonmilitary-options-on-syria.html.

33　"Wait and Sea: An Awkward Visitor," *Economist,* January 14, 2012, http://www.economist.com/node/21542793.

34　Barack Obama, interview by David Sanger and Peter Baker of the *New York Times,* April 5, 2010.

Chapter 15: Restraining the Tiger, Containing the Kims

1　State Department cable, dated February 28, 2009, classified "confidential," available at http://wikileaks.org/cable/2009/03/09STATE300049 .html.

2　Daniel Dombey, "Gates Warns over Chinese Stealth Aircraft," *Financial Times,* January 9, 2011, http://www.ft.com/intl/cms/s/e93c9c20-1bb1 -11e0-9b56-00144feab49a,Authorised=false.html?_i_location =http%3A%2F%2Fwww.ft.com%2Fcms%2Fs%2F0%2Fe93c9c20-1bb1 -11e0-9b56-00144feab49a.html&_i_referer=#axzz1sGXsgi2C.

3　I am indebted to my colleague Michael Wines for many of these insights, which he and I wrote about in the *Times* shortly after Gates's visit. See David E. Sanger and Michael Wines, "China Leader's Limits Come into Focus as US Visit Nears," *New York Times,* January 16, 2011, http://www .nytimes.com/2011/01/17/world/asia/17china.html.

4　Edward Wong, "In China, Inflation Eases as Growth Slows," *New York Times,* March 9, 2012, http://www.nytimes.com/2012/03/10/business/ global/china-inflation-economic-growth-forecast.html.

5　"Hillary Clinton's Silence on Human Rights," *Washington Post,* February 24, 2009, http://www.washingtonpost.com/wp-dyn/content/arti cle/2009/02/23/AR2009022302412.html.

6　Jeffrey Bader, "Obama Policy Toward China and Asia," speech given at the Fairbank Center for Chinese Studies, Harvard University, Cambridge, Mass., November 21, 2011.

7　George Parker, "EU Needs Big Hitter, Says Miliband," *Financial Times,* October 26, 2009, www.ft.com/cms/s/0/ee315f94-c262-11de-be3a -00144feab49a.html.

8　Michael Hirsch, "Thank You, G2: Why the US–China Relationship Is Not Only the Fulcrum of the World Economy, but a Good Thing After

All," *Newsweek*, November 16, 2009, http://www.thedailybeast.com/newsweek/2009/11/16/thank-you-g2.html.

9 Dennis C. Wilder, "How a 'G-2' Would Hurt," *Washington Post*, April 2, 2009, http://www.washingtonpost.com/wp-dyn/content/article/2009/04/01/AR2009040103039.html; and Mark Landler, "US Is Not Trying to Contain China, Clinton Says," *New York Times*, January 14, 2011, http://www.nytimes.com/2011/01/15/world/asia/15diplo.html.

10 For the best accounting of North Korea's illicit activities, see IISS Strategic Dossier, "North Korean Security Challenges," available at http://www.iiss.org/publications/strategic-dossiers/north-korean-security-challenges-a-net-assessment/press-release.

11 By necessity this is a very telescoped history of Bush's fascinating encounters with the North Koreans. For a far lengthier discussion, see my account in *The Inheritance* (New York: Crown, 2009), 267–344.

12 This anecdote and those that follow I first reported as part of the *Times'* "State's Secrets" series. See David E. Sanger, "North Korea Keeps the World Guessing," *New York Times*, November 29, 2010, http://www.nytimes.com/2010/11/30/world/asia/30korea.html.

13 Clinton's reticence is discussed in Jeffrey Bader's short, excellent memoir, *Obama and China's Rise* (Washington, DC: Brookings Press, 2012), 33.

14 Ibid., 38–39.

15 Sanger, "North Korea Keeps the World Guessing."

16 Noam Scheiber, "Peking over Our Shoulder: Our Chinese Shareholders Get Nosy," *New Republic*, September 15, 2009, http://www.tnr.com/article/economy/peking-over-our-shoulder.

17 Helene Cooper, with Michael Wines and David E. Sanger, "China's Role as Lender Alters Obama's Visit," *New York Times*, November 14, 2009, http://www.nytimes.com/2009/11/15/world/asia/15china.html.

18 Bader, *Obama and China's Rise*, 80.

19 David E. Sanger, "Gen. Tso's Default Chicken," *New York Times*, July 9, 2011, http://www.nytimes.com/2011/07/10/sunday-review/10sanger.html.

20 Bader, *Obama and China's Rise*, 57.

21 "Oil Riches Languish on China's Doorstep," Bloomberg News, November 11, 2011, http://www.bloomberg.com/news/2011-11-10/oil-riches-languish-on-china-doorstep-as-clashes-delay-drilling.html.

22 Jonathan Holslag, "Chapter Two: Engaging the Hegemon," *Adelphi Series* 50 (issue 416, 2010), 29–74.

23 Banyan, "A Half-Pike up the Nostril," *Economist*, September 30, 2010, http://www.economist.com/node/17155658.

24 "China's Aggressive New Diplomacy," *Wall Street Journal Online*, October 1, 2010, http://online.wsj.com/article/SB10001424052748704483004575523710432896610.html.

25 Ministry of Foreign Affairs of the People's Republic of China, "Foreign Minister Yang Jiechi Refutes Fallacies on the South China Sea

Issue," July 26, 2010, http://www.fmprc.gov.cn/eng/zxxx/t719460.htm. See also "Foreign Minister Warns of South China Sea Issue," *People's Daily*, July 26, 2010, http://english.peopledaily.com.cn/90001/90776/90883/7079915.html.

26 "Washington Warned over South China Sea," *Global Times*, July 26, 2010, http://www.globaltimes.cn/china/diplomacy/2010-07/555737.html.

27 Bader, "Obama Policy Toward China and Asia."

28 Dai Bingguo, "Adhere to the Path of Peaceful Development," Chinese government official translation, http://it.china-embassy.org/ita/zl/yjjj/t807349.htm.

29 Bader, "Obama Policy Toward China and Asia."

30 Austin Ramzy, "State Stamps Out Small 'Jasmine' Protests in China," *Time*, February 21, 2011, http://www.time.com/time/world/article/0,8599,2052860,00.html. See also Andrew Jacobs, "Chinese Government Responds to Call for Protests," *New York Times*, February 20, 2011, http://www.nytimes.com/2011/02/21/world/asia/21china.html.

31 Liu Yongming, "Just Look at How the US 'Changes Faces' in the Middle East," *People's Daily Online*, February 25, 2011, accessed November 26, 2011, http://english.peopledaily.com.cn/90001/90780/91343/7300546.html.

32 Liang XiZhi, "Special Report: 100 Days into Middle East Turmoil," Xinhua News Agency, March 27, 2011, http://news.xinhuanet.com/english2010/world/2011-03/28/c_13800638.htm.

33 Chris Buckley, "China Calls for Domestic Unrest to Be Defused," Reuters, February 21, 2011, http://www.reuters.com/article/2011/02/21/us-china-unrest-idUSTRE71K0PQ20110221.

34 Jeffrey Goldberg, "Hillary Clinton: Chinese System Is Doomed, Leaders on a 'Fool's Errand,'" *Atlantic*, May 10, 2011, http://www.theatlantic.com/international/archive/2011/05/hillary-clinton-chinese-system-is-doomed-leaders-on-a-fools-errand/238591/.

35 Richard Haass, "China's Greatest Threat Is Internal," *Financial Times*, December 28, 2011, available at http://www.cfr.org/china/chinas-greatest-threat-internal/p26930.

36 David E. Sanger, "North Koreans Unveil New Plant for Nuclear Use," *New York Times*, November 21, 2010, http://www.nytimes.com/2010/11/21/world/asia/21intel.html.

37 The White House, Office of the Press Secretary, "Remarks by President Obama and President Lee Myung-Bak of the Republic of Korea in Joint Press Conference," March 25, 2012, http://www.whitehouse.gov/the-press-office/2012/03/25/remarks-president-obama-and-president-lee-myung-bak-joint-press-conferen.

38 Choe Sang-Hun and David E. Sanger, "Rocket Failure May Be Test of North Korean Leader's Power," *New York Times*, April 13, 2012.

39 The best biographical account of Xi's early life is contained in Jeremy

Page and Mark Peters, "Heartland Return for Chinese Leader," *Wall Street Journal*, January 31, 2012, http://online.wsj.com/article/SB10001 424052970204573704577186992329708730.html.

40 Wang's essay is worth reading in full. It is accessible at http://www .brookings.edu/~/media/Files/rc/papers/2012/0330_china_lieberthal/ 0330_china_lieberthal.pdf.

Epilogue

1 "Threatening a Sacred Cow," *Economist*, February 10, 2011, http://www .economist.com/node/18114525.

2 David E. Sanger, "The Price of Lost Chances," *New York Times*, September 8, 2011, http://www.nytimes.com/2011/09/08/us/sept-11-reckoning/ cost.html.

3 "Threatening a Sacred Cow," *Economist*, February 10, 2011.

4 "Estimated Impact of Automatic Budget Enforcement Procedures Specified in the Budget Control Act," Congressional Budget Office, September 12, 2011, http://www.cbo.gov/publication/42754.

5 David M. Herszenhorn and Robert Pear, "What the Health Care Bill Really Costs," *New York Times*, October 29, 2009, http://prescriptions .blogs.nytimes.com/2009/10/29/a-health-care-bills-cost-the-reality/.

6 David E. Sanger, "The Price of Lost Chances," *New York Times*, September 8, 2011, http://www.nytimes.com/2011/09/08/us/sept-11-reckoning/ cost.html.

7 James Fallows, "Obama Explained," *Atlantic*, March 2012, http://www .theatlantic.com/magazine/archive/2012/03/obama-explained/8874/.

8 Remarks—Secretary of State Hillary Rodham Clinton Delivers the Forrestal Lecture at the Naval Academy," April 10, 2012, available at http:// www.state.gov/secretary/rm/2012/04/187693.htm.

INDEX